REVOLUTIONARY BODIES

Suspensions: Contemporary Middle Eastern and Islamicate Thought

Series editors: Jason Bahbak Mohaghegh and Lucian Stone

This series interrupts standardized discourses involving the Middle East and the Islamicate world by introducing creative and emerging ideas. The incisive works included in this series provide a counterpoint to the reigning canons of theory, theology, philosophy, literature, and criticism through investigations of vast experiential typologies—such as violence, mourning, vulnerability, tension, and humour—in light of contemporary Middle Eastern and Islamicate thought.

Other titles in this series include:

REVOLUTIONARY BODIES

Technologies of Gender, Sex, and Self in Contemporary Iran

K. S. Batmanghelichi

BLOOMSBURY ACADEMIC
LONDON • NEW YORK • OXFORD • NEW DELHI • SYDNEY

BLOOMSBURY ACADEMIC
Bloomsbury Publishing Plc
50 Bedford Square, London, WC1B 3DP, UK
1385 Broadway, New York, NY 10018, USA
29 Earlsfort Terrace, Dublin 2, Ireland

BLOOMSBURY, BLOOMSBURY ACADEMIC and the Diana logo are trademarks of
Bloomsbury Publishing Plc

First published in Great Britain 2021
This paperback edition published in 2022

Series Design by Catherine Wood
Cover image © Newsha Tavakolian/ Magnum photos

ISBN: HB: 978-1-3500-5002-0
PB: 978-1-3501-9538-7
ePDF: 978-1-3500-5003-7
eBook: 978-1-3500-5004-4

Series: Suspensions: Contemporary Middle Eastern and Islamicate Thought

Typeset by Deanta Global Publishing Services, Chennai, India

To find out more about our authors and books visit www.bloomsbury.com and
sign up for our newsletters.

Miss na miss kita talaga: For Filomena, Olivia, Jocelyn, and Annie

CONTENTS

ILLUSTRATIONS

ACKNOWLEDGMENTS

No labor of love, now twelve years and counting, is the culmination of the effort and intellect of one woman. This project was an orchestrated effort of countless hands and voices, from the librarians who patiently took my requests to the custodial workers who chatted with me, keeping me company late at night, as I worked through different movements of this book. Indeed, making sense of this goliath project often felt like a group effort, accented by the spirited opinions of many heroes. I count no peripheral characters in its genesis: there are many to whom I owe my heartfelt respect, credit, and loyalty.

I begin by expressing my sincere thanks to Hamid Dabashi. From him, I learned to toughen my stance and strengthen my intellectual core as a graduate student. Much gratitude goes to Gil Anidjar, whose courses on deconstruction ignited my intellectual growth. I also express deep appreciation to Marnia Lazreg, Neferti Tadiar, Partha Chatterjee, Homa Hoodfar, Gayatri Spivak, and Katherine Ewing. From near and far, each has helped me sharpen my feminist, critical eye, inspiring me to stand on my own two feet, despite the chaos.

I would like to convey special thanks to Professor Shirin Ahmadnia. Contemporary sociology in Iran would not exist without her insight. Zari T., Leila F., and Fourogh A. will forever comprise the triumvirate of friends and research partners who helped me navigate through tight spots, translations, and the National Library in Tehran. I also extend thanks to Rassa Ghaffari, whose eyes allowed me to revisit municipal parks from across continents. To the great Agha Mansourian and Mojtahed Shabbestari: the latter's philosophy classes helped me connect the dots in more ways than I can count; the former's compassion and humility demonstrated to me how to cultivate true relationships—both in sickness and health.

Many years ago, Jason Babak Mohaghegh approached me about one day seeing my research published in book form; how thankful I am to him and Lucian Stone for their encouragement and patience.

As this work reared its many faces, across different times and spaces, I owe much credit to the institutions that helped me to continue writing and reflecting on its content and purpose. I recognize the invaluable support from Columbia University's Department of Middle Eastern, South Asian and African Studies; the Institute for Religion, Culture and Public Life; the Whiting Foundation; the Brooklyn Institute for Social Research; and the University of Oslo's Institute for Culture Studies and Oriental Languages.

Thank you to Newsha Tavakolian for generously providing her artwork and Nahid Siamdoust for her part in making this happen.

To the wonderful "editors and technicians" who meliorated the many drafts of this project: Though their names have grown in number, I would be remiss not to mention some of them here. Many thanks to Leila Mouri, Anahi Alviso-Marino, Elizabeth Johnston, Yasmine Ramadan, Babak Orandi, Erline Maruhom, Travis Lindhorst, Alireza Mortezai, Joshu Harris, Laura Muggeo, Masoumeh Naseri, Kevin Stoy, Kellie Bryan, Shirin Saeidi, Erin Wilson, Eftychia Mylona, Depeche Mode, Matteen Mokalla, Erik Skare, Jessica Roda, Moumita Sen, and my NORA classmates. Their love and faith carried me to the finish line.

I will never forget the kindness of my extended family in Iran, including all cousins, uncles, aunts, the exemplary Ameh, and the Sarlak family. Each essentially moved mountains to ensure both my safety and academic integrity; from them, I learned to let go, laugh at myself, and try again and again.

To my parents, the late Olivia and Massoud, I am enthusiastically indebted. No two other people in the world could have shown me the values of hard work and raging against the machines, theoretical and material. I would also like to thank my hero sister Suzanne, brother Jordan Kaveh, Mama Marija, and Baba Nabil.

Finally, to my partner-in-crime Sami and our Lina: *Ljubim vaju neizmerno.*

A NOTE ON TRANSLITERATION

The transliteration method in this work is a simplified version of the *Encyclopedia Iranica*'s (EIr) own transliteration system for Persian. I have made allowances for pronunciation and have omitted diacritical marks. I transliterated short vowels "a," "i," and "u" in Persian words as "a," "e," and "o." Neither long vowels, "a," "i," and "u," nor diphthongs, such as "ey," are written differently. Names of individuals are rendered as they are most commonly used and known in sources.

Consonants				Vowels	
ء	ʾ	ض	ż	آ	ā
ب	b	ط	ṭ	وُ	u
پ	p	ظ	ẓ	ِى	i
ت	t	ع	ʿ	ـَ	a
ث	t̲	غ	ḡ	ـُ	o
ج	j	ف	f	ـِ	e
چ	č	ق	q	ه	a
ح	ḥ	ک	k	وْ	ow/aw
خ	k̲	گ	g	ىْ	ey/ay
د	d	ل	l		
ذ	d̲	م	m		
ر	r	ن	n		
ز	z	و	v		
ژ	ž	ه	h		
س	s	ى	y		
ش	š				
ص	ṣ				

INTRODUCTION

A June afternoon in 2007 featured the usual suspects: shoppers lingered in storefronts, only to be ushered inside by the force of pedestrians as heat rays stretched across the pavement. Traffic in Tehran's Haft-e Tir Square remained at a standstill as drivers waited impatiently for red to turn green. A frenetic cross section located in the middle of the capital's business district, the square was named to commemorate the victims of the 1981 bombing of the Islamic Republic Party's headquarters. Yet for many generations of Iranian women, it is also known as Tehran's central manteau (overcoat) shopping district. Both designer knockoffs and contemporary youth couture can be found displayed side by side in tiny accessory shops.

Public chatter and online blog posts were bustling with commentary on the presence of headless mannequins and mutilated breasts suddenly appearing in window displays throughout town. Curious, I took to the streets on that summer day and searched for these displays, and almost immediately came upon store mannequins whose heads and breasts had indeed been lobbed off. Female mannequins in particular, albeit wrapped in exquisite designs and adorned with faux jewels and Louis Vuitton patterned scarves, had been crudely cut from different angles as if haphazardly cut by saws and knives ill-suited to the task of modification.

Peeking out as jagged plateaus covered in fabric, the breasts were unlike anything previously seen in the city's window storefronts. Some breasts looked like cutoff spherical mounds. Others resembled miniature tree stumps. Equally alarmed and amused, I asked friends and relatives if they had noticed anything peculiar about these displays. One friend darkly quipped, "Oh, the mannequins have breast cancer!" This joke, though made lightheartedly, intimated both ambivalence and effort at normalizing the out of the ordinary: in this instance, a nonhuman object stricken with disease was spoken about as something natural and in this way appeared oddly acceptable.

Such "rough cuts" had become widespread in shopping districts across the capital by 2008: the result of a government public morality campaign beginning in 2005 under the controversial presidency of conservative Mahmoud Ahmadinejad.[1] Under the crackdown, mannequins deemed curvaceous were forbidden from being displayed (particularly those dressed revealingly), and soon boyish body shapes with minimal curves were mounted in their stead. These moves clearly reflected an emerging trend taking shape in the state's gender policy.[2]

Reminding a woman to "mind her hejab"—meaning, to make sure her hair and certain areas of her body were not exposed—had been extended to any living and nonliving representation of the female body. Public monuments featuring female characters and other three-dimensional public artworks deemed "naked" were grouped into a deviant sexuality category. For instance, large installations were subsequently covered and, in some cases, veiled to hew more closely to official definitions of modesty. Shouldering these very actions was the notion that a woman's femininity and sexuality could potentially endanger the preservation and maintenance of public morality.[3] In countless treatises, essays, and speeches, Shi'a religious scholars (ulama) and Iranian officials have stated, as a matter of fact, that the female body stirs both desirable and undesirable emotions in men. There were also a number of televised lectures by leading Iranian Shi'a clerics denouncing representational art depicting women. Even a woman's hair was viewed as a catalyst for arousal, for it holds symbolism of female sexuality.[4] All women held an ipso facto insidious power to provoke spontaneous arousal in men—encapsulated in the Arab-Islamic concept *fitna*, or sexual sedition luring men and women away from their more virtuous paths. A woman's body was perceived as taboo-laden, and it therefore must be appropriately managed, controlled, hidden, and in certain cases, reformed. Hence the wider public message being circulated about women in general was clear: any depiction of the female physical form—even a nonhuman model perceived to be dressed immodestly—would not be tolerated for display, lest it entices (male) onlookers' desire. Further, policies continued to be implemented through "modern and effective means and methods"[5] to reform male-female interactions and physical appearance so as to maintain not just public morality but also the ideal family unit.

Nearly a generation has passed since the controversy of headless mannequins dominated the Iranian online media and blogosphere. These days a mannequin without a head is simply a dummy designed for its utility—that is, to sell clothes, not sex. And the subject of female mannequins with rough cuts is no longer contentious; the controversy seems to have been folded into the annals of post-1979 history, another example of a gender policy that constantly reconfigures its projections of morality, public space, and gender relations to fit some amorphous and regularly shifting norm that has been loosely assigned to the Islamic faith and Iranian culture. Clothing storefronts across Iran rarely display full-bodied female mannequins; instead, they are presented in various states of alteration: many sport half-heads or no heads at all. Mannequins have flattened chests, and, in some instances, they have been completely replaced with wire frames shaped to resemble human forms. Although recent attention is preoccupied with the precarious diplomacy and mutual animosity between Iran and the United States, for a time, opinions about headlines of headless mannequins were part of everyday chatter, even ridicule, as Iranians described the new lengths to which government authorities attempted to control public morality.

Puzzled by these many examples of official preoccupations and hypersensitivities toward mannequins' perceived sexualized torsos, I began investigating decades-long state policies related to gender and sexuality under various administrations regardless of their ideological proclivities. What values and perspectives were being incorporated into constructing these policies to regulate and discipline women's behavior and sexuality in particular? How are concepts of "deviance" and "problematic" sexuality incorporated into official government policy—and, by extension, how have these regulatory measures uniquely impacted women from highly marginalized populations, including prostitutes, temporary wives, and those who are HIV-positive? Yet the further down the rabbit hole of inquiries I proverbially went, the more I observed repetitive narrations of permissible and accessible kinds of realities, lifestyles, and desires. Through this constant iteration, demonstration, and visualization for the public, did they become realized as socially and "culturally" acceptable behavior and practice?

Revolutionary Bodies: Technologies of Gender, Sex, and Self in Contemporary Iran is the result of a multiyear investigation on disciplinary technologies of sexuality employed by seemingly incompatible regimes, from the Pahlavi dynasty to the clerical-led Islamic Republic of Iran (hereafter, IRI). It investigates the conditions and contexts which made these "rough cuts" of women's bodies possible, both corporeal and imagined, and observes how they were marinating in the same cauldron of questions on morality, intimacy, sexuality, and deviance that have vexed Iranian society since the 1940s. It examines specific regulatory methods of five unique sites whereby the subject of sexuality occupies a controversial center—popular women's magazine *Zan-e Rouz*, former red-light district *Shahr-e No*, a proposed chastity house, a de-"feminized" store window display, and a nongovernmental HIV-AIDS organization in Tehran. These historically situated vignettes convey how certain disciplinary technologies used to regulate sexuality repeatedly emerge in recycled forms throughout consecutive political regimes. *Revolutionary Bodies* offers a glimpse into how these modes have been used to promote positive ideals about health, family, and security for the Iranian citizen and general body politic. It thus prominently inserts itself into current debates on the discourse of sexuality in modern and contemporary Iran, and appeals to social historical narratives in order to illustrate the impact that global forces like sexual disease pandemics, sex trafficking, postwar reconstruction, and consumerism, among others, have had on their construction, implementation, and timing of usage. Ethnographic material helps locate these regulatory modes operating within the level of praxis, whereby Iranian women converse about how they individually experience, challenge, and appropriate disciplinary modes into their daily lives.

Mapping the Theoretical and Ethnographic Fields

There is an extensive body of literature on the sociopolitical aftermath of the 1979 Revolution. The pioneering works of Ali Ansari, Ervand Abrahamian, Saïd Amir Arjomand, Asef Bayat, Hamid Dabashi, Nikki Keddie, Ziba Mir-Hosseini, Minoo Moallem, Afsaneh Najmabadi, and Parvin Paidar are still heralded as furnishing some of the most substantive research and analysis on the Islamic Republic's main political and social actors, its economic structure, and institutional changes taking place immediately after the revolution.[6] Most of these studies privilege the role of politics and the economy over the inner dynamics and experiences of the social domain. Furthermore, they rely primarily on textual and visual sources, such as government documents and photographs, respectively. Covering especially important ground in the fields of Iranian and Middle Eastern studies, these scholars have applied various levels of analysis. The majority have rarely studied sexuality in terms of the disciplinary methods applied to regulate and modify social relations. They seldom factor ideals of health and modesty, nor do they consider spatial constructs into their analyses of the legal and political transformations taking place during the postrevolutionary period.[7] Moreover, this body of literature is typically divided between pre- and post-Revolution; there are few authors who trace the ruptures and connections between these periods, comparing these movements by increments of decades.[8]

One of the prime issues addressed by scholars writing on "the women question" in the Islamic Republic is the infringement and modification of women's civil and political rights after Ayatollah Khomeini and his legion of supporters came to power in 1979.[9] Janet Afary, Minoo Moallem, Valentine Moghadam, Hamideh Sedghi, and Najmabadi individually discuss different aspects of the state's social and political intolerance, highlighting gender-discriminatory passages in Iran's civil and criminal codes, as well as in Shi'a doctrine and jurisprudence.[10] Afary, Moallem, and Moghadam have written extensively on the usurpation of women's rights in the face of government restrictions, such as compulsory *hejab* and sex segregation in the public sphere.[11]

Most scholarship on gender and sexuality in modern Iran highlights the significance of hygiene, nationalist symbols, and religious beliefs, which were pervasive in the late nineteenth and first half of the twentieth century, during the formative years of the modern, Iranian nation-state.[12] For example, Najmabadi's *Women with Mustaches, Men without Beards* is a study of the centrality of gender and sexuality, exploring the shaping of Iranian modernist culture and nationalist discourses from the late nineteenth century, fostering an anxiety-ridden, heteronormalized patriarchal order.[13] Similarly, *Sexual Politics in Modern Iran*, written by historian Afary, is a historical survey of 200 years of diverse sexual practices from the Qajar period to the first term (2005–09) of Iran's president Mahmoud Ahmadinejad. Afary chronicles the evolution of the discourse of sexuality, maintaining that the construction of heterosexuality in Iran was greatly impacted by modernizing, political, and social interventions taking place domestically and influenced by Western notions of sexuality. In the late nineteenth century, a notion of "normative sexuality" occluded homoerotic practices in Iran, leading to new sexual norms and practices.[14]

The subject of sexuality in particular is a recent scholarly enterprise within Middle Eastern studies and Iranian studies. There is landmark research on the study of gender and sexualities in conversation with scholars working on Euro-American lesbian/gay/queer studies.[15] Notably Kathryn Babayan, Joseph Massad, and Najmabadi have offered critical interventions on the different genealogies of sexuality, questioning theoretical and epistemic assumptions about the knowledge and knowledge production of sexuality for peoples of the Middle East.[16] Although written over a decade ago, most of their works have contributed significantly to challenging universalizing treatments of sexuality, situating the discourse within larger colonial and imperialist contexts. Babayan and Najmabadi's *Islamicate Sexualities: Translations across Temporal Geographies* is a pioneering anthology on "a new field of historical knowledge and site of knowledge production—that of Islamic sexuality studies."[17] *Islamicate Sexualities* offers alternative models for studying Islamicate sexuality by "crossing paths" between Middle Eastern studies and sexuality studies, employing sources from medieval literature, history, psychoanalysis, comparitivisms, and translation.[18] Likewise, Massad's intervention, *Desiring Arabs*, examines Orientalist scholarship on Islamic and Arabic homosexuality, asserting that the notion of sexual identity was a function of modernity. Massad critiques Euro-American attempts to universalize the term "sexuality," arguing that the term is itself an epistemological and ontological category. And, it is a product of specific social formations and histories of the Euro-American cultural and political experience, which traveled to the Middle East by way of European colonialism.[19]

The literature on the construction of sexuality discourse in the post-1979 Islamic Republic consists of a handful of works on the following subjects: same-sex desires and transsexuality; family planning population policies; shifts in the sexual norms of Iran's urban populations; the success and failures of popular, modern artists before and after the revolution; and permanent and temporary marriage practices during the Republic's formative years. Hammed Shahidian has written a chapter on the contesting discourses of sexuality in postrevolutionary Iran.[20] Kamran Talattof has also studied developments within the discourse of sexuality in Iran, tracing the histories of nonelite and popular cultural actors prior to and after the revolution and commenting on the silencing and stigmatizing of an open, intellectual discourse on sex, sexual health, and sexuality in the IRI.[21]

Scholars integrating ethnographic research have added much-needed nuance to the study of sexuality in contemporary Iran. The writings of Homa Hoodfar, Shahla Haeri, and Najmabadi are noteworthy contributions.[22] Haeri's *Law of Desire* is a pioneering anthropological study on temporary marriage arrangements (in Arabic, *mut'a*) discussed in Twelver Shi'a ideology and experienced by Iranian women.[23] Interviewing women and high-ranking ayatollahs in Qom, Haeri discusses the legal and experiential understandings of *mut'a* (in Persian, *sigheh*) to understand how sexuality is constructed in religious and public discourses. Shi'a ulama, in maintaining that *mut'a* is intended for sexual pleasure (unlike permanent marriage, which is intended for procreation), justify its practice based on a masculine understanding of what female sexuality ought to be: "not in and of itself, but always in relation to male sexuality."[24] Although published in 1989, this work is still *the* authoritative text on *mut'a* in practice, and, by extension, on the discourse of sexuality from the perspective of Shi'a legal and ideological paradigms.[25]

Since the publishing of *Law of Desire*, there have been a few, albeit vital, contributions from anthropologists and sociologists based in Europe and the United

States who study gender and sexuality and integrate fieldwork into their research. They have researched indigenous women's movements, women's participation and resistance during the Iran–Iraq War, and social customs and rituals in urban spaces. In this group, I accent the works of Najmabadi, Roxanne Varzi, Shirin Saeidi, and Pardis Mahdavi.[26] Najmabadi's publication of *Professing Selves: Transsexuality and Same-Sex Desire in Contemporary Iran* is a groundbreaking study of the contemporary discourse and practices of transsexuality in contemporary Iran, using ethnographic material. Situating these practices within a longer historical trajectory, she studies transsexuality's discursive creation within a matrix of social, medical, political, religious, and legal domains, and notes the emergence of new, paradoxical "social spaces" for "a variety of 'not-normal' people."[27] Concerning the topic of Iranian subcultures, academic debates were stirred by Mahdavi's controversial claims regarding the sexual practices of upper-middle-class Tehrani youth, whose customs and attitudes according to her demonstrated the existence of a burgeoning "sexual or sociocultural revolution."[28]

For recent and important sociological research in Persian, pertaining to the discourse of the body and sexuality in Iranian society, we have thus far relied on a handful of social scientists based in Iran, namely Soheila Shashahani, Shirin Ahmadnia, and Fatemeh Sadeghi.[29] (Their research methodology, thesis objectives, and research findings are often scrutinized—for the purposes of being accepted for publication—by officials within Iran's Ministry of Education and Ministry of Culture and Islamic Guidance.) There are, additionally, many researchers in the public health sector who have written extensively on prisoner populations, drug addiction, and sexually transmitted diseases (STDs) in Iran for the purposes of acquiring statistical data and analysis.[30]

Sadeghi in particular has examined shifts in sexuality discourse of young, urban Iranian women.[31] Although observing changes in their private and public lives, Sadeghi attests that these changes do not testify to radical breaks in social conventions of the past. She has however observed the Islamist state's politicization of sexuality in the second decade of the Islamic Republic, noting, "The Islamist project [in Iran] has been also inclined to homogenize and discipline sexuality on the basis of what is legitimate and illegitimate in the Sharia."[32] Moreover, she argues that the morality police's scrutiny of heterosocial relations has replaced the guardianship duties of traditional families in this domain.[33] Consequently, relations have become privatized, moving courtship from public spaces to homes and cars, for example. This shift into private spaces has resulted in younger generations participating in a "precocious sexuality."[34]

Regulating Sexuality in Iran

Cultural anthropologist Shahla Haeri observes, "In Iranian society, sexuality comes to be a cultural cynosure, because of which, it is simultaneously perceived as precious and treacherous to its original master."[35] To "*come* to be a cultural cynosure" (emphasis mine) means to move into a tenuous space, where shifting perceptions determine the boundaries of acceptability for a woman's sexuality. For Haeri, sexuality's precarity is its essence; its perceptible contradictions are necessarily dependent on the shifting gaze and reflection of the (heterosexual male) beholder. By extension, sexuality's force lies in its instability as an identity marker not just for men and women but also for those things that come into its range of association—in this case, a mannequin with protruding spherical rounds. This means that its regulation across time and space has been both messy and unpredictable, like the decision to saw off the "sexuality" marker of a female mannequin to promote public morality. Questions sparked by Haeri's comment are as follows: How have Iran's clerical authorities come to regulate such a fluid, mobile concept as sexuality? How did a negative trope about women and their purported deviant sexuality lead to a top-down decision to disfigure nonliving female forms as an expedient method of regulation? Further, how did life-size dummies made of plastic and fiberglass and intended for displaying clothes in a storefront come to be understood as threats to public morality? Had nonliving things designed to display clothes anthropomorphized into sexual talismans taunting the morals of an entire society?

Elizabeth Bernstein and Laurie Schaffner remark, "Sexuality is *regulated*— governed, directed, and made more uniform—through the rule of law as well as through media, nongovernmental organizations (NGOs), educators, and others engaged in the 'helping professions.' Sexuality is also regulated by diffuse state policies seemingly unrelated to questions of gender and erotic intimacy." (Emphasis in original) In *Regulating Sex: The Politics of Intimacy and Identity*, they advise, "In order to understand the regulation of sexuality, we must situate it within its broad political context, exploring the mutual constitution of public and private, family and nation, and sexual and social life."[36] Bernstein and Schaffner speak to the necessity of identifying factors that, despite their apparent opposition to each other, are equally consequential in impacting social policies and social tensions emerging from debates around sexuality. [37]

In light of their direction, the most obvious starting point to commence this inquiry would be to look at, for instance, how sexuality discourse and practice have been impacted by Islamic ideals supposedly enshrined in the foundational documents of the Islamic Republic.[38] The IRI constitutional dictum, "good moral values based on the Islamic faith,"[39] formed the conceptual rubric guiding Ayatollah Khomeini's reformation of Iranian society into an Islamic society. At the time of the 1979 Revolution, embryonic government bodies, such as the Supreme Council of the Cultural Revolution, began devising policies in which the state's ideals of Muslim women, as pious, modest, and self-sacrificing mothers and wives,[40] became socially, religiously, and legally enforced.[41] However, as this book illustrates, the regulation of sexuality is directly related to historically situated and interwoven discourses of women's status, health, morality, modesty, religion, and modern reform that are not bound to the time constraints of grand revolutionary narratives.

Looming large within this work are writings on space, power, sexuality, prostitution, and gender that, individually and in conversation with each other, have helped to theoretically ground this topic. One cannot consider the regulation of sexuality without taking into account how flows of capital, labor, technology, information, drugs, and culture impact the implementation and efficacy of certain policies. It is imperative to discern how different regulatory modes situated within this discursive matrix are constructed, implemented, rejected, and remodeled during and beyond historical events. This means surveying moments of social, political, and economic crises throughout Iran's modern history, from the rule of Muhammad Reza Pahlavi (1941–79) to the present-day Islamic Republic, and recognizing examples of similitude. Hence, I have chosen to move away from the oft-repeated, facile statement about the 1979 Revolution that a clear break in political and social trajectories happened, cleanly distinguishing the state policies of one regime from the next. Stepping into this domain of inquiry whereby similarities and continuities between two regimes are observed has enabled an analysis that Marnia Lazreg has inspiringly described as "[exploding] the constraining power of categories."[42] As such, I am able to discern the formation and implementation of unlikely technologies of regulation in sites and spaces that bear little connection—at least at first glance.

Introducing Bodily Technologies

Throughout *Revolutionary Bodies*, I engage theoretically with the concept of "bodily technologies" to discuss the construction and implementation of regulatory and disciplinary modes employed in modern and contemporary Iran. Gill Valentine's own definition of bodily technology is "the solution[s] to the problem of the deviant body."[43] She employs this term when referencing physical and sensory aids, such as a hearing aid and wheelchair, in *Social Geographies: Space and Society*. Valentine describes how bodily technologies assist "'disabled' individuals . . . categorized as socially inferior and a 'problem' for society."[44] A wheelchair, for instance, is a bodily technology that holds the power to improve a body that needs assistance in being more able-bodied. Germane to the Iranian case study, Valentine's terminology is useful in perceiving the utility of a chestless mannequin (meaning, one without protruding breasts) as having its own disciplinary function: it encourages public morality and modesty. In effect, it acts as a preventive measure to help onlookers from becoming sexually aroused, or at least admiring a mannequin's breasts. In other cases, a veil too could be regarded as a provisional bodily technology. For example, one might consider the gigantic sheet fashioned into a scarf and placed on a public monument to cover its female character's hair as a bodily technology assisting in controlling the gaze of a deviant bystander. Or, consider also a popular women's magazine designed to encourage a modern lifestyle, or to return to one's Islamic faith. For many of these bodily technologies, the default assumption is that the reader, the viewer, and the audience are incapable of independently reforming and assisting themselves. Perceptions of their "non-normality" are based on them becoming "normal" or "capable." Thus, are there alternative examples of bodily technologies that assist in "curing" the deviant body—or, by extension, those populations perceived as "sexually deviant"? How have Iranian officials treated certain communities when they are described as carrying contagion—for instance, of venereal disease and sexual promiscuity?

As a case in point, recall Iran's century-old policy on prostitution over two regimes. Even though in 1979 prostitution was banned, its criminalization has neither halted the rise in prostitution nor prevented the sex trafficking in urban areas and across Iran's borders. Prostitution in the discursive Iranian context has been traditionally and uniquely couched in Shi'a ideological frames of reference. At the same time, the role and figure of the (female) prostitute has featured in Iran's nationalist rhetoric on reform, hygiene, maternity, citizenship, and health throughout the last century. For the Pahlavi state, the regulation of prostitution involved policing prostitutes' behavior and not their clients. Many prostitutes were quarantined in red-light districts under both police protection and Ministry of Health supervision as preventive measures to curb the spread of STDs. Two days before Ayatollah Khomeini's return from exile on February 1, 1979, Tehran's red-light districts were set ablaze; by month's end, provisional revolutionary courts outlawed prostitution and ordered the demolishing of brothel sites. Even still, as mentioned earlier, prostitution continues to be a pressing domestic and international issue for the Iranian government and clerical leadership.

By investigating and tracing the shifts, gaps, and continuities in regulatory policies on prostitution, one discerns the salient tensions preoccupying state, clerical, and popular discourses on sexuality. One demonstrable tension is a demarcation of normative from abnormal human behavior, impacting both the Shi'a ideological and popular conceptualizations of sexuality and the men and women involved in prostitution—who enter by choice or by force.[45] Are prostitution and other forms of sex work considered deviant work? Is there a conceptual space for such practices to be conducted and accepted? How does the official response to prostitution connect to government attitudes toward married couples? What positive ideals are emphasized to ensure that men and women embrace regulatory policies on their sexuality, health, and social relations, subsequently internalizing these ideals? Moreover, how do women perceive, experience, and confront these bodily technologies and their impact—especially in cases when they encounter additional discrimination and stigmatization because of government regulation?

Revolutionary Bodies: The Narrative Pivot

The central argument of *Revolutionary Bodies* is that the scope of practices, methods, and technologies used to regulate and experience sexuality in contemporary Iran are manifold and diverse, conflictive and collaborative, and seldom reflective of the state's ideological imperative of an "Islamic sexual morality." Understanding their makeup, target audiences, and shifts and continuities in content and usage is vital to unpacking how disciplinary technologies condition certain forms of isolation, concealment, and stigmatization over time. The subject of breastless mannequins is only the proverbial tip of an iceberg. The historical narratives of how sites and modes of regulation mutate into each other, breaking form to join with others, offer evidence to certain patterns of gendered governmentality, whereby women and their bodies are at stake. One clearly sees an extensive network of constantly reconfigured and retested government "red lines," leading to the emergence and consolidation of social spaces of exclusion—both physical and conceptual. In many instances, certain women, mostly prostitutes and women living with HIV, are forced to remain "in crisis" and face societal ambivalence and stigmatization for their own self-preservation.

One proposed conclusion of *Revolutionary Bodies* is that through both inclusionary and exclusionary practices of state authorities and their affiliated institutions, those objects and persons labeled deviant, taboo, immodest, and obscene are continually subject to reformation, readjustment, and instability through their association to "non-normal" sexuality. On a macro-level, this means that the moral jurisdiction of the state designates which bodies are clean, pious, favorable, and worth memorializing. Via state modesty and public morality campaigns, women and their bodies (and by extension their nonliving representations like mannequins) are designated as embodying shame, and thus necessary recipients of easily administered and convenient reform. This also means that whatever power the state possesses has been administered through vast manipulations and erasures of the public (social) memory, the public (social) body, and the private (physical) body. The effect is that certain bodies go into hiding, they become absent, or they resort to a kind of mutilation. Through the initially haphazard Islamization process of the postrevolutionary period, which in later decades morphed into a state project of mere political expediency and gender control, women's bodies became the overt expression by which an Islamist state could commence its disinfection or *paksazi* or cleansing process. Thus, women's revolutionary "bodies," understood as material entities in their many states of representation, compliance, and resistance, were intended to be physically and publicly forgotten through legal and extralegal policies, structures, development, destruction, and, moreover, compulsory forgetting. *Revolutionary Bodies* endeavors to tease out these "forgotten" narratives and acknowledge their invaluable permanence.

Interventions and Methodology

In order to ground my analysis of the written material, I conducted ethnographic fieldwork in Tehran over a five-year time span, between 2006 and 2011. In this period, I also scoured archival materials, analyzing magazine articles, photographs, and official portraits published since the mid-1960s, when Iran underwent modernization reforms under the second Pahlavi regime (1941–79). I reviewed the Ministry of Health, public health, and media materials on women's health, sexual education, and HIV/AIDS. In addition, I enquired into the IRI's policies on modesty, clothing, and veiling, as well as articles and images in women's journals and fashion magazines that were popular in the past forty years (e.g., *Zan-e Rouz* and *Ettela'at Banevan*). Finally, I turned to speeches and writings of religious officials—some of whom have held or presently hold leadership positions in government—to supplement the extant literature on policies of compulsory *hejab* and "Islamic modesty," as well as the writings on the subject of human sexuality from high-ranking Shi'a ulama.

Much of this historical material required further contextualization and what I like to call experiential mapping, whereby conversations with Iranians who experienced the revolutionary reforms from Pahlavi Iran to Islamic Republic of Iran elucidate the print material I engaged. Thus, initially I spoke with mostly older Iranian women who perhaps might be able to recall their own memories, not just by reading *Zan-e Rouz* and other female-targeted journals but also by recollecting on the shifting norms and codes of conduct that they observed during the transition from the Pahlavi monarchy to Khomeini's Islamic Republic. Our semi-structured interviews turned into longer conversations about their personal navigations around the IRI government's "red lines." More often than not, they broached topics that illustrated very complex constructions of and experiences with social custom, identity, personhood, health, and power. The immediacy and potency of these individual accounts were invaluable for offering diverse interpretations of sexuality and sexual practices.

At the time, I had many contacts residing in Tehran and the neighboring suburb of Kharaj, the former where I had intermittently lived and worked since 2003. Word of mouth helped put me in contact with women whose ages ranged from eighteen to eighty-five from across the socioeconomic and religious spectrum—from high-society housewives to women who travel three hours to clean their homes, from the very pious to the nonreligious. I also spoke with clothing shop managers in Haft-e Tir Square about government and morality police's policies on mannequins. Semi-structured interviews were conducted in mostly Persian in their private homes and offices. For this work, I have changed their names and omitted certain details in order to preserve their privacy. In total, I interviewed eighty-one women about body perception and breastfeeding experiences, touching on issues of sexuality, marital relations, modesty, and health. In addition, I interviewed ten men, the majority of whom were related to the female interviewees via family or work. For this work, I wanted to present detailed accounts of interviewees so the reader gained a more nuanced account of their personal backgrounds and the various conditions and constraints in which they lived. The reader thus will find four in-depth interviews with Iranian women in the work's ethnographic section. I chose to focus on these interviews because my interlocutors offered detailed, extensive opinions about their daily experiences, relationships histories, and health practices at different moments during my fieldwork. It was very important for me to recognize how informative the dozens of intimate conversations I had have been to my understanding and without which this work would have not been possible.

As a way to both clarify and focus the interviews, I asked women general and specific questions about motherhood and their bodies, not once initiating the terms sex or sexuality during our interviews in case they felt uncomfortable discussing such topics. I had decided that if these women wanted to bring up sexuality themselves, then I would follow their lead and ask related questions. Our conversations naturally segued into tangential topics like breastfeeding and personal health maintenance. Both topics sparked some to recall stories of intimate encounters and to explain their feelings toward their spouses. I found that the concept and topic of breasts in particular served as a common denominator for the majority of married women, generating stories of intimacy, sensuality, pain, marital relations, motherhood, and childhood memories. It elicited a variety of anecdotes, many of which revealed a woman's particular understanding of her self-worth, personal relationships, and desires. Plus, personal breasts served as a good conversation starter for the sawed-off mannequins' breasts were being displayed in window shops throughout the city. For the majority of respondents, they had meaningful, even acerbic, comments about this phenomenon.

Reforming and Defining Sexuality: Five Narratives

The following five chapters are vignettes of the historic struggle over redefining and reforming sexuality in contemporary Iran; though seeded in the past, their tendrils extend into the present. Chapter 1, "Reform: An Art of Visual Persuasion," discusses the methods of "semiotic control" that originate in the mid-1960s, encouraging Iranian women to become modern citizens. This chapter maps how Iranian women and their bodies are represented through the processes of first, modernization, and second, Islamization. It analyzes a selection of recurrent and illuminating drawings and advertising images from *Zan-e Rouz*—a women's weekly magazine published from the late Pahlavi era (1965–79) until the present day. What becomes evident is the continuity in the modes of regulation. Each attempt to culturally transform women into boundary-making objects of the Iranian nation—be she a Westernized, modern woman or a veiled, pious daughter of the Islamic Revolution—was based on the expectation that women would be naturally receptive to reform. Chapter 1 identifies how thematic images aimed at cultural reform under the Pahlavi dynasty were recodified by government officials and media institutions in the Islamic Republic for first, to promote the values of modesty, family, and piety to Iranian women, and second, to perform their regulatory and disciplinary purpose.

The next two chapters move the reader to a two-part exploration of the discourse of prostitution in Iran, analyzing the role of the prostitute in satiating male sexual desires from the Pahlavi period to the present-day Islamic Republic. Chapter 2, "Red-Lights in Parks: A Social History of Park-e Razi," investigates the inner dynamics and spatial transformations of a red-light district in southern Tehran, which was once a societal landmark called the "Citadel" of *Shahr-e No*. During the Pahlavi years (1925–79), it operated quite openly as a government-regulated brothel district. In 1979, it was demolished and later developed into a large family park, Park-e Razi (Razi Park). Chapter 2 explores the social history of this site, when it was once a century-old red-light district. Key figures in *Shahr-e*

No's history, such as brothel madams and high-level clerics and politicians, are highlighted, along with the shifting inequalities and interactions of this space. By outlining the social and historical processes affecting *Shahr-e No*, the reader arrives at the entrance of a much larger debate over the role of prostitution and the expectation of female sexuality across the Pahlavi era and the IRI.

Chapter 3, "Safety Valves and Postrevolutionary 'Prostitution,'" returns to the site of *Shah-re No* and begins with the criminalization of prostitution in 1979. Despite being banned, prostitution eventually increased under the policies of the Islamic government. This is attributed, in part, to several shifts in the official position toward prostitution in moments of economic crisis and in the midst of postwar rehabilitation. It is also due, in large part, to the patriarchal, heteronormative assumptions held by Shi'a ulama about male sexuality. During the first two decades of the Islamic Republic, to solve the problem of high unemployment, a rise in the number of unmarried veterans, and the anxiety of unbridled sexual activity among the youth, government officials began suggesting that Iranians enter *sigheh* arrangements (temporary marriage in Shi'a Islam). This practice was then extended, intentionally as it is argued, to allow temporary marriages to women working as prostitutes. From criminalization to regulation, the change in policy enabled the sites of prostitution to mutate and thus be absorbed by other spaces and paradigms.

The penultimate chapter, entitled "Naked Modesty and the Reformation of Statues," explores the regulatory methods of erasure and modification through the handling of artistic representations of women under the Islamic Republic. The removal and/or modification of statues depicting women illustrate the great lengths to reconfigure public space as a sexually regulated and modest setting. As concrete examples, this chapter highlights how public space is redesigned to express and reinforce positive "Islamic revolutionary values" in the face of growing domestic opposition to social policies and the pressure of global forces, such as the internet and consumerism.

The fifth and final chapter, "When HIV/AIDS Meets Government Morality," is the last site of inquiry for this work. Divided into two parts, it first provides a historical overview of HIV/AIDS discourse in Iran, and it then studies the experiential side of bodily technologies related to morality, modesty, and marital relations from the perspectives of a select group of Iranian women living with HIV. Despite the increasing numbers of HIV infections countrywide, public health and NGO efforts to ameliorate the living conditions and health care of specifically HIV-positive women are in a nascent stage. Many of these efforts are often impeded by contradictory data and mixed messages coming from religious authorities and state officials, coupled with the disease's stigmatization and overall public ignorance about HIV/AIDS and its "high-risk" groups. This means that those who carry the virus face a particularly unique dilemma: How does one break down a social stigma of a STD when one is generally perceived to be the physical manifestation and carrier of that disease?

Chapter 1

REFORM

AN ART OF VISUAL PERSUASION

Did the 1979 Revolution mark a cessation or continuation of regulating women using certain bodily technologies for the purposes of reform and discipline? How women's sexuality and femininity came to be regulated and desired in the policies and visual imagery of the Islamic Republic bore striking similarities to how they came to be reformed, disciplined, and conceptualized during the Pahlavi years. Identifying both unique *and* similar modes of regulation to corroborate this "un-transformative trajectory," so to speak, is this chapter's purpose. In emphasizing this continuous process, I discuss the state enterprise of transforming women and their bodies into malleable, consuming objects that require radical change—whether by a "Westernized" public culture during the Pahlavi regime or by Islamist ideology in the Islamic Republic. In this chapter, I document how this leitmotif formed well before 1979 as part of a routine reshaping of women's desires, lifestyles, and femininity during the 1960s.

Hamid Dabashi and Peter Chelkowski examined the rich iconography of the Iranian Revolution in *Staging a Revolution: The Art of Persuasion in the Islamic Republic of Iran*. Sorting through revolutionary slogans, banknotes, banners, posters, and other graphic material, they studied the integration of Shi'a beliefs in mobilizing massive protest politics, culminating in the end of the Pahlavi dynasty. Their project ignited a similar direction for this work, albeit one exhumed from a compelling single source: *Zan-e Rouz*, a popular Iranian women's journal whose publication continued despite changing government regimes and editorial boards. Since its first issue in 1965, *Zan-e Rouz*'s history has spanned more than five decades. When the two manifestations of the journal (prerevolutionary and postrevolutionary) are analyzed as one archive, their evolution in content, visual presentation, and readership are read as a historic cache comprised of popular, typical, and illuminating images of continuous and not disparate periods of regulation.

The selection of photographs and articles from this journal shares informational, propagandist, comedic, consumerist, and pop-cultural characteristics. As a collection, they provide contrapuntal evidence to the idea that the Iranian woman underwent such a transformative overhauling in 1979. For, it is commonly held that this year marks the moment she comes into a revolutionary consciousness, abandoning her consumerist, sexualized ways for the persona of a pious, overtly sexless yet maternal woman of IRI. The evidence rouses other possibilities: studying photographs and articles in this influential magazine from 1965 to 1986 suggests that the transformations and subtle shifts in the concept of "Iranian women" were more unitary in presentation and message. In fact, throughout both regimes, women were presented as abstract, sexualized, consumerist, and desirous. More so, their reform was necessarily dependent on a vast enterprise of producing identifiable personality types consistent with the ideological agendas of each period. In many instances, women were encouraged to accept the novel reshaping of their bodies and the overhauling of their interests and identities as prerequisites for their entrance into a "better life." This undertaking was initiated, defined, and refined through collaborative efforts of state institutions, with varied assistance from editorial boards of major magazines, to communicate to and convince a broad audience the necessity of modern progress, reform, and ideology.

Reviewing Zan-e Rouz in History

Ronald Inglehart and Wayne Baker note, "Well into the twentieth century, modernization was widely viewed as a uniquely Western process that non-Western societies could follow only in so far as they abandoned their traditional cultures and assimilated technologically and morally 'superior' Western ways."[1] The Pahlavi regime "promoted a pseudo-modernist orientation that equated Westernization with modernization, and which increased technological, economic, political and cultural dependence upon the West."[2] According to the modernization paradigm in which the Pahlavi-era project of reform operated, women had to become Westernized in order to be more socially desirable and acceptable. The process would necessitate their bodies' submission to particular codes of conduct and styles of dress as an expression of the ideal and modern Iranian women.

The year 1965 marked *Zan-e Rouz's* inaugural year of publication, when the weekly entered the panoply of print publications targeting female audiences and showcasing Iran's modern course.[3] The brainchild of journalist and editor in chief Majid Davami, its founding was closely tied to the auspicious growth of *Kayhan* (The Universe), an evening paper, which later became an institution and Davami a publishing magnate within a span of thirty years.[4] Both *Kayhan* and *Zan-e Rouz* were financed by academic and newspaper publisher Mostafa Mesbahzadeh, a Sorbonne-trained jurisprudence scholar and former senator under Muhammad Reza Shah.[5] Mesbahzadeh dreamed of turning Iran into a news-making, journalistic tour de force. He sought to cultivate an Iranian newspaper milieu in which Iranian publishers and journalists were no longer under pressure from pro-British and Soviet forces, which at the time were subsidizing the distribution and publication of many of Iran's dailies.[6] *Kayhan* distinctly reported on events important to Iran's ruling constitutional monarchy, which simultaneously led to favorable advertisement for the Pahlavi regime.[7] Through its domestic expansion, it evolved into a semiautonomous publishing company, known as the Kayhan Institute, which launched a range of magazines that targeted different generations and genders of audiences, in Iran and abroad.[8] The English-language newspaper *Kayhan International*, created and based in London, was followed by *Kayhan Varzeshi* (Sport), *Kayhan Farhangi* (Cultural), and *Kayhan Bacheha* (Children).[9] *Zan-e Rouz* was the last to be launched, focusing on a seemingly underrepresented audience within the general readership of *Kayhan*: Iranian women.[10] As the authoritative older brother-figure to its lesser-known sister *Zan-e Rouz*, Kayhan Institute offered a ripe gestational space in which the women's magazine would generate itself and find purpose. This business venture into female-targeted magazines proved fruitful. By 1979, the average circulation of *Zan-e Rouz* had reached 250,000 while newspaper *Kayhan* was reported at one million.[11]

State-funded radio, television, and publishing[12] were key to this process of constructing desires for modern and upper-class lifestyles. The Pahlavi state seemed to be in "the mood of a consumption-oriented environment."[13] With the aid of advertising images, print, and broadcast media, the regime sought to emphasize raising Iranians' "social knowledge" to enhance the public's reception of its modernization policies.[14] To do so would involve an overt collaboration among government, consumerist, and corporate interests.[15] Investing in the publishing industry, for example, meant that the government would not only become a substantial source of revenue for magazines, but it would also dictate the limit and scope of their editorial content—likely an important factor for editors in the decision-making process about featured content at magazines like *Zan-e Rouz*.[16] Underlining this union of forces was the threat of financial doom, which bore consequences for news editors and influenced magazine content and editorial direction. Haleh Esfandiari recalled this very tension in her memoir. Reflecting on her tenure as a journalist at *Kayhan*, she wrote, "The government was a source of advertising revenue, and it set policies that could affect everything from *Kayhan*'s ability to purchase newsprint abroad to Mesbahzadeh's considerable land holdings. Increasingly the shah and the government showed less tolerance for even the mildest criticism, and the grip on the media of the emboldened Information Ministry grew tighter."[17]

As a popular magazine under the direct guidance and sponsorship of the royal family, *Zan-e Rouz* operated in part as a state ideological outlet to construct a consumer society, meaning that a highly stylized femininity and sexuality went hand in hand with Pahlavi Iran's paradigm of modernity. Although first identifying itself as a journalistic space dedicated to improving Iranian women's social and political status, *Zan-e Rouz*'s editorial board soon clarified its ultimate purpose and direction: Several issues after its launch, the magazine's content began to highlight more fashion and popular culture; their advertisements featured household commodities and beauty regimens. This about-face was deliberate in the context of a reform-minded Pahlavi leadership. The intention was to quickly develop Iran into a modern, capitalist society, moving away from its agrarian roots and promoting education, literacy, development, and economic restructuring via a fourteen-year reform program the Shah called the *Enqelab-e Safid* (White Revolution). Images of gleaming kitchen appliances, perfumes, makeup, and fashionable European clothes were described as basic commodities meant to achieve a modern Iran. This aspect of commodity culture helped construct cultural ideas about modern lifestyle, self-improvement, glamour, and how things should be.[18] *Zan-e Rouz* positioned itself within the glitz and glamour of an advertising, celebrity cosmos.[19] Beauty advertisements selling products from Germany and America were plentiful, supplementing articles on self-improvement and the rising stardoms of actresses Sophia Loren and Elizabeth Taylor. There were feature articles on hairstyle trends, from the beehive to the bouffant styles, offering advice to readers on the most appropriate occasions to wear them.[20] Women were similarly advised on how to better maintain their skin, via the application of requisite vitamins and creams, to ensure a dewy, youthful appearance.[21] A woman's public image and body image awareness were consistent themes in *Zan-e Rouz*'s prerevolutionary days.[22] In the late 1970s, there appeared to be even more articles on beauty maintenance, body language, and etiquette.

This enterprise of modernization necessarily entailed reforming men's and women's desires and interests. Hence in order to cultivate the concept of a "modern Iranian woman," magazine content, including advertisements and feature articles, were central to reorienting women's manner and style of dress, or their social habits. However, to humanize this message for female audiences, enter Her Royal Highness, *Shahbanu*.

Emancipating Women through Shahbanu's Image

Since the Constitutional Revolution (in Persian *Enqelab-e Mashruteh*, 1905–11), a new formation of the model Iranian citizen was being constructed and subsequently promoted among the country's diverse population of Azeris, Baluchs, Persians, Kurds, and many others.[23] Under the realm of Reza Shah Pahlavi, the father of Muhammad Reza, the authorities amplified their communications to Iranians the characteristics of a modern lifestyle, calling attention to Western fashions, motherhood roles, and household responsibilities. This articulation of modern life was wrapped in women's citizenship duties to the nation-state. In a modernized Iran, tribal and spousal affiliations were secondary and tertiary identity markers; instead, women owed their progress and allegiance to a larger institution, the Iranian state.

By the mid-1960s the Pahlavi family with Muhammad Reza at the helm had initiated both extensive reforms and a countrywide campaign promoting their imperial heritage as successors to dynastic conquerors of Asia Minor from the sixth century BCE.[24] The Shah and his third childbearing wife Farah Pahlavi—*Shahbanu* (meaning "Empress," a Sassanid title), as she was called by the moniker-loving Iranian press—co-opted the majestic narrative of Cyrus the Great—acclaimed hero of the Achaemenid Empire—to promote this royal lineage to the Iranian public.[25] Abrahamian writes,

> [The Shah] declared that Iran was at the gates of the Great Civilization; its future would be more glorious than its past—including the Achaemenid, Sassanid, and

Parthian empires; its standard of living would soon surpass that of Europe; it would produce a way of life superior to both capitalism and communism; and indeed within a generation it would be the world's fifth most powerful country—after the USA, Soviet Union, Japan, and China.[26]

The metonymic association of the modern Pahlavis with ancient Persian kings and their beloved queens, despite the passage of more than a dozen centuries, was recast into a contemporary fantasy of a modern, Westernized, and Persian king and queen. Ancient grandeur became contemporized for a female audience through the iconic figure and presentation of Empress Farah, whose daily schedule became news fodder and thus a matter of public concern.

During her royal tenure as queen, Farah Pahlavi was captured in photographs as loving wife, mother, charity worker, and approachable leader. Unlike her husband, who was often photographed in military regalia, she was pictured wearing modern fashions popular among the elite classes. "The Queen represented the ideal stereotype of the emancipated Iranian woman," the late historian Parvin Paidar commented, "and, as such, had everything that the Shah desired in a woman. As a woman she was beautiful, feminine and elegant; as a wife she was loyal, subservient and caring; as a mother she was devoted and conscientious. She believed that her prime responsibility in life was looking after her husband and children but her role as the Queen required her to take an interest in extra-familial affairs. She left the serious business of the state in the hands of her husband and took up 'feminine' pursuits such as a social welfare, education, art and culture."[27] Women's magazines like *Zan-e Rouz* projected her ideational force onto a mass audience. Photos capturing intimate moments with Farah Pahlavi inside the palace walls helped shorten the distance between the monarch and her people.

Becoming modern involved cultivating a consumer breeding ground on which both Pahlavi reforms and consumer marketing campaigns could meet a wider Iranian audience. Along with the expansion in radio and television programs and sales, publishing in general and women's magazines in particular were apt forums to advertise Iran's integration of global capital. The language of this integration, however, was in the vernacular of rights and emancipation. The latter subject was particularly attractive to reformers set on disseminating a novel state "feminist" project. The groundwork for improving women's status was achieved through advertising a different way of dress and behavior, which was believed to help women transition from traditional to modern ways of living. Consider the opening greeting of the first issue of *Zan-e Rouz*. Addressing their readers, the weekly's editorial board praised "Her Majesty the Royal Highness Pahlavi" for inspiring its efforts to elevate women's status:

In this present era when Iranian women face great purpose, with abundance of freedom and equality, they should now endeavor to elevate themselves, their own status, and personal sense of what they should provide for their country.

Her Royal Highness Farah Pahlavi is hopeful that this journal, *Zan-e Rouz*, would guide and advise Iranian women to reach their goals. We hope to try, using as much power as we have in this path, to make ourselves proud and honored before the society of Iranian women. Her Excellency *Shahbanu* (Farah Pahlavi) is our greatest supporter in this endeavor.[28]

From this brief introduction, the weekly journal acknowledges its semiautonomous status by linking itself to royalty. In what may be read as both an opportunity to stroke the ego of a royal and having special access to the Queen, the clear reference of her approving their mission statement suggests that the editors understood their elevated purpose. They had assumed the responsibility of being a modernizing force for a readership comprised of fans of the royal family. This assumption persists throughout *Zan-e Rouz*'s content until the revolution. Upon closer inspection, the preceding statement transmits multiple problematic messages about women's status in Iran. In addition to the obvious textual messages, there were a number of subtextual messages. First, the magazine board greeted women as a collective entity, erasing any differences among them; their aspirations were treated as communal, as part of a "society." Explicit was its praise of the freedoms bestowed upon Iran's women, assumedly granted by the monarchial state; absent was any mention of real criticism directed at the Pahlavis. Rather, this introductory greeting reads as a written pledge to uniformly support and disseminate Iran's modernization efforts. For Iranian women were purportedly not sufficient as they were, as the greeting infers. The queen and this weekly helped them strive to improve their status. Without such guidance, Iranian women would hypothetically not reach their potential and, in part, be led astray from their objectives of national service and socioeconomic development.

Framing the Queen from Different Angles

In the prerevolutionary issues of *Zan-e Rouz*, Farah Pahlavi was presented as a fashionable and glamorous Iranian woman. An empress "of the people," she embodied a majestic, yet approachable persona, and thus through her symbolic figure, the Pahlavi state-initiated reforms of Iranian women via her image. *Zan-e Rouz* gave access to the pomp and circumstance as well as behind-the-scenes coverage of her life as monarch. Several issues were dedicated to her interactions with the public. In one striking photo spread, the queen was photographed meeting with *chador*-wearing provincial women—her designer outfit contrasting their regional dress.

In other settings, her service as the "nation's mother" was documented through "private" portraits of her with her young children. Consider the photographs from Figures 1.1 and 1.2—both taken circa 1965. The same scene is replicated in Figure 1.2, though it was shot from another angle. Figure 1.1 is a photograph of the front cover of the inaugural issue of *Zan-e Rouz*. The photo was not published in the magazine and was likely an outtake from the photo shoot. In any case, images like Figure 1.1 seldom graced *Zan-e Rouz*'s covers, for later issues featured a variety of models, singers, and cultural icons.[29]

When inspecting the images and having little contextual information, the identities of these three subjects may not be so obvious. Yet for an older generation of Iranians, they would be easily identifiable: Empress Farah Pahlavi and her young children, Farahnaz and Reza. Figure 1.1 is a provocative illustration projecting the image of perfect domesticity with the Queen Mother. How they are seated, what they are doing, and how they are presented offer an intimate peek not only into royal life but also into how to live as a modern, Iranian family. Notably absent from this family photograph is a male presence—meaning no father, husband, or male figure is present in the scene's foreground or background. The omission of Muhammad Reza Shah from this portrait reinforces the importance of the central character of this photograph as the queen and her responsibilities toward her children.

Through the photographer's lens, the viewer observes a precious moment among royal family members, presumably captured in a palace salon or library. There is a sense of balance between foreground and background; the subjects and the setting occupy roughly equal areas in the frame. The bouffant-haired queen, seated with her bare legs crossed, appears to be guiding her children through an engaging story. She appears equally engrossed in reading, and in Figure 1.2, she is depicted pointing to something in a book.[30] In both photos she has wrapped her arms around her children, and they seem mutually transfixed, undisturbed by the fact that their reading time is being observed and photographed by others. While sheltered by their mother's embrace, daughter Farahnaz sucks her thumb, leaning on her mother's lap. Her brother Reza, smartly attired in a light blue V-neck sweater, also leans in, apparently mesmerized by his mother's reading and pointing. The scene suggests a normal and habitual activity between a doting parent and child. Yet this moment of tenderness between mother and children communicates more

Figure 1.1 *Zan-e Rouz* cover page featuring Shahbanu.

Figure 1.2 *Zan-e Rouz* cover page featuring Shahbanu, from another angle.

than just family habits and pastimes; it also showcases the Pahlavi's unique lifestyle and more so, their utter modernity.

When positioned side by side, both images reveal subtle and marked differences in tone, effect, and narrative structure. In Figure 1.2, the viewer's central focus is the three individuals because the photograph was shot at a side-angle; as a result of this positioning, the scene feels more intimate. Additionally, there is more contrast in the black-and-white image; the subjects' faces are brighter, and the background is darker, creating a heightened, dramatic effect. Because the image is both visually stark and a medium shot, the main characters in this scene are in full frame. The viewer's interest is narrowed, and the shot provides more details about the royal family's facial expressions and gestures. Where they sit is also significant in this pictorial illustration of modern life. Note the decorative accoutrements of technological advancements in the background that are enhanced by the color hues: a wooden entertainment center is staffed with books, handicrafts, and vases. To the right of the figures, a fuller view of the TV screen gleams in the background; to the left, several books align the shelves, tilted ever so slightly as if to signal their daily usage and haphazard placement. A *Zan-e Rouz* magazine reader-viewer would have been able to perceive more details of the subjects' surroundings in Figure 1.1, whose background lighting is not dimmed like in Figure 1.2.[31]

"The photograph itself," writes Pierre Bourdieu, "is usually nothing but the group's image of its own integration."[32] In *Photography: A Middle-Brow Art*, Bourdieu analyses the social practice of taking pictures among the French social classes.[33] Photography developed into a structured cultural activity promoting social norms and codes of conduct among the bourgeoisie. A photographic image should not be treated as having just an objective illustration of a group of people at a particular event; it has a didactic and instructional purpose: to project an image of social cohesion through a produced collective memory of an event. For instance, the way people are positioned in photographs illustrates prestige, nostalgia, and class consciousness.

Bourdieu's discussion of the staging of characters in photographs is insightful in our endeavor to configure how pictures of Farah Pahlavi with her children help cultivate an image of an upper-class life and promote to the public its consumerism, fashion sense, and embrace of technology. Observe the household objects that surround the queen and her children, which are clearer in Figure 1.1. What appear to be decorative accents found in any home library or family salon are, in actuality, luxury goods not yet present in a cross section of Iranian households. At the time, "media images began to reflect growing foreignness of the physical and social environment, including architecture, clothing, food, social values and mores, and the growing social class divisions of consumption and attitudes," explains Sreberny-Mohammadi.[34] The television, in particular, is a special object in this photo; its style is appropriate for the era, but its presence would have been a rarity in Iranian households.[35] Figure 1.1 thus should be perceived as an advertisement for the products and comforts of modern-day kingship. Unlike advertisements for household appliances published in newspapers, these images depict the activities and lifestyle of an upwardly mobile royal family. The photos thus carried a unique, ideational force of luxury that, on the surface, was intricately modern, consumerist, intimate, active, and tacitly Iranian. Hence a queen reading to her children was a special event, worthy of a front-page cover story. In many ways, these images were visual souvenirs for mass consumption.[36] Both offered instructional cues for Iranian women on the importance of family pastimes in modern Iran, but only one enabled them access and information about Iran's journey toward "a better life." As such, the Iranian public peered into the queen's life, observing the idyllic setting of her household. They witnessed her family life, conducted in an orderly, peaceful, and refined setting.

Zan-e Rouz's Photoscape: Advertising Lifestyles

When perusing almost two decades' worth of issues, the inaugural *Zan-e Rouz* is an anomaly. While the first cover page extols a quiet, intimate moment of Pahlavi domestic life and motherhood, subsequent issues followed a different course: Iran as fashion center, embodied through the figures of hip cover models whose features viewers would not assume to be stereotypically Persian—meaning they did not have dark eyes and hair. In the second issue alone, a light-skinned, green-eyed model is dressed in brightly colored, 1960s Western fashions, exhibiting an exuberant and carefree manner. Gone is the royal valorization of pristine, family-centered homelife intimated the previous week.

Given the distinct shift in aesthetic direction and feature content, *Zan-e Rouz's* editorial staff were likely catering to a small niche of Iranian women's interests. The preponderance of articles emphasizing high-society life indicates that its true target audience was in fact Iran's upwardly mobile—the small network of urban elite and aristocratic families with direct ties to the Pahlavi regime and not regular Iranian women. In editions of the magazine from the late 1970s, many of the articles appeal to the interests of this upper class—that, or the desire to promote an upper bourgeois life to the general Iranian public.[37] In one illuminating example, an article described how Iranian female tourists faced social pressure after visiting boutiques in London and Paris.[38] The author depicts Iranian tourists as lavish spenders who shopped extensively just to prove, upon their return to Iran, that they could afford luxurious travel and thus did so only to become the envy of their peers. It was suggested that female tourists should minimize their shopping during vacation and instead enjoy sightseeing. In no part of the article did the author discuss how infrequent, improbable, and expensive international travel and shopping were for the majority of Iranians.

Interestingly, there were a few sections of the magazine that stood out for their recognition of nonelite Iranian women. In one short-lived column,[39] women were asked about their career interests, lifestyles, and romantic inclinations. Nine women were asked sixteen questions about their lifestyle habits and, specifically, their hobbies.[40] Their answers about pastimes included dancing, living simply with their parents, and being academically successful. When asked to identify their leisure activities, they named shopping, entertaining, and beautifying. The similarities in their responses conveyed that these gendered and consumerist pastimes were universal desires for the majority of Iranian women, irrespective of class, background, circumstance, and upbringing. Noticeably, surrounding the grainy black-and-white photographs of each Iranian respondent, there were stylized advertisements of European and American models and actors leaping from the pages.

Ramadan: The Art of Fasting and Remaining Beautiful

Alongside modernization reforms initiated in the mid-1960s came the flourishing of a revolutionary and forceful visual culture. In the theater of Iran's White Revolution, almost anything was subject to reform. The Pahlavi state's rapid modernization program sought a range of structural changes, from the state's economic and agricultural infrastructure to the shape of a woman's body. In fact, modernization was achievable for both the profane and spiritual. Consider Figure 1.3. Even the Islamic holy month of Ramadan was open to modification. A drawing that accompanied an article entitled "Fasting: The Best Regime for Achieving Health and Balance of the Body," it featured in *Zan-e Rouz*'s special edition, which commemorated the ninth month of the Muslim calendar, when believers observe fasting from dawn until sunset. The article's tone and content make obvious that fasting was a common method of dieting—and one openly discussed. "Fasting," the author quips, "is the best medicine for one's struggling with weight gain."[41] Written in a first-person narrative, the article's opening sentence reads, *Man dokhtar-e chaghi hastam* (I am a fat girl). Following this proclamation, the author informs the reader about fasting rituals across the globe.[42]

In no part of the article was fasting described as ritual practice; it seemed to hold even minimal spiritual significance. Instead, fasting during Ramadan was described as a dieting fad that accommodates the desires of a modern, Iranian woman. For the author's primary assumption was that the reader of *Zan-e Rouz* was a weight-conscious believer, and thus Ramadan was an opportune time to slim her burgeoning waistline. For when she fasted, her body physically improved. Her pimples apparently vanished; the pounds melted off. Her skin began to take on a dewy appearance, potentially shaving five to ten years of age off the dieter.[43] Indeed, by practicing self-restraint, she learned to eat less and achieve *ta'adol jesmi* (physical or bodily balance)—the union between her spirit and body. In this way, fasting was articulated as a modern, gendered strategy of improvement summed up in this question: What are the physical benefits to fasting during Ramadan? Chiefly, a desirable body.

Figure 1.3 drives home this point. It is meant to illustrate a typical predicament that Muslim women faced during Ramadan—their struggles choosing between

Figure 1.3 *Ta'adol jesmi.*

sweet indulgence and spiritual obligations. Yet note how this message was conveyed in the aforementioned article and its accompanying image. Certain tropes and stereotypes about femininity, body image, female sexuality, and piety were deployed in both. Their function bears a disciplinary quality, encouraging women to reform their physiques to meet a dual objective: desirability and religious observance. Upon closer inspection of the drawing itself, these themes become more evident. Notice the suggestive position in which the female subject—presumably the main character from the article—sits; her body is half covered in what appears to be a prayer *chador*.[44] Lush, pinkish hues are contrasted by the dark and light shadows, a visual effect which accentuates her physical shape underneath the cloth. Though the woman's body is not fully visible, its contours are. The viewer's gaze zooms in on her perfectly round breasts; they pop out of her V-neck blouse, held in place by a green garnet nestled between them. Hovering behind her is a portrait of a bearded spiritual guru, ostensibly in meditative pose and presumably from a distant land, though styled in some 1970s-era garment. He sits in the center, above her, as an ideal guide for her spiritual self. She is also flanked on both sides by two different vices. Edible desires linger in the background to her left; to her right, there is an open room to serenity, illustrated by snowcapped mountains perching over valleys. In this scene, the projection of edible desires is mixed into a sexually suggestive piety.

Indeed, the overall depiction of this character implies that beneath any Muslim-Iranian woman's *chador* lies the voluptuous body of a believer. She is represented as being simultaneously open, sexually suggestive, and at least on the surface, religiously observant. And somewhere in the background lurks the desirous male gaze; it is transfixed by the idea of what stirs underneath these layers. It even motivates a woman's perpetual labor to fast in order to remain an object of desire, to keep slim and enticing during Ramadan. Ironically, there is no mention in the article of the possibility that any of these reflections on fasting and weight loss would be deemed inappropriate or questionable in the eyes of practicing Muslim women.

Other articles promoting beauty maintenance include diagrams of exact body measurements of the ideal female form, which further reinforce the objectification of women. As demonstrated in Figure 1.4, a color-coordinated diagram accompanied the article "Chic, Beautiful and Cute." It described the ideal hand to elbow and waist to buttocks ratios to educate women on the most beautiful body composition and forms.[45] Another article about body and beauty perfection explored different styling techniques, such as dyeing one's hair color a lighter shade to match the popular European and American styles of the period.[46] Additionally, *Zan-e Rouz* integrated advertisements into its articles, showcasing new consumer goods and providing readers with commentary on how these products, from household appliances to new kinds of makeup, tested in homes. It appears that the most newsworthy topics often related to what could be sold to the general public. Advertisements about bodily improvement—the maintenance of a slim body, as illustrated in Figure 1.5—demonstrated the simple ways to maintain an attractive form through the purchase of stylish brassieres and

Figure 1.4 Body perfection chart.

Figure 1.5 Slimming garment advertisement.

undergarments—items that were imported from Europe and America sometime in the mid-1950s.[47]

Prerevolutionary issues of *Zan-e Rouz* sought to not only promote ideas about a woman's appearance but also her behavior. The magazine published numerous articles on etiquette, often including instructions on appropriate conduct for social

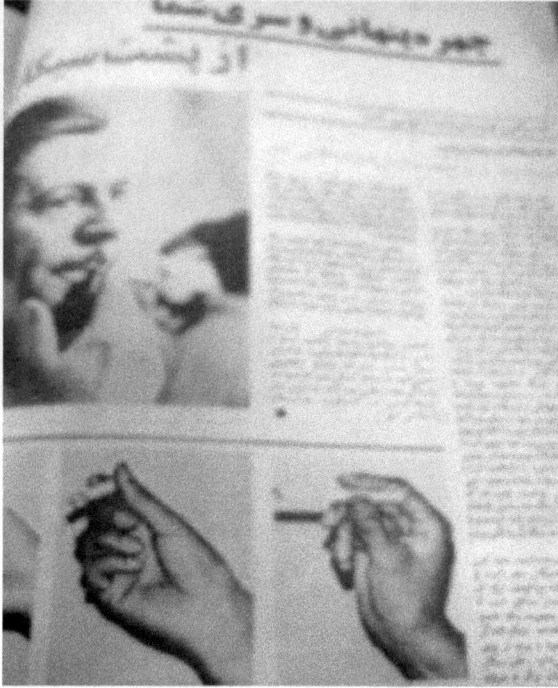

Figure 1.6 *Az posht-e cigar* article.

settings where others would observe (and likely judge) women's behaviors. How a woman maneuvers her body, even in the slightest movement of her hands, is material for observation and analysis. For instance, when hosting a successful dinner party, a woman should project the image of a reputable wife and homemaker who excels in the domains of family, cooking, and household chores and perfecting social norms.[48]

The magazine also gave advice on how to read people through their body language. Long before smoking was considered a social taboo and public health hazard, *Zan-e Rouz* was advising women on how to decipher the body language of a man or woman holding a cigarette. From the positioning of a cigarette in one's hand, it was possible to extend norms of sociability to an Iranian public. This advice featured in the article "Chehreh-ye Penhani va Seri-ye Shoma: Az Posht-e Cigar," as demonstrated in Figure 1.6.[49] The author implied that smoking cigarettes expressed a glamorous lifestyle, especially when the hand was extended and its silhouette became elongated by the presence of a slender white stick.[50] Yet if the cigarette were held incorrectly, the disreputable character of the cigarette owner would be understood and the viewer would have been forewarned.[51] Though the efficacy and impact of this mini training module is unknown, it suggests nevertheless that *Zan-e Rouz* intended to translate this purportedly socially acceptable and desirable lifestyle to its readers, promoting smoking as a passport to women's emancipation, glamour, and seduction.[52]

Caricatures in Service of the Male Gaze

Pivotal to women's acceptance of modernization was their education in its style and content: from fashionable hairstyles and appropriate hand gestures while smoking to household chores and perfection of marital responsibilities, women were instructed how to "better" themselves through the magazine's caricatures and articles. The modes of disciplining women's bodies were accomplished through presenting them as sexually desirable, followed by teaching women new and refined forms of etiquette and body language. Through the development of the television and advertising industry in Iran and the proliferation of color magazines targeted to female audiences, Iranian women were given visual proof of the sheer possibilities of being and looking modern.

In a magazine that aimed to present material consonant with the goals of "Today's women," especially in its desire to improve their social status, there were numerous caricatures of women that promoted misogyny by criticizing women's physical features. In the joke section of the weekly, specifically, there were repeated themes centered on the force of the heterosexual male gaze and the pressure it exerted on women to maintain certain physiques that men found attractive. *Zan-e Rouz* included caricatures that, on the surface, made light of male-female relations yet simultaneously illustrated a familiar awkwardness when men appeared to be sexually disappointed by women's bodies. In many of these caricatures, women's bodies were the prime target of admiration, shame, ridicule, and desire. For a magazine that alleged "to advise and guide women to reach their goals," there was no expressed critique or commentary about their humiliation and sexual objectification.

In the following examples, first illustrated in Figures 1.7 and 1.8, men's expectations of women's bodies were the main themes behind male-female interactions. Breast perfection—manifest by the appearance of ample breasts—motivated male expectations of the perfect, desirable female body and shape. No figure better illustrates this perfection than the figure given here where a women's

Figure 1.7 Breast expectations caricature.

از خواص آهن ربا !

لبخند

Figure 1.8 The power of magnets.

bosom is fully revealed. Figure 1.7, a black-and-white caricature printed in 1978, tells a one-scene story about a man's deflated expectations in the presence of a naked woman.[53] Here, a portly, middle-aged man appears confused after entering a bedroom because his expectations do not match what he sees before him. In his mind, he has envisioned the torso of a buxom, naked woman awaiting his arrival. Standing at the doorway, he sees a small-breasted woman and her lithe figure. The sight of her deflates his expectations of what he had imagined her to be. The woman still looks eagerly at him, as the expression on his face can be interpreted in two ways: the first, of disappointment; the second, of the insignificance of the woman herself. Remarkably, even in the man's imagination, the woman is not full-bodied to include her head and lower torso. Instead, his imagination only sees an ample bosom greeting him in the bedroom.

This peculiar attention to breasts recurred in another caricature from the same issue's joke section. Figure 1.8 presents a two-scene narrative, which is in effect a before and after shot. In one scene, a bespectacled man, dressed in a tuxedo, smiles admiringly at a woman wearing a strapless gown. The female character resembles a Jessica Rabbit-type character; she has exaggerated features and a buxom figure. Noticeably, she does not appear to have a nose. Instead, her face has only two doe-like eyes and provocatively pouted lips. The first scene presents the characters in the middle of a conversation, intimating that the man is listening intently to her, as his eyes are directed at hers. Yet this intent listening is only strategic. In the very next scene, the same man is holding a horseshoe magnet in his hand. Its force is so strong that the dress's jeweled pendant has been forced away from her gown, revealing perky breasts. The magnet now makes visible that which the male gaze had already imagined: her erect nipples.

Though the male audience was not explicitly mentioned in any of the content of prerevolution *Zan-e Rouz*, the countless advertisements and images on breast and body perfection that were directed at women speak to an overemphasis on valuing men's opinions of them. Many images featuring women were consistently mediated through a male gaze: how they dressed, wore their hair, revealed their bodies, and so on were fundamental to women learning how to please men. In some manner, women were educated in these proverbial schools of Pahlavi modernization to value and develop themselves ultimately to service men, not women. Understanding what social and beauty norms gave men pleasure meant that it was purportedly women's responsibility to satiate men's desires. That an Iranian woman should consistently exhibit a sexual vulnerability and need for improvement for the betterment of the modern Iranian man should not be denied.

Transitioning into an Islamic Republic

The association between high-life Tehran and upward mobility led to a grand concealment of the truth—of unsightly slums, of surmounting poverty on the peripheries of modernized reform, and of a dictatorship that eventually thrust Iran toward revolution. By the 1970s, the Pahlavis were the richest entrepreneurial family in Iran.[54] In the midst of an agrarian reform-driven White Revolution, an oil boom brought a gamut of changes that drastically adjusted the standard of living for many Iranian families.[55] A village flight from rural to urban sites ensued. Tehran was unprepared for the influx of migrants and the housing necessary to settle into metropolitan life. As Abrahamian has noted, "The sudden fivefold increase in the oil revenues inflated people's expectations and thereby widened the gap between, on one hand, what the regime promised, claimed, and achieved, and, on the other hand, what the public expected, obtained, and considered feasible."[56] According to Paidar, "[The Pahlavi regime] had always suffered from a degree of externality to society . . . [because it] managed to alienate most sections of society as a result of ruling through a combination of authoritarianism, favoritism, and patronage."[57]

Critique of the Pahlavi regime also focused, in part, on the growing moral and economic degradation of Iran; the modernizing plans of the Pahlavi monarchs were argued to have "ingratiated Iran to Western corporations and had imported a western mode of life," writes Shirin Deylami.[58] It was claimed that Iranian society had subsequently become stricken with a Western malaise, or "westoxified" (in Persian, *gharbzadeh* or stricken by Western culture).[59] The issues of women's presence and roles in society were particularly contentious for certain intellectuals and prominent religious scholars of the revolutionary period. As Valentine Moghadam writes, "The idea that women had 'lost honor' during the Pahlavi era was a widespread one."[60] The manner and style in which women dressed and behaved in public became scrutinized and thus identified as a typical characterization of a "westoxified" woman. According to Afsaneh Najmabadi, the *gharbzadeh* woman, in particular, "in its crudest form, she was identified with a woman who wore 'too much' make-up, 'too short' a skirt, 'too tight' a pair of pants, 'too-low-cut' a shirt, who was 'too loose' in her relations with men, who laughed 'too loudly,' who smoked in public."[61]

The prominent social, literary, and political writer and critic Jalal Al-e Ahmad (one of the few secular intellectuals to be praised by Khomeini[62]) proposed a cultural alternative to this *gharbzadeh* woman: the concept of a "modern-yet-modest" woman who was unlike the "painted dolls of the Pahlavi regime."[63] Al-e Ahmad argued that Westoxification had resulted in, according to Shirin Sedigh Deylami, a "libertine culture of sexuality without developing a juridical and political role for women."[64] Although he died a decade before the revolution, many of his ideas on *gharbzadegi* (Westoxification) were in harmony with those of the leading Shi'a clergy who became increasingly critical of the Shah and Iran's Westernization. Prominent revolutionary ideologues such as Ayatollah Khomeini and Ayatollah Morteza Motahhari, for example, called for a modest direction and more respectful treatment of Shi'a women.[65]

Fast-forward to the 1979 Iranian Revolution: magazines promoting this *gharbzadeh* woman character promptly ceased publication; in publishing hibernation, they worked on revamping style and content. Soon after, *Zan-e Rouz* in particular transformed into a platform showcasing a steady flow of images and content on veiled Muslim women who were "authentic."[66] Within two years after the revolution, women were pictured wearing loose overcoats, trousers, and veils, exposing just their hands, feet, and faces. Photographs and other visual media heralded the success of the revolution, commonly featuring the following visual motifs: wives in domestic settings; grieving mothers of veterans; and militant women marching in demonstrations, clad in *chadors*, "with their hands held high in exhortation."

The 1979 revolutionary period in Iran's modern history is analyzed as a watershed moment animating drastic political, economic, and social changes. It is often defined as a time of great historical ruptures, exemplified by the return from exile of charismatic Ayatollah Ruhollah Khomeini (1902–89), who upon his return to Iran, took the helm of a popular movement against the inaccessible, pro-Western dictator Muhammad Reza Shah Pahlavi.[67] Once revolutionaries secured control of state institutions and commenced the project of institutionalizing Khomeini's doctrinal concept of *velayat-e faqih* (Guardianship of the Jurist), some scholars have regarded this period as a breakaway point from Iran's modern course—from the progressive, liberal initiatives of the Pahlavi state to the radicalism and fundamentalism of an Islamist government run by high-ranking Shi'a ulama.[68]

The same dramatic script documenting epistemic shifts is cast onto the narrative of Iranian women's status after the revolution, especially with regard to their civil and political rights. Analysts contend that compulsory *hejab* (Islamic head covering), enacted gradually within three years after the revolution, set in motion the curbing of women's rights and the disciplining of their femininity and sexuality, to the chagrin and protest of many.[69] During anti-Shah demonstrations, the Islamic *hejab* became an important symbol of resistance to the imported "culture" and a symbol of rejection of Pahlavi values.[70] Ayatollah Khomeini had designs to reform Iran into an Islamic Twelver Shi'a society with a theocratic government. He and his hard-line supporters sought to consolidate their power even further through what Paidar refers to as a "rapid Islamization"—a strategy intended to "strengthen the Islamic features of society whilst the clergy was in leadership position and popular, and to delegitimize prerevolutionary secular concepts."[71] Since 1981, when the Islamic Republic adopted a constitution intended to foster an "Islamic society,"[72] one whose rules were enforced to comply with religious law, certain aspects of social life came under direct supervision of the state.[73] Subsequently compulsory veiling was reasoned as a beneficial method of protection for women. For Khomeini insisted, "As for women, Islam has never been against their freedom. It is, to the contrary, opposed to the idea of a woman-as-object and it gives her back her dignity."[74] Women were thus encouraged to dress modestly if they sought to be respected, honored, and no longer subjected to the objectification they experienced under the Pahlavis.[75]

As Iran's newly drafted constitution spoke of "drawing inspiration from the revolutionary and fertile teachings of Islam . . . to [raise] the level of ideological awareness and revolutionary consciousness of the Muslim people," great steps were taken to introduce and institutionalize Khomeini's doctrine of Islamic government to the Iranian public, of whom a large percentage were unaware as to how this would manifest as state policies.[76] What resulted, in part, was the formulation and implementation of ordinances and public statements on model citizenship that reflected what were loosely defined "Islamic values." Through the state's emphasis on modesty, sex segregation, appropriate attire in public space, and the sanctified family unit, state policy had a direct and fundamental impact on the lives and lifestyles of many Iranian women.[77]

Zan-e Rouz Enters the Islamic Republic

After Khomeini's clerical followers consolidated power, a massive enterprise in eradicating traces of the Westernized government and its network of secular institutions ensued.[78] In mainly institutions of the military, government agencies, and mass media, swift changes took place virtually overnight. The new Islamist government purged members of the *ancien regime* and began to employ a volunteer corps of revolutionaries who sought to radically transform Iran into a more just, independent, and Muslim country. Calls to strengthen the institution of the family—and specifically facilitate women's roles within the domestic sphere—reverberated in the halls of state institutions, which underwent radical, cultural revolutions of their own.[79] Certain semiautonomous companies, like Kayhan Institute (publishers of the magazine *Zan-e Rouz*), though not a direct apparatus of the state like television and oil divisions, underwent drastic changes in staff, membership, and institutional objectives. On the national level, revolutionary clerics and their supporters emphasized the establishment of a mass media that was both informative and expressed the ethical values defined by the constitution of the Islamic Republic.[80] At the same time, a national constitution was being drafted, insisting that in an Islamic Republic, women would not be treated as "an object or instrument in the service of promoting consumerism and exploitation." She would, instead, "recover her momentous and precious function of motherhood, rearing of ideologically committed human beings," and "[assume] a pioneering social role and [become] the fellow struggler of man in all vital areas of life."[81]

While other women's magazines were closed down due to diverse reasons, such as government pressure or lack of staff and funding, *Zan-e Rouz* survived after having overhauled its editorial board and overall objectives. The weekly reformed itself in the 1980s as an Islamic lifestyle magazine, entering the revolutionary print media enterprise. Editor Shahla Ansari took control of the journal in 1980, followed by Firuzeh Gol-Mohammadi and then feminist Shahla Sherkat until 1991.[82] The new editorial board initiated a drastically different agenda from its prerevolutionary past. Iranian human rights lawyer Mehrangiz Kar recalls, "The weekly *Zan-e Rooz* (Today's Woman), had, like a modern woman who had suddenly become pious and weighted down with the *hejab*, transformed."[83] She observes, "It continued to be published, only now its cover seemed tired and dark."[84] No longer would magazine articles report on pop singer Googoosh and beauty pageant contestants. Photographs published in *Zan-e Rouz* incorporated an Islamic coding into its visual topography of women's bodies. Veiled women were photographed at work, in village settings, engaging in handicraft, wearing traditional clothing, or in their homes. They were depicted in stereotypically traditional settings deemed more suitable and representative of the lifestyle that a Muslim, Iranian woman in the modern Islamic Republic would have.

In postrevolutionary editions of *Zan-e Rouz*, content featured the methods in which to foster Islamic social virtues, including sections on respecting women and their roles as Muslims, wives, and mothers and maintaining chaste and modest relations between the sexes. Moreover, the magazine's advertisements changed considerably in content, design, and look; they no longer include photographs highlighting lingerie, American appliances, and fashion trends. Instead, a typical print ad would feature wedding attire, sewing classes, day care, real estate, and potential marriage suitors, too. Arts and crafts sections, such as *khayati* (sewing), were too expanded. Content-wise, articles were focused on novel methods to enhance women's spiritual health, reporting on topics such as *rouh-e zan* (woman's soul) and establishing a new column entitled "women in the family," to highlight their unique role within this social unit. The number of photo spreads and news reports on Islamic attire and clothing typically worn by Iran's indigenous, tribal communities were also increased.

The new direction for *Zan-e Rouz*—now reincarnated as a magazine catering to a distinctly Muslim female audience—was meant to reinforce the notion that the newly coined Islamic Republic was promoting a nativist, spiritually inclined and family-oriented version of Iranian woman. Moreover, the magazine became a platform for theological debates, wherein Qur'anic exegesis and feature articles on legal interpretations of *hejab* and women's rights in Islam were central to its content.[85] Regarding the latter, the incorporation of rights discourse from the Qur'an in post-1979 editions of *Zan-e Rouz* offered a popular and literary forum on which to promote the revolution's ideological tenets, which were enumerated in both its national constitution and in the mission statement of its Cultural

Revolutionary Council. This committee, established by the Islamic Republic's ideological founder Khomeini, began setting expectations for state media, stipulating that it should reflect and support good morals based on faith and also raise public awareness through the proper use of mass media. For these reasons, the majority of postrevolutionary *Zan-e Rouz*'s content highlights Muslim women's piety and family roles.

Ideological Subjects in the Islamic Republic of Iran: From Bodies to Body Parts

Ashraf Zahedi has argued, "To revive authentic Islamic beliefs as the foundation of a new society, it was necessary to reeducate Muslims, particularly women."[86] The following illustration, printed within one year after the revolution, best exemplifies Zahedi's point regarding the types of instructional methods and material created to instruct and guide women, specifically. Figure 1.9 is an illustration that accompanied a February 1980 article in *Zan-e Rouz* entitled "Woman, in Three Mirrors" from the section, "Knowing the Right Islam in the Domain of Women."[87] The drawing is meant to depict how women operate in different socioeconomic and ideological systems—in this case, those of capitalism, communism, and Islam. Moreover, it conveys positive values for women representing the Muslim faith and to some extent, how women within this structure should achieve and embrace these values.

Figure 1.9 "Women in Three Mirrors."

As understood by reading the article accompanying this drawing, the three female figures are not meant to depict women as they appear in human form; in fact, they portray symbolic and generic prototypes. Each figure is a representative member of a distinct ideological system that is practiced in different geographic areas. The leftmost figure is a generic American woman, followed by her Soviet counterpart in the middle, and lastly, a woman from a Muslim country. While it is not certain this last country represents Iran (for its country flag bears different features), it is clear through the inclusion of Arabic and the message it communicates, via the *shahada*, which is the most important Muslim proclamation of faith meaning "There is no God but God," that this female figure is a member of the *ommat* (the worldwide community of Muslims bound by their faith).[88] Assuming that each flag corresponds to a particular ideological system or way of life, it is then surmised that the American woman heralds from a capitalist system, and her Soviet and Muslim counterparts represent the systems of communism and Islamism, respectively.

Viewed in juxtaposition, these figures reveal two underlying assumptions about women's participation in certain ideological systems: first, that their roles, values, and worth can be both limited to and depicted through the use of their requisite body parts; second, that women are represented as the boundary-making objects of a state's ideological system and political agenda. In each figure, symbolic body parts are blackened to emphasize the values associated with a particular ideology. For the American, her values are expressed through the exploitation of her physical appearance, which is illustrated in the illustrator's accentuation of her bodily shape. The article supports this claim, referring to American women as easily "usable," especially in a capitalist system that encourages them to project their sexuality into the public domain. By comparison, the Soviet and the Iranian/ Muslim prototypes are more favorably depicted. While the Soviet woman uses her arms, representing her labor power, the Muslim figure uses both her intellect and emotions, depicted in the drawing of her brain and heart.

Zan-e Rouz had made the case that among the women of the world, in particular those women living in superpowers the United States and the Soviet Union in the 1980s, the Muslim woman was superior to both—and by extension, so was the Islamic Republic. Indeed, it was the Muslim female subject who was exemplary among these three. For in an Islamic system, she would be able to exploit her mental and emotional capacities, which distinguished herself from her counterparts. Moreover, standing next to the *shahada*, she was supported by a community of faith that endowed her with these specific capabilities and values. The inclusion of the Qur'anic injunction of the *shahada* means that she, too, had "Truth" on her side, signifying her obedience to God's absolute words.[89] As such, her strengths lay not in her physical appearance, but in the union of her head, heart, and God to determine her value and worth. This message was thus conveyed to any *Zan-e Rouz* reader, who became engaged in a one-way conversation about the benefits of membership in such a powerful and influential Islamic society.

Beyond the primary meaning conveyed by both the illustration and article, there are many underlying messages that register a darker reading of this representation of women. Clearly the juxtaposition of female prototypes demonstrates an underlying assumption about women's worth—that its significance is best expressed by its association with a particular system or ideology, be it of Western origin or not. Likewise, the figure of woman is constrained by the expectations and details of these three prisms, or "mirrors," as the article's title suggests. Hence, women do not represent themselves; they represent entire systems. As an example, the Muslim woman is depicted as a collective entity and *not* as an individual. Thus, women are presented as having an absence of choice, in moving fluidly between each system and more so, to variegate which mental and physical capacities they wish to exploit.

In this paradigm, an Iranian-Muslim woman's exclusion from and inclusion into a particular ideological community are dependent on how she proves her worth in relation to the ideal character imagined by that Islamist system. This restrictive articulation of Muslim women is a device for an ideological system to impose itself onto a symbolic woman who then becomes a model for female citizens. More so, the control of female bodies and behaviors were central to the projection of success for this state Islamization project; women were quickly expected and made to alter their beings, from purportedly Westernized, capitalist-leaning individualists of the Pahlavi era to ideal, traditional Muslim women. This however presented special challenges for Iranian women—especially in a frenzied postrevolutionary context wherein new social norms and expectations were being hammered out helter-skelter.

Demonstrating Modesty through Caricature

During the reign of Reza Shah, father of Muhammad Reza, the state attributed Iran's "backwardness" to traditional practices like veiling that promoted Muslim women's modesty. Modesty discourse of the state took other forms once Islamists ascended to power in 1979, given their attempts to "reconstruct and re-strengthen hetero-marital sexuality," writes Shahidian.[90] In Khomeini's Islamic Republic, modesty was heralded as a gendered marker of resistance against the sexual objectification of women.[91]

Writings on sexuality are closely tied to state attempts "to regulate people's identity and behavior, and challenges to cultural norms, social practices, and dominant gender roles."[92] Shi'a *ulama* used the language of protecting women from being exploited and leading them to a morally virtuous path.[93] Within the purview of Shi'a Islamic thought, modesty is considered a quality of forbearance that believers should aspire to embody and manifest in their appearance, behavior, and reflections. To express modesty does not mean the simple limitation of one's wealth or acquisition of material goods or wearing clothing that hides the body. It also necessarily entails the development of social virtues in trusted human institutions, such as the family.

In the Qur'an, Motahhari argued, Shi'a women's value was defined by their familial roles, as wives and mothers. Assuming these responsibilities would ensure society's overall well-being and help define men's familial roles, too.[94] Outside the family domain, Motahhari argued that the *hejab* was an "important device created to preserve the separation of the sphere of the 'family' from 'civil society' and it was women's responsibility to preserve it."[95] The process of transforming a woman's Westernized body into a modest configuration involved applying several visual and editorial techniques to construct and style a prototypic image of a Muslim female subject. Islamist-lifestyle magazines were optimal forums to spotlight a new visual reality for the figure of a Muslim woman.

As a way to signal *Zan-e Rouz*'s nonexploitative treatment of women, article content integrated many of the motifs popular among Iran's clerical authority: piety, modesty, family, and morality, among many others. Evoking these values would mean modifying societal behavior by introducing and, in many cases, emphasizing norms of conduct. For example, early editions of postrevolutionary *Zan-e Rouz* published several articles against makeup usage, discontinuing coverage of beauty products and hairstyle trends. Interviews with regime representatives were included in the magazine's content, which can be interpreted as its endorsement of the government. In one particular article, a *Zan-e Rouz* journalist interviewed a female parliamentarian from the Islamic Council.[96] In the interview, she connected makeup usage to the pitfalls of American imperialism and consumerism and lambasts women in "Third World countries" who wore makeup. She claimed their emphasis on their physical appearance had made them vulnerable to exploitation by consumerist nations, and thus encouraged Iranian women to lift themselves up.[97] To reject the trappings of a consumerist society, she advised women to become "unaccustomed" to makeup usage in order to promote their inner spiritual capacities.[98]

Another method of communicating Islamic values to Iranian women was achieved by standardizing the way they appeared in both images and in public. For print media, this was actualized through modifying women's bodies in images using various techniques, like streamlining their curves and drawing objects over women's faces. A woman's breasts, hips, arms, posterior, and legs were especially scrutinized because, according to some religious scholars, they are considered *awrat*, an Islamic term denoting sensitive or intimate body parts that must be covered in order to prevent sin.[99]

Of the *Zan-e Rouz* issues I reviewed, dating from 1980 until 1986, photographs (whose original negatives featured European and American models in Western attire) were extensively doctored. Almost every image (and every female featuring) in the magazine underwent some kind of reconstruction. *Awrat* areas in particular were usually covered by extra clothing, which was often superimposed onto or drawn over the original image. In many cases, veils and trouser legs were added on bare legs, and skirts and sleeves were elongated. Save the feet and hands, arms and legs were no longer exposed, as they were considered naked and thus inappropriate for public viewing. Additionally, print models were given "Islamic" makeovers. Now wearing *hejab*, they wore very minimal makeup. More so, the presentation of toned down and unaccentuated women's faces conveyed their disinclination to beautify themselves for the admiration of men, other than their husbands.[100]

In many images, the natural curves of her body shape, such as the hip and posterior areas, appeared to be flat or downsized. Certain anatomical features of the body were also removed or obscured, such as nipples and navels.[101] In cases when no photograph existed, simplistic drawings are used to depict female figures or specific body parts. In certain instances, when body parts were excised and thus missing from the original figure, a cartoon would be superimposed onto it. The next four illustrations document each of these techniques, starting with the design method used to reduce a woman's bodily curves.

Reconvening its columns on health and body maintenance after the revolution, *Zan-e Rouz*'s editors continued publishing step-by-step exercise regimens to promote healthy lifestyles and physiques of its readers. Figure 1.10, for example, is a 1980 illustration of a husband and wife team posing in various stretch positions found in the *Varzesh* (exercise) section from postrevolutionary editions of *Zan-e Rouz*.[102] The captions accompanying each exercise provide narrative snippets about a married couple seeking to lose weight. As a solution, the author suggested working out together to achieve both marital unity and weight loss.

In Figure 1.10 specifically, many of the techniques used to modify women's figures into ideal representatives of an Islamist system are evident, especially in the streamlined presentation of a woman's curves. Notice how the woman's breast area is variously represented in different scenes. When the female character is seated, with one leg raised, her chest is evident in the twisting of her body. In one specific pose, both man and woman's bodies join to form an upside-down heart, evidenced by the empty space formed between their legs.[103] As shown in Figure 1.10, in which the female subject pushes her body up off the floor, her breasts vanish. Her body is streamlined to look like that of her male exercise partner. This depiction results in

Figure 1.10 Couples exercising in IRI *Zan-e Rouz*.

the desexualization of her body—her body shape is rendered formless, appearing linear.

By 1985, women's bodies were depicted in outline form and illustrated with less detail in the face and body in the magazine's *Varzesh* section, as shown in Figures 1.11 through 1.13.[104] And just one year later, in 1986, characters no longer wore full-bodied leotards as an example of exercise attire. Instead female characters were depicted wearing appropriate Islamic dress, such as headscarves, *manteau* (long overcoat), and in many cases, trousers, as shown in Figure 1.13.

As shown directly earlier, the woman is depicted as a faceless, veil-wearing caricature that performs exercises with an automatic motion. Her body is devoid of any demonstrable curves, since the artist drew straight lines for her chest. Figures 1.11 to 1.13, representative of how the *Varzesh* section had transformed by the mid-1980s, are particularly striking because it is clear that the illustrator took great pains to draw women without any stereotypical female body shapes and features. In other words, the illustrated female characters are bare renditions of entities that categorically look like women. As shown in Figure 1.13, the only identifiable gendered marker is a headscarf.

Moallem contends that the veil became an immediate visual marker for staging difference between men and women and more so, between the Westernized woman and her purported opposite: the modest, pious Muslim subject.[105] For women entering public and official spaces, compulsory *hejab* became nationwide policy almost two years after the revolution.[106] *Zan-e Rouz* editors appeared to have anticipated this policy change because, by 1980, the

Figure 1.11 Working out in IRI.

شنا:

به رو دراز بکشید، بدنتان را روی پنجه‌های پا و کف دستان در امتداد شانه‌ها به حال تعادل در بیاورید. حال آرنجهایتان را خم کنید تا زاویهٔ ۹۰ درجه ایجاد کند و با فشار به حالت قبل باز گردید. اگر این حرکت بدین صورت برایتان دشوار است، می‌توانید بدنتان را روی کف دستان و زانوان به حال تعادل در بیاورید و مانند قبل پایین و بالا بشوید.

Figure 1.12 Working out in IRI.

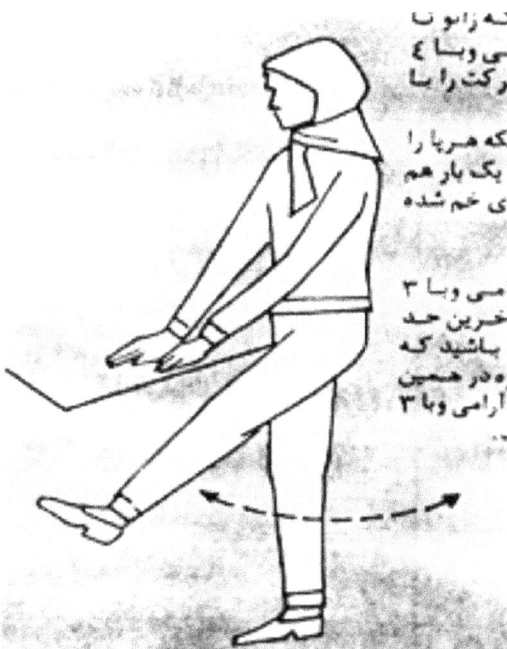

به زانو تا
سی و بـا ع
حرکت را با

که هر پا را
یک بار هم
ی خم شده

امی و بـا ۳
خرین حد
باشید که
ه در حین
آرامی و با ۳

Figure 1.13 Working out in IRI.

Figure 1.14 *Ba yek kot* advertisement.

hejab—or some version of a headscarf—featured in many of its photo spreads and illustrations. Effectively any image or representation of a woman meant for public display was held to the same standard as that of a woman on the street: both would observe Islamic *hejab* to promote and preserve Muslim identity. Notably, during the third decade since the revolution, this would be reasoned as preserving public morality.

As an illuminating example of how the *hejab* is incorporated into the project of staging difference, consider Figure 1.14. When photographs could not be easily doctored given the rudimentary graphic design technology of the early 1980s, artists drew acceptable images over that which the magazine wanted to hide, obscuring exposed limbs and hair. The end result however often looked like an awkward caricature bearing nonhuman features. Figure 1.14 is a *Zan-e Rouz* illustration of female characters dressed in contemporary coat fashions for the 1980 fall season.[107] Departing from colorful photo displays from the Pahlavi era, *Zan-e Rouz* introduced cartoon renditions of models to illustrate the upcoming fall season line of women's jackets. Here, fashion entered the realm of the imaginary: the illustrator obscured the female figures' faces by superimposing butterfly hats to convey that their heads were appropriately modified—and ultimately covered.[108]

Islamization Meets Consumerism

The headline *Ba Yek Kot* (With One Jacket) runs across the photo spread, as evident in Figure 1.14. The title denotes a message of fashionable frugality. Cartoon models pose in different outfits while wearing the same jacket. The main idea being expressed is that a modern Muslim woman need not buy many clothes; by purchasing the right jacket, she can wear one item of clothing in a variety of styles. With the rising tides of anti-consumerism, *Zan-e Rouz* editors now endeavored to promote a non-extravagant lifestyle—in this case, to accommodate one's wardrobe with what one already had, and not with items that one did not need.

Indeed, switching from the prerevolutionary marketing of makeup and couture designs from European companies to then promoting goods and behaviors perceived to be reflective of an Islamic lifestyle was not executed without compromise. By "Islamicizing" illustrations, *Zan-e Rouz* continued promoting the accents of a more pious lifestyle. Yet, the very fact that the magazine advertised products to potential customers meant that the consumerism, lambasted as a corrupting force in Iranian society prior to the revolution, was not eradicated with the founding of the new state. Advertising was a major source of revenue for the magazine, as was the case during the Pahlavi era. The notion that Iran becoming an Islamic Republic would mean the cessation of this need for revenue, or that Iranian women would stop consuming or caring about fashionable clothing, is not supported by the evidence found in the journal itself. In fact, postrevolutionary issues of *Zan-e Rouz* continued to have numerous print advertisements for beauty and weight regimens and plastic surgery, though no longer featuring pictures of women as it did before the revolution. These ads featured alongside its Islamicizing message which, in theory, should have opposed such open consumerism. The magazine's fashion images may have conveyed that they were catering to a Muslim readership; however, the advertisements strewn throughout the pages were also targeting an audience of female consumers.

By the early 1980s, butterfly-esque *hejab* no longer featured in *Zan-e Rouz* fashion spreads and female models wearing veils became the visual marker for women featured in advertisements, regardless of their origin or religious dispositions. In effect, all visual representations of women printed in images and advertisements for public consumption were made to wear the veil. It is an automatic insertion, and, as shown in Figure 1.15, the *hejab* acts as a cover-up stamp, marking the female subject's transformation into a default postrevolutionary Muslim subject. Figure 1.15 is a photograph of an advertisement for male and female robes from *Zan-e Rouz's* sewing section. The photograph is obviously doctored—where a female model's head should be, a cartoon head with a veil is drawn in.[109]

When comparing both male and female models, the starkness in their presentations suggests an extra sensitivity toward the depiction of the woman's body. While the male model appears at ease, as if dressed in a luxurious bathrobe, the female model is both rigid and out-of-scale. The man's figure remains untouched, and upon closer inspection, there are even chest hairs visible in the opening of his robe. Wearing a bulky jacket, the female model is not in the original form she was photographed. Her "real" head is completely cut off. The positive space—in art, the space that is occupied by an element or a form that is the intended focus of that image—is filled in with a depiction of a *hejab*-wearing caricature. In effect, the female figure is depicted as part-cartoon, part-human next to her fully human, male counterpart.

Figure 1.15 Adding hejab to ads.

Reforming Contentious Women's Bodies

For the *Zan-e Rouz* images highlighted in this postrevolutionary period, the body of any woman is a site of contestation in need of editorial and visual transformation. This is demonstrated not only in the technique of presenting women's bodies as abstract prototypes but also in the didactic articles and advertisements teaching Iranian women how to become modest Muslim women via changing their appearance and behavior.

There have been numerous studies on compulsory *hejab* and its historical contestation, acceptance, and usage among women in different social classes, ethnic groups, education levels, and religious backgrounds.[110] At this moment, I do not seek to add to this extensive scholarship, especially to the valuable reflections on the concept of *hejab* as it has been articulated in the Iranian political context. What I draw attention to is its inclusion as a design technique in the collection of disciplining tools used for women's bodies in *Zan-e Rouz*. Earlier, I mentioned the method of minimizing natural curves of women in photographs and images to diminish the hint of their sexual appeal to the desirous male gaze. When the contours of breasts and buttocks are pared and trimmed, there is little way of distinguishing between the bodies of men and women in different scenes. The effect of streamlining women's bodies is the construction of ostensibly genderless bodies, which purportedly are no longer viewed as sexually explicit or sexually arousing. What are other conceptual pitfalls and repercussions to this resculpting of women's body shapes to reflect an ideological point of view? By depicting women's figures as contourless abstractions, bodies become stand-in representatives for women who do not communicate difference; they do not speak back. Instead, they reveal compulsory compliance to regulations of conduct and appearance, flouting historical trends and precedence. In other words, when transforming *to* an Islamic subject, one is expected to abandon her origins and identity prior to that metamorphosis.

As these images demonstrate, representations of women's bodies in postrevolutionary editions of *Zan-e Rouz* were doctored and reconstructed to reflect an ideal, Islamic female subject. Often through subtle didactic methods, modesty was drawn onto female figures, in cartoons, advertisements, and photographs. With the addition of a *hejab* and articles on family values to accompany these images, new norms of sociability were being reinforced to *Zan-e Rouz*'s audience. However, these tactics should be perceived, too, as examples of disciplinary technologies, outlining the Islamist regime's parameters for modest conduct and appearance specifically for the female subject. Underlining this strategy was the anticipated fear of arousal in the face of female sexuality; ostensibly, there would be many unforeseen consequences if photographs and illustrations of women's bodies were to be left unaltered, their heads unveiled, or their limbs exposed. The viewer would assumedly be confronted with an array of indecent thoughts.

Piecing Together Pre- and Post-1979 Hegemonic Narratives of Women's Bodies

The era of the late 1960s until the final steps into the 1979 Revolution marks a momentous period in the evolving, visual landscape of Iranian women's bodies. The state-administered techniques of modernizing women in the 1960s and 1970s were very similar to the reform techniques applied in the redesigning of the female subject during the inaugural years of the Islamist regime. Thus, what may appear to be a stark contrast in the representation and treatment of women and their bodies from the prerevolutionary to postrevolutionary periods was, as I have documented, only skin-deep.

The post-1979 modification of the figure of woman as a modest rendition did not, in essence, signal a structural change or reversal in the conceptual treatment of women. Yes, more Iranian women were visually (and compulsorily) veiled after the revolution. However, in the domain of women's magazines, the novel iconography of Iranian women in the Islamic Republic speaks only to the *appearance* of new norms of sociability defined by an Islamist ideological framework. In truth, the representation of Iranian women's bodies as veiled, all the while fulfilling ideal prototypes subject to fundamentalist control of women's gender roles in Islam, was merely a reactive adaptation of a Pahlavi-era leitmotif. The techniques used to construct a postrevolutionary Islamic female subject were in fact crafted during the modernization reform period of the Pahlavi era. The conceptual foundation underlying women's liberation and improved social status was the expectation that Iranian women were malleable and receptive to reform. In both Iranian regimes, women were exposed to reforms of their conduct, lifestyle, and hobbies—whereby consumerism and Muslim identity made them realizable.

When looking at the sample of postrevolutionary images from *Zan-e Rouz*, one can easily argue that a verifiable "Islamic coding" of the figure of woman is evident in the post-1979 stylization of women's bodies as veiled and streamlined. In other visual media, this term has been used to define the representation of the figure of woman in postrevolutionary Iranian cinema. In the 1998 article "Body-less Faces: Mutilating Modernity and Abstracting Women in an 'Islamic Cinema,'" Dabashi notes, "[For] [v]eiled women who had participated in the revolution from its earliest stages [,] soon after the revolution . . . posters began to propagate an 'Islamic' code on the emerging vision of a revolutionary woman."[111] In postrevolutionary Iranian "Islamic cinema," he argues that the figure of woman is the "site of relentless contestation between a metaphysics of concealment and an aesthetics of revelation."[112] For Dabashi, in this aesthetic paradigm, "danger" and "Truth" are integrated into constructions of the figure of woman as taboo.[113] This culminates in anxieties and fears about the exposure of women's bodies, which in turn leads to the mutilation or erasure of representations of women from public space and, in its most visual example, it leads to the *hejab* visually overtaking women's bodies by fully covering them. To ensure that a woman's body is not the source of social disorder—in that by evoking illicit desires in the viewer—women's bodies are "absented," covered by "layers and then more layers of dark and prohibitive scarves." Dabashi observes,

> Behold the forcefully absented presence of the Iranian woman on the wide but ever narrower screen of an "Islamic" cinema, the post-Islamic-revolution impossibility of being feminine, the censorial brutality of mutated bodies, carefully cut off and concealed from faces that must now speak and envision, act and convey, the entire task of a denied body.[114]

Dabashi's usage of "Islamic coding" is a useful segue into concluding this chapter. As I mentioned earlier in its introduction, the year 1979 is regarded as a watershed moment in Iranian history, when a revolution fundamentally changed the country's political, social, cultural, and economic institutions. Because I pushed back the timeline, so to speak, into the 1960s, I was able to cast a wider frame of reference for the purposes of reading, both visually and contextually, the many representations of women from before and after the Iranian Revolution.

What should by now be transparent is that the dual state and media enterprise of producing norms and values entails the heavy investment in women. This is true for issues of *Zan-e Rouz* published under the direction of the Pahlavis and under the editorial leadership of Khomeini's supporters. Although this magazine does not account for the whole range of publications that constitute Iran's print media industrial complex, it nevertheless provides a linear terrain on which to pinpoint the shifts and similarities in each regime's method of reform on a popular level. From how a woman is positioned on a chaise to the way she holds a cigarette, from her modest style of dress to how she stretches her limbs, these are all examples of the methods of socialization and regulation pursued by successive regimes. What they similarly demonstrate is the projection of an idealized, normalized Iranian female character who is in need of instruction on how to dress, how to socialize, how to be informed, and how to properly "become" a true modern woman—regardless if she is an Iranian citizen before or after 1979.

Central to many of these reform and advertising campaigns—be they campaigns to sell products to a modern consumer or to endorse a pious way of life to a female believer—is that in order for women to grasp how to reform, one must guide and frame the parameters of their improvement. As a visual and material platform upon which to promote a new Iranian female citizen, *Zan-e Rouz* was perhaps an ideal medium. By targeting a female audience through stylized images and narratives of the modern Iranian woman, *Zan-e Rouz* operated as a visual guide for mapping out a modern woman's interests, fashion sensibilities, and political inclinations. Under the Pahlavis, the self-promotion and "modernization" of Iranian women were manifest in the updating of their physical appearances and through the imposed transformation of their hobbies, interests, and desires. The inclusion of Empress Farah Pahlavi in its inaugural edition marked a naissance of the modernization process for Iranian women during the White Revolution. Indeed, the state enterprise for constructing a modern woman character had found a perfectly fashionable, female citizen and archetype to convey and encourage new norms of sociability for the Iranian public.

From the sampling of *Zan-e Rouz* images explored in this chapter, women are depicted through cartoons and photographs of abstraction; they are abstract because their representation is never truly real. It is often staged, mutilated, and illustrated as a nonhuman prototype—stylized in a way to attract and/or deflect the gaze of the reader, the bystander, or the consumer. Though the physical appearance and ideal characteristics of this female citizen change, come 1979, the rationale behind their need for reform, in fact, remains the same. That women subsequently were subject to an "Islamic coding"—for instance, their heads covered by *hejab* or their arms sleeved—is an important, albeit relatively minor detail given Iran's extensive history of introducing and implementing reform measures designed to educate, reeducate, and/or underestimate women in order to compliment a particular political or ideological persuasion. A continuous motif among the Khomeini-inspired reforms was the notion that Iranian women would require and subsequently embrace their transformation during the formative years of the Islamic Republic into idealized, religiously pious, and maternal characters. Despite the outcome of these measures, the reasons behind these methods of reform and regulation seemed eerily similar to those of the Pahlavis. In an effort to prevent women's exposure and objectification, *Zan-e Rouz* editors after 1979 operated on the same assumption from the Pahlavi era: that women could learn from prototypes how to embrace certain values, how to understand their roles in a particular religious system, and how to restructure their desires in order to match an overtly patriarchal authority and national project of cultural revolution.

Chapter 2

RED-LIGHTS IN PARKS

A SOCIAL HISTORY OF PARK-E RAZI[1]

In the middle of the night, Iranian security forces raided a downtrodden area of East Tehran's District Four.[2] This was in March 2000, three years into Muhammad Khatami's first presidential tenure. For almost two decades, authorities had tried in vain to quell the area's black market activities. A place notorious for rampant drug use and the illicit sex trade, it had evolved into a makeshift red-light district. In an effort to *paksazi kardan* (cleanse the district), police forces rounded up residents living in subpar conditions, many of whom slept in cardboard boxes and lived among trash. District Four[3]—known colloquially as *Khak-e Sefid* (White Dust)— had a notorious reputation.[4] Locals were described as behaving in a particularly intimidating street manner, often in line with the area's notoriety as a den for criminal activity, prostitution, and drug use. This only aggravated the police's suspicion, for bad behavior was said to be rubbing off on new residents. Yet with little warning, the area disappeared into the night. Homes were destroyed. Though some residents were financially compensated, those remaining lived in provisional shelters; others suspected of black market activity were transferred to detention centers.

Midnight raids were not out of the ordinary in the seedy districts of the capital, where drug usage and knife crimes were often reported. More than ten years earlier, in 1989, authorities had raided the *Mahal-e Jamshid* (Jamshid District), in the southwest area of central Tehran; reportedly around 4,000 persons were arrested. Though the identities and occupations of the apprehended cannot be confirmed, the few available reports suggest the existence of an unmanageable sex trade in urban areas of Iran. Of those detained in the Jamshid district, 800 were apprehended for suspicion of being prostitutes.[5] In 2003 alone, forty-one brothels in Tehran were also raided, of which seventy-two men and eighteen women were apprehended for participation in the sex trade. The same year, 1,080 brothels were shut down countrywide, and almost 6,700 people were arrested for prostitution-related charges.[6] Although not openly discussed by authorities, eradicating former sites of societal corruption was instrumental to the policy of defining and maintaining public morality.[7] Women referred to colloquially as coming from *najeeb-khaneh*[8] (prostitute's home) were particularly targeted, rounded up en masse so that suspected prostitutes could be separated from everyone else—apparently, the morally inclined. Yet despite these efforts to demolish enclaves of prostitution, the sex industry is itself nowhere near its end.

Long before the 1979 Revolution, red-light districts were already well-known fixtures. Official maps, government reports, and social worker and historian accounts document that a nascent brothel district had formed in the late Qajar period (1785–1925). In March 1786, Tehran—at the time, a group of villages that were selected by Qajar patriarch Agha Muhammad Khan for his capital—was en route to becoming a metropolis.[9] The "town's population swelled by the courtiers and soldiers," and soon the lure of industrial jobs brought rural migrants pouring into the city, forcing the expansion of the city limits.[10] Concomitantly, on a site known as a pastoral residence for royal officials, women who came from mostly rural, economically depressed backgrounds were brought to the area to live and work as prostitutes in 'azab-khaneh (private brothels).[11] By the 1920s, these brothels formed a sizable group of houses, known as *Shahr-e No* (New City), an area known as Tehran's largest red-light district for almost a century.[12] Elsewhere in Iran there were other incarnations of *Shahr-e No*—designated zones around town where prostitution was solicited.[13] In the 1960s, when Pahlavi officials introduced a series of nationwide reforms in the education and public health sectors, among others, red-light districts in particular became sites of government regulation. University researchers, doctors, social workers, and ministry health officials were sent to study and monitor the residents and activities of *Shahr-e No*. Prostitutes were subsequently checked for venereal infections, and some were sent to rehabilitation and skills training programs. Yet these measures did little to ameliorate their lives; instead, government intervention had the effect of institutionalizing an industry built upon the notion that male sexual desires needed a relieving space.

Before the fall of the monarchy, much of the opposition's criticism against the Pahlavi government was based on claims that the regime had supported "dens of moral corruption"—meaning cinema houses, private brothels, red-light districts, and entertainment clubs in cities across Iran.[14] The Gomrok neighborhood in southwest central Tehran, where the *Shahr-e No* quarter was located, was reportedly set afire for that very reason.[15] After Khomeini's supporters consolidated and increased their own power, special revolutionary courts emerged, ordering all brothels closed, demolished, or both. In 1979, prostitution became illegal. *Kanun-e Hemayat-e Eslami* (Centre for Islamic Protection) officially closed down the quarter.[16] Apprehended prostitutes were hastily tried in closed-door proceedings, with their punishments determined by an Islamic criminal code.[17] Yet the criminalization of prostitution did little to halt the industry's growth in the postrevolutionary period. The services provided in the red-light district and other brothel areas simply went underground, or remained in plain sight. More than three decades on, prostitution is still arranged in public, often in city parks and in full view of police, officials, and local denizens. In fact, the exact location where *Shahr-e No* once stood is now the manicured public park known as Park-e Razi (Razi Park), where undercover sex workers and potential customers easily mingle in the midst of families picnicking on lawns.

The re-manifestation of prostitution in this park is the culmination of many intersecting factors. Notwithstanding economic reasons, there is a more nuanced aspect for why prostitution has spread in Iran since being banned in 1979. According to popular and high-ranking Shi'a clerical discourses on the subject, prostitution is generally understood as a key practice in maintaining social order. At the same time, in Shi'a ideology, there is an understanding and expectation that female sexuality is reactive and yielding to male sexuality.[18] In the presence of a woman, a man cannot help but desire her, and thus it is the "woman's nature to want to be taken."[19] The responsibility hence falls upon the woman to satiate his desires, reining in his "animal"[20] sexual urges. Sex with prostitutes is therefore justified in the face of rampant male promiscuity. Historically, this particular interpretation has undergirded much of the reasons for the regulation of sexual commerce. Under Muhammad Reza Pahlavi, the Ministry of Health mandated health checkups of prostitutes and conducted many of these procedures on the grounds of *Shahr-e No*. Conversely, under the spiritual and political leadership of the late Ayatollah Khomeini and presently Ayatollah Ali Khamenei, the regulation of prostitution has been vehemently rejected. However, legal exceptions are allowed to accommodate sexual relations conducted outside of a permanent marriage. And, as will be later discussed, there are identifiable social and economic circumstances that have justified the drawing up and implementation of new modes of regulation.

What is unique about the historical narrative of *Shahr-e No* in particular, and the discourse of prostitution in general, is not that sex sells in the IRI. Rather, it is that the sex industry continually mutates itself soon after its brothels are destroyed and prostitutes are arrested. The reasons for this regeneration are institutionally and conceptually based and perhaps best exemplified by the following idiosyncratic statement made famous in the revolutionary period. At the time of the Gomrok fire, a popular Shi'a cleric and contemporary of Khomeini came to *Shahr-e No*'s defense. Ayatollah Mahmoud Taleghani is widely known to have uttered the oft-repeated line: "Every house needs a *mosterah* (toilet)." Its meaning is commonly interpreted that in every society (or, metaphorically, house), a space for excess must exist as an output for human aggression, sexual release, folly, or sin.[21] In other words, prostitutes figuratively embody the proverbial toilet—their role and function are that of a human repository for the discharge of male sexuality. In regard to *Shahr-e No*, Taleghani's metaphor speaks to an underlying acceptance—by a well-respected cleric and national figure—that brothels and prostitutes are requisite for maintaining some level of social order. And for many Iranians, his quip—and its repetition ever since—reinforces this popular understanding about prostitution and its societal relevance. Thus the *mosterah* should be tolerated and incorporated into daily life—provided, of course, that its activities are conducted in private. This was apparently the justification for *Shahr-e No*; its more than a century's existence was generally tolerated and put under government regulation.

After the 1979 Revolution, with the main site of prostitution eliminated and prostitution criminalized, it is commonly reported that the sex industry moved into plain sight, albeit operating under different conditions. Ethnographic fieldwork illustrates this view; on the former land of *Shahr-e No*, which has been turned into a family park, prostitution actively continues on the very same contested site. Perhaps one of the primary reasons for prostitution's recurring presence in this particular space lies in the continuity—and not rupture—of a normative conceptualization of human sexuality that prevails in the contemporary Iranian context: the recognition that a physical outlet for male sexual expression, in which women "of the periphery" play a formative and functional role, must coexist and cooperate with the "morally acceptable" norms and conduct of the time. In such a frame, there are many questions over which to ponder: What became of the prostitutes and/or of the conditions that pushed the sex district into full operational mode in the first place, after *Shahr-e No* was demolished and purposefully erased from the official historical record? Were they expected to disappear or self-reform once the site was transformed into an Islamic family park? From a quantitative perspective, have the rates of prostitution subsequently abated since the district's destruction in 1979? Moreover, what do these particular interrogations into the history of *Shahr'e No* and its subsequent redevelopment reveal about the unsavory links between—and contestations over—clerical authorities, police protection, government morality, male sexuality, poverty, and public memory in the postrevolutionary Islamic Republic?

Vali Mahlouji writes, "The erasure of the urban neighbourhood signified the initiation of a programme of cultural cleansing that transformed the Iranian landscape. At the core of this cultural revolution was a redefining of sexual and gender urban mores."[22] Yet, crucial to understanding the institution of prostitution—its constraints, social support networks, cultural and political impact, and/or how it operates in contemporary Iranian society—is charting the intersections of economic exchange, sex, gender, poverty, law, religious doctrine, and disease that are elaborated through the piecing together of *Shahr-e No*'s history, detailing, for instance, its processes of development, demise, and "Islamically acceptable" modification. When analyzing how different institutions, agents, and interests become interconnected and modified over time, the "cultural cleansing" and "transformations" of the Iranian landscape appear merely superficial; the subcutaneous layers have in fact remained intact, with sexual mores and appetites for illicit sex satiated in more diversified forms and, as observed at Razi Park, in plain sight. In brief, the prostitution industry continues to thrive in present-day Iran, no longer contained within the "citadel" of *Shahr-e No*.

In what follows, I aim to document the kaleidoscopic history of Iran's most controversial red-light district, *Shahr-e No*, examining primary, secondary, and tertiary players and powers operating in the district from the early twentieth century until the contemporary period. I mark a slight turning point in 1979, when the site was demolished, but follow the continuities in its historical narrative, considering its many spatial and conceptual transformations, until the site is reconfigured into the modern-day public leisure space of Razi Park. I underscore the disciplinary technologies employed by two consecutive regimes (Pahlavi and Islamic Republic) both to regulate the sex industry and reinvent a century-old landmark into a workable site of government regulation and reform—be it one designed to express modern development, or to convey a moral triumph over

Western decadence. In an effort to explore the mentalities that structure the diverse understandings and experiences of the "space" of *Shahr-e No*, I frequented the park in 2011, interviewing its patrons and reflecting on "ideological and societal concepts physically emplaced and enacted"[23] at that specific location. This ethnographic section acted as a natural segue into a larger discussion on the possibilities of meaning behind, first, *Shahr-e No*'s transformation into a "morally righteous" park and, second, the reinforcement of historical ghettos constructed to satisfy and safeguard male sexuality. On some level, *Shahr-e No*'s reformulation and strategic transformations are interpreted as attempts to sustain female-embodied heterotopias, ironically constructed by seemingly different regimes. The human geographic concept of heterotopia, which Foucault elaborates as "a space of illusion"[24] that is perceived as natural by society, although nonetheless designed to control, discipline, and punish—essentially to regulate social behavior—provides a useful lens through which to examine the contradictory measures taken by state and clerical authorities to deal with public health fears, socioeconomic pressures, and in particular, uncontrolled (male) sexual energy.

Regulation of Prostitution during Reza Shah Pahlavi Reign (1925–41)

In the first half of the twentieth century, the infamous *Shahr-e No* district was publicly regarded as a zone where prostitution, drug abuse, *khalafkari* (deceit and mischief),[25] and sexually transmitted diseases (STD) were rampant. According to one social worker's account, most of the women prostitutes were addicted to opium and arak.[26] They were also accused of spreading venereal diseases (VD).[27] Outbreaks of syphilis in particular were commonly reported, as the disease had become more widespread by the turn of the century and had been steadily increasing.[28] In one report, an Iranian doctor surmised, "[T]he prostitute carries the poison of this dangerous disease [syphilis], and death is considered the best end to it."[29] By the mid-twentieth century syphilis and gonorrhea were common afflictions among Iranians, for whom condom use was both costly and a social stigma.[30] Contracting gonorrhea in particular was of heightened concern, for it potentially led to sterility and affected young couples hoping to expand their families.[31] Less reported was the fact that women of all social classes were impacted by rising VD rates. Not only were increasing numbers becoming infected by their husbands (as a result of their extramarital sex), but children were also being born with syphilis-related disabilities.[32] "To put the problem of VD in perspective," said investigative reporter Hedayatollah Hakim-Olahi, "three hundred thousand inhabitants of Tehran, or 40 percent of its population, had VD in 1946."[33]

Concerns over the spread of VD were especially high among the military, and the blame was again directed at prostitutes.[34] According to Willem Floor, the Pahlavi government attempted in 1933 to register the prostitutes themselves in *Shahr-e No* and also threatened to ban brothels and arrest any officer found with a prostitute.[35] In October 1933, it was reported that a law was passed, although not signed by the Shah, to make brothels illegal and have them shut down in three months' time.[36] The proposed regulations would require prostitutes to carry identification cards with their signature and the date of their last hospital visit. This order was soon revoked. It was only in 1941 that a law on the prevention of venereal and contagious diseases was passed by the parliament; however, it was evidently poorly enforced due to lack of funding and training.[37] By the 1960s, the cases of VD had not abated. According to a 1963 report, they were as high as 80 percent in rural areas.[38]

The Pahlavi-era method of regulation for prostitution was shaped, to some extent, by European contagious disease legislation and influenced by public health regulatory measures enacted by European and Ottoman governments during the nineteenth and early twentieth centuries. In the nineteenth century, a policy of "regulationism" of prostitution commenced in continental Europe and spread throughout the British colonies. As Muge Ozbek has observed, "The regulationist regimes targeted prostitutes, not their clients, as the primary conduits of venereal disease within a gender-biased discourse of social hygiene."[39] These policies were justified as pragmatic responses "to the threat of venereal diseases and the problems of security and social order."[40] European governments began abandoning polices of toleration in favor of regulationism—except for Victorian-era Britain—and legalized prostitution by "allowing brothels legal or quasi-legal status and giving prostitutes special licenses."[41]

Regulatory policy in general meant registering prostitutes, mandatory health examinations, and administrative surveillance.[42] Ozbek contends, "The existence of prostitution was accepted as a 'necessary evil' that should be tolerated as toleration allowed the state stricter control of prostitutes in order to protect public health and social order."[43] As an immediate example, in the late 1870s, the Ottoman municipal government began requiring prostitutes to carry unique identity cards designating their special status among the general population. Brothels were also obliged to register as licensed businesses with municipal commissions.[44]

Across continental Europe, the regulation of prostitution was initially based on concerns over the spread of sexually transmitted infections among the armed forces in the nineteenth century. In France, Napoleon I ordered the inspection of prostitutes following his armies in an attempt to control VD.[45] During France's Second Empire, his step-grandson and nephew, Napoleon III, ordered the establishment of a national registry of prostitutes and that their health be regularly inspected.[46] In Victorian England, vagrancy laws criminalized prostitution. Certain behavior considered as morally unacceptable—believed to be the conduct of "fallen women," or women who were perceived as social outcasts and sexual deviants—was outlawed in 1824. If prostitutes and beggars were caught idle or acting disorderly in public, they were charged with vagrancy. In such cases, punishment was one month of hard labor; in other cases, prostitutes were sent to Anglican penitentiaries for social reform.[47] Nascent social purity campaigns pushed for the abolition of prostitution and deviant sexual acts, as they were claimed to be an affront to family values and led to widespread social corruption.[48]

In 1864, the British Parliament passed the Contagious Diseases Acts intending to curb the spread of sexually transmitted infections in the military.[49] The Acts led to arbitrary police arrests and compulsory medical examinations of women to check for venereal disease. Following their repeal, British military and civilian officials introduced a series of restrictions that recognized women as "disloyal conduits of sexual infection, and men in the armed forces as their victims."[50] Worried that sexually transmitted infections would reach its troops stationed in British colonies and naval bases, the British government encouraged Singapore, the capital of the British Straits Settlements and a main British naval base in East Asia, to legalize a system of segregation and isolation of Japanese and Chinese prostitutes. The ordinance was designed to protect British soldiers from the "ravages of uncontrolled sexually transmitted diseases."[51]

For the Pahlavi state, regulation of prostitution had also involved policing prostitutes' behavior. These actions were reasoned to be essential, pragmatic measures to control the "necessary evil" of prostitution. Prostitutes were quarantined in a red-light district, where police supervision could be conducted at specific sites.[52] Underlying the Pahlavi policy was the protection of public health through curtailing the spread of VD among prostitutes and *not* their clients.[53] Rather than scrutinize their male customers or, say, addressing the subject of male promiscuity, authorities were suspicious of sex workers. The Ministry of Health ordered them to get monthly medical checkups and procure identity cards[54] (though medical examinations were not regularly conducted).[55] Absent in these measures were calls to encourage the general public to take preventive health measures, such as condom usage.[56]

Regulation of Prostitution during Muhammad Reza Shah Pahlavi Reign

While Muhammad Reza Pahlavi (1941–79) was monarch, the regulation of prostitution became integrated into the modernization and reform agenda implemented throughout the 1960s known as the White Revolution. Earlier, in 1949, the Shah had announced his main purpose as Iran's ruler, namely, "the restoration of dignity and a better life to the people of Iran."[57] In 1963, "a better life" was translated into top-down modernization and development projects, outlined in a six-point executive order addressed to the Iranian people.[58] A few years after, state-administered land, economic, cultural, and social reforms commenced, the last of which were ostensibly designed to improve Iranian women's status.[59] This entailed eliminating illiteracy, extending suffrage rights to women, revamping public health policy, and setting up vocational training programs for poorer communities. Initially, these progressive reforms did not address the issue of prostitution or include social welfare programs for female prostitutes. By the late 1960s and early 1970s, Princess Ashraf Pahlavi, twin sister of the Shah,[60] figure-headed a program funded by the government's Fourth Development Economic Plan to provide educational assistance and training for a small number of female prostitutes.[61] Set to improve literacy and teach domestic trades, such as sewing, the program aimed to enable them to return to society as functional, socially accepted citizens.[62] Nevertheless, these policy measures did little to break the cycles and conditions of poverty that these women experienced.[63] Khosrou Mansourian, a social worker who documented living conditions at *Shahr-e No*, remarked that little progress was made to alleviate their poverty and improve prostitutes' literacy rates.[64] According to one report, prostitutes who attended vocational workshops had left the red-light district only to continue the same activities in other parts of Tehran.[65]

The Brothels of Shahr-e No

Uneven socioeconomic development in the 1960s and 1970s fueled a growing city population in the midst of an urban construction boom.[66] The influx of rural migration, fueled by officials' demands for domestic, industrial development, meant that a thriving sex industry grew to cater to the labor force.[67] Especially in impoverished quarters of Tehran, prostitution was becoming rampant.[68] Alongside this wave flourished a sexual vocabulary about women in the sex trade; for the term "prostitute," the words *jendeh*, *fahesheh*, *rouspigar*, and *zan-e marufe* were all variants of a gendered terminology primarily dependent on male promiscuity and the demand for paid sex.[69] Red-light districts at the time were unspoken enclaves located not only in the capital but also in provincial cities such as Abadan, Bandar Abbas, Ahvaz, Esfahan, and Shiraz. Except for Tehran's district, most areas of prostitution were located on the outskirts of cities and had "virtually no street lights at all, red or otherwise," notes Kamran Talatoff.[70]

The "toilet" of Taleghani's day was known colloquially by the euphemism *Shahr-e No* or "New City." A designated space of sexual transaction and transgression, it was tacitly accepted, but not openly discussed. Still there was no denying the distinct presence of prostitution in Iranian society. For the most famous of the New Cities was located in what is now central Tehran—its name differentiated from other *Shahrha-ye No* by the terms *Qal'eh* (fort or castle) *Shahr-e No* or *Qal'eh Zahedi*, a name attributed to a Pahlavi statesman and general, Fazlollah Zahedi.[71]

Qal'eh[72] *Shahr-e No* is best understood as a designated heterotopia. In Foucault's analysis of space, heterotopia is conceptually understood as a site of "other," meaning relational spaces constructed by societies to house, contain, and deal with "otherness."[73] Similar to prisons, nursing homes, and brothels, for instance, heterotopias function as both an escape from a society's real self and also an illusion of its best self. Bodies confined to these spaces are considered weak, undesirable, vulnerable, and remaining separate from normative society.[74] As a physical site of both isolation and exclusion, it is generally reserved for individuals in a state of crisis, such as adolescents and the elderly. For Foucault, brothels are distinguished as "extreme type(s) of heterotopia."[75] Though the notion of an "ideal self" or "ideal society" is compromised when heterotopic sites are subject to investigation. For those living on the margins to remain segregated from "normal" society, certain forms of discrimination, segregation, and unequal power dynamics must be continually sustained in these "other" spaces. In other words, that the sex trade reforms itself after 1979, reemerging as new "sites" in other Tehran districts is no surprise; heterotopias are reactualized through untempered power relations irrespective of ideology or regime change.

In its heyday, *Shahr-e No* was a microcosm of urban city life; with its own hierarchical system of madams and pimps, the area also had cafés, theaters, groundskeepers, and police protection. A citadel-like enclosure on Jamshid Street in the Gomrok district (where Razi Square now stands), *Qal'eh Shahr-e No* housed at one time an estimated 4,000 prostitutes[76] living in squalid, cramped quarters.[77] From north to south directions, the area was made up of approximately twelve alleyways; from west to east, it covered the space of three major streets—in total a surface area of about 135,000 square meters.[78] This town-within-a-city was initially a pastoral haven of the political elite. During the late Qajar period, the land was known as a retreat for the Qajar royal family.[79] At the time, a well-known local named Zal Muhammad Khan reportedly managed the area.[80]

Famed social historian Ja'far Shahri writes that *Shahr-e No* was not yet an identifiable brothel district in the late nineteenth century. But by the turn of the century, it was well-known where to find the best prostitutes—women who were considered the cleanest (*paktizetarin*)—and they were located in the district.[81] He writes, "Indeed the official number of brothels was 850 of which 4421 prostitution rooms were attributed to the *Shahr-e No* area."[82] The worst prostitution houses, located in *payeen-e shahr* (poorer downtown areas), were found in the areas of Chaleh Meydan and Chaleh Silabi (See Figure 2.1). Brothels were scattered across Tehran, and their protection by

Figure 2.1 1969 map of *Qal'eh Shahr-e No* district.

the police ensured their ongoing business. According to Shahri, police contracts with brothel owners made certain that prostitution rings would survive.

By the time Reza Shah seized power in 1925, the number of brothels ballooned as ownership fell increasingly into the hands of private citizens. The district's reputation worsened as young women, the majority of whom originated from Iran's central provinces, were brought to *Shahr-e No* for sex work.[83] When British and American intelligence orchestrated a coup d'état to re-hand the throne to his son Muhammad Reza on August 18, 1953, *Qal'eh Shahr-e No* was already a well-known local institution. The area gained its "citadel" status around 1958 once national chief of police Fazollah Zahedi (who later became Iran's sixty-third prime minister) ordered the construction of a brick wall around its premises, designed to separate the prostitutes from the rest of Tehran society.[84] By this very construction, *Shahr-e No* becomes a designated heterotopic space—separate from "ideal" society, yet integrated into the netherworld of public life as a government-regulated red-light district.

Reporting on Life Inside Shahr-e No

Although the literature on the conditions of brothel life post-Revolution is scarce,[85] pre-Revolution research was substantive as academics and fieldworkers from social and public health sectors investigated and regulated the conditions of *Qal'eh* prostitutes. A social worker by the name of Sattareh Farman Farmaian[86] published a groundbreaking report in 1969 on the conditions of prostitutes in the district during the Pahlavi period.[87] Farman Farmaian's report is important not only for its detailing of *Qal'eh* daily life but also for providing sociological data about the prostitutes. After conducting interviews with 1,548 sex workers, she compiled information on the prostitutes' living conditions and sex work, some of which included their awareness of sexual intercourse, prophylactic usage, marriage status, and even spending habits.[88]

Taking cues from prostitution discourse in America—many of her theoretical sources are based on publications from the American Social Health Association (ASHA)[89]—Farman Farmaian provided what is still considered to be the most in-depth analysis of the conditions of prostitution inside *Qal'eh*. Funded by the *Vezarat-e Keshvar* (Ministry of Interior), Farman Farmaian investigated five locations where sex workers were prevalent—the largest section of this report is dedicated to conditions inside *Qal'eh*.[90] Most of this research documents prostitutes working on the streets, in restaurants and bars, residing in the district, and based in private brothels spread throughout the city. At the time of the report's publication, prostitution was specific criminal offense in the Pahlavi penal code.[91]

Living Conditions inside the Brothel District

Relations inside *Qal'eh Shahr-e No* were certainly no lover's paradise. Black-and-white photographs of war photojournalist Kaveh Golestan provide some powerful images of life inside the "citadel." Golestan famously remarked, "I want to show you images that will be like a slap in your face to shatter your security. You can look away, turn off, hide your identity like murderers, but you cannot stop the truth. No one can."[92] Women resided in cramped quarters, assigned to single rooms in houses that had about six to seven rooms each. Every house typically had a *hayat* or courtyard.[93] There are mixed reports on the length of time women resided in this district or even if the "citadel" was more like a work-site than a living compound.[94] Described as a "waste ground or public toilet," conditions inside the compound were so grim that one report described a pile of rotting, postcoital tissues left alone in a *hayat* (courtyard).[95]

According to Farman Farmaian's study, the area was a dilapidated, hierarchical microcosm wherein social roles were clearly defined by key figures operating inside the area. *Sahebs* (male pimps) and *nae'eb khanoms* (madams) were in charge of *Qal'eh*'s management. They confiscated a percentage of the prostitutes' wages and acted as their liaisons to the world outside the district. As detailed in Farman Farmaian's report, both clients and *Qal'eh* management followed certain role-playing and protocols throughout the transactions.[96] For instance, a potential customer would enter the *Qal'eh*, and shortly a madam would appear, beckoning him to meet her in one of the houses' *hayats* (courtyard area) or come inside the

Figure 2.2 1969–70 Farman Farmaian rendition of the concentration of prostitution-related activity in Tehran. Farman Farmaian, *Rouspigari dar Shahr-e No-e Tehran/Prostitution in Tehran's Shahr-e No*, 49/6/25, p. 25.

home. Prostitutes would stand in requisite positions; they were often visible from the window balconies or sitting near the front door—"as if on display," recalled Mansourian—for the potential customer.[97] When a woman was found appealing to him, a bartering session between the madam and customer ensued.[98] After a price was agreed upon, the madam would hand him a token, which he would then give to the prostitute with whom he chose to have sexual relations. The prostitute in turn handed all tokens accumulated at the end of the day to the elder *Maman* (madam-figure) of the house. A veteran among the prostitutes and well-known by customers, *Maman* would place the token in her leather or nylon purse; by day's end, the number of tokens were tallied in order to divvy out the sums owed to each prostitute. Moreover, police would confiscate a portion of the madam's profits because protecting women came at a price. Women who provided sexual services for male customers charged a daily rate of up to 600 riyals (or 60 tomans).[99,100] Serving some 16,000 men each day, they worked between three to twelve hours per day—some close to eighteen hours.[101] (Some children were offered at a discounted hourly rate of forty to fifty tomans.)[102]

Shahr-e No transformed into a distinct red-light district once its perimeters became fortified by walls and its entrances guarded by patrolmen. At least two guardsmen stood at *Shahr-e No*'s only entrance on Sohrab Street (now Helal Ahmar Street) and inspected men and women hoping to enter. Prostitutes hoping to leave the premises of their own volition had to exit at *Shahr-e No*'s sole entrance.[103] Escaping was usually their only recourse to pursuing a life outside the quarter. Prostitutes who fled were eventually arrested by police, beaten, and sent back to *Qal'eh*.[104]

The Women of Shahr-e No

Both young and old women who ended up in *Qal'eh* were primarily from rural areas and poor families; they had minimal literacy and virtually no schooling.[105] Sold into the sex trade, many had not given their consent nor had any knowledge they were being trafficked.[106] In some cases, their own husbands and parents tricked them or sold them into prostitution.[107] Little girls, as young as six years old, were sold by their parents to traffickers and madams and brought to live and work in the district.[108] Some of the older women prostitutes had arrived at *Qal'eh* as divorcees, having had little or no financial support from their families.[109] Added to the mix of *Qal'eh* denizens were also female runaways and orphans, whom opportunistic characters collected from the provinces, raped, and brought to *Shahr-e No*, such as Abdelmahmoud Arab and Erbab Jamshid.[110] Throughout the district's history, gigolo-types (both male and female) would ultimately force these women into sexual servitude as compensation for their housing; gigolos held these women against their will and ordered them to pay back debts that they owed either to the gigolos or to their own parents.[111]

In Farman Farmaian's report, social workers had asked prostitutes their reasons for entering the sex trade. Their responses are illuminating: 572 said they were fooled; 415 were sold; 311 had no guardian or immediate care; 41 had desires for wealth; and 72 answered they became prostitutes for "pleasure," or *lezat* in Persian, which is neither explained by Farman Farmaian nor by the interviewees.[112] Although not elaborating on their reasons, the report illustrates that there was some dimension of choice in deciding to enter and remain within the sex industry. Long before sex workers' rights initiatives in the mid-1980s pushed for international conventions to include self-determination and state protection of the industry,[113] the survey responses indicate some of the women's self-awareness in deciding to enter and work in *Shahr-e No*. Another interesting find is that the majority of the prostitutes had minimal awareness of sex: only 157 were aware of what sex was, whereas the remaining 1,389 expressed ignorance.[114]

Intrepid Pari Bolandeh of Shahr-e No

An untold number of powerful hands participated in economically and materially sustaining *Shahr-e No*, suggesting that political influence and corruption extended deep into the Iranian political system.[115] Certain female figures inside *Qal'eh* also attracted attention and received clemency that originated well beyond its domain. Being business savvy, madams were able to invest in commercial and political opportunities outside *Qal'eh*. One of the most recognized of these madams was a prostitute by the name of "Pari Bolandeh (Pari the Tall)," the catchy moniker of Sakineh Qasemi.[116]

Nicknames like hers were hard to come by. During Reza Shah Pahlavi's reign, women were not typically referred to by their full names. According to formal custom of the time, they were referred to by their relationships to the closest male relative. *Khanom* (wife) or *dokhtar* (daughter) of *Agha* (Mister) was a more appropriate reference, ensuring that a respectful distance be maintained at all times between *mahram* relations.[117] However, state modernization attempts altered many of these customs. Once Reza Shah demanded that Iran Westernize itself, through force and legal ramifications, women were ordered to unveil in 1936.[118] Prostitutes were exempt from this ordinance and allowed to wear the *chador* as a way to distinguish themselves as women who were not chaste. But Pari Bolandeh was a tradition-breaker; she capitalized on this era of state-administered modernist reform. A tall and slender woman, she was known for her brazenness in promoting her employees' sexual services. Originally from Ghazvene, she appeared to be a respected figure in her community, having managed brothels from several properties throughout Tehran. Her reach even extended into the field of politics. During the American-orchestrated coup to overthrow Prime Minister Mossadegh, Qasemi participated in demonstrations against the pro-Soviet Tudeh party, which were organized by Pahlavi state authorities. Pictured demonstrating along with athletes from *zur-khanehs* (traditional gymnasiums of urban Persia)[119] and other prostitutes from *Qal'eh Shahr-e No*, Qasemi publicly chanted "Death to Mossadegh" and called for an end to his nationalist policies.[120]

The 1979 overthrow of the Pahlavi regime meant the swift cessation of Pari Bolandeh's madam activities and political activism. Arrested and tried in the Islamic

Figure 2.3 *Kayhan* announcement of the execution of Pari Bolandeh, photographed in black *chador*.

revolutionary courts, she was executed by a firing squad[121] on July 12, 1979, along with two other female associates, Saheb Afsari (also known as Soraya Tarkeh) and Zahra Mafi (also known as Ashraf Cheharchesme or Ashraf Four Eyes).[122] Although details of the court proceedings are scarce (few facts about her court case and execution were released in *Kayhan* newspaper), it was reported that after several closed meetings, Branch One of the Islamic Revolutionary Court in Tehran found her guilty of administering and abetting the illegal prostitution of girls, deceiving women, operating brothels, and spreading corruption among generations—or, as the judgment read, "corruption on earth."[123] In the last known photograph of her (Figure 2.3), taken some time before her execution, she appears downcast, wearing a *chador*.[124]

Male Clientele: Recalling Shahr-e No's Past

For male patrons of *Shahr-e No*, gaining entrance into the brothel district meant access into a somewhat exclusive club of mischief, revelry, and obtaining sexual experience. Although politicians, celebrities, and even clerics were spotted entering *Qal'eh*, male laborers were reportedly the most frequent patrons. (Mansourian disputed this claim, stating that men from various social stratum and political persuasions used *Shahr-e No*'s services.) Men sought such services because it was claimed—and implicitly accepted—that given the extended periods away from their marital beds, their sexual tension needed release.[125]

According to former male patrons I interviewed for this study, *Qal'eh* had once provided an opportune space for a man's sexual rite of passage.[126] From ten interviews conducted with mostly middle-aged men based in Tehran, all of whom were teenagers or in their early twenties at the time of the revolution, I heard many diverse explanations for why they chose to enter *Qal'eh*.[127] Primary motivations were spontaneity, sexual rite of passage, and youthful curiosity. In one interview, Jamal, a middle-aged craftsman, admitted that his friends—and not he—were frequent visitors of *Qal'eh*.[128] Yet during my interview with his close female relative, she recalled discovering a doctor's prescription for syphilis treatment in his pocket when he was fifteen years old. She presumed it was unlikely his infection happened from having sexual relations outside of *Shahr-e No*. For some of the male interviewees, sneaking around the premises, either alone or with a group of friends, was just enough experience to weave into a nostalgic memory about youthful adventure. One male respondent spoke of how *Shahr-e No* offered an entrance into the world of sexual experience; he described how a friend's father purchased the services of a *Shahr-e No* prostitute to rid his son of his virginity. Another interviewee named Nader, a middle-aged computer engineer from East Tehran, recounted that at age fifteen, he accompanied an older group of male friends to *Shahr-e No*. Though he insisted he did not personally engage in any sexual activity and was there out of curiosity, he recounted a story in which a young man fell in love with a prostitute and the lengths he traveled to help her escape the premises. Thirty-something Farhad, a web designer whose older cousins would confide in him stories about their *Shahr-e No* experiences, expressed sympathy for the prostitutes. Farhad argued that the quarter's destruction would mean the prostitutes would soon be forgotten. When I asked him to elaborate, he mentioned that before the revolution prostitutes had an actual site to work; now their work had dispersed throughout Tehran.

Yet not all males were allowed entrance into the district, according to Mansourian. Age and masculine appearance were key factors. Police officers standing at the gates would check if a male had fully entered puberty by rubbing their bare hands across his cheek and chin. If an officer felt hair stubble, then the male was permitted inside to use *Shahr-e No*'s services. Those too young to produce a sign of a beard or any facial hair were reportedly turned away.[129]

The Demolishing of Shahr-e No

As the tide of Pahlavi dissent culminated in the co-opting of a people's revolution in the name of Ayatollah Khomeini's Islam, prostitutes fared no better. Public condemnation of them swiftly rose to the level of riots, with angry crowds gathering around *Shahr-e No* within the first days of the revolution. *Qal'eh*'s denouement proved both gruesome and spectacular: After a failed attempt to set fire to the district in November 1978,[130] three months later in early February 1979, an angry mob was reported to have attacked its residents, setting the district ablaze after attempts by police and firefighters to quell the riots were unsuccessful. (Mehrangiz Kar claims that the riots were the work of Islamic revolutionary extremists who had come to "destroy the roots of moral corruption.")[131] There were two confirmed deaths.[132] Soon after, Ayatollah Sadegh Khalkhali—himself notorious for the swift condemnation and execution of political prisoners and activists during his brief tenure as chief justice of Iran's first revolutionary courts—denounced the area and ordered bulldozers inside it to level the district for its illegal and un-Islamic activities.[133]

Park-e Razi: Cleansing the Site of Prostitution for a Moral Leisure Area

Today, the *Shahr-e No* narrative has faded into the shadows of public memory. Ask most Iranians under the age of thirty about this district, and they will likely puzzle over its existence and history.[134] Inquire instead where Gomrok district is located, and more likely the response will be, "It's near a park!" Prior to 1979, this form of response would have been impossible. The name Gomrok was heavily associated with the notorious sex district, and although its name has not been altered, for two generations of Iranians born in the postrevolutionary period, its contemporary connotations resonate quite differently.

In the site of *Shahr-e No* now stands a multi-acre, manicured park known as Park-e Razi (Razi Park) and a hospital complex both of which are located in Tehran's District Eleven (Figure 2.4). In the northeast lies the Farabi Teaching hospital, now affiliated with the Tehran University of Medical Sciences. The hospital was reportedly well-known in the Middle East for performing advanced surgical techniques in ophthalmology.[135] More than 25 hectares (about 61 acres) of the original *Qal'eh* site (almost 108.7 acres) were developed into a park in 1997, and currently it bears no physical resemblance to its prerevolutionary form. Unlike the majority of formerly inhabited lands in Tehran which after the revolution and the Iran–Iraq War were intensely developed into office and apartment buildings—for land development has been a lucrative business—a large section of the area was transformed into a family-friendly culture, leisure, and athletics haven.[136] Its grounds include a cultural exhibition center, a public library, cinemas, a marketplace for traditional Persian crafts, the intermittently operational amusement park of Shahr-e Bazi (Play City), and a man-made lake fit with a lighthouse and a neon-lit bridge on which park patrons and fishermen can observe swan gondola rides (Figure 2.7). The park also hosts a children's playground area (Figure 2.6), prayer spaces, and a lecture hall, as well as Astroturf soccer fields and an open-air calisthenics section for public use. From the park's main entrance on Kargar Street (Figure 2.5), petty businessmen are found sitting on benches with their satchels open, selling snacks and trinkets to passersby. Traditional and fast-food restaurants line avenues reaching to the main square, where a statue of Persian medieval scholar and physician Mohammad ibn Zakariya al-Razi peers over a rotunda. Park-e Razi's surrounding area is still relatively poor, surrounded by a mixture of rundown two-story buildings, vacant shopping centers, local banks, and family-operated businesses selling odds and ends.[137]

The Tehran Parks and Green Space Organization runs most of the capital's 800 parks, providing maintenance, landscaping, and beautification services. The

Figure 2.4 November 2019 aerial view of Park-e Razi, Tehran.

organization even produces its own newsletters about park-related topics and the psychological benefits to being park patrons. For instance, it published the article, "The Importance of Green Spaces and Its Effect on Human Mentality," praising municipal parks as symbols of heaven and health. They are places where individuals escape to nature for peace, leisure, and relaxation.[138] The article cites reasons why visitors frequent parks: to take inspiration and calm from the psychologically pleasant green colors surrounding them.[139]

Park-e Razi is however operated by a different municipal authority. Since 2005,[140] it has been uniquely managed by a state cultural organization, *Sazman-e Farhangi Honari Shahrdari-ye Tehran* (Cultural and Arts Organization of Tehran Municipality), which has administrative offices located near a park entrance. The organization describes itself as a "center for cultural activities in Tehran and administrates over 300 cultural centers" across the city.[141] As a state institution, it also has its own publishing branch. (For the thirty-second anniversary of the revolution, it commemorated the occasion by publishing a 600-page chronology of revolutionary milestones from state-media sources, which it planned to sell during the anniversary's demonstrations.)[142] According to a news report, the Sazman has special plans for Park-e Razi, transforming it into the "cultural pole of the capital."[143] Currently, the park hosts art and film exhibitions and offers cultural, educational, and religious programs, such as the spring season 2012 lecture series on *hejab* and chastity called *Gohar-e Efaf* (The Jewel of Chastity) (Figure 2.8) (Figure 2.9).

In the last four decades, the Iranian government has pursued a policy of constructing Islamic communal leisure spaces through reinventing monuments and landmarks from the Pahlavi era, thus expunging from communal records their prerevolutionary pasts. City parks are often perfect sites to execute these aims. More than public meeting points for relaxation and sport, they offer people easy access to state-funded and administered public programs and facilities, too. Eradicating and then redeveloping a century-old site of prostitution into a familial park and hospital complex is one method of projecting the triumph of Islamic values over the corrupt, symbolic political capital of the Pahlavis that these sites formerly embodied. According to the Islamic Republic's revolutionary narrative, while the Pahlavi state promoted "dens of moral corruption," Ayatollah Khomeini's

Figure 2.5 Pedestrian sign at the Kargar Street entrance of Park-e Razi.

Figure 2.6 Painted car sitting at a side entrance of Park-e Razi.

Figure 2.7 Neon-lit bridge overlooking man-made lake of Park-e Razi.

version of an Islamic state, by contrast, promoted religious and family values.[144] The deliberate transformation of *Shahr-e No*'s land into a recreational public park is one of many illuminating examples. In its place is now a utopian and remodeled landscape that forges a new collective memory and social cohesion via a carefully designed ideological space where history can be both erased and reimagined. The

Figure 2.8 View of paintball ad and Park City Ferris wheel, Park-e Razi February 2019.

Figure 2.9 Park visitors picnicking in Park-e Razi February 2019.

remodeled site is a cursory reincarnation, disguising an attempt to build over a "primary" site for the purposes of dismissing and revising facts about what exactly went on in that location for many generations. As Robert Sack has argued in his discussion of spatiality and social life,

> When place, and not only the things in it, is a force—when it influences, affects, and controls—it is a primary place. Primary places involve human actions and intentions and have the capacity to change things. Unlike a secondary place, which can be replaced without remainder by substituting the objects and interactions in its area, a primary place cannot be replaced. Primary places are delimited, they possess rules about the things to be included and excluded, and they have meaning.[145]

In this theoretical paradigm, Park-e Razi is a secondary place. The material fixtures of a children's playground and prayer space are temporary replacements, meant to nurture an Islamic identity ground in piety, family, and Muslim community. This is best exemplified in how the Cultural Arts Organization of Tehran Municipality narrates the history behind Park-e Razi. According to a 2012 description posted on its website (which has since been removed), the park's identity is mediated through Islamic revolutionary discourse.[146] The organization praises the revolution for positively transforming the land where *Shahr-e No* once stood:

> Historically, this area is one of the important areas of cultural heritage, if one counts the Ghazvin gates, the Garden of Kings, and Sheikh Hadi and Moniriyeh Streets. Before the revolutionary period, the cultural background of this neighborhood was very bleak because of the existence of Jamshid quarter and other profound social problems. However, with the glorious advent of the Islamic Revolution (*Khorshid-e Enqelab-e Islami*) and through the efforts of the municipality, it was transformed from a corrupt area into the biggest leisure and sports center in the city.[147]

Indeed, prostitution is not explicitly cited here; instead, a street name also associated with the brothel area—Jamshid—is mentioned, although it is no longer a common reference point for Iranians under the age of thirty-five. As a strategy of replacing the prerevolutionary history by superimposing an Islamic identity and a new beginning for that site, the illicit past is ostensibly absolved through a process of spatial cleansing. The actual area of *Shahr-e No* transforms into a purported prostitution-free green space that accommodates families, athletes, and library patrons. In this zone, Islamic family values are cultivated and nurtured through the ubiquitous planning of the state; according to park director Behnam Khadem, people come to the park to "get away from many of the societal problems."[148] To a certain degree, visiting Park-e Razi is unlike visiting other parks spread across the city—it is inscribed within the domains of the state, functioning as a platform to promote its ideals. The Cultural Arts Organization integrates religious and state programs into the recreational activities that the park offers, which means that a particular definition of "recreation" is being disseminated. As such, the park offers a new social and spatial reality, where Islamic tenets are made accessible and thus reinforced to the general public. In other words, if a visitor wants to learn about the revolution, Persian handicrafts, and the subject of modesty from the state's perspective, then the park facilities provide such a space for learning about these topics. Hence, visiting Park-e Razi involves much more than an escape to nature for the benefits of health and leisure.

Recalling Shahr-e No's Past from Park Residents

Although demolished, *Shahr-e No* remains somewhat alive in the vivid storytelling of older generations who dare mention its name; newspaper clippings and history books also offer glimpses into its history, albeit piecemeal. Attempting to learn more of its social history and observe the physical transformation that the Gomrok district had undergone, I visited the park multiple times and asked visitors about their knowledge of the brothel district and Park-e Razi's past.[149] During those trips on several afternoons in August 2011, the park was virtually empty, presumably because it was very hot and also in the middle of Ramadan.[150] In another period, this would have been unusual; during weekends—for Iranians, Thursday and Friday—public parks were generally packed with families and young people mingling, playing sports, and picnicking.

At the park I conducted eight on-site interviews with park patrons (six men and two women), whom I met while they were seated on benches at different locations in the park. Each person was a denizen of the park's surrounding neighborhoods. The two women interviewees were in their late twenties and early thirties and were both strangers to me and to each other. The men, however, seemed to be acquainted with one another, as each offered suggestions about the next person with whom I should speak. Of the six men, five were above the age of sixty and told me that they sat in the park as part of their daily ritual. The last interview I conducted in the park was with a gondola conductor who introduced me to a middle-aged security guard—coincidentally, one who had formerly worked at *Shahr-e No*.

When I inquired individually if they had heard of *Shahr-e No*, they all responded that the park was constructed over its remnants. I spoke with a thirty-year-old mother, who was waiting for her son to finish a game of football. She admitted she was too young to know details about the red-light district; however, she said that prostitutes were known to frequent the park in the early mornings and late evenings. In one part of the park, canopies shield tables and benches, and certain areas are not well lit. She pointed out that prostitutes and potential customers gather there discreetly to arrange meeting times and meeting places.

The people I spoke to offered few personal details about the red-light district; this topic caused uneasiness particularly for the elderly men.[151] For instance, after animatedly detailing the layout of the park and describing mischievous activities of young couples there, an elderly divorced man suddenly lowered his voice when describing the area before 1979. He said, briefly, "bad things happened here," and promptly ended our conversation. In other interviews with male park visitors, the details tended to be more illustrative of the illicit sexual conduct—such as men and women engaged in petting and fornication—that they had witnessed while visiting the park. According to the 21-year-old gondola conductor and the security guard who was a worker inside *Shahr-e No*, elderly prostitutes are spotted occasionally in the park, sitting on benches near the man-made lake. The conductor claimed that there was a particular protocol men and women would follow if they sought casual or paid sex: they would sit on opposite ends of the benches and discreetly flirt, while arranging the specifics of paid sexual encounters. When I asked for more details about these women—namely, their ages and cities of origin—the men separately told me that although the majority were young prostitutes, there were some rumored to have worked in *Shahr-e No*. According to their accounts, some women had returned to the site to continue sex work after having difficulty finding employment after the revolution.[152]

During the time spent in the park, speaking with social workers and park revelers and walking around the area, it became vividly clear to me that despite *Shahr-e No*'s physical destruction and renovation into a park, the legacy of prostitution still lingered. Although this new site looks and feels nothing like its predecessor, it is still a quotidian presence because transactions for illicit sexual activities are made and conducted in various sections of the park. Moreover, it resists official narratives, which purport that the sex industry belonged to a bygone era and had been erased. The former "toilet" of Taleghani's days was, in fact, in this postrevolutionary moment, a renovated heterotopia, its concrete walls turned into a manicured and counterfeit green space, but still propagating the same illicit activity. Government morality and careful urban planning could not whitewash the more-than-century-long history and soul of this space, where a constellation of competing interests undermined and *reinforced* consecutive social orders from the Pahlavi period to the present day.

My lengthy discussions with the park's patrons about the prerevolutionary history of Park-e Razi and their acknowledgment that prostitutes still "worked" in the area provide an important and subversive public counter-narrative to the state's attempt at infusing Islamic family values in the construction of Park-e Razi. Clearly, the physical erasure of *Shahr-e No* had only physically transformed the site where activities in the sex trade were practiced. The ongoing presence of prostitution suggests that the renovation of the space and the attempt to eradicate the sex industry were in reality a cosmetic effort, doing nothing to address the underlying socioeconomic factors and conditions, which gave formation to the need for such a space in the first place. Vilifying prostitutes and demolishing sex districts with bulldozers were surface (and ultimately) perfunctory measures which momentarily sought to disguise two very critical issues, both equally worthy of engagement: male sexual promiscuity and the tacit acceptance of prostitution in the overall cohesion and maintenance of the existing social order.

This historical discussion of Tehran's erstwhile red-light district and its more contemporary transformation is not meant to locate and sensationalize the underworld of a thriving sex industry, operating openly in a Tehran park, in an

Islamic Republic. By merely acknowledging the presence of sex workers in parks, no radical redirection is offered in how the discourse on prostitution operates and is handled inside Iran. As discussed earlier, there have been, internationally, various methods of tolerance and regulation of prostitution and persons involved in the sex industry. The unique feature about prostitution discourse in contemporary Iran, in relation to the memory of *Shahr-e No*, is the overtly politicized, spatial transformation of a former sex site—a physical and overt brothel catering to men—to a green park intended for pious, family-oriented patrons. From the ashes of a burned-down red-light district, a public park was constructed to represent and symbolize a new direction in values, distinct and profoundly counter to its prerevolutionary past. Now promoting religious chastity and modesty, these green spaces were designed to celebrate spiritual and mental health, and a return to nature. Yet, the elimination of prostitution in its previous form did not equate to an eradication of its memory or of the practice of illegal sexual interactions between men and women. When intersections of social, cultural, economic, and political factors merge into a zone once highlighted as a place for human excess, it seems the transformation of that particular space into a pious alternative neither excuses nor denies the very existence and continuation of the need for such human excess.

In the next chapter, the subject of prostitution in the postrevolutionary period continues. I follow the destruction of the Pahlavi "citadel" of prostitution and study how a unique reformulation of illicit sex between men and women appears. I discuss the Islamist state's reform policies from 1979 until 2008, which targeted *Shahr-e No*'s sex workers, who, after the revolution were reported to have been offered a chance at rehabilitation in the newly formed Islamic Republic. Although the actual "site" of Taleghani's "toilet" in some manner vanishes, the conditions and circumstances that enable prostitution to proliferate years later suggest something equally troubling—that, within both Pahlavi and Islamist regimes, prostitution is an institutionally and conceptually accepted feature and necessity.

Chapter 3

SAFETY VALVES AND POSTREVOLUTIONARY "PROSTITUTION"

Islamist Reform Meets the Sex Industry: An Introduction

There are two parallel, yet intimately codependent, discourses motivating one another in this chapter: the state discourse of prostitution and that of temporary marriage, in Persian vernacular known as *sigheh*. For both, it is reportedly the notion of an insatiable, consuming sexuality that underscores why the sex industry in contemporary Iran continuously disrupts social order, leading officials to seek out "Islamic solutions." Interestingly, following the destruction of *Shahr-e No*— once identifiable as *the* conceptual and physical site of prostitution in the Pahlavi era—a reconfiguration of prostitution discourse occurred using legally Islamic marriage contracts to curb heterosexual men's and women's perpetually activated sexualities. Given this, the reports that prostitutes and clientele returned to "mingle" in a former sex district-turned-family park are no surprise. For many reasons, state attempts to eradicate the sex industry was an improbable task, even despite the demolition of a blighted area known as the "Citadel." The reasons for such lie in how the discourse of prostitution has been mediated in the postrevolutionary period, intersecting with other discourses on the rehabilitation and reform of not just "fallen women" but also of veterans, youth, and the economy. At the same time, these discursive rays have intersected, been buttressed, and/or clashed, depending on the speakers and audience, with Iranian Shi'a discourses of family, marriage, chastity, and human sexuality.

It goes without saying that there is something peculiar to postrevolutionary Iran's historical processes of disagreement and negotiation over the very contentious issue of prostitution. While ongoing debates grapple with proving or denying its existence and prevalence in Iranian society today, many of the country's high-ranking clerics and officials have made specific utilitarian and political calculations in the face of postwar economic calamity and societal trauma, suggesting the sex industry had never left town, so to speak. At certain points during their decision-making processes, they have repeatedly lassoed into their realm of possibilities a temporary solution that has been consequential for the lives of a whole spectrum of humanity, "prostitutes" included. To clarify, I mean *sigheh*, or temporary marriage, which entered public discourse multiple times over the past four decades when officials sought remedies to address, Islamically, multiple social and economic dilemmas. In doing so, postrevolutionary reform technologies and public policy initiatives integrated certain default assumptions about men and women into discussions on protecting social order, preventing societal ills, and offering Islamic "safety valves." Concomitantly, any discussion about contemporary practices of prostitution necessarily involves the very important factor of paid and temporary sexual unions made possible via legal, short-term marriage contracts offered in Shi'a Islam and increasingly made use of in the Islamic Republic.

This chapter focuses on the sparks of discursive activity, when prostitution discourse bisects with conversations on criminality, penance, marriage, chastity, and financial security. Through this, a metanarrative emerges, linking the social realities and practice of *sigheh* with those of prostitution. As a punishing war with Iraq saw no end in sight, fueling multiple economic and social crises, government officials moved to bolster the economy, interlacing talk of the necessity of marriage for those financially wary. Then, a unique semantic justification for the traditional practice of marriage emerged, emphasizing a time constraint. The functional role of wife was concomitantly reconceptualized as a temporary partner, stirring controversy about a state-approved method of regulation for paid, sexual arrangements that was both Islamically legal and thus useful. It is through this process that the structural tenets of an Islamic marriage become wrapped into a dual state project of Islamization and regulation.[1] Suddenly, prostitution was interwoven into state rehabilitation and reform programs. I contend that through this discursive nexus, the "ghettoization" of women's sexual labor (in which their bodies provide sexual gratification for men) is teased into the framework of Shi'a legal discourses of marriage and uniquely communicated as public policy. In essence, Iranian authorities encouraged *sigheh* as a policy solution to address social dilemmas because of certain default assumptions they carried about women's sexuality, receptiveness, and function in preserving public morality and social order.

Returning to Pahlavi Sites of Body Traffic

After the fall of the monarchy, what became of Iran's prostitutes in the midst of these structural changes? In the very first month of this transitional period (1979–82), brothel districts were immediate casualties. Two days before jubilant celebrants greeted Ayatollah Khomeini at Tehran's Mehrabad airport on February 1, newspapers printed images of the city's red-light district on fire.[2] By month's end, once provisional revolutionary courts were established, vice areas were ordered demolished. Places known for body traffic—sites where illegitimate, opposite sex interactions of the *namahram*[3] sort took place, such as city intersections, cinemas, brothels, and commercial centers—came under monitoring by the new revolutionary state. Seemingly all manner of heterosexual interaction conducted in public spaces was subject to some type of Islamization reform and regulation. For those accused of *zedd-e arzesh-e enqelab-e eslami* (being against Islamic revolutionary values) punishment was severe. Ad hoc revolutionary courts sentenced intellectuals, activists, writers, madams, and members of the Pahlavi establishment to death.[4] As reported in the newspaper *Ettella'at*, "Any action that is pleasing to God is valuable; any deed that contradicts God's command is anti-value."[5] Najmabadi explains, "Execution of prostitutes, men and women accused of adultery, drug smugglers as well as drug addicts, are all part of the same campaign to 'cleanse society,' and expunge from it all these 'points of corruption.'"[6]

To erase vestiges of the Pahlavi state, the Supreme Council of the Cultural Revolution[7] began implementing institutional changes to restructure Iran as an identifiably Islamist nation-state.[8] "Islamic criteria," later enumerated in the national constitution, formed the rubric through which the state designed and implemented new cultural, political, and economic policies for its nascent theocratic republic.[9] Radical transformations in Iran's legal, economic, and social structures followed. Soon powerful *ulama* (Muslim scholars or clerics) fully entered the political fray, after decades of subjugation and exile by the Pahlavi leadership and secret police.[10] Given top leadership and ministry positions, they helped draft the country's constitution and assumed their positions as vice-regents or "heirs to the mantle of the Prophet."[11] "After the Islamic Revolution," writes Ervand Abrahamian, "The clergy had the field to themselves, since recent socioeconomic developments had dissolved the traditional ties between the rural magnates and their clients, between landlords and their peasants, and between tribal chief and their tribesmen."[12] They helped form a judiciary system staffed by *mujtahids*[13] and local court clerics, replacing the Pahlavi-era secular court system (with secular university-educated judges).[14] This judiciary became the legal bastion of the Islamic state, interpreting and applying the Khomeini-approved doctrine of a theocratic government run by a senior-ranking Shi'a Ayatollah who holds the position of *velayat-e faqih* (Guardian Jurist). Additionally, the Supreme Judicial Council (which was later unified in the position of the Head of the Judiciary in 1989) directed all courts to abide by Islamic legislation. In 1982, Iran implemented a *shari'a*-based penal code (*Qanoun-e Mojazat-e Eslami*) for an experimental period; punishments were revised in accordance to their specifications in the Qur'an.[15] But in Paidar's view, the institutionalization of Khomeini's ideological doctrine faced several setbacks, for "the process of transition entailed a gradual disintegration of the discourse of revolution, and the post-revolutionary transitional period became the scene of intense debate over the new culturally authentic and economically and politically independent society, and the place of women within it."[16]

Theorizing the Prostitute as "Other"

Erving Goffman attests that "society establishes the means of categorizing persons and the complement of attributes felt to be ordinary and natural for members of each of these categories."[17] Individuals who cannot conform to socially constructed norms are judged as deviant and stigmatized. The former term is typically used to describe those "as declining voluntarily and openly to accept the social place accorded them, and who act irregularly and somewhat rebelliously in connection with our basic institutions."[18] The latter is described as "an attribute that is deeply discrediting," and according to Goffman has three typologies: physical deformities, a problematic character, and a tribal or racial affiliation.[19] Prostitutes are placed in the second category, along with drug addicts, gypsies, and the urban unrepresented poor, among others.[20]

Sex workers and their clientele are seen to deviate from behavior that is deemed to be morally and legally unacceptable.[21] Often subjected to the "whore stigma," they are associated with "disease, dirt and pollution, which can fuel hostile attitudes and acts of violence."[22] Further, according to Shannon Bell, this maligned characterization of the prostitute is strategically positioned as an "other." The prostitute is viewed through a prism of normative and abnormal human behavior—concomitantly, exposing contradictory assumptions about human sexuality.[23] Bell finds this to be a discursive outcome of a modernist discourse that dichotomized women into "good" and "bad" characters.[24] In her view, "modernity through a process of othering has produced 'the prostitute' as the other of the other within the categorical other, 'woman.'"[25] The hierarchal, binary opposition of masculine and feminine, which is "at the heart of the foundational metaphysics of Western thought," is reproduced within this dichotomy of good and bad woman and reproduced in feminist and modernist writings. She observes, "Prostitutes were analyzed and categorized in relation to the bourgeois female ideas: the good wife and the virginal daughter. The prostitute might be the same, she might be different; often she was located on a continuum somewhere between sameness and difference, but she was always the disprivileged other in relation to the determinant site: wife, mother, daughter."[26] This process of othering runs through both feminist and modern constructions of the prostitute body, which was "actively produced as a marginalized social-sexual identity, particularly during the latter half of the nineteenth century and the beginning of the twentieth century."[27]

Keeping in mind Goffman's and Bell's analyses, a comparable conceptual portrait of "prostitute" as whore, sexual object, insult, outsider, and paladin of decadence and moral corruption abounds in both pre- and postrevolutionary political discourses in Iran.[28] Not unlike their treatment in other cultural contexts, prostitutes and those involved in the sex work industry are historically vilified, and the literature from the modern and contemporary Iranian context is quite extensive. The female prostitute as societal antagonist featured prominently in modernist literary discourse, especially in the writings of nationalists, religious scholars, and modernist women's advocates during the late nineteenth century until the early 1970s, when Iran underwent state modernization and economic development.[29] The prostitute was the antithesis to the idyllic Muslim, Iranian woman character, which *Shi'a* clerics supported as an "ideal type model for Iranian women."[30] For Iranian nationalists and women's advocates, prostitutes featured in national discussions in the first half of the twentieth century about women's citizenship and motherhood; these themes typically incorporated the topics of hygiene, reproductive politics, and sexuality.[31] They were specifically accused of spreading sexually transmitted diseases (STDs), destroying the marital home, and spoiling new generations (as it was believed that infected men could spread syphilis to their wives and children).[32] In the 1960s, a treatise on female criminality identified a female-specific category of traits considered injurious and unbecoming of the ideal Muslim woman. In this work, prostitutes are viewed with particular disdain. The 1962 publication of Qadisih Hijazi's *Barrasi-ye Jara'im-e Zan dar Iran* (An Investigation of Women's Criminal Activity in Iran) was one of the first "book-length Iranian treatise[s] on female criminality," according to historian Cyrus Schayegh.[33] A devout Muslim raised in a clerical family, Hijazi argued that "criminal-women" failed at being mothers, unlike "mother-women" who excelled in child-rearing and maintaining pious, crime-free domestic lives. Prostitutes did not have any socially acceptable place or role.[34] Schayegh describes her purview of female criminality as ground in her condemnation of women who rejected their main purpose in life, to be mothers:

> A woman's original crime is a sin against her body, a body that does not truly belong to her, a body she has to look after for society's sake. Prostitution is morally condemnable, medically dangerous, and socially harmful. A woman's attempt to subvert her body's basic purpose—reproduction—drives her insane and endangers society.[35]

Here, the prostitute's crime is her rejection of reproduction. According to Hijazi, prostitutes provided sex for male pleasure, although not to maintain social order, or to propagate mankind. Their immoral acts made them anti-role models who strayed from their social, familial, and biological duties.

Prostitution on Tehran's Streets

Iran's state media uses an official terminology for prostitution and the women involved in the sex industry. Prostitution is officially translated as *khod-forushi* (selling oneself) and *tan-forushi* (selling of the body). Yet, instead of using the definitions *ruspigar* or *ruspi* for a female prostitute, euphemisms are used.[36] The terms *zan-e kheyabuni* (street woman), *dokhtar-e ferari* (a runaway girl), and more recently *zanan-e asibdideh-ye ejtima'i* (socially harmed women) are mentioned in state media and government agency reports.[37] The unspecific terminology is reflective, in part, of an official reticence to admit the existence and prevalence of prostitution countrywide. To date there are no independently confirmed statistics on the number of prostitutes nor is there any systematic research on prostitution in Iran.[38] In 2002, unofficial estimates claimed that approximately 300,000 prostitutes were working in Iran.[39] In 2007, they claimed that approximately 84,000 prostitutes reside in Tehran alone.[40] Government officials dispute unofficial figures, claiming that this part of the social issue is part of a Western plot to corrupt Iranian youth.[41] Their responses usually manifest in two ways: either they deny the existence of prostitution or they provide lower estimates, pointing to inaccuracies and exaggerations in unofficial statistics.[42] For instance, Tehran's chief of police

Hossein Sajedinia reported in 2011 that there were only 200 "street women." Iran's Wellbeing Agency disputed this number, reporting that about 400 female prostitutes are arrested annually in Tehran.[43] Medical researcher Zargooshi quoted an anonymous official who claimed that, outside the capital, about 2,000 prostitutes were working in Kermanshah.[44] Similarly, in a rare instance of official recognition of this social issue, government official Homayun Hashemi from Iran's Social Welfare Organization, a government-run body, admitted, "Certain statistics have no positive function in society; instead, they have a negative psychological impact. It is better not to talk about them."[45]

Despite official hesitation to recognize the issue of prostitution, there are many available sources that elaborate the conditions and circumstances in which Iranian women, be they married or single, participated in paid-sex activities on a temporary basis, or had entered the sex industry as self-employed sex workers or linked to organized sex rings. Gender studies scholar Sholeh Shahrokhi has written extensively on *mahfels*, or places where female runaways and self-employed prostitutes seek refuge after fleeing domestic abuse and other problems.[46] In December 2011, Dr. Habibollah Masoudi Farid, the director general of the Societal Victims Bureau of the State Welfare Organization, reported that 50 percent of women involved in prostitution are married and consider themselves middle class.[47] His findings offered more recent data about the status of women sex workers in Tehran, which showed that the majority of women sex workers were generally poor, illiterate, and unmarried.[48] (Recall Varvayyi's dissertation, which discusses what transpired following the illegalization of prostitution in 1979 and the living conditions of street prostitutes working in various sites throughout Tehran.) Farid suggested that economic survival was no longer the main reason for entering prostitution; recently, more prostitutes turned out to be middle-class women with moderate salaries who prostitute themselves as a "second job."[49] According to Amnesty International, "Married women are sometimes forced into prostitution by their husbands to feed their drug habits or as a result of an abusive relationship. If arrested, they risk being charged with adultery and, if convicted, execution by stoning."[50] Analyst Saieed Madani expanded Farid's assessment during an interview with Iran's *Sharq* newspaper. He reported that "95 percent of women sex workers in Tehran" were literate.[51] The medium age for women sex workers had dropped by three years, wherein girls between the ages of fourteen and fifteen were reportedly entering the sex market.[52] (This drop in age is significant, given that in July 2000, the average age of prostitutes had dropped from twenty-seven to twenty years.)[53] Among the population of female prostitutes who were interviewed, 11.7 percent claimed they were virgins the very first time they prostituted. In addition, 11.8 percent of the female sex workers were presently living with their own husbands.[54] However, for those women who chose prostitution even though they had modest incomes, Madani cited two reasons: economic mobility and accumulation of material wealth. The reasons why a woman entered the sex market were based not only on economic necessity but also on enhancing quality of life and increasing material possessions.[55] Indeed, both Madani and Farid emphasized that these women were at the beginning of the spectrum of prostitute types. Once they entered the "cycle" of the profession, they would become exposed to drugs and STDs and would need additional psychological care.[56]

Additionally, there were many reports on government measures and police activities to shut down prostitution rings alongside articles on the community assistance and public health organizations set up to provide safe havens for sex workers.[57] Articles featured interviews with civil servants who spoke on record about the existence of an intricate and vast network of domestic and international sex trafficking and prostitution rings that traverse Iran's geographic and virtual borders.[58] As quoted in a 2014 interview with *The Guardian*, Dr. Farid (mentioned earlier) estimated that there were over 8,000 extant sex rings in Tehran alone.[59] Although Iran's state press did not typically report on this subject, outside press outlets have reported on police raids of brothels and prostitution networks in Tehran.[60] In 2002, Agence France Presse reported that Iranian authorities were stepping up their raids of prostitution rings. Police commander Mohammad Bagher-Ghalibaf said, "[The police] are ready to pick up all street women and prostitutes in less than 72 hours across the country."[61] In June 2002, the Basij paramilitary forces made a rare public announcement that raids on brothels had resulted in 48,900 arrests.[62] Even the elite Revolutionary Guards were involved in the prostitution crackdown, raiding four prostitution rings "centered on Tehran which had been sending young Iranian girls to France, Britain, Turkey and Arab countries of the Gulf and arrested more than 100 people."[63] Clearly, there is domestic sex work going on in Iran, despite the official government proclamations to the contrary—and Iranians are aware that brothels exist. In 2001, a reporter from *The Hindu* interviewed an elderly gentleman, about the "peculiar gender situation" in Iran. The journalist noted his response: "There was a long pause and then, as if he had decided that there was no more delicate way to express himself this gentleman said, 'Teheran had the biggest red-light district in the Middle East before the revolution. Do you think this has all gone away?'"[64]

Revolutionary Reform of "Fallen Women"

Initially it seemed that in the early years of the Islamic Republic, officials fully intended to make prostitution "go away." Denouncing and punishing those who strayed from a righteous path were knee-jerk reactions leading up to the revolution. Scorn was particularly directed at wealthy and middle-class women who were condemned for having lost their moral standing during the Pahlavi era.[65] During mass demonstrations, popular slogans denounced the treatment of women as "sex-objects."[66] The Pahlavi dynasty was labeled as the "spreader of prostitution."[67] Throughout the revolutionary period (1978–82), the female prostitute continued to garner mixed public sympathy. Prostitutes maintained a precarious social position—either they were pitied as victims of social ills, or they were treated as leading a "pathological" life in need of a cure, writes Shahidian.[68] Women sex workers were also judged to be already promiscuous, unethical, and impious—characteristics that conflicted with the ideological construct of the Muslim mother and family, foundational features of the Islamic Republic's constitution.[69] Even the word "prostitute" became a slur. When a woman was called such, it connected her to all that was anathema to the Islamic Republic's model female citizens—women of piety, character, and family values who espoused revolutionary ideals.[70] In 1980, Khomeini condemned the Pahlavis by associating their government with entrapment and sexual pandering: "In the name of freedom, progress, and civilization, Reza Khan and Mohammad Reza Khan led all our youths to prostitution but took all their freedoms away."[71] By all accounts, postrevolutionary Iranian authorities regarded prostitution—and anyone associated with the corruption of society—as a criminal, morally vacant, and socially deviant, Westernized lifestyle and condition.[72]

By 1982, strict punishments were identified in Iran's criminal code to warn potential offenders of their fates in the event they were caught, prosecuted, and punished for abetting illicit sex.[73] In the penal code itself, the crime and punishment of prostitution are cited in the section *ghavadi* (pimping).[74] Prostitution is considered a crime against public morality and chastity—and therefore a capital offense.[75] Any person who facilitates prostitution or encourages immoral acts, establishes or manages brothels, or facilitates travel abroad for the purposes of prostitution is subject to punishments, including lashing and in certain cases, stoning.[76] In Islamic jurisprudence, illicit sex falls under the umbrella category *zena* and includes the acts of adultery, prostitution, premarital fornication, and homosexuality. Sex between an unmarried man and woman is explicitly forbidden and is punishable by prison, lashing, or execution by stoning. The penal code designates criminal sexual activity as *hodoud* (literally in Arabic, restrictions or limits) crimes—meaning that specified forms of punishment are outlined in the Qur'an and *hadith* and thus should be applied.[77] However, it is important to note that certain conditions must be met for these punishments to be applied. These include the use of proper procedures, such as fair and reliable witnesses, and the determination of the "circumstances" of the case.[78]

Simultaneous to the formulation and implementation of an Islamic jurisprudence-based criminal code, which handled prostitution-related offenses, lawmakers and clerical authorities began pursuing the route of rehabilitation to control prostitution. To understand this better, we return to the gripping months during the revolutionary period, after *Shahr-e No* is demolished. Though little is published in Persian and English on the individual fates of *Shahr-e No*'s prostitutes, there are some key academic sources that offer general information about the resurgence of the sex industry after the revolution. For those prostitutes from the red-light district not imprisoned, many were reportedly given a second chance, provided they accept a specific kind of Islamic reform. Haeri reported that they entered rehabilitation programs wherein some were transformed into *sigheh* (temporary marriage) wives.[79] Presented as a kind of rebirth for "fallen women," the program sought to reform them into pious, useful members of society and ostensibly to help them return to a morally guided path.[80] Historian Paidar also mentioned the incipient government policy toward prostitutes immediately after *Shahr-e No*'s razing. Because prostitutes were no longer concentrated in red-light districts, concerns grew that the sex industry would openly penetrate city life. Paidar describes the manner of reform that these women faced:

> [The Islamic Republic's] Bureau [for Combating Corruption] adopted a carrot and stick policy towards prostitution. It announced that prostitutes who chose to repent would be assisted to marry and "return to the warm embrace of family life," or be provided with jobs in specially set-up workshops. Those who chose to "continue their wicked ways, causing perversion of the country's youth and betraying the blood of the martyrs of the Revolution, would be punished by revolutionary courts."[81]

The Bureau For Combating Corruption was set up to cleanse postrevolutionary Iranian society of the "manifestations of 'Westernized' gender relations"; it also sought to stop the "free relationships between men and women."[82] According to Haeri, the Bureau's special rehabilitation workshops focused on training former prostitutes to embrace their maternal and spousal responsibilities[83]—for their reform necessitated accepting gendered roles of mother, wife, and sister which the Islamic Republic's religious authorities encouraged.[84] With room and board provided, former prostitutes were educated in household tasks, such as ironing and washing. They were also pushed to reestablish family bonds, gain employment, and marry.[85]

> One of the main intentions driving this program was to reform prostitutes by resettling them into the most honorable setting: the domestic sphere. Here, a woman's obligations to her family ensured the safe maintenance of a pious household. Women learned to embrace "instinctual" maternal sensibilities, such as child-rearing. By accepting Islam as a guiding force, former prostitutes were believed to have been rehabilitated and reintegrated into the *ummat* (Muslim community)—from which they were presumably occluded during their work as prostitutes. The emphasis on reforming prostitutes generated much public sympathy; subsequently donations poured into this revolutionary program.[86]

The details of this program are indeed sparse, for relatively, few written records in Persian are available. Much of the information circulates within the realm of public memory and discourse, often surfacing during private and tangential conversations about *Shahr-e No*'s revolutionary history. In one exceptional case, the topic of *Shahr-e No* was the subject of a university thesis on street prostitution in contemporary Tehran. Doctoral candidate Akbar Varvayyi, at the University of Tehran in the School of Law and Political Science, composed the 2008 thesis, "*Barrasi-ye Avamel-e Ruspigari-ye Kheyebani dar Tehran-e Bozorg* (Investigation of the Beginning of Street Prostitution in Greater Tehran)."[87] This work provides key information about former *Shahr-e No* residents, including the prostitutes' main sources of income and housing for instance. Varvayyi recounts that after prostitutes became homeless, they began pouring into neighboring areas. *Mahal-e Jamshid* (Jamshid district) and *Meydan-e Shush* (Shush Square), for instance, became provisional residences.[88] Many of the prostitutes found work in parks or on roadsides; most were runaways or had a history of drug usage. After an undisclosed number of years, authorities grew weary of the tarnishing of the area's reputation. There were reports of makeshift brothels and other illegal activities. Arrests soon followed, and those suspected of criminal activity, including approximately 800 women believed to be working as prostitutes, were detained. According to Varvayyi, their fates were mixed: some faced imprisonment or were shot; others became vocal supporters and activists for the government; and some entered low-wage earning jobs, working as domestic help or seamstresses.[89]

Introducing Sigheh

Also available to prostitutes in the early years after the revolution was an alternative program touted as an "ultimate rehabilitation."[90] The slogan, as described by Willem Floor, was "productive labor makes free."[91] According to Haeri, the government needed to find a quick solution to minimize the rising numbers of single veterans unable to find wives and/or sexual partners. As a method of providing a sexual respite for veterans of the Iran–Iraq War, they began encouraging temporary marriage among the former prostitutes. *Sigheh* is the Persian colloquial term for a fixed-term temporary marriage in Shi'a Islam. In what Haeri has described as "penance *sigheh*," prostitutes were brought to northern Tehran mansions for "rehabilitation and purification."[92] While in rehabilitation centers, they were encouraged to marry Revolutionary Guards, temporarily—which many did, both willingly and unwillingly.[93] Women were also told that veterans of the war would be granted a place in heaven—suggesting that marriage to a veteran would mean a shared spot.[94] Another report noted that "[s]exual *sigheh* was also applied as a means of both repentance and punishment. In prisons too, women prisoners who were virgins were forced into *sigheh* with their jailors before being executed, since according to [the State's] religious beliefs they [the prisoners] would otherwise go to heaven."[95]

Khomeini offered special praise to women who demonstrated this kind of sacrifice in the name of revolutionary causes supporting the Islamic Republic.[96] In a mother's day speech addressing women, he acknowledged "that brave young girl whose magnanimous spirit overflowed with sincerity and genuineness [who] said: 'Since I cannot go to the war front, let me pay my debt to the revolution and my religion through this marriage.'"[97] Although he did not distinguish this marriage as a *sigheh* union in this particular case, he still highlighted a woman's responsibility in galvanizing the war effort through her act of sacrifice. This is exemplified by her marrying a would-be martyr—or, in other words, veterans of war, who were praised as the revolution's ultimate paragons of self-sacrifice.[98] In the same vein, reformed women who married veterans could "[reintroduce *sigheh*] into society from a completely new perspective, 'purifying' the institution of some of its negative cultural connotations."[99] Khomeini was not alone in his approbation of *sigheh*; the same sentiment was echoed by other esteemed figures of the revolution, including Ayatollah Morteza Motahhari, who found it to be one of "the most progressive and farsighted aspects of Islamic thought."[100]

The use of and need for *sigheh* are specifically addressed in official discourses of the economy and postwar rehabilitation, especially germane to discussions on providing provisional and exigent methods to regulate sexuality and maintain social order.[101] But much of these conversations are based on default assumptions about the parameters of marriage and the kinds of possibilities for legitimate and socially acceptable male and female relationships in Islam. Normative understandings of an Islamic marriage describe it as a contract of exchange based on duties and rights, wherein sexual access and compensation factor into the husband-wife relationship.[102] In the words of Shi'a *mujtahid* Muhaqqiq Hilli, marriage is "a contract whose object is that of dominion over the vagina, without the right of possession."[103] In Twelver Shi'ite ideology, there are two main forms of marriage: permanent (legally known as *nikah mut'a*) and temporary (known as *mut'a sigheh*). A Muslim man is limited to four permanent wives—ideally, if he can afford such a circumstance. In either marital union, men pay money or valuables to gain exclusive right and access to sexual relations with women.[104]

Meant for sexual pleasure, *sigheh* is unlike a permanent marriage whose objective is mainly procreation.[105] Shi'a legal consensus is that this kind of marital agreement (*'aqd*) is legitimized via a fixed-term contract between a Muslim man and an unmarried woman, "be she a virgin, divorced, or widowed," writes Haeri.[106] Both parties in a *sigheh* arrangement determine the contract's expiration, the precise nature of the services rendered, and if financial compensation will be exchanged.[107] The predetermined time period can last from as little as one hour up to ninety-nine years.[108] Once the contract expires, a woman must wait the expanse of two menstrual cycles to assure that, in the event of a pregnancy, the father is identifiable and held accountable.[109] Moreover, unlike permanent unions, a temporary marriage requires neither the presence of witnesses nor its registration, and it can be verbally agreed upon. A Muslim man has the right to maintain multiple *sigheh* partnerships at any time, irrespective of the fact that he is permanently married or not, or even if he has more than one permanent wife. An unmarried Muslim woman can have only one male *sigheh* relationship at a time.[110]

Ayatollah Motahhari argued that *sigheh* was "one of the brilliant laws of Islam."[111] It is sanctioned by leading Shi'a Jaf'ari jurisprudential interpretations of a Qur'anic verse—chiefly *al-Nisa* 4: 24.[112] *Hadith* sources, too, cite that the Prophet Muhammad permitted *sigheh*. However, the Shi'a believe that Caliph Omar, whom they do not acknowledge as the rightful blood heir and next in line to the Prophet, had outlawed the practice.[113] Further, Shi'a *ulama* have specified the circumstances within which legitimate and lawful interactions between men and women in a *sigheh* union are permitted to take place—such as in the event of long periods of travel like a pilgrimage or an educational sojourn.[114] Because sexual segregation is a committed priority of the Iranian *ulama*, maintaining propriety between *namahram* (non-blood or kin-related) parties is legitimized through this form of legal consent.[115] The consent in this marriage means that both parties agree to either a sexual or nonsexual (platonic) interaction.[116]

Undergirding this promotion of *sigheh* is the notion that human sexuality is inherently insatiable—in other words, that men and women are voracious, consuming subjects of sexual desire. It is largely argued that the overall aim of *sigheh* is to satisfy sexual urges.[117] "Islamic ideology on marriage and sexuality," writes Haeri, "is celebrated by the Shi'i *ulama* as being positive, self-affirming, and cognizant of human needs. . . . Celibacy, on the other hand, is considered evil and unnatural."[118] Shi'a *ulama* justify *mut'a* marriage on the basis of human nature, which is dichotomized into male and female sexualities. The distinction between the two helps maintain social order.[119] *Sigheh* unions are temporary, preventive solutions to the "animalistic" sexual needs of men—necessary in times when their sexual desires reach insatiable levels.[120] In "Shi'i ideology, the man is assumed to be driven by his sexual drives, to have 'animal' energy."[121] Male sexual drives are also described as "volcanic" and in need of containment and satisfaction through morally acceptable means.[122] Women, by contrast, are perceived to be the sources of energy, to be "nature itself . . . something that is life giving and life threatening, frightful and fascinating."[123]

Yet in this dichotomy of sexualities, male sexuality—if conducted within the confines of a legal marriage contract—is considered legitimate, natural, and expected. It is instinctual and central to the propagation of an orderly Muslim society. By contrast, female sexuality is perceived as a form of "enslavement" because "'by nature' they cannot refuse to yield; it is their nature to want to be taken."[124] Mir-Hosseini adds, "Control of women's sexuality finds its legitimacy in the *fuqaha*'s (Muslim jurists) conception of marriage."[125] For unrestrained sexual relations between two non-married persons encourage vice, uncontrolled urges, which could potentially lead to psychological unrest.[126] Sexual relations between a husband and wife however offered the best example of male-female, spousal complementarity in a controlled and "traditional" framework.[127] Thus to satiate these desires and instincts, temporary sexual partnerships are pursued, sanctioned by Islamic law and doctrine, and even encouraged by Iranian authorities.

Recasting Sigheh: Supporting Veterans and Iran's Economy

After *sigheh* was integrated into government-administered rehabilitation programs, there were three distinct moments when officials began acknowledging and then publicizing their support of temporary marriage. These episodes, presented hereafter chronologically, exemplify how the state integrated temporary marriage in both discussions of uncontrollable, human sexual desires—of veterans, self-sacrificing women, the unemployed, the unmarried, and the youth—and socioeconomic duress. Rather than reiterating *sigheh*'s curbing of errant, human sexual practices, government officials instead emphasized finding Islamic solutions to address societal problems. Interestingly, many have been quiet or deny *sigheh*'s connection to prostitution despite the evidence to the contrary.

By 1988, Iran's casualty-heavy eight-year war with Iraq had culminated in high numbers of veterans and widows in need of social and public assistance. Journalists were already reporting about impending social crises in 1985, having written articles on the decreasing number of marriages, apparently resulting from a cocktail of economic problems, housing shortages, and decreased incomes.[128] Iranian president Hojatoleslam Ali Akbar Hashemi Rafsanjani (*d.* 2017) responded by suggesting that *sigheh* was the answer, and restating this point during public engagements. A heavyweight in Iranian politics, given his leadership roles in the deliberative bodies of the Expediency Council and Assembly of Experts, Rafsanjani garnered international attention after discussing the topic in a series of speeches, television appearances, and newspaper interviews he gave in 1983, 1985, and 1997.[129] He expressed concern about the societal consequences stemming from fewer marriages taking place, stating that society would face more problems due to untamed sexual problems and sexual instincts. (According to Paidar, there were also other concerns that these problems would contribute to "an increase in venereal diseases, especially since prostitution had gone underground.")[130] For him, *sigheh* was Islam's "safety valve to prevent explosion."[131] "It is not there for men to satisfy their voluptuousness and ruin their families," he cautioned.[132] During a pivotal interview with *Zan-e Rouz* magazine in 1985, he again iterated *sigheh*'s ideal purpose.[133] This was reaffirmed while speaking to American journalist Mike Wallace during a 1997 interview with the CBS program "60 Minutes," wherein he clarified his views on temporary marriage. When asked about how *sigheh* functioned in Iranian society, Rafsanjani explained,

> This corruption in ethics, which is so common in the West, in Islam has been organized in a controlled manner and a legal way. It has been considered that under certain circumstances, when a man and woman aren't able to marry on a permanent basis, they need to satisfy their instincts. We believe this is a solution to sexual problems. . . . They need to satisfy their instincts. It is not possible for everyone to have a permanent marriage. [For instance] occasionally some are travelers, some do not have the financial potential. There are many things. There are women losing their husbands, and overall, there are many people who need to satisfy their instincts on a temporary basis. This could be accomplished through an official agreement or contract between two parties . . . for whatever the time. This brings an order to the relationship. The fate of the child would be clear, it addressed the idea of the woman in respect of her expenses and she will not be able to marry for a while. Psychologically speaking, this is a legal act, not a forbidden act that everyone is fearful of. . . . In the Shi'ite school of thought, all *ulama* accept this. We believe this is a solution to sexual problems.[134]

His elaboration of *sigheh*'s advantages in alleviating social dilemmas (including sexual tension) had no significant weight on Iranian public opinion. It was reported that the public was generally disapproving toward temporary marriage, viewing those unions as similar to male-female relationships formed in Western cultures.[135] Although his comments stirred a lively debate in the local press, *sigheh* was not a trending topic for more than a decade.[136] Paidar observes, "Cultural disapproval of *sigheh* prevented its legitimization and institutionalization during the first decade of the Islamic Republic despite state propaganda in its favour."[137]

Come the 2000s, financial grievances had augmented in the face of mounting international sanctions, coupled with government economic mismanagement. These factors motivated young couples to delay entering permanent marriage. More than ever, Iranians were finding themselves unemployed, outpriced, and outpaced by the skyrocketing housing prices. Their university degrees had not been golden tickets into financial stability.[138] During the first presidential term of conservative politician and former mayor of Tehran, Mahmoud Ahmadinejad, in 2007, *sigheh* was again broached publicly. A repeat in economic problems surmounted, followed by increased worries that the specific demographic of young Iranians was facing disastrous consequences unless they found long-term stability. Young couples were encouraged to enter temporary marriages to avoid prolonged courtships in which they would be tempted to engage in premarital sex. At a conference in Qom, cleric Mustafa Pourmohammadi, then minister of the interior, announced that the government should promote *sigheh* among the youth, as it would provide a stabilizing and preventive force in the face of society's moral corruption.[139] Pourmohammadi said, "We must not be afraid in promoting the temporary marriage of youth in a society in which God rules; this problem must be bravely addressed across the country."[140] In another media report, he elaborated further:

> The increase in the marriage age in this country has caused many problems. Is it possible that Islam is indifferent to a 15-year-old youth into whom God has put lust? We have to find a solution to meet the sexual desire of the youth who have no possibility of marriage. Islam is a comprehensive and complete religion and has a solution for every behavior and need, and temporary marriage is one of its solutions for the needs of the youth.[141]

Here, Pourmohammadi concentrated on the progressive nature of Islam, perceived to offer Muslims solutions for modern-day dilemmas, using Islamic institutional structures and tenets.[142] Explicit in his reflections on temporary marriage was the prevailing assumption that human sexuality naturally requires satiation. As such fulfilling sexual desires was best handled through heterosexual marital relations—or as Shahidian has defined, "healthy hetero-marital" unions, designed in accordance to Shi'a marital traditions.[143] In this framework, human sexuality is viewed as normal as long as it is confined to specific marital arrangements. In the event that sexuality should err toward deviant expression—meaning that couples should engage in premarital sex or be tempted by lust—temporary marriage is a sufficient mechanism to help subdue errant sexuality.

A point worth mentioning: while temporary marriage was promoted as an available, Islamically approved alternative to entering illicit sexual relationships, young women were not factored into this campaign. State officials did not encourage them to quench their desires by entering temporary marriages. It remains taboo for women to enter *sigheh* and even more unusual for women to announce they have entered a *sigheh* relationship.

Deterring Prostitution through Khaneh-ye Efaf

The increase in prostitution compelled certain religious officials to propose unique forms of regulation. This strategy was a reversal of an approximately three-decade policy of criminalizing prostitutes. In 2002 Ayatollah Mohammed Mousavi Bojnordi, a former member of the Supreme Judicial Council, was quoted as saying, "We face a real challenge with all these women on the street. Our society is in an emergency situation." In an interview with *Etemad* newspaper, he stated, "If we want to be realistic and clear the city of such women, we must use the path that Islam offers us."[144] Just as Rafsanjani had argued, Bojnordi reasoned that Islam, as a model and all-encompassing life system, was capable of responding to every societal dilemma, including prostitution.

The same year, independent news organizations inside Iran began publishing reports that the government was intending to regulate prostitution through the establishment of *khaneh-ye efaf* (chastity houses). The basic idea behind this program was that women and men would convene in small and private centers, being monitored by government agencies, and conduct sexual activity in legal and religiously sanctioned brothels.[145] The proposals were based on "providing safe sex for men of the city."[146] Initially the government was silent about these reports; it would not officially confirm that there were any designs for such a program. Only after media reporters began piecing together more details did the authorities begin to relay any information.[147] According to the research findings of WomeninIran,[148] now a defunct feminist social science and journalism research group based in Tehran, several government agencies were involved in designing and implementing this program.[149] WomeninIran reported that the judiciary, Tehran municipality, and the Ministries of Corrections and the Interior were each participating in this government plan.[150] However, among this group, the only ministry to offer information to the press was that of the Interior, which emphasized the prevention of disease and sexual health of Iranians.

Ashraf Bornudi, the Society Deputy for the Minister of Interior, argued that a "specific strategy" needed to be designed with which to address the relationship between men and women nationwide, especially concerning protecting their health.[151] According to a preliminary plan for *khaneh-ye efaf*, prostitutes would be provided with a health card, which they would receive after obligatory health checkups. This card would grant them access to public health facilities affiliated with the Ministry of Health. Couples would then go to special centers, such as hotels, where they could consummate their union without police interference.[152] In August of the same year, it was apparently agreed that the Social Council would begin collecting expert opinions on these legalized brothels. By the end of the month, an internal memo had circulated around government agencies discussing plans for licensing a particular institute to handle *sigheh* contracts. Proponents of this plan argued that "chastity houses" would help eradicate social corruption.[153]

Researchers from WomeninIran reported widespread disapproval from the public.[154] *Markez-e Amar-e Mosharekat-e Zanan* (The Statistical Center for the Participation of Women), a Tehran-based women's advocacy group, challenged the ministry's plans, stating that sexual contact was just one way in which sexual diseases could spread. They argued that the ministry's focus on the prevention of AIDS through this route would be ineffective.[155] After news of these plans leaked to the public, it ignited much controversy, prompting immediate denials from officials. Hojjat al-Eslam Rahami, then head of the Political Conscience division of Iran's security forces, announced that the chief architect behind these proposed chastity houses had been identified and arrested.[156] The arrest—which cannot be independently confirmed if, in fact, it did happen—was perhaps an attempt to placate public disapproval while simultaneously denying that the plan had any official government approval, or even existed. It is generally believed that plans for *khaneh-ye efaf* were abandoned soon after.

Indeed, the controversy surrounding the proposals for chastity houses was generated from the possibility that the government intended to begin regulating legitimate brothels in the Islamic Republic. But these plans were also problematic because implicit to this policy was the involvement of particular demographic groups. According to WomeninIran, the likelihood that destitute women and female runaways would participate was strong.[157] One could only speculate if the authorities had known about this and so indirectly provided a location and reason for these women to seek sex work as a quick source of income.

That said, state and clerical rhetoric has repeatedly downplayed the link between *sigheh* and prostitution. Shi'a clerics generally view *sigheh* as a sexual safety valve, which is available to Muslims in certain circumstances. The late Mohammad Kazem Shari'atmadari, the leading Grand Ayatollah in Qom and whom Haeri interviewed in 1978 for her fieldwork, asserted that *mut'a* was not legalized prostitution. He claimed, "this to be an erroneous understanding, typical of what foreigners think about *mut'a*."[158] For Ayatollah Sayyid Reza Borghei Mudaris specifically, *sigheh* was available to financially strapped persons—for instance, a widow who "answers her needs because if she doesn't, she will have psychological problems."[159] In other cases, men who could not afford a permanent marriage should consider *sigheh*, as well as a "married man with domestic problems who needs 'a kind of medicine."[160] Likewise, Haeri contends that calling *mut'a* another variation of prostitution is a mistake, commenting, "The problem is more complex than the apparent similarities might suggest."[161] Yet by denying the connection between the two, one ignores significant data on changing social behaviors and the diverse demographic groups that partake in temporary marital arrangements. Further, there is recent evidence that officials, to some extent, are aware of the problems associated with prostitution and have responded, accordingly. As case in point (and thus, as a direct critique to Haeri's foregoing statement) is the proposed establishment of chastity houses. Why would the Ministry of the Interior incorporate *sigheh* into this program if officials had not considered using temporary marriage in some significant way, a method by which paid sex could be legitimized and thereupon lead to the regulation of the sex industry in part? Evidently, the distance is great between government officials' public opinions of *sigheh* versus popular, civil society, and academic discussions on how it is practiced and *by whom*.

Sigheh in the Face of Social Realities

There are many important debates circulating in scholarly and public discourses about how *sigheh* is seamlessly interwoven into discussions on women's sexuality, prostitution, economic stability, and extramarital affairs. "This form of marriage," writes Haeri, "lend themselves to a wide range of manipulations, negotiations, and interpretations of the institution on both symbolic and practical levels."[162] The academic literature on *sigheh* points to a general consensus: it is not a marriage worthy of celebration. In a permanent marriage, sexuality "is celebrated by Shi'a *ulama* as being positive, self-affirming, and cognizant of human needs."[163] *Sigheh* is generally frowned upon by most social circles. Mir-Hosseini describes it as a "socially defective marriage."[164] In an interview with the American magazine *Mother Jones*, Mir-Hosseini reiterated this point, explaining that "women who enter this kind of marriage never talk about it."[165] The stigma is even more pronounced when the dynamic of the temporary contract is sexual in nature. Women are more likely to hide or deny their participation in this arrangement.[166] Paidar explains, "Those who practiced it tended to keep their activities secret and this also applied to the clerics who fervently defended its philosophy."[167] Haeri adds, "*Sigheh* is a pejorative term that has been colloquially applied to a woman who is temporarily married, but the term is not applied to a man."[168] In fact, women who do become *sigheh* do not usually celebrate this kind of union.[169]

However, Shahla Sherkat, a prominent women's activist and former editor and publisher of *Zanan* magazine, expressed a favorable opinion of it.[170] For her, *sigheh* had a potentially transformative effect on societal understandings toward women's sexuality. Sherkat argued that *sigheh* offered a particularly emancipatory direction for perceptions on a woman's virginity and sexual rights. In a *New York Times* interview, she enumerated its benefits, taking unique stances on *sigheh*'s advantages in curbing youth political protest, among other things: "First, relations between young men and women will become a little bit freer. Second, they can satisfy their sexual needs. Third, sex will become depoliticized. Fourth, they will use up some of the energy they are putting into street demonstrations. Finally, our society's obsession with virginity will disappear."[171] Several research studies conducted in Iran suggest that these benefits have yet to materialize in a meaningful way.[172] According to the 2009 research findings published in the monthly journal *Gozaresh*, from a group of Iranian social scientists affiliated with the Sociological Society for Women's Studies, the primary reason that women agreed to enter a temporary marriage was financial compensation. Moreover, there were crucial differences in how this compensation was realized, depending on the demographic group. As stated in the *Gozaresh* article, "Women who are *sigheh* usually have a history of societal hardships or are divorced or they have husbands who have problems with addiction, betrayal, and family violence; or, they do not accept responsibility."[173] Additionally, there were emotional and financial reasons that drew women into temporary marriages—the primary reason being financial, since they received little help from Iran's welfare organizations to mitigate their economic duress.[174] They found that *sigheh* partners were typically poorly educated.[175] Likewise, they had a poor general knowledge of sexual health; diseases such as AIDS and hepatitis were unknown to them.[176] This ignorance could be attributed to the limited, sexual health education programs in Iran's school curriculum.[177]

In another study, researchers found that people were entering temporary marriage because it was more financially feasible. Permanent marriage was postponed simply because it was too expensive to get married. Dr. Ali Asghar Kayhania, a psychologist and family counselor, said that the rise in *sigheh* unions happened because men were decreasingly unable to pay the *mehriyeh* (dowry), which they would have had to provide in a permanent marriage. It would have been out of their financial reach.[178] Moreover, fewer men were becoming homeowners, or their families could not afford to purchase properties for them. Thus, the idea of a newly (permanently) married couple resettling in a new place was increasingly unrealistic. As a secondary solution, young women agreed to temporary marriages because they did not want to incur additional hardships for their partners, who would otherwise have been responsible for compensating *mehriyeh* in the case of divorce.[179] (Rising gold prices also affected a man's decision to enter a permanent or temporary marriage, especially if the *mehriyeh* amount agreed to by the bride's parents would have been a financial impossibility for the groom.)[180]

Sociologist Parvaneh Hooshmand suggested that financial sustainability was a secondary reason underlining *sigheh* partnership. Her research found that the chief motivating force behind entering a *sigheh* is material desire.[181] Interviewing fifty urban middle- and upper-class women on the practice of temporary marriage, her research suggests that temporary marriage was being used as sexual currency. In brief, sex was offered in exchange for housing, a meal, or even easy cash.[182] Hooshmand claimed that in a *sigheh* arrangement, sexual intercourse meant material gifts were expected—or that women must have used sex as a method to convince their temporary "husbands" to give them something they want.[183] She argued that this expectation of an exchange did not appear in long-term or permanent marriages, wherein sex was not included in the quid pro quo.

A 2006 report published by the government's Statistical Center of Iran, an organization responsible for census-taking and preparing statistics of state policies and programs, studied men who participated in *sigheh* relationships. According to its findings published in *Ebtekar News*, married men were more inclined to have *sigheh* partnerships than those who were single.[184] Among Iran's general population, the number of men and women between the ages of twenty and sixty constituted thirty-seven million people. Within this population, two million had *sigheh* relationships between the ages of twenty and fifty. Of the male respondents, more than two-thirds who pursued temporary marriage were married men, whereas less than one-third of the male correspondents were single.[185]

The preceding research suggests much diversity in practice and public opinion about *sigheh*. It also points to the little mentioned topics of financial compensation and security. Fatemeh Sadeghi, a political scientist and former professor at Islamic Azad University, maintains,

> in our [Iranian] society many women agree to become *sighehs* mostly because of distress due to economic pressures and the inability to provide their own means of subsistence. When a woman becomes a man's *sigheh* under such circumstances, she is in essence engaging in a fundamentally unequal exchange. It is her distress over providing her means of subsistence that forces her to agree to become a *sigheh*. On the other hand, given the disagreeable character of *sigheh* in our culture, many of these women are compelled to keep the relationship a secret from neighbors and family members. It is even worse when an unwanted child results from the relationship.[186]

Here, Sadeghi is making a larger point on the gender and power dynamics interwoven into *sigheh* arrangements: women in particular enter temporary marriages to secure their own welfare and for financial protection. It is not simply unbridled human sexual desires that motivate people to enter into temporary unions, as certain officials have argued. Hence Sadeghi's analysis calls into question official promotion of temporary marriage for the main purpose of curbing and/or satiating the lustful inclinations of Iranian youth, among others.

Exploding Categories of the Temporary Wife

To state that prostitution is illegal in the Islamic Republic is to equivocate about its actual presence. The authorities have seemingly endorsed policies that now make it too easy to link prostitution with something being publicized as a legitimate "Islamic" practice. This is not to say that clerical authorities fully encouraged sleeping with "fallen women"—nay, quite the opposite. Some clerics were proponents of temporary marriage for the purposes of maintaining social order. Therefore paid, sexual liaisons conducted within the framework of Islamic legal tradition were fine, even if also politically expedient. Yet a result of this semantic tango was that in times of economic duress, encouraging temporary marriage was often buddied up with paid, temporary sexual arrangements—which, in many parts of the world is generally understood as a form of prostitution. Indeed, regulating and legitimizing prostitution is a delicate issue of social, economic, and political significance. At the height of the Iranian Revolution, many considered it a societal blight. Its practice and regulation were blamed on the liberal, Westernized policies of the Pahlavi regime, and it was often presented as an example of the overall moral decline of the Iranian people during this reign. Ayatollah Taleghani regarded prostitution as a social necessity, akin to the fundamental presence of a toilet in a house.

In the postrevolutionary era, prostitution is both conceptually and physically emancipated from saturnine dwellings of red-light infamy. These days, it bears the faces of the middle class, credited in part to an Islamic marital tradition being used like a permission-slip to conduct extramarital affairs. For many, *sigheh* is perceived as a legitimized form of prostitution irrespective of what the clergy insists, that Islamic legal tradition legitimized these temporary unions for society's use. For others, it is regarded as a requisite means to obtain economic mobility and financial security. Beyond its many uses and interpretations, its impact on prostitution cannot be denied. After 1979, the physical site of prostitution entered a conceptual leviathan subject to politically convenient motives. Money being exchanged for sexual services was reconfigured as just a procedural activity performed during a legal, marriage contract. Increasingly more clerical and official commentaries on human sexuality and marriage popped up, identifying the theoretical and legal sources upon which to support *sigheh* for young adults, veterans, and men, in general. By 2002, there were reports of clandestine, government proposals for chastity houses. The custom and institution of *sigheh* entered the uncharted terrain of social reality, where diverse sexual practices and human relationships softened government red lines designating appropriate and morally guided conduct in an Islamic society. An immediate consequence of this strategy of encouraging and accommodating *sigheh*—perhaps unintended—was that the concept of (female) prostitute expanded. The concept of prostitute roped in a wider range of women from varied socioeconomic backgrounds—meaning, it is no longer clear *who* and *what* constitutes and qualifies as a sex worker and as sex work. In lieu of a prostitute located within a red-light district, the contemporary version of "prostitute" has penetrated traditional, domestic spaces, taking on the title of "wife"—albeit temporarily.

Chapter 4

NAKED MODESTY AND THE REFORMATION OF STATUES

President Rafsanjani[1] did not mince his words: "A cleric could not walk through the university with those scenes on the grass, in classes, in streets. We could not go to government offices. If you stood in front of a desk, you would commit a sin, because there was a nude statue [an unveiled woman] behind the desk."[2] When a cleric stood before an unveiled woman, the encounter was one of sexual impropriety; the opportunity for decadence abounded. Assumedly the presence of an unveiled woman evoked unnecessary temptation, especially for a believer seeking to maintain his piety and moral constitution. Although he did not specify the impending sin, it must nevertheless be avoided. Yet to evade such an encounter, there were only two possible solutions: either the believer should not enter official spaces where he would come across women who were "naked" or women should not be permitted to present themselves as "nude statues" in the workplace.

The legal enforcement of compulsory *hejab* showed that the latter option was, in fact, the only possible remedy. Reflecting on the Islamicization programs enacted once Ayatollah Khomeini rose to power, Najmabadi surmises, "The notion was now emerging of the importance of possessing some singular morality that would help purify a society perceived to be hopelessly corrupt, as opposed to backward."[3] Decrying unveiled women who entered public space as being naked was a tactic often used by many of Khomeini's hard-line followers to discredit and shame those who opposed observing Islamic *hejab*: women who refused to wear the *hejab*, "[flaunting] their naked bodies in the streets," and behaving in a manner perceived to be destructive to Islamic values.[4] *Kayhan* editorials denounced them as "corrupt, seditious, dangerous and destructive of public honour and chastity."[5] During a March 1979 speaking event, Khomeini claimed that Islamic agencies would be committing sin if they allowed women to enter office spaces while being *lokht* (naked).[6] Though the general definition of *lokht* means "naked," "bare," or "nude,"[7] the mentioned usages of the term are references to being in public and not wearing an Islamic head-cover.

If we momentarily set aside Rafsanjani's anecdote, and instead focus on the metaphor he invoked (of an unveiled woman as a "nude statue"), then we are able to extrapolate other possible scenarios whereby the analogy similarly resonates, inviting related questions on morality, space, and shame. Do statues of women, situated in city squares, evoke the same level of disapproval and shame in the viewer as Rafsanjani presumed the presence of an unveiled woman would? Would the viewer likewise feel sinful as if s/he acted improperly? If such were the case, what would be the institutional approaches to modifying public space and the objects that inhabited those sites in order to ensure that men and women would not end in gazing upon these objects—in effect, to shield them from temptation and immoral thoughts?

Much of the literature on the status of women in postrevolutionary Iran has focused on the issue of compulsory *hejab*, analyzing the policy's impact on women's freedoms and daily lives. Generally, these studies enumerate and contextualize the ways in which sex segregation and veil ordinances affected women's mobility, dress, and civil and political rights. Ever since Ayatollah Khomeini declared that Iran would be governed by laws adhering to Islamic criteria, compulsory *hejab* has been a contentious sociopolitical issue. Ashraf Zahedi has argued that this specific policy was "part of the regime's agenda to institutionalize the female identity espoused by the Authenticity Movement which promoted the wearing of hijab as 'moral cleansing.' Concealing female hair became the clerics' immediate 'political project.'"[8] Ziba Mir-Hosseini has said, "paradoxically, the enforcement of *hejab* became a catalyst here: by making public space morally correct in the eyes of traditionalist families, it legitimized public presence."[9] A woman's entrance into heterosocial public space necessitated her observance of a new verbal and bodily language, whereby disciplinary tactics such as sex segregation and compulsory *hejab* certified her legal and legitimate presence in this space. Val Moghadam argues, "But the legal imposition of *hejab* was not about protecting women, and it was certainly not part of any struggle against male sexism: it was about negating female sexuality and therefore protecting men. The idea that women had 'lost honor' during the Pahlavi era was a widespread one."[10] Though the extensive debate on compulsory *hejab* should not be limited to the reflections of these scholars, they do speak to an overarching trend in the academic literature on women in postrevolutionary Iran that emphasizes *hejab* ordinances and the material and legal ripple effects they had for Iranian women. An extension of this debate, seldom addressed, is the regulation of sexuality through the disciplinary modification of objects erected in heterosocial public space—for instance, the veiling of a "nude" female statue in a public square. In what ways have the postrevolutionary state's conceptualizations of women's bodies, female sexuality, and public morality led to a restructuring of public space and more so, how those sites are remembered?

There is an extensive history of the destruction of landmarks by powerful elites competing over a nation's social and political capital. This is especially true for monuments captured by the collective memory of a people, for whom a historic victory or an esteemed leader has been commemorated by a marble monument and placed in the center of major squares and thoroughfares. By commemorating societal achievements and ideals, these statues are designed to reflect national heritage and pride—of artistic value and wartime significance. Yet timing bears heavy consequences on the visual object of that square: as political regimes pull one hero down from the pedestal and raise another up, the threat of extinction looms large. The hero of one regime swiftly becomes the antagonist of another;

new symbols manifest, new identities are crafted, and legacies are rewritten in an effort to erase all vestiges of the fallen regime.[11]

In the midst of regime change from dynastic to clerical leadership, many Pahlavi-era landmarks and monuments were destroyed. Sculptures of Persian historical and cultural icons were vandalized—a notable instance was the beheading of the sculpture of famed, Iranian classical poet, Ferdowsi, located in central Tehran's Ferdowsi Square.[12] Although statues of women in particular were not subject to the same manner of destruction in the early years after the revolution, they were dealt with in accordance to the state's social policies enforcing an "Islamic code of public appearance."[13] For sculptures of women, this was often translated into material reform by tempering any "obscene" exhibitions of the body[14] and refashioning them as modest, thus making them suitable for public viewing. Designating which presentations of statues fell under this category has varied, from their purported nakedness for being displayed without *hejab* to the way their shape hints at the existence of a female bosom. From the perspective of certain clerics underscored throughout this chapter, public space was considered an arena suitable only for displaying objects consistent with Iran's "societal standards" and exemplifying Islamic values. Hence any object that contradicted these values should not be exhibited. In the past decade, the same criticism has been directed at all lifelike representations of women, such as mannequins in storefronts, which have been accused of advertising inappropriate (and unlawful) relationships between men and women.

In an attempt to diversify scholarly discussion on the regulation of sexuality in contemporary Iran, I do not limit myself to the discussion of the social control of compulsory *hejab*. Instead, I focus on other cultural, religious, legal, and spatial dimensions within this regulatory framework that determined how and to what extent women's bodies and their representations were disciplined. In this chapter, I review the alteration of specific statues, monuments, and mannequins to point out the strategic application of "Islamic criteria" in the face of robust social change. In what follows, I discuss the controversies surrounding mannequins and three sculptures—*Mard-e Neylabakzan* (The Flute Player), *Mojassameh-ye Fereshteh-ye Azadi* (*Angel of Freedom*), and *Zan va Mard-e Keshavarz* (Woman and Man Farmers). These three public artworks were once prominently displayed in Tehran's public squares and in front of ministry and municipal buildings. Their subsequent renovation in the postrevolutionary period illustrates how public works of art—especially those representing women—went from being recognized as part of a national, cultural heritage to suddenly being identified as suspicious, immodest, and obscene objects. The historical narrative behind this process of modification in the name of promoting "Islamic values" of public morality, chastity, and modesty aids in contextualizing how and in what ways public space underwent significant transformations through the regulation of sexuality. Studying these pieces helps identify the shifting understandings toward female sexuality alongside the legal, authoritative, and sculptural methods used to recodify monuments into gender-neutral objects suitable for a morally guided, Muslim public sphere.

From here on, I elaborate the government's efforts to restructure the physical and social dynamics of public space so that the people and objects interacting and situated, respectively, in that space conform to an "Islamic moral imperative." Though reportedly posing as threats to the chaste communal space being projected by the Islamist government, after the revolution, those artworks transferred to unknown locations and spared from destruction underwent strategic renovations specific to the regime's principles. A handful of their narratives are addressed here, tracking their modification in the name of "Islamic modesty."

Gender Paradigms of Space and Social Organization in Tehran

How is public space[15] mediated in contemporary Iran's state and religious discourses?[16] Islamic laws on modesty are translated through not just the modification and regulation of social interactions taking place in public but also the prevention of any tendencies that might initiate immoral relations from happening in the first place. In theory, citizens entering public space would neither gaze upon immodest statues nor interact inappropriately with the opposite sex because temptation would not manifest in their path. This compunction for preserving a modesty of heterosexual interactions forms much of the foundational rubrics of Iran's social policy, born out of an Islamic conceptual paradigm of gender relationships known as *mahram* and *namahram*.[17] Although this framework is an imperative in Shi'a discourse, this does not mean that this provision is necessarily and fully observed, accepted, and/or practiced by Iranian men and women. However, a brief illustration of a dominant social organization of space is worth our attention.

The Islamic legal terminology of *mahram* and *namahram* designates marriageability between men and women. Kinship relationships determine the extent and manner of social interaction between opposite sexes.[18] *Mahram* denotes a legal "relationship by blood, marriage, or sexual union."[19] Parents, for instance, are *mahram* to their children, as are brothers and sisters to one another.[20] A *namahram* relation is denoted as "any person of the opposite sex whose kinship does not represent an impediment for marriage."[21] Men and women, who are both unrelated to each other, can become *mahram* to each other through marriage. Haeri explains, "The *mahram/namahram* paradigm, or rules of segregation and association of the sexes, is one of the most fundamental and pervasive rules of social organization, social relations, and social control in Iran."[22] The clerical leadership's and state agencies' implementation of this gendered paradigm has been translated into the veiling of women before men who are *namahram* to them.

Yet the construct of *mahram* and *namahram* does not fully make intelligible how apparatuses of the state reconfigured public space to be a so-called Islamic arena by invoking the ideal of modesty. This recoding of public space—its meaning, purpose, and parameters—was the outcome of a unique process, involving the demarcation of redlines that integrated gender, ethical, religious, financial, and political factors. In the IRI, urban spaces in particular intermix forces of commerce, traffic congestion, lifestyle differences, and at least on the surface, religious fervor. It is also an arena in which codes of conduct and social norms are observed and disobeyed under the watchful eyes of a clerical leadership and its extensive apparatus of guidance patrols and regime supporters. Iranian citizens are expected to interact in a manner that is mindful of sex segregation policies (*siyasat-e tafkik-e jensiyati*)—including but certainly not limited to regulations on public modesty and *hejab*.[23] In this purview of urban space, sexuality that potentially incites arousal is sinful and might possibly have legal ramifications. Which is why for many believers, to guard one's gaze is a necessary tactic in fending off unlawful lust and *tahrik* (arousal) between the sexes.[24] As Hamid Dabashi has written, there is a "serenity of a distanced gaze"[25]—of an image, object, or person that does not provoke temptation, but just *is*. In public space, the heterosexual gaze must keep its distance; it should not submit to temptation and desire. The eyes of a believer must be directed away from the object of desire (to "guard their gaze")—even if this viewing should fall upon the statue of a woman in a public square. For even gazing upon this statue would be an act of temptation, for it would lead one astray by kindling prurient thoughts and illicit actions.[26] Hence to control (and subdue) the gaze, the assumption is that one must exterminate the potential source of moral corruption—and, as illustrated by the next example, the statue of a heroic woman erected in a famed city square.

Effacing the Feminine of Baharestan Square

Forest and Johnson have argued, "Official memorials, monuments, and museums play a unique role in the creation of national identity because they reflect how political elites choose to represent the nation publicly. By erecting memorials in public space, states and interest groups attempt to define the historical figures that become national heroes and establish the historical incidents that become the formative events of a nation's identity."[27] How did a postrevolutionary government come to monopolize and transform public opinion, and by extension the collective memory about certain monuments in public squares that were once heralded during the Pahlavi era? For answers, consider first the postered landscape of Tehran, a metropolis checkered with billboards so central to communicating state narratives about war, family, and faith—all of which are wrapped into the oft-repeated phrase "the success of the Islamic Revolution." Across the capital, advertisements and panels of revolutionary slogans are featured on the walls of highway overpasses and apartment buildings, declaring the state's ongoing commitment to Ayatollah Khomeini's revolutionary ideology.[28] As a visual topography and pictorial archive, they narrate a historic story of triumph and a reminder of continued efforts to preserve his legacy in the face of pro-West, secular incursions.[29] Notably, to ensure this new direction and legacy for the Iranian-Muslim nation, monuments of both symbolic and secular heroines were removed from public space. In their stead were monuments erected that featured Islamic philosophers, war martyrs, and veiled mothers—icons likely more in line with state attempts to present Iran as an

Islamic nation.[30] This is perhaps most evident in the postrevolutionary narrative of reform for Tehran's storied Baharestan Square.

Newspaper headings reported June 24, 2009, as a bloody day of protest in Baharestan Square.[31] Less than two weeks after the presidential reelection of Mahmoud Ahmadinejad, protests continued to swirl in the streets; city squares became crucial meeting points for both dissenting citizens and security forces, whose fist-to-fist battles were photographed and videotaped, and later broadcast on major international news programs and posted and commented on across the internet. Two days earlier, a young woman by the name of Neda Aqha Soltan was shot in the head and died instantly. Public anger skyrocketed, as video images of her death went viral. Government threats of reprisal were not initially successful in deterring Iranians from joining opposition rallies in public squares[32] (Figure 4.1, Figure 4.2).

Baharestan Square was one of several popular gathering spaces where protesters have held opposition rallies and faced heavy consequences in the process.[33] For more than a century, demonstrations have taken place in front of parliament's old headquarters, which directly face the square.[34] The square has an extensive political history in the modern formation of the Iranian nation-state—spanning from the early twentieth century's Iranian Constitutional Revolution to the present Islamic Republic. It was once the site of one of Tehran's oldest structures, the palace of Mirza Hossein Khan Sepahsalar, Iran's Prime Minister from 1871 to 1873. In recent years the authorities have used the square to stage military and artillery shows. In September 2008, they hosted an exhibition of its "sacred defense," showcasing a yellow-colored missile in the center of the square, flanked by armored vehicles and positioned underneath a giant poster of Ayatollah Khamenei, Iran's Supreme Leader and *Vali-e Faqih* (Supreme Jurist).[35]

Figure 4.1 Baharestan Square, June 2011.

Figure 4.2 Baharestan Square, December 2010.

Since the square's construction, several statues of politicians and cultural icons have been located in its center. At present, a statue of Ayatollah Seyyed Hassan Modarres, a supporter of the Constitutional Revolution and a former mentor of Ayatollah Khomeini, is the square's central attraction.[36] The bust of this early twentieth-century cleric is a relatively recent addition; three decades prior, a winged statue, known as *Mojassameh-ye Fereshteh-ye Azadi* (Angel of Freedom), was erected in that very site.[37] The statue was a gift to parliament from Sardar As'ad Bakhtiari (1856–1917), a powerful democratic reformer and tribal leader during the Constitutional Revolution, and later installed in front of the parliamentary buildings in 1937 (1316).[38] While reviewing images from women's journal *Zan-e Rouz*, an important archive highlighted in the first chapter, I stumbled upon a doctored photograph of Baharestan Square, printed three years after the revolution[39] (see Figure 4.3). The photograph and accompanying article were published in the February 1982 edition of *Zan-e Rouz*, in the section "*Begoo! Begoo!*" (Say! Say!), which was dedicated to reader commentary about local domestic and political affairs. In this section, readers voiced their complaints and offered suggestions to officials from the Ministry of Labor and other state organizations. (For instance, in this issue, a reader criticized the incompetent method of ticket collection on city buses.) It was challenging to locate other evidence that provided background details about its very existence.[40] The statue itself depicted a defiant pose of a female figure charging forward against the wind, wrapped in swarms of fabric billowing below her feet. As shown in Figure 4.3, an "x" mark was drawn directly on the statue's bust apparently to prevent the reader from clearly viewing it. (For emphasis, I deliberately circled the "x" marking in figure 4.3.) This censorship reflected a new editorial direction for *Zan-e Rouz*, which no longer published images that suggested and depicted any kind of immodesty. Although

Figure 4.3 *Angel of Freedom* Statue, Baharestan Square, 1982.

not explicitly stated, it was likely that *Zan-e Rouz*'s editors found the exposure of women's bodies—specifically their breasts—inappropriate for its readership, even if the majority were in fact women. The "x" marking was one example of this new policy that did not publish images of women's bodies deemed unsuitable for public viewing; initially, this meant that they expected images of women to present them as modest and not necessarily as veiled. As discussed in the first chapter of this book, in 1980, *Zan-e Rouz* relaunched itself as an Islamic lifestyle magazine, publishing articles and images of women whom they characterized as natural homemakers, self-sacrificing mothers and sisters of the revolution, and pious Muslims observing Islamic *hejab*.

Figure 4.3 is striking not only for being censored but also for the title and reader commentary accompanying it. Below the photograph reads the headline *Mojassameh-ye Azadi-ye Shahanshahi dar Meydan-e Baharestan* (Imperial Statue of Freedom in Baharestan Square). It is not certain if this particular title reflected an editorial decision to change the statue's name, for its previous moniker as *Angel of Freedom* was no more. Presumably this alteration was intended for two reasons: one, to illustrate a major shift in permissible representations of women that could be published in print media after the revolution, and two, to present a pejorative image to readers of the statue's true origins, which has been associated with the heavily criticized imperial dynasty of the Pahlavis. In any case, located underneath the photograph is a short commentary from a concerned *Zan-e Rouz* patron, based in Tehran:

> Thank you to those who are responsible for the page, "*Begoo Begoo*," it has been some time that I've wanted to write a letter and request a response from municipal officials. The issue is that every time I pass by Baharestan Square, my eyes fall upon the scenery of the square and the statue of the winged-woman, whose shape and appearance are against public modesty. I don't understand how such a statue exists on one side, in front of the buildings of education, whose great mission is to educate and to foster humanity. On the other side is located the Imam Khomeini Relief Foundation, as well as the Central Committee. I don't know what kind of concept and message this is sending, based on our Islamic, revolutionary rituals and doctrine. This statue reminds us of the Pahlavi's free woman.[41]

After complaining about why the statue had not yet been removed, the reader voiced their expectation: "I hope that these words of caution can be useful for the *sazandegi* (reconstruction) of the slogans and dress[42] of the Islamic society." The reader closed by writing, "Hopes for the success for all of those who are committed to Islam." Evidently, this person found the presence of an unveiled, curvaceous statue to be intolerable and thus alerted government officials using the magazine's platform. More so, as the reader suggested, the *Angel of Freedom* was a barefaced reminder of the backward values of the Pahlavi regime, after it infringed new standards of modesty and public morality. Evidently, the crystallization of Iran as a legitimately Islamic society could not be realized unless such objects no longer challenged its revolutionary ideals and were thus removed.

Making Statues Modest: Nakedness in State and Religious Discourses

Responding to a reader complaint about a nude statue seemed miniscule compared to overhauling all social interactions and public spaces, among other things. The latter required a massive mobilization of forces and state apparatuses countrywide. How did the postrevolutionary authorities mandate a "culture of modesty," a phrase dealt with later in this chapter, to ensure it was reflected in public works of art? For statues representing women in particular, did such methods require the mere addition of a veil? The answers are nestled in the history of the construction and implementation of laws and prohibitions governing social interactions between the sexes and how they came to be understood and soon internalized in the first decade after the revolution. In the early summer of 1979, the clergy-dominated Islamic Republican Party (*Hezb-e Jomhouri-ye Eslami* or IRP) had just formed to assist in mobilizing political support for Ayatollah Khomeini and help popularize his doctrine and teachings.[43] Simultaneously, the leadership of a Supreme

Council of the Cultural Revolution (discussed further in this chapter), staffed by hard-line proponents of Khomeini, set forth new societal redlines prohibiting a wide range of political and social activities.[44] These provisions gave expression to ideal standards of morality maintained in a Shi'a religious society. For Iran's ruling clerical authority, citizens were automatically identified by their religious beliefs and practices—their primary identity being Muslim subjects. They were encouraged to abide by good moral values based on faith, family, revolution, and the preservation of public morality.[45] As new restrictions of sex segregation were put in place, by 1982, the authorities announced that Iranian women should observe compulsory *hejab* in public, or face fines and forms of punishment. Alongside these policies were public campaigns about how to lead a moral life— for instance, recall the articles on behavior and modest dress in post-1979 issues of *Zan-e Rouz*. Subsequently sculptures and other works of art, especially those pieces that depicted the human body in two-dimensional form, fell within the purview of these initiatives. Deriding uncovered body parts (such as limbs, buttocks, and hair) was all the rage, with terms "pornographic" and "immoral" hurled in their direction. To display these objects would mean that once again they would be led astray from the morally righteous path to an Islamic society.

Islamic jurisprudence (*fiqh*) scholars have relied on certain rules of modesty to reach a consensus that the exposure of one's private parts is *haram* (religiously forbidden). Disagreement exists over the identifiable areas of the body that are considered *awrat* areas, meaning those body parts that should not be left uncovered during *namaz* (prayer), or in the company of *mahram* and *namahram* men and women.[46] For some *fiqh* scholars, this means the vagina, penis, and buttocks are regarded as private; for others, women's entire bodies are *awrat*.[47] Shi'a understanding of *awrat* is based on the religious commentaries of the sixth Imam, Ja'far al-Sadiq, which consider *awrat* to include women's bodies, save their faces and hands.[48] This definition of *awrat* is mutable, depending upon the activity being performed and in front of whom. For example, Ayatollah Khomeini—who was a *marja'e taqlid* (Shi'a source of emulation or Grand Ayatollah)[49]—specified that during prayer, the *awrat* of a woman became her entire body, including her head and hair, except for her face, hands, and feet.[50] Given this, a Muslim woman is expected to cover her body completely with a full-length, loose-fitting garment. In the Iranian context, this clothing has usually been understood to be a *chador*. In other cases, determining *awrat* depends on the company present. In *Tahrir al-Vasileh*, Khomeini asserted that it was *haram* to be naked when intending to engage in pleasure and incest, with the exception of undressing or being naked before one's spouse.[51] (The Qur'an encourages married couples to enjoy looking upon their partners' bodies. By contrast, in private interactions between unmarried, *namahram* and *mahram* men and women, being naked is a sin. Women in particular are expected to be covered from navel to the knee.)

Grand Ayatollahs (*maraji'e taqlid*) have issued fatwas guiding the circumstances when parts of the human body should be exposed and when they would be harmful for others to see; opinions are also provided on appropriate clothing for believers to wear, depending on the occasion.[52] The late Grand Ayatollah Mohammad

Taqi Bahjat[53] issued a fatwa that "men must cover their private parts from other men," although covering the rest of their body was not *vajeb* (necessary). Grand Ayatollah Naser Makarem Shirazi (who, in 2006, issued a fatwa against women entering football stadiums in direct challenge to President Ahmadinejad's calls to allow them access) stated that some workout clothing had negative consequences on *akhlaq* (morality and manners) and for this reason should be avoided.[54]

Conforming Art and Modesty: Hejab-Wearing Monuments after 1979

A matrix of clashing motivations underlined the vandalism and destruction of artworks, monuments, and other landmarks in the postrevolutionary period. The main reasons were politically and ideologically motivated, on pace with anti-Pahlavi demonstrations and the suspicious fires of cinema houses[55]—at the time, deemed dens of immoral activity—prior to pro-Khomeini revolutionaries securing control of a popular movement against the Pahlavi regime. They were based on one of the religious arguments pertaining to the prohibition of the production and veneration of idols and figurines, be they of living or nonliving things, of which statues and artworks were included.[56] The Prophet Muhammad banned the worship of deities, calling upon Muslims to abandon polytheistic traditions and accept the oneness of God. As narrated by *hadith* traditionalist scholar al-Bukhari, the presence of statues discourages angels from entering a Muslim home.[57] Shi'a *fiqh* scholars have argued that by creating sculptures, artists would mold them in their likeness and thus be inclined to worship something other than God—He, who is already perfect and inimitable.[58] According to Grand Ayatollah Makarem Shirazi, sculptures of human bodies and animals were problematic; however, paintings of them were allowed. In certain cases, the sculpting of human beings is permitted as long as these sculptures or statues are used specifically as materials for war propaganda, as dolls for children, as medical education tools, and as robots that are not used for entertainment purposes but for extending human life.[59]

In mounting demonstrations against Muhammad Reza Shah Pahlavi, artworks and landmarks in particular were targeted by anti-revolutionary slogans against the regime's opulence and its propagation of anti-Islamic, pro-Western values. Certain statues commemorating Pahlavi heroes and statesmen were subsequently vandalized and removed from their original sites for not only emblematizing a pre-Islamic heritage and legacy but also honoring political figures perceived to be corrupt and enemies of the revolution. In other instances, modern-art sculptures tied to Pahlavi values were subject to denunciation and vandalism during the revolutionary period. Solicitation and patronage of modern-art sculptures had reached a zenith during Muhammad Reza Shah's reign.[60] Armenian-Iranian artist and curator Marcos Grigorian organized Tehran's first biennial exhibition in 1958.[61] Iranian artists traveled back and forth between European capitals and Tehran, training in sculpture and painting ateliers.[62] "The highly active 1950s," writes art historian Maryam Ekhtiar, "were followed by the equally spirited 1960s and '70s. These decades saw the opening of Iran to the international art scene, as local artists participated in art fairs, founded galleries, and courted foreign collectors."[63] After successful exhibitions in Paris and Italy, many Iranian artists returned to Iran, having been commissioned by the Pahlavis to sculpt some of the country's cultural and political icons into marbled works of art.[64] Among this group of artists were the sculptors Parviz Tanavoli, Jalil Ziapour, Jazeh Tabatabai, and Bahman Mohassess.[65] Clerics and partisans of Khomeini claimed that many of their works projected allegiances to the former monarchy and were perceived as advertising anti-Islamic revolutionary messages.[66]

Well into the third decade of the Islamic Republic—many years after the artists had died or left Iran—a particularly interesting controversy emerged concerning the alleged obscenity and anti-Islamic orientation of artworks featuring naked torsos and exposed intimate areas and created in the 1970s. *Mard-e Neylabakzan* (The Flute Player), as shown in Figure 4.4, was damaged because it was regarded as obscene and contrary to Islamic values—the same accusations made of the Pahlavi dynasty before its demise. Standing at 4 meters tall, The Flute Player by the late sculptor and painter Bahman Mohassess depicted a, two-horned mythical creature playing a flute.[67] Originally sculpted in Rome in 1975 (1353) and commissioned by Empress Farah Pahlavi, the artwork was gifted to Tehran's City Theatre and remained at the theater's entrance until its removal after the revolution.[68] Although the reason for its removal was never officially announced, the figure's exposed buttocks and genital area were likely the cause; left uncovered, the sculpture was criticized for promoting nudity and immodesty. Museum officials initially stored the piece in the stage area of the theater (it was later transported to a storage facility in Tehran's Museum of Contemporary Art), while deliberating a more suitable exhibition space for the sculpture. Should

Figure 4.4 Front angle of *Mard-e Neylabakzan*.

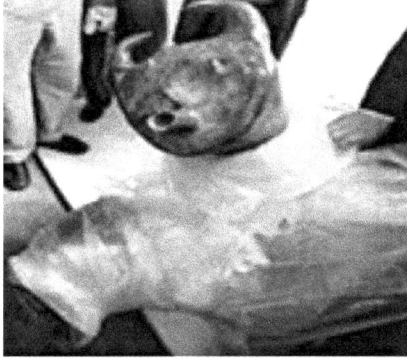

Figure 4.5 2010 leaked photograph of damage to statue *Mard-e Neylabakzan*.

officials keep the statue in front of the city theater in its present state? Or should they sculpturally remedy the figure? One proposal suggested placing *tonikeh* (underpants) to cover the figure's posterior; however, its poor design did not solve the problem of the exposed backside. *The Flute Player* remained in storage until a photograph of the statue leaked online showing that it had been defaced: the flute player's two hands were missing, and the nose-flute extension was no longer attached (see Figure 4.5). When this happened, museum officials provided contradictory statements about the sculpture's status. Initially they denied reports of any damage, insisting it was safely packed away in storage.[69] However as public speculation grew, museum director Dr. Habibollah Sadighi, in a 2008 interview with *Iran* newspaper, stated that among the museum's collection, several pieces of art, including The Flute Player, were scheduled for repair. The museum even offered a public invitation to sculptor Mohassess to return to Tehran to conduct its restoration.[70] (Mohassess had immigrated to Italy in 1969.) Sadighi neither disclosed the culprits behind the damage nor offered any motive for why it might have been intentionally destroyed. Rather, he suggested that the damage might have occurred during the renovation of the City Theatre.[71] Sadighi conceded, "In addition to being repaired, some part of [the statue] has a specific nakedness. Even though it is not erotic, it must still fit the standards of our society so that we can display it in the garden of Tehran's contemporary art museum." Insisting that the work would not be censored, he emphasized, "As the director of creative arts, I want to preserve the quality of the statue and also display it—what can I do except ask the artist himself to repair it and adjust it in accordance to societal standards."[72]

Sadighi's call to adjust modern-art sculptures to suit the Islamic Republic's "societal standards" reads like a cryptic warning directed at Iranian artists to comply, though short on details explaining how. What's more, his commentary about the vandalism was unclear. Was the vandalism of The Flute Player an anomaly, or representative of a larger campaign to punish artists popular before the revolution who had created pieces that fell outside the state's conventions of Islamic modesty?

Indeed, translating the ideal criteria necessary to achieve an Islamic modesty was no smooth process. For public works of art, especially featuring female characters, their prominent display in front of key government buildings first involved public condemnation followed by the chance of being granted a modesty makeover, so to speak. Once strategically covered, presumably as a method to subjugate the female sexuality that they projected, officials began to consider reinstalling them in public.

Man and Woman Farmers Meet Islamic Reform

This next example is that of *Zan va Mard-e Keshavarz* (Woman and Man Farmers), an oxidized bronze monument sculpted by Dariush Sane'izadeh and depicted in Figure 4.6.[73] Located at the far corner of the courtyard of the Museum of Contemporary Art in Tehran, it was located during the Pahlavi era near the front entrance of the Ministry of Agriculture on Keshavarz Boulevard. The statue depicts a farmer couple surrounded by a collection of symbols from industry and agriculture, ones typically found in communist iconography. Notice the sheaf of wheat and a cogwheel, as shown in Figure 4.6. Though *Zan va Mard-e Keshavarz* does not necessarily express the working-class struggle of a proletariat couple, it still evokes a feeling of collaborative work being enacted by male and female farmers who are engaged in the quiet act of watering a sprout.

After the revolution, its communist symbolism elicited criticism from a particular faction of Khomeini's supporters who wanted its immediate removal. Their reasons were attributed to four factors related to appearance, dress, symbolism, and an unknown relationship. Visually speaking, the artwork depicts an unveiled woman wearing a short-length skirt surrounded by communist symbols.[74] This recognizable homage to another ideological movement that had no connection to Islam aggravated the religious and ethical values being avowed by government officials. Moreover, the exact relationship between the couple was unclear; though we know them to be farmers, we are not certain if they represent a married or unmarried couple. This ambiguity was likely unacceptable to officials, who were unwavering in their attempts to present clear-cut and chaste relations between the sexes. While accusations that it promoted indecency and societal corruption increased, pressure mounted to have it removed from public space.[75] The challenges it explicitly posed against the ideals propagated by an Islamist regime were too much; it was eventually removed. The details behind the subsequent attempts to "Islamically" modify are presented next.

Alterations of *Zan va Mard-e Keshavarz* occurred in the midst of public ridicule. Officials were initially perplexed over how to restyle the sculpture into an appropriate statue for display; preserving the female figure's modesty and adhering to compulsory *hejab* were prime among their concerns. They made several attempts to reconfigure its structure by changing the attire of the male and female characters. Officials first covered the entire statue with burlap canvas. Yet its awkward placement on the sculpture, at the time located in front of the Ministry of

Figure 4.6 Two photographs of *Zan va Mard-e Keshavarz* sculpture in the courtyard of Tehran's Museum of Contemporary Art, October 2011 and December 2019.

Agriculture, roused visitor curiosity as museum patrons inquired about what lay underneath the cover.[76] The tarp was subsequently removed, and a smaller piece of burlap was placed on the female figure's head to resemble a *rousari* or headscarf. As for her *lokht* (naked) legs, officials placed specially designed trousers, also made of burlap, over them. People ended up pillorying it, joking that the woman farmer appeared to be covered in mud.[77]

Despite the efforts to change the sculpture's appearance, officials decided it had minimal value and thus had it removed from the ministry's offices and transferred to the front entrance of the Museum of Contemporary Art. In this new site, the sculpture again came under fire, as new complaints arose protesting the work's exhibition and its potential to corrupt the mind.[78] The piece was moved to the far corner of the museum's sculpture garden, where it remains and is still visible from Tehran's North Kargar Street. In the end, the modest transformation envisioned for this artwork was ridiculed, its modification process abandoned, and ultimately it was left alone, untouched.

What is significant about the modesty modification narrative of *Zan va Mard-e Keshavarz* are the naive assumptions, motives, and haphazard manner in which the alterations took place. Cleary underlying the act of placing an Islamic *hejab* onto this work was the belief that a garment (here, headscarf) would magically and instantly transform an allegedly obscene object into a representation of chaste and uncomplicated Muslim family values. The ease with which these artworks were expected to be modified echoed the manner in which Iranian women in particular were believed to be immediately receptive to their reform and regulation via the state's Islamization programs and measures. Such dependence on communicating these gendered expectations extended into other domains: from outlining appropriate marital relations to curbing sexuality; from micromanaging appearances to conduct; and from redefining and repurposing objects in public space to name a few pivotal examples—all for the aim of distinguishing Iran's present from its deviant past.

To reach some understanding of the theoretical cultivation and reinforcement of what came to be understood as a new form of "societal standards," I turn to the concepts of modesty and *hejab*, which were engaged as core Islamic values in the postrevolutionary period and fundamental to the social engineering of constructing a chaste Iranian society that ensued. As evidenced by their repetition and emphasis in official state documents, these concepts became identified as revolutionary, positive values enshrined in Iran's national constitution. Tracing their mediation over time via certain state regulatory bodies illustrates not just their malleability in meaning and impact but also their exploitation as disciplinary technologies to compel uniformity of conduct and appearance for both living and nonliving things. This is especially true during periods of the clerical establishment's resistance to reforming (liberalizing) Iran's political system.

Postrevolutionary State Policy of Hejab and Modesty: Designating Protocols and Societal Standards

Since the early 1980s, legal mechanisms, ad hoc revolutionary committees, and paramilitary forces answering to high-ranking members of the clerical authority have been used to implement and enforce a hegemonic vision of Iran as a religious society under the absolute authority of the *Velayat-e Faqih*.[79] Soon after Khomeini's return to Iran upon the collapse of the Pahlavi dynasty—a triumphant event referred to by many Iranians as the "success of the revolution"—neighborhood-watches formed in major cities, working both as security and as informal committees.[80] While aiming to keep their communities safe, given the breakdown of the Shah's police force, some of these committees (such as the *Komiteh-ye Enqelab-e Eslami*) also acted as the "eyes and ears" of Khomeini's supporters in government. As enforcers of the "fundamentalist moral and religious standards upon the residents in their neighborhood," *komiteh* were the precursors to the morality police known as *Gasht-e Ershad*,[81] a government police force—typically clad in dark green uniform—that polices activity deemed illegal or in contravention to the cultural and gender policies of the state.[82] In 1992, three branches of the government's security forces merged to form the police force, known as the *Nirou-ye Entezami-ye Jomhouri-ye Eslami-ye Iran* (Security Forces of the IRI or the police). (*Gasht-e Ershad* is a subbranch of this force.)

In the 1990s, the clerical leadership became even more sensitive to the liberalizing attitudes of Iranians who appeared to be loosening their adherence to Islamic *hejab*, thus fearing eminent societal corruption if *hejab* policy was not designed, implemented, and enforced. (This was a few years before reformist Mohammad Khatami was elected president and news reports proliferated of loosening restrictions on *hejab* policies in public.) In a May 1992 missive addressed to the head of parliament, *Majles* Chairman Mehdi Karroubi, the minister of Culture and Islamic Guidance Mohammad Khatami, and the ministers of the Budget, Finance, Industry, and the Interior established new guidelines of "cultural and societal goals" for preventing "the corruption of public morality."[83] The Ministry of Culture and Islamic Guidance (MCIG, hereafter) designated further restrictions on which clothing items were considered inappropriate to be worn in public places and at "centers of cultural production." New prohibitions banned the usage of see-through veils or veils showing exposed necks and mismatched or colorful shoes.[84] Restaurants, salons, photography studios, and agencies were also obliged to observe these guidelines.

Fostering a Culture of Hejab and Modesty

In December 2011, at a meeting for officials from the women's affairs bureau in Shiraz, the director of Fars province's office of the MCIG, Mahmoud Alishavandi, announced that a culture of "*hejab* and modesty" should be encouraged when creating works of art.[85] Emphasizing art's impact on impressionable audiences, Alishavandi suggested that the creation of art should include the themes of "*hejab* and modesty," which he argued were valuable in society.[86] These thematic elements, which are presently fundamental social policy, date back to the late 1990s. From 1982, there were already state policies on observing Islamic *hejab*; however, no specific laws or regulations determined how exactly this policy should be implemented and observed in varied social settings. It was only in 1998, a few months after the landslide victory of Khatami, that the Iranian government formulated a broader policy framework on *hejab* with which to cultivate a religious lifestyle and to protect revolutionary-Islamic values.

These edicts came at a time when reformists had won the presidency in 1997, and three years before they had gained a majority of seats in parliament.[87] The reformists' preliminary efforts at liberalizing social and political facets of the Iranian state culminated in the loosening of press restrictions and, at least momentarily, making overtures to improve relations between Iran and America and Europe.[88] Amid these sociopolitical changes, the tempo on the street was similarly animated. For many women in Tehran, Khatami's presidency was an opportunity to tamper with the state's dress code restrictions and establish nongovernmental advocacy organizations to push for changes in discriminatory parliamentary bills.[89] Secular women and religious women who participated in the reformist political movement—primarily from the middle and upper classes—began sporting a range of dress styles, such as shorter manteau and trousers, bright-colored scarves, and for some women, tighter clothing overall.

The rapid social changes and public resistance to social and legal restrictions conducted on the streets prompted the Supreme Council of the Cultural Revolution—hereafter, the Supreme Council—to reinforce its Islamist agenda to realign a disobedient public. The Supreme Council, whose membership is determined by the Supreme Leader and which, until 1989, was founded and led by Ayatollah Khomeini,[90] is the central government body responsible for guiding Islamization policies in educational, cultural, and industrial sectors. Though the Supreme Council is chaired by the country's president, its decisions can be overridden by Supreme Leader Ayatollah Khamenei. For more than two decades, it has sought to expand and strengthen the "influence of Islamic culture" in a Shi'a Muslim society.[91] The main objective of their policies is to fortify "human, religious and spiritual values and heartfelt beliefs,"[92] which has thus far meant concentrating on identifying and reinforcing Iranian-Muslim society's moral roots and behavior. This very program entailed the institutionalization of *farhang-e efaf* (culture of modesty)[93] throughout Iranian society by delineating cultural guidelines and implementing security measures that deter social corruption and preserve national morality.[94]

The pairing of the terms *hejab* and *efaf* first appeared in both official and legal documents of the Supreme Council in February 1998; however, it became a wider campaign slogan for cultural reform in the 2000s.[95] In 1998, the Supreme Council commenced a national campaign of *farhang-e efaf* via the text *Ousoul va Mabani va Ravesh-ha-ye Ejraee-ye Gostaresh-e Farhang-e Efaf*/The Principles, Foundations, and Executing Methods in Spreading a Culture of Modesty. The Supreme Council emphasized in this document the importance of one's education in Islamic principles and the fortification of family structures for the aim of constructing a "culture of modesty." Throughout the text, there are appeals to ideal representations of the Muslim family. The institution of the family itself is underscored as a natural, cohesive unit within which a culture of modesty should be consolidated "in thought and spirit."[96]

The campaign also helped define and structure social policy by integrating popular revolutionary-era terms expressed in Iran's national constitution. The main goal was to establish a "system of modesty that aimed to make the modesty of Iranian women the hallmark of the new Shiite nation."[97] In a rather extensive explanation of its goals, the Supreme Council affirmed,

> It is necessary to attract the attention of the general public, especially the youth, to the role of modesty and *hejab* in order to create an independent, cultural and national identity for the country and nation; [it is also necessary] to attract their attention to the positive, political effects of this independence [as well as to understand] the enemies' aims in advocating a culture of nudity, which is a method of cultural attack, by mentioning and describing the evidence and historical incidents [of this attack].[98]

By the mid-2000s, the official campaign to foster a culture of modesty had to be thoroughly reassessed. In July 2005, the Supreme Council designated forty-seven objectives in *Rahbord-ha-ye Gostaresh-e Farhang-e Efaf/Guidelines of Developing or Spreading a Culture of Modesty*, establishing guidelines for developing this culture of modesty in education, family, social awareness, and regulations of clothing. Objective 8 clarified this philosophy by pointing to the positive cultural, social, mental, and ethical consequences of *efaf* and *hejab* in "various arenas of life."[99] It also warned that when a society did not abide by these principles, such intransigence would be an "unsettling" force to the moral principles of family in society.[100]

Less than six months into Ahmadinejad's presidency, these guidelines were repeated as standard features in Iran's social policy. The Supreme Council enumerated a list of requirements for each government agency and designated how each was individually responsible in "fostering and preserving a chaste culture."[101] In the introduction of *Qanoun-e Rahkar-ha-ye Ejraee-ye Gostaresh-e Farhang-e Efaf va Hejab/The Law of Executing Solution for Developing a Culture of Hejab and Efaf*, *hejab* was introduced as one of the "most valuable cultural and societal manifestations of the Islamic-Iranian civilization."[102] Of primary importance was elevating the *hejab* in the general public, which the Supreme Council found needed refining when implemented in the domains of media, education, cinema, theater— among many others.[103] It left little room for misinterpretation or ambiguity by devising guidelines that were both broad and specific: from specifying the kind of attire worn in official and public settings to designating certain practices as good and "bad *hejab*" (mal-veiling),[104] which included wearing makeup in the workplace.[105]

Whereas both the 1998 and 2005 documents emphasized the importance of the *hejab* and wearing Islamic covering in its objectives, the titles of these documents mentioned only *efaf* or modesty. In fact, the term *hejab* is listed under the umbrella category of *efaf*. In 2006, this emphasis changed, when both terms were present in the title of the executing orders of the Supreme Council. This dual emphasis of *hejab* and modesty signaled that the Supreme Council had begun to regard both concepts as equal and interconnected in the enterprise of reforming Iranian society.

Additionally, as outlined in *The Law of Executing Solution for Developing a Culture of Hejab and Efaf*, the Supreme Council sought to "give authenticity to the culture of modesty through various appropriate cultural and artistic products."[106] In this text, the Supreme Council indicated the exact roles of government ministries and agencies for the purposes of institutionalizing a culture of "*hejab* and modesty."[107] In Objective 4, the Supreme Council stated that they should introduce proper cultural standards for advocating a culture of modesty. These standards should be in line with the "national, religious culture" and also should provide the "necessary contexts for the advocacy of ideal types of appropriate, Islamic covering through the efforts of institutions, which are responsible for making these patterns."[108] Moreover, under the General Principles section of this text, the Supreme Council affirmed one of its main objectives: to "[strengthen] the moral foundations, principles, foundations of the education for parents—specifically mothers on the topics of modesty and *hejab*—by creating a sensitivity in them regarding the idea [behind this law] is the preservation of chaste culture."[109]

Devising and implementing strategies for this social policy of *hejab* and modesty fell upon executing government agencies. Security forces (*Nirou-ye Entezami*) were put in charge of announcing to the public the limitations and legal criteria of modesty and bad-*hejabi*—and also recognizing when infractions took place.[110] They subsequently began policing cinema houses, stadiums, and other public places for acts and dress of impropriety. Ultimately, the security forces would "[make] society aware of the positive ethical and social effects of *hejab* and modesty . . . by creating cultural and artistic products and advertisements."[111] As per the responsibility of policing sculptures, this was the duty of the Ministry of Economy and Properties, whom the Supreme Council had designated to be in charge of banning the importation, production, exhibition, and supplying of sculptures, toys, mannequins, and pictures that advocate anti-modesty, such as paintings, carpets, newspapers, and other products.[112]

A close review of these policies suggests that the specifications of the *hejab* and modesty ordinances were defined and reassessed once social reality began to challenge the Supreme Council's vision and narrative that Iran was (and should be) a modest Islamic society. Increasing public resistance, demonstrated in the altering of styles of dress worn in public, presented a direct challenge and threat to the political elites' control of this narrative. The presence of a woman using heavy makeup, wearing a bright-colored *hejab* and a curve-hugging *manteau*, jeopardized not only the sanctity of public space but also the founding values of the Islamic Republic. The examples of potential threats to the state's version of modesty appeared to multiply: from statues of women in city squares to more recently, fashionable women walking on the street. (The latter became known by the term *mankanha-ye khiyabani* (street mannequins) for being colorfully dressed and/or heavily adorned in public.)

This body of regulatory policy of the Supreme Council of the Cultural Revolution has had far-reaching effects, even in the realm of nonartistic renditions of the female body—such as lifeless dummies or mannequins displayed behind a storefront window. In the next section, I discuss the strategies of Islamicizing mannequins as a prerequisite for their being displayed in storefronts. The story of their modification differs from the aforementioned examples of monuments

Figure 4.7 Partially severed head of a female mannequin on Vali Asr Street, Tehran August 2009.

and statues, as the transformation of a mannequin into a "modest form" was determined by quick, back-and-forth negotiations between store owners and officials. The tactics employed by both parties illustrate the mutability of social policies on modesty and *hejab*, in addition to the state's inconsistent and incoherent conceptualizations of women's bodies that appeared to support these policies (Figure 4.7).

Islamic Mannequins and Bodies in Commerce

Haft-e Tir Square is the bustling *manteau* (overcoat) district located in central Tehran. Stores offer a variety of designs: intricately jeweled scarves; a *manteau* for every occasion; and knockoffs of European and American brands. Competition here is fierce, for over thirty stores selling *manteau* vie for customers' business. For the shops encircling this square, often the most outrageous and well-styled window displays attract the most customers. Amid the commotion, mannequins in window displays stand out. Because magazines censor clothing advertisements (certain body parts are obscured from view and heads are covered in scarves), storefront displays are optimal forums for potential customers to envision how clothing would drape on female figures. Yet for many Iranians, the freedom to envision something as simple as an overcoat dressed on a mannequin has been steered by religious and political redlines (Figure 4.8).

Figure 4.8 Mannequins with cutoff breasts, 2006.

In the early months of President Ahmadinejad's first term, the MCIG began clamping down on window displays that exhibited inappropriately dressed and adorned mannequins. Clerics and authorities believed the unregulated displays of the life-size statues would evoke illicit thoughts in passersby, thus encouraging society's moral depravity.[113] Thus they authorized the police to prevent "the promotion of prostitution through mannequins and models."[114] Subsequently all public exhibitions featuring women's fashions, including catwalks of dress exhibitions, were thoroughly inspected and regulated.[115]

In September 2008, the same ministry, under the leadership of Mohammad Hossein Saffar Harandi, published extensive guidelines for catwalk models in a seven-part report, *Dastour ol'amal-e Sodour-e Mojavez-e Barpaii-ye Namayeshga-he Mode va Lebas dar Keshvar* (Rules for the Permission of Clothing and Fashion Exhibitions inside Iran).[116] Among the list of prohibited behaviors included the banning of fashion runways themselves, as they were charged with promoting non-Iranian and non-Islamic influences—typically code words for the state's disapproval of "Western" hegemonic culture—popular in satellite programs broadcast by Iranian communities living outside Iran. Harandi announced that models and designers would no longer be permitted to emphasize the curves of a woman's body when designing and displaying new fashions. To implement these new standards, models were told that they "should avoid any behavior that would distract visitors' attention from the clothes put on display," according to the "Guidelines for Fashion and Dress Shows."[117] Also mentioned in the directive, "The wearing of tight and body-hugging clothes and types of makeup that are incompatible with Islamic and Iranian culture are prohibited"[118] (Figure 4.9, Figure 4.10, Figure 4.11, Figure 4.12, Figure 4.13).

Figure 4.9 Half-headed mannequins with severed breasts in Haft-e Tir Square, Tehran June 2010.

Figure 4.10 Display case of veiled mannequins with severed breasts in Haft-e Tir Square, June 2010.

Figure 4.11 Window display near Haft-e Tir Square, June 2010.

Figure 4.12 Faceless mannequins with flattened chests near Haft-e Tir Square, June 2011.

Figure 4.13 Half-headed mannequin on Vali Asr Street, October 2011.

Three years before these guidelines were published, in 2005, officials in the *Gasht-e Ershad* division of *Nirou-ye Entezami* were implementing a policy of inspecting mannequins in window displays of popular shopping districts in Tehran. The arrival of spring signaled a new inventory of clothes to be showcased in shop vitrines. In clothing emporiums across Tehran, shop owners began redesigning their window displays to feature the season's latest "must-haves." *Gasht-e Ershad* patrolled shopping districts, paying close attention to shortened shirt sleeves and skirt lengths that exposed a mannequin's shape and body parts. They warned shop owners: if mannequins were found placed immodestly in storefronts, they would be fined or shut down. The threats of closure and reduced business and profit[119] initiated what Fataneh Farahani has described as a process of "Islamicizing mannequins" in window shops—a modification process that began between 2005 and 2006. Shop owners moved swiftly in order to meet the plainclothes officers' expectations.[120] First, a few inches were added to short skirts displayed on mannequins.[121] At the time, their shapes were still curvaceous, and hair was still visible from underneath the *rousari*. Officials still found fault with the mannequins' hairstyle, hair color, and the fact that they were not fully veiled. "Within a few weeks," mannequins were displayed bald, "leaving their luscious hair behind in storage rooms."[122] Soon their heads were fully covered by veils, and any unruly hairs were tucked underneath scarves.

As these modifications diminished the selling power of the mannequins, on which shopkeepers and designers advertised the upcoming fashion season, owners sought other methods to entice potential customers inside. Without this main showpiece, shop owners became creative out of necessity. Some owners chose to enhance the mannequins' makeup, which again drew the ire of the officials. The authorities responded by ordering them to minimize the eyeliner and lipstick because they "claim[ed] that the lips of women were aphrodisiac and their eyes stimulating."[123] And finally when matching the authorities' expectations seemed improbable, owners began contemplating buying expensive government-approved mannequins. However, some shopkeepers decided to remove the mannequins entirely from their displays, and, in other instances, they began to consider displaying headless mannequins on which to exhibit fashion items.

Despite these many changes, officials disapproved of the mannequins, finding fault chiefly with the curvature of the mannequins' breasts that was still noticeable underneath the garments. In lieu of buying new mannequins, storeowners decided to slash the chest area, as it was more cost efficient (see Figure 4.8).[124] However, this solution did not satisfy the authorities; breasts were still visible underneath the clothing in their jagged forms (see Figures 4.8 to 4.11). In other cases, "little coils" were used to assume the shape of a wire breast.[125] "The coils," Mehrangiz Kar observed, "displayed the mutilated gender of the mannequins."[126]

The back-and-forth negotiations between shopkeepers and authorities exemplify the haphazard construction and arbitrary interpretation of certain social policies seeking to enforce modesty onto mannequins. It also suggests that the conceptualization of a "modest" woman's appearance for public display was neither standardized nor easily identifiable. In fact, officials acted without a firm policy in place—often extemporaneously—and thus could not fully explain to storeowners (or even themselves) the proper display of a storefront mannequin. Moreover, every rough alteration of the mannequin proved to be more comical and conspicuous in its outcome. For example, once the mannequins' breasts were sawed off, their serrated appearance drew special attention, inviting curiosity, guffaws, disbelief, and condemnation in press and blog reports, not to mention daily conversations.

The most recent depictions of mannequins' forms are found in Figures 4.11 and 4.12. As the photographs show, the mannequins' bodies appear streamlined; the chest area in particular bears little resemblance to the typical female form—what were once two round breasts now appear to be a flat surface covered by fabric. Representations of female bodies are now depicted as shapeless, revealing what appears to be the slight cleavage of an adolescent girl. Moreover, full-sized, female plastic mannequins no longer come in all shapes and sizes. Often mannequins are deliberately displayed with missing hands, legs, and heads. In their latest manifestation (from June and October 2011), half-headed female mannequins are displayed with flattened chests, hairless, and almost always with a scarf wrapped around their heads (see Figures 4.9 and 4.10).[127] ("Iran's concern over the mannequins coincides with high levels of plastic surgery in the country," remarks Nina Power, "as young women attempt to wrest control over their bodies by way of oddly homogeneous rhinoplasties.")[128]

A Culture of Modesty and the Crisis of the Human Body

The struggle to maintain an aesthetic value in compliance with societal standards determined by clerical authorities and administered by state agencies demonstrates the complexities and crisis that renditions of the human body present in preserving a modest and chaste Islamic culture. The underlying assumption is that, even a dummy—a nonhuman entity with humanlike features—disturbs the ideal of modesty being projected onto an Iranian public. Imposing a "culture of modesty" is a method of disciplining both men and women not only in how they dress but also in their behavior and social interactions.[129] However, exhibiting a modest self is not just a requirement of both sexes; it also extends to their representations in art. Just as Iranian women (and men) were subject to ordinances of veiling and sex segregation in official spaces, statues and mannequins of women were subject to obligatory modifications so that they complied with the clerical leadership's categorical ban of any forms of nudity and "erotic" art.[130]

The transformation process in which monuments are subject to reform is similar to the destruction and subsequent metamorphosis of red-light district *Shahr-e No* into a family-themed park. Those landmarks of public art that were spared from being vandalized were offered a second chance at public exhibition, provided they underwent the process of modesty reform. In such instances, officials attempted to redesign pieces that adhered to the Supreme Council's articulation of an Islamically sanctioned visual and bodily aesthetics. The implicit understanding was that the public's gaze must be shielded from any suggestion or expression of female sexuality.

The state's tendency, via its public policy and morality campaigns, has designated the human body (and its nonhuman representations) as something shameful. As stated by Mehri Honarbin-Holliday, the female body, in particular, is used as "the state's instrument in order to dictate cultural behaviors."[131] Still, one cannot walk the streets of Tehran without sensing and realizing the importance of bodies—their manipulations, their troubles, their politicization, their projected martyrdom, and their socialization. In Tehran's public spaces, there is always *something to see*—an object or person on which to gaze, evoking a mixture of bemusement, affirmation, vindication, and confusion. Billboards of martyred men and painted slogans of the Islamic Revolution on walls throughout the city hang above Iranians, young and old, sporting dramatic styles and weaving through traffic. Here, Tehran bears witness to how living and nonliving bodies are constituted, reconstituted, projected, and denied expression as the regime pursues its ideological project to transform this capital into an "Islamic city."[132] Yet this title has had little impact on this city of "paradox."[133] For the diverse inhabitants who traverse and maneuver through it daily, it is a home and theater to a widely contradictory Islamist ideology that has become intimate with secular, consumerist, technological, sexual, and global forces.[134]

Chapter 5

WHEN HIV/AIDS MEETS GOVERNMENT MORALITY

In Iran, myriad pressures have led to a culture of secrecy and anonymity for those living with HIV, the Human Immunodeficiency Virus that causes AIDS (Acquired Immune Deficiency Syndrome), even more than in most other societies.[1] Disclosing an HIV-positive status in Iran can potentially arouse suspicions and lead to assumptions about one's sexuality, lifestyle, educational background, religious conviction, and socioeconomic status. Writing on cultural stigmas associated with HIV/AIDS, researcher Robert Crawford has observed, "At the heart of the cultural politics of AIDS is a contestation over the meaning of the self. It is a politics about identity and difference, about the boundaries of personhood which distinguish legitimate from non-legitimate identities, and about the meanings upon which identities are constructed, managed, and reworked."[2] For Crawford, HIV/AIDS is a boundary marker, one that differentiates "unhealthy" from the "healthy." It is an illness associated with many presumptions about "deviant" sexuality and excessive sexual behaviors.[3] Such comments resonate with the cultural politics of HIV/AIDS in the Iranian context. Because transmission of HIV is generally believed to occur through unprotected sexual relations, HIV is often associated with unethical and/or "high-risk behavior," such as illicit drug use, sexual promiscuity, and fraternizing with criminal networks.[4] Hence HIV/AIDS in Iran is both popularly and officially treated as a taboo-laden disease, supposedly concentrated among key populations of injecting drug users (IDUs) and female sex workers not using protection.[5] Government policies and clerical rhetoric do little to publicly discourage or denounce stigmatization and discrimination against those living with the disease even in the face of a rapid increase in the population that has been affected. Negative associations are particularly impactful for women, whose reputations are tarnished by accusations that they engaged in "immoral" behavior leading to their contracting HIV.

Worldwide, women account for 50 percent of people living with HIV (PLWH), while young women aged fifteen to twenty-four are particularly vulnerable to HIV infection rates, accounting for 22 percent of all new HIV infections.[6] In the Middle East and North Africa (MENA) region, women comprise an estimated 40 percent of adult PLWH cases—the majority of whom are infected by their husbands or partners who engage in high-risk behaviors and are mostly unaware of their HIV-positive status.[7] Minoo Mohraz,[8] a professor of infectious diseases and head of

Iran's HIV/AIDS Research Center, reported that the number of women diagnosed with AIDS was up by 30 percent since 2012.[9] Recent statistics published by Iran's Ministry of Health and Medical Education (MOHME) reveal that 8.7 percent of the 23,497 registered cases of HIV patients are women.[10] Moreover, as reported by MOHME acting director Dr. Mohammad Hossein Nikman, the majority of them are spouses of IDUs.[11] Khosrou Mansourian, a social worker and HIV/AIDS advocate, estimated that Iran had entered a "third stage of HIV/AIDS epidemic," whose rise in HIV cases he attributed to unprotected sexual relations among youth populations and married couples.[12]

Albeit informative, these statistics do not explicate the social settings within which HIV infection takes place. In Muslim-majority societies like Iran, rights and duties in an Islamic marriage involve *nafaqa* (maintenance) and *tamkin*,[13] which is defined as "a woman's obligation to live under her husband's roof and to surrender herself to him when he desires sexual intimacy."[14] "A woman is called 'untamed' if she refuses to satisfy the desires of her husband."[15] According to the UNAIDS report *Standing Up, Speaking Out*, which surveys the status of HIV/ AIDS in the MENA region, there is a complex set of social, cultural, and economic factors placing many women at risk. The authors explain, "Cultural norms that favour men, mistakenly cloaked in religion and reflected in national law in many countries, increase women's vulnerability. This is particularly true when it comes to questions of sexuality, in which women are held to double standards of virginity and sexual monogamy. . . . Social constraints—particularly on unmarried women—make it difficult to access sexual and reproductive health services, including HIV prevention and testing."[16] Due to the high concentration of HIV-positive cases among Iran's IDUs, prisoners, and prostitute demographics, the Iranian government has allocated most funds to these target populations; hence specialized funding and social support rarely reach HIV-positive, unmarried women and widowed mothers. Even though health and public health officials have started to acknowledge the existence of an emerging demographic of married HIV-positive women, this has not yet translated into significant and proportionate financial support; nor has it resulted in aggressive public health policies that include HIV/AIDS awareness and prevention campaigns to combat the disease.[17]

Since the virus's domestic detection more than three decades ago,[18] Iran's HIV/AIDS policies and advocacy projects have been mired in opposing political, religious, and social conflicts. HIV and AIDS—as well as STDs in general—are viewed as security issues due to the ways in which they reveal hidden (and likely image-tainting) realities about life in an Islamic Republic. Given the state's targeted reforms in HIV/AIDS treatment programs for its IDU demographic, it appears that clerical authorities and MOHME reports associate HIV/AIDS transmission in Iran more with drug abuse and addiction than with sexual intercourse.[19] To speak frankly about sex and sexual practice would require the government to "recognize the occurrences of premarital sexuality, prostitution, and homosexuality—to which heavy legal penalties apply."[20] Moreover, public statements about HIV/ AIDS from Iran's clerical authority can be tinged with fire and brimstone rhetoric. As a potent example, the influential Grand Ayatollah Abdollah Javadi-Amoli announced that "God had punished [Western] society with HIV/AIDS for legally permitting homosexuality. . . . Problems like AIDS didn't exist before."[21] Presently, few *marja'e taqlid* have issued *fatwas* on HIV/AIDS prevention methods for the general public.[22] As Pardis Mahdavi has observed, "In a country [such as Iran] where high value is placed on 'proper' and 'moral' behavior, admitting a disease whose mode of transmission is primarily through unprotected sex and IDU is difficult."[23] From reticence to speaking publicly about sex and sexuality to denial about the actual number of domestic HIV cases, the official response to HIV/AIDS has been far from transparent, let alone consistent.

Central to this study of technologies of gender, sex, and self in contemporary Iran is talking to women who come from diverse backgrounds and inquiring about their individual experiences—in effect, to understand how they construct intricate and often shifting viewpoints on modesty, femininity, and their bodies, especially when culturally and politically sensitive issues like HIV/AIDS are considered. Indeed, when Iranian women living with HIV talk about issues of sex and sexuality, their narratives do not just reflect life experiences impacted by an HIV diagnosis but also reveal certain tensions in official, clerical, and public discourses on femininity, motherhood, modesty, and sexual morality. As a quick example, in Iran, there is a vast societal apparatus (including peers, family members, clergymen, and officials) that encourages women to be sexually available to their husbands. When women are not made aware of their reproductive choices or even the benefits and/or necessity of prophylactic usage,[24] simultaneous to hearing official advice on modesty in public and "guarding one's gaze,"[25] these messages have the potential to create a dangerous public health situation. In fact, in the past decade, the rising number of women infected with HIV has become topical for Iranian health advocates and researchers.[26] University-funded and MOHME-approved cross-sectional studies on HIV-care and prevention among "high-risk groups" as well as research on cultural attitudes about the disease are too many to list.[27] Yet, where are the details illustrating the actual conditions and circumstances under which HIV transmission is taking place? Are married men passing it to their wives? Are they angry and blame their husbands for the disease? Given that the burden of sexual morality and motherhood falls upon women, how do those living with HIV cope with these expectations? How do they feel or claim that HIV has changed their own perceptions of their bodies? More so, does religion help them to cope with the illness or does it add another layer of blame?

Researchers have yet to tackle these crucial questions and their implications, in part because sexuality is treated in "theocratic" Iran as a politically and socially contentious subject.[28] Thus data on the circumstances under which infections take place for women in particular, or even how they live with HIV, is rarely reported nor is this information easily accessible. This neglect to the plight of HIV-positive women has put single parents living with HIV especially at risk. Many do not have a proper understanding of HIV/AIDS and are not even aware of its consequences, subsequently penetrating many areas of their lives. Facing possible homelessness, joblessness, ostracism, and familial abandonment, "[they] are afraid to openly disclose their illness, due to the negative biases regarding the disease in society. Those who do disclose their HIV infection are deprived of the simplest social services (e.g. refusal by dentists or other physicians to provide medical services, rejection from jobs, deprivation of children from school registration)."[29]

The previous chapters of this book investigate both conceptual and physical sites wherein disciplinary technologies were employed to structure and reinforce ideals of family, marriage, modesty, citizenship, and becoming "modern" since the late Pahlavi period into present-day Iran. I have charted how certain patriarchal and heteronormative understandings of women and female sexuality determined social policy, visual reform, spatial contexts, and the dominant historical narratives from the 1960s to well into the postrevolutionary period. This final chapter turns to the experiential side of bodily technologies, wherein discussion centers on intersecting issues of sexuality and HIV as they interlace with social, cultural, economic, political, and religious variables and come to animate women's lived experiences. By the concept "lived experience," I mean how "people become social entities and how they attend to one another and the products of human endeavor in the course of day-to-day life."[30] To illustrate, I enter the "proverbial pit of the taboo" by reflecting on the insights on sexuality, bodily perception, dress, marriage, and modesty from the perspectives of HIV-positive widows of female-headed households who attended wellness and health strategy workshops, which I detail later in this chapter. Moreover, using ethnographic material, I discuss how a distinct group of women living with HIV dealt with their illness without necessarily highlighting its importance.

Much of the findings here are based on ethnographic fieldwork I conducted in Iran from summer 2010 to winter 2012. While researching sexuality and prostitution discourses in Iran, I often came across the side issue of HIV/AIDS, especially after attending meetings and workshops held at *Anjoman-e Hemayat va Yari-ye Aseeb Didegan-e Ejtemai-i* (Society for the Protection and Assistance of Socially Disadvantaged Individuals, hereafter SPASDI), a nongovernmental, charitable, and advocacy organization in Tehran and formerly led by founder and director Khosrou Mansourian.[31] Although my data is larger than here in this chapter, I make use of the anecdotes of four participants, namely Farah, Akram, Maryam, and Masoumeh. Given the stigma attached to HIV and that it is a taboo subject, I look at my interlocutors' coping strategies, and listen to their reflections not only on accessing better care but also on their individual efforts to move beyond the stigmatization of their illness and instead concentrate on empowering and safeguarding themselves through community-building, social acceptance, and financial stability, to name a few. In what follows, I sketch the social and political challenges of HIV/AIDS in Iran. I highlight the discrepancies found in official and nonofficial statistics and analysis, and I detail ministry health agencies and HIV/AIDS advocates' attempts to reduce the rising rates of infection. I then discuss the dissemination of misinformation on the disease, underscoring certain efforts by clerics to find religiously inspired and practical solutions to combat HIV and address the stigmas associated with the disease. Thereafter, I enter the ethnographic section of this work, in an effort to understand how a unique group of women come to perceive and experience motherhood, sexuality, and modesty, among other topics.

Situating HIV/AIDS in Contemporary Iran

Sources provide varying accounts of the first documented case of HIV in Iran, indicating that the first case happened sometime between 1985 and 1987 as a result of contaminated blood during a blood transfusion.[32] Thereafter, consecutive waves of HIV infections hit different demographic populations at different times, across Iran. The first wave, ending in the mid-1990s, was marked by infections among hemophilia patients who received tainted blood transfusions.[33] (According to a MOHME 2010 report,[34] until 1995 less than ten new cases of HIV were identified, annually.[35]) The government began charting demographic shifts in the general public's sexual behaviors almost ten years after it realized that rates among "high-risk" groups[36]—in official health reports, identified as primarily intravenous or injecting drug users (IDUs) and prisoners—were reaching epidemic levels.[37] An incident marking the "second wave" of HIV in the mid-1990s necessitated an immediate change in public health attention and strategy. In Kermanshah-Khanuj prison 250 prisoners tested positive for HIV.[38] The reported occurrences of needle-sharing among inmates presented a potentially dangerous public health scenario if prisoners were released without being diagnosed. As a result, health officials began implementing practical strategies for treatment and prevention.

At the time, the epidemic was regarded as "concentrated" in the subpopulation of IDUs from state penitentiaries.[39] Clerics, public health advocates, and government officials sought to curb the soaring numbers of infections among IDUs, and encouraged a more "typology-suggested intervention."[40] Subsequently needle exchange, methadone maintenance, outreach programs, and harm reduction therapies were introduced and strategically implemented for an incarcerated demographic that was, in many respects, physically quarantined in prison.[41] Even prisoners' families were provided complimentary medical care.[42] With these reforms, official perceptions of HIV-infected drug addicts began to be transformed. Public health workers lobbied clerics, judges, and government officials to treat drug addiction as an illness and humanitarian issue. Judges began ordering rehabilitation for treating substance abuse instead of jail time.[43] If convicted drug users went through rehabilitation programs, their sentences would be reduced or dropped altogether.[44] This shift in policy represented a radical approach to state-level methods of discipline and punishment,[45] which treated drug addictions and HIV/AIDS as signs of moral depravity and corruption.[46] Public health reforms began to treat people with drug addictions as "vulnerable" patients, in need of comprehensive public health guidance and support.[47]

When major reforms in the nation's penitentiary treatment programs were implemented for the general public, HIV/AIDS policies changed nationwide. These measures ran parallel to the liberalizing reforms of Iran's fifth president,

Mohammad Khatami. By 2001, MOHME and participating agencies had created a National Strategic Plan, concentrating on "age appropriate information and education, voluntary counseling and testing, harm reduction, HIV/STI care and treatment and strengthened HIV related applied studies."[48] Two years later, the clerical leadership and government institutions began to accept the possibility of a rising HIV rate, which led to expansions in university-approved research studies on the epidemic and more programs to reach members of the general public affected by the disease.[49] In August 2006, localized support centers, known as *Bashgah-e Yaraneh-e Mosbat* (Positive Clubs), were set up for HIV-positive patients, focusing on HIV harm reduction and creating local strategies for the problems of stigma and discrimination.[50]

Iran's various ministries also pledged to assist in maintaining infection rates at less than 0.1 percent among the general population and below 25 percent among high-risk groups by the end of 2010.[51] Triangular clinics were established to incorporate accessible services such as HIV/AIDS treatment and care (including treatment with antiretrovirals);[52] voluntary and confidential testing; and information on HIV/AIDS, STD, and drug dependence.[53] (However, in the provinces' urban centers of Esfahan, Shiraz, and Mashhad, testing centers were less available).[54] Iran's HIV/AIDS and public health experts also began presenting their findings and prevention methods at international research and NGO conferences; they showcased innovative HIV/AIDS prevention and care programs, such as methadone maintenance treatment and triangular clinics operating in Iran.[55] (Many of these researchers were university-funded and affiliated with Iran's Center for AIDS Research.)[56] Also at these conferences, Iranian researchers collaborated and shared teaching and prevention strategies with HIV experts from different countries. These combined efforts among government officials, social scientists, and public health advocates were believed to be the reason behind the improvement of domestic HIV/AIDS treatment and subsequently decreasing domestic rates of HIV infections.[57]

In parallel, Iranian officials began speaking about HIV/AIDS as a matter of public interest, subsequently launching a MOHME-administered media campaign to inform the general public. MOHME started releasing official, annual statistics on the reported cases of HIV/AIDS infections, via Iran's media agencies, including the Iranian Students' News Agency (ISNA), Mehr News Agency (MNA), and the IRIB.[58] State television and radio commenced mass media programs through "teaser" health campaigns.[59] These campaigns publicized World AIDS Day, which is celebrated annually on December 1.[60] Health clinics were supplied with brochures on AIDS awareness. Across Tehran, giant billboards were decorated with red ribbons—the universal symbol for HIV/AIDS advocacy—in major thoroughfares and parks.

The public health community also helped mobilize public awareness. HIV/AIDS advocates began pushing for the widening of public access to HIV/AIDS-related information by promoting prevention methods, such as condom use.[61] Health officials initially focused on reaching out to specific demographic groups to stimulate changes in knowledge, attitude, and behavior—namely, teachers, trainers, high school and university students, couples intending to permanently marry, and "high risk" populations,[62] including IDUs, prisoners, and sex workers who were provided cursory instruction about HIV prevention and care.[63] By 2006, policy reforms for HIV/AIDS curriculum were proposed in schools and workplaces where AIDS-awareness pamphlets and handbooks were approved for distribution. Qom-based[64] Shi'a clerics even endorsed the booklet.[65] A 2012 official review of this education curriculum concluded that HIV is still considered a taboo in the education system, in spite of the HIV/AIDS curriculum that commenced in 2006.[66] In one qualitative study, researchers found that "because of unreasonable fears among most Iranian people that AIDS education promotes high risk behaviors, sex education about HIV transmission has no place in schools and universities in Iran."[67] Even despite official campaigns to improve HIV/AIDS awareness during Khatami's administration, other obstacles jeopardized how much access and knowledge about the virus and its prevention Iranians could obtain, given the state's control of information output. Two major roadblocks seemed to impede campaign efficacy and outreach. The first is related to discrepancies in government estimates of the number of people in Iran living with HIV/AIDS versus the figures presented in international monitoring reports by Iranian health officials. The second pertains to clerical dissemination of HIV/AIDS information and their actual involvement in providing HIV community support. The next two sections enquire into these matters.

Who Counts? Statistical Discrepancies in HIV/AIDS Discourse

"Obtaining an estimate of the number of people infected with HIV in a country or region is important for the purpose of evaluation, programme planning and advocacy," writes the Joint United Nations Programme on HIV/AIDS (UNAIDS) and the World Health Organization (WHO) Working Group on Global HIV/AIDS and STI Surveillance.[68] UN member states employ different surveillance systems of their respective HIV epidemics, although reporting systems intend to "provide information that will increase and improve the response to the HIV epidemic."[69] Early warning indicators of a possible epidemic can also be determined, and among concentrated demographics or subgroups, "surveillance can provide valuable information for designing focused interventions."[70] Iran's MOHME has generally followed procedure, although qualifying that estimating the number of HIV-infected cases and at-risk groups "[could] play a decisive role in clarifying the political orientation of prevention with respect to the size of each at-risk group, the gravity of the problem in each of the groups, the change in the conditions of the epidemic among them, and the identification of the program's blind spots."[71]

Yet little critical attention has focused on the discrepancy between the official HIV statistics provided by the MOHME and the Center for Disease Management—two domestic institutions that release official HIV/AIDS statistics—and the data they have reported and published for review by international aid agencies. The discrepancy in part lies in the government reports on the actual versus estimated cases of Iranians who are HIV-positive. Health officials provide different health statistics for different audiences. Take for instance MOHME monitoring and epidemiological reports from 2004 to 2012 reports, which they prepared for UNAIDS, WHO, and UNDP in order to satisfy Iran's reporting obligations for membership in (and funding from) these agencies. According to Iran's HIV/AIDS progress reports, HIV/AIDS statistics for English-language audiences are much larger than reported in their domestic monitoring reports, written in Persian. In 2003, Iran estimated 31,000 PLWH.[72] By the end of 2005, Iran reported a range of 60,000 to 70,000 cases.[73] In a 2008 epidemiological report for the UNAIDS/WHO Working Group on Global HIV/AIDS and STI, Iran reported an estimate of 86,000.[74] For 2009, in another country monitoring report, MOHME estimated 83,000.[75] In Iran's 2012 progress report for UNAIDS, health officials reported 23,497 registered PLWH cases by September 2011, and 93,250 estimated for 2010. They forecasted that by 2015, the figure would increase to 126,300.[76]

By contrast, consider the following research findings: In 2003, a study from University of Tehran's Medical Sciences reported that official figures were approximately 5,000 people infected with HIV/AIDS.[77] HIV/AIDS experts disputed this figure, stating it was likely five times more.[78] Iran's Center for Disease Management stated that by late 2004, official figures were around 9,800 HIV-positive cases and 374 cases of AIDS.[79] In 2006, according to feminist journal *Zanan*, Iranian officials reported 13,357 known cases.[80] Three years later, in 2009, MOHME reported an increase in HIV cases, reporting around 20,000 cases of HIV countrywide.[81] Hossein Ali Shahyari, Acting Director of the Health Commission for the *Majles* (Parliament), disputed MOHME's data on the reported number of HIV-positive cases in 2009. As cited by *Farda News*, an online Persian-language news portal, he claimed the range was "five to seven times this number, equaling almost 100,000."[82] The most recent estimate from a 2012 joint-report from the MOHME and the Center for Disease Management cited 23,125 known domestic cases of HIV—of which 8.5 percent are women and 91.5 percent are men.[83] By the MOHME's own admission, there was a wide gap between the official figure for the identified cases of HIV versus the number of estimated cases. The ministry's monitoring reports attributed this challenge to limitations of diagnostic services, which require expensive tests.[84] In a 2012 monitoring report, for instance, "special software" was reportedly the reason for the new and larger estimates.[85]

Iran-based experts from the fields of medicine, public health, and social work, as well as journalists writing on women's health or other health-related issues, were cognizant of this underreporting and its ramifications. Public health employees, medical researchers, and HIV/AIDS advocates responded by going on record, conducting interviews with domestic and international media outlets while pushing aside the potential backlash or the fear of losing their jobs for speaking out. Their objective was to encourage MOHME to accurately publish the number of HIV cases—which are already published in regional and international AIDS reports—for the general public. And when they were not successful in reaching this objective, they published counter-statistics to dispute official MOHME reports. Masoud Mardani, a member of Iran's AIDS National Committee reportedly said,

"According to a statement by the World Health Organization, we have to multiply this figure four or five times to reach the real figure of those infected with AIDS in Iran."[86] As of 2018, only 36 percent of Iranians knew their HIV status, and among them, only 20 percent were receiving treatment.[87]

Monitoring HIV: Clerical Involvement and Islam as the Answer

During official gatherings of Friday prayer in Tehran, when sermons are usually broadcast on state television, the Shi'a clerical establishment (including Grand Ayatollahs, Ayatollahs, and Hojjataleslam clerics) has not yet commented on the HIV epidemic and the rise in domestic cases of HIV. The responsibility of disseminating information to the general public has typically fallen upon lower-level clerics in the vast hierarchy of the clergy, who have addressed social issues to their local communities.[88] In areas where MOHME resources are not comprehensive or readily accessible, these clerics fill in necessary social roles by informing the public of taboo topics, such as HIV.

MOHME officials reported in 2011 that there was an "increasing trend of community leaders, i.e. religious leaders, who [were] subsequently addressing issues such as prevention, stigmatization, and discrimination at the local and grass-root levels in Iran."[89] Likewise, a 2011 UNAIDS report praised clerical participation, distinguishing it as exemplary within the region. UNAIDS previously recognized "the support of the ayatollahs in Iran for harm reduction programmes for people who inject drugs. With their support, the country's harm reduction programme has become the most extensive and effective in the MENA region."[90] As described in the report,

> In Iran, religious leaders are active participants in a project on psychosocial support to people living with HIV. This project, which is funded by the Global Fund to Fight AIDS, Tuberculosis and Malaria,[91] is working with Islamic leaders on understanding the psychological and social aspects of HIV and providing them with the necessary knowledge and communication skills to support people living with HIV. As part of an initial needs assessment with participants, this project found that 83% of religious leaders believed in the participation of religious leaders and figures in psychosocial support for people living with HIV.[92]

However, the preceding assessment only referenced the intentions guiding Islamic leaders' participation and did not elaborate their actual participation in offering support services for PLWH. Furthermore, the statement did not mention the results of such support, nor did it convey the precarity of their participation under different presidential regimes. According to a 2008 study, conducted during Ahmadinejad's first presidential term, most conservative religious leaders were opposed to safe-sex curriculum, the promotion of condom usage, and needle exchange programs, fearing that such education promoted acts prohibited by

Islamic tenets. (These forbidden acts include premarital sex, homosexuality, and intravenous drug use.)[93]

"The best prescription in the struggle against AIDS is Islam," remarked cleric Hojjat al-Eslam Mohammad Taghi Sarfipour, a leader of Friday prayer from the city Pol-e Dokhtar in Lorestan Province.[94] In a 2010 interview with semiofficial Fars News Agency, Sarfipour discussed the presence of AIDS in his community, deeming it "one of the worst phenomenon we're facing." As a solution for the prevention of the spread of HIV, he suggested that believers seek guidance and direction from the religious sources in Islam. "Islamic teachings," he clarified, "are very good for reaching human growth and evolving as human beings, which has been ordained for us. If we follow these orders well, we'll never suffer from moral decline and incurable diseases."[95] Sarfipour's statements echoed statements of other religious leaders in Iran, who appeared to use religious frames of reference to understand and deal with HIV/AIDS. The suggested methods of controlling the HIV/AIDS epidemic necessarily involved one's adherence to social and moral principles discussed in Islamic texts and teachings. One would therefore observe a pious and moral lifestyle, whereby monogamy, abstinence, and being faithful become deterrent mechanisms.[96]

Studies have shown mixed results about the efficacy of such strategies. In MOHME's 2015 monitoring report for the United Nations General Assembly, they acknowledged that among 15- to 24-year-olds, only 11.7 percent correctly identified ways of preventing the sexual transmission of HIV.[97] A population-based study in Iran found that about 80 percent of the respondents agreed with the notion that the lack of religious and moral commitments could result in AIDS infection.[98] In a study by Mohammadi et al., boys who regarded themselves as "religious" had less knowledge of sexual issues compared with those who regarded themselves as being "somewhat religious" or "not religious."[99] And despite recent studies expressing public desire to learn more about HIV/AIDS through an evidence-based approach to HIV/AIDS policy and research, the clerical establishment has not changed its course.[100]

Much evidence has also pointed to an overall reticence among Iranian officials to acknowledge rising numbers of HIV-positive statuses among their general (non-incarcerated) population. Despite the top-level and community-specific strategies implemented to mitigate the rates of infection, according to Mahdavi, "for many years the government refused to comment on the incidence of HIV in Iran, and researchers interested in this topic were discouraged from investigating the issue."[101] This resistance to publishing comprehensive PLWH data inside Iran is rooted in certain legal, social, cultural, and religious factors that, collectively, have led to the continued stigmatization of the HIV-positive community. Consider the following constraints: Iran's religious authorities forbid premarital sex, and it is punishable by law. Similarly, talking about HIV/AIDS is largely based on the assumption that the virus is directly related to extramarital sex—which is forbidden.[102] Family reputation is also important in maintaining social status and ties. An HIV-positive diagnosis would likely tarnish one's familial reputation and lead to discrimination and/or being ostracized. More so, an HIV status likely jeopardizes one's marriageability, and in a society that values marital roles[103] and the institution of the family, this has reportedly resulted in severe levels of depression and anxiety, especially among women living with HIV.

Accessing Healthcare, the SPASDI Way

Iran's state, religious, and public discourses regard women living with HIV as occupying a particularly vulnerable position, one linked to drug and other criminal networks and high-risk behavior. In 2011, Iran's acting director of the MOHME reported that the majority of women living with HIV were spouses of IDUs.[104] According to UN regional reports on HIV/AIDS, "a large proportion of women living with HIV in the MENA region are believed to have acquired their infection from their spouses who practice high-risk behaviors."[105] They did not specify if this spousal activity involved a higher prevalence of infection through injecting narcotics or practicing unsafe sex with their wives and/or others. Given that the majority of state resources have been allocated to certain demographic groups, for many Iranian women widowed by AIDS and now HIV-positive themselves, accessing health care and forming support networks have meant seeking assistance from Iran's NGO community. They seemed the most willing, capable, and least resistant to providing social services to PLWH.

Since its founding in 1999, SPASDI (mentioned earlier in this chapter) has evolved from a nonprofit organization determined to "help prevent social disorders, protect the foundation of the family, and offer support to vulnerable individuals and families who are victims of social disadvantages" to one also committed to the protection of women and children with HIV.[106] Because of Iran's mounting societal problems due to poverty, prostitution, homelessness, AIDS, and divorce, Director Mansourian[107] individually steered the organization toward providing crucial services not provided by the Iranian government. SPASDI has offered professional counseling and a confidential hotline service, professional rehabilitation for children with mental and physical disabilities, self-help workshops, art exhibitions, and AIDS special services. In 2007, it began concentrating on tackling the controversial issue of HIV/AIDS after observing more women urgently requesting its services. Alarmed by the rising number of HIV-positive cases among married women, Mansourian rejected the MOHME's description of the current phase as "concentrated" among key populations like IDU and female sex workers. He argued that "the most vulnerable and harmed victims of AIDS" were namely single mothers infected by their drug-addicted husbands and widowed following their deaths.[108] He explained,

> Many of these victims don't have a proper understanding of HIV-AIDS and its implications for them. Moreover, they are afraid to openly disclose their illness, due to the negative biases regarding the disease in society. Those who do disclose their HIV infection are deprived of the simplest social services (e.g. refusal by

dentists or other physicians to provide medical services, rejection from jobs, deprivation of children from school registration).[109]

In many ways, SPASDI mediated state HIV/AIDS health policies by being the on-the-ground forces that not only took their situations seriously but also offered long-term support. The director often repeated, "The fundamental principle is to teach fishing, while providing fish." In brief, SPASDI provided mothers the necessary support and training to aid in financial independence and healthy lifestyle changes for them and their children.

Notably, obtaining help from this nonprofit was not an easy task producing immediate results. HIV-positive widows, seeking emotional support and financial assistance, were typically introduced to SPASDI via both word of mouth and recommendations from state hospitals, such as Tehran's Imam Khomeini Hospital. Women who inquired about their social services were immediately informed that they would agree to the following: They would not dramatize their HIV diagnosis or its impact. They would have to begin the long process of breaking down social taboos associated with the disease by radically overcoming their own assumptions and ignorance of it.[110] Through individual efforts, they would improve societal awareness of HIV, educating friends and strangers on basic facts and methods of transmission. And, eventually, they would let others know they were HIV-positive.

Accepting and then affirming one's HIV status was a fundamental SPASDI principle. The organization expressly discouraged being silent about HIV-positive diagnoses—they reasoned that not disclosing this information created and increased the risk of it spreading.[111] Often volunteers (although none who were HIV-positive) wore pins and T-shirts emblazoned with "I am HIV-positive." This was done not only in recognition of the global effort to destigmatize the illness and increase public awareness but also to show solidarity for the women and children at the center who were living with the virus.

Notes on Interview Protocols

For almost thirteen months, I attended SPASDI's weekly educational workshops for PLWH mothers and became integrated into their NGO cosmos. My attendance first involved partial observation and, in the first six months, minimal participation with the group. Initially the director and social workers were concerned that my presence would unsettle the workshop participants. To assure the mothers' safety and comfort, the director and I agreed that I would observe the workshops and, after brief introductions and consistent attendance for several months, I would be allowed more interaction with the group. Any outside conversations with group members would require their individual permission, along with that of the staff. Moreover, if anyone were to voice concerns about my presence to the director or workshop moderators, I would agree to depart on friendly terms.

My observer status quickly disappeared after the initial meeting. The moment the mothers learned I spoke Persian and was personally connected to the director,[112] they began to inquire about my family background, education, research interests and project, and even my love for Persian food. At first, our conversations and interactions were limited to my answering their questions. Save smiling, I was quiet and did not individually approach any participants. I instead helped the workshop moderators, pouring tea and distributing sweet snacks. The moderators were often dismissive of my silence, often asking my opinions about HIV/AIDS training and advocacy methods in New York. After a few occasions whereby I expressed ignorance, I was gently advised to return home and conduct research, which I obliged. The following weeks, the moderators allotted five to ten minutes for me to divulge whatever information I had assembled on mothers and children living with HIV and the medical resources available to them through New York's municipal health agencies. At every moment I hesitated and expressed my inadequacy in delivering or explaining this information; it appeared that this was inconsequential. The brief information sessions were used by the moderators as opportunities for the mothers to feel comfortable with my presence and most certainly my intentions—that, for example, I would fully commit to participation with respect and humility. Once the meetings ended, many of the women asked me questions about my personal life and my Iranian father. Because I was single (and thus this nonmarital status piqued their curiosities concerning my potential marriageability in my thirties), I was asked about potential mates, when I wanted to have children, and future plans once I completed my doctorate. After over a year of mutual acquaintanceship, we warmly greeted one another and caught up.

In September and October 2011 (the last two last months of my research stay in Tehran) Mansourian agreed to my personally interviewing the group of mothers, provided I abide by three conditions. First, the NGO's staff would preapprove my interview questions, and second, I needed each woman's personal permission.[113] The permissible questions, from the questionnaire I had originally designed,[114] included questions on perceptions of street mannequins, breastfeeding techniques, and personal philosophies of the body. Any direct questions about the relationship between bodies and politics was not permitted. I was also not allowed to discuss sex, nudity, underwear usage, or gather any information about their bodies. These topics were deemed too personal and potentially embarrassing for women who were not comfortable speaking about such topics to family members, let alone strange researchers. The director encouraged me to instead focus my questions on motherhood and breastfeeding, for, in the words of staff members, these topics would be well received by the group. It would enable them to speak more specifically (and animatedly) about their experience as mothers.

Lastly (and perhaps the most paramount), I would agree to not dramatize their HIV-positive status—meaning I would not focus my questions on their health status. Although Mansourian knew the general concept of my project, he wanted to be certain of my careful and empathetic treatment and analysis. He reasoned that HIV should not be an isolated characteristic of their lives and experiences, and thus I should not sensationalize the disease during our interviews. ("You should speak to them just as you would speak to someone who has diabetes, cancer, or a common cold—humanely, just as you treat your sister or your mother," he advised me.) If the women themselves felt inclined to bring it up in conversation, then it was their prerogative and thus permissible. I agreed to respect all three conditions. One week in advance of conducting any interviews, Mansourian and the seminar moderator Fatemeh S. informed the participants that I intended to conduct confidential, voluntary interviews over the next few weeks from late August until late September 2011. Of the sixteen participants from *Madaran-e Hami-ye Salamat*, I spoke with nine women from the group, followed by interviews with four female members of the staff.[115] The next sections are testaments to our dynamic and stimulating conversations.

Monday Mornings for Madaran

To assist mothers living with HIV, SPASDI held mandatory hour-and-a-half sessions every Monday in a support program and network they call *Madaran-e Hami-ye Salamat* (Mothers Advocating Health; abbreviated to *Madaran*, hereafter). The workshops were part of a pilot program for a group of twenty HIV-positive widows and mothers, providing them with crucial, long-term support, skills-based education, and financial assistance. A volunteer corps of social workers and retired nurses chaired each session. According to Mansourian, this support was a lifesaving intervention mainly because government funding offered precious little support for the widows' sustenance, and other NGOs such as the popular, Tehran-based NGOs like *Zanan-e Solh* (Women of Peace), *Banoo-ye Bartar* (Superior Women), and *Anjoman-e Hemayat az Kodakan-e Kheyabani* (Society for the Protection of Street Children) focused on short-term, tangible results.[116]

For the last few workshops in the summer of 2011, the director brought in health experts to teach these women how to eat more nutrient-rich foods and improve their dental hygiene. Staff members spoke extensively about fortifying their immune systems with exercise, nutrition, positive thinking, and spotting drug addiction. Often moderators showed informational videos on these subjects, followed by short lectures on self-confidence, self-awareness, and compassion. They repeatedly discussed these themes in an effort to promote positive self-esteem among the group members. When it came time for group discussion, conversations were often speckled with personal tales about their children and economic hardships—or, during other candid moments, about flirtatious advances of male admirers. Almost every week, the moderator asked questions about each person's state of mind, health status, and if they had any particular difficulties and thoughts they would like to share. Soon after, one of the group's mothers—who had volunteered the previous week to prepare the next week's group activity based on a particular theme—would take over discussion. These brainstorming sessions were often interrupted by whispers and side conversations between women or between women and their little children. (Children would often be present in the last thirty minutes. No longer wanting to remain on the upper floor's nursery, they shyly entered the room, edging closer to their moms.)

A discussion session led by Mansourian was often informative, enthusiastic, and filled with a medley of anecdotes. On the occasions when he was present, the level of seriousness and concentration heightened. I noticed that the moment he entered the workshop room, the mothers would immediately sit up straight, adjusting their *rousaris* and *chadors*, neatly tucking into their scarves any wanton hairs.[117] Side conversations would promptly halt. Any group member arriving late typically waited near the room's entrance, preferring not to enter until his lectures had finished. A typical lecture featured inspirational stories, as common reference points, from the Qur'an and *hadith*. On other occasions, Mansourian's stories referenced Iranian television shows and films to complement these anecdotes.[118] He also pointed to individual mothers, referencing their children, or relaying their stories of success and overcoming obstacles. Mansourian had an encyclopedic knowledge of each member's personal history, after having spent years working to provide them social services tailored to their circumstances. In the workshops I had attended, he consistently addressed the women with respect. By the meeting's end, many members asked his help to solve any problem they faced in their homes, neighborhoods, and at government health agencies. Once he departed, the women relaxed their positions. Tea and sweets were served during this break time, when women updated each other and carried on having personal conversations, or shared stories with the entire group. In more than half of the meetings, certain mothers reported on their CD4 white blood cell count.[119] When a woman's CD4 count was low, the typical reactions were an outpouring of compassionate words and actions. At most meetings, a number of women were absent. The reasons for this were varied—some health-related and others financial and personal. According to my interviews with two of SPASDI's social workers, in some cases, mothers stopped showing up after fearing their families would find out about their health status.

But the seminars were not just information sessions about healthy approaches to living with HIV. They were also opportunities to share positive news, to form a supportive community and network, and to become financially independent. It was often throughout the seminars that Mansourian and his organizers expressed joy upon hearing news that two participants had just remarried—in one case, a member had gotten remarried to an HIV-negative man who knew of his wife's condition and willfully practiced safe sex with her. (This happened very rarely.) According to the director, "This is a success, given the fact that even remarriage for healthy divorced or widowed women is faced with lots of cultural barriers in Iran, let alone for HIV infected women."[120]

There was also news of financial stability and progress made in raising awareness about the illness. Because SPASDI administered personal loans from private donors to women seeking stable housing, some of the mothers were able to buy their own small apartments. A few of them received smaller loans from the organization itself in order to start a home-based, small business. At a meeting, a participant spoke of her excitement after selling her handicrafts at the annual show-and-tell event marking the end of Ramadan. SPASDI encouraged women to be guest speakers at this event, before an audience of donors, relatives, friends, government officials, and religious intellectuals supportive of Mansourian's work. (At the last two events I attended, Mohammad Mojtahed Shabbestari, renowned Shi'a philosopher and once a close ally of President Khatami, was in attendance and also delivered a congratulatory speech to SPASDI and the mothers.)

The Mothers of SPASDI as HIV Advocates?

When I first met the women from *Madaran*, they were all at various stages of their lives and of the illness. Many of the mothers, hearing about the NGO via word of mouth or from the medical staff at Tehran's Imam Khomeini Hospital, had entered the organization under severe psychological duress, having suffered from financial problems, depression, and family isolation. Some had struggled with a lack of emotional support from family members who avoided mentioning their HIV diagnosis, or told them not to return home. In most cases, women traveled great distances to reach the center in Tehran. Kermanshah, Qom, Karaj, Mashhad, Bandar Abbas, and Quchan were some of the cities and towns from where they originated and some still resided. Yet traveling long distances was the least of their worries. Facing single-parenthood, they also had to focus on maintaining high CD4 levels[121] and those of their children, many of whom were also HIV-positive. Moreover, there was navigating the state's leviathan health care and welfare network, which provoked much frustration and concern if they wanted to continue receiving monthly antiretroviral treatment.

The recently widowed Akram, a thirty-year-old resident from Kermanshah, often traveled 500 kilometers with her children in tow to reach the center by its 9:30 a.m. start time. Her second husband—a drug addict and former prisoner who died from AIDS—had passed away three months before our interview, and her attendance at SPASDI was based, in part, on her need for financial assistance from them, as she was a homemaker. Most participants were widowed after their spouses died from AIDS-related complications. For the majority of *Madaran*, their spouses had contracted HIV through IDU, sexual relations with men and other women, or by other means during a period of incarceration. There was only one exception to this member profile: a middle-class woman in her late twenties who sought SPASDI's emotional support services. Never married, she did not disclose to group members how she contracted the virus.

Unlike the shy Akram, 49-year-old Maryam was a vocal and consistent participant of *Madaran*, regularly debating with moderators (and me) in side conversations and in hushed tones. Her throaty smoker's voice and acerbic quips of the tongue hinted to vast and intense life experiences. Originally from Shiraz, and now a Tehran resident, she was punctual and often the last to leave meetings. In workshops, she mentioned the especially difficult period of her life when she frequently injected the drug *shisheh* or "glass" (the colloquial terms in Persian and English for crystal methamphetamine). Raised in a family of boys, Maryam emulated the freedoms of her brothers and their friends, admittedly enjoying socializing with a "rough crowd" and wanting to "date a lot," unlike her more "traditional" female cousins, she remarked. Her life began to unravel after falling deeper into drugs and subsequently lying and stealing in order to sustain her habit. After losing her husband to AIDS-related complications, she sobered up, maintaining sobriety for almost a decade. At the time of our interview, she had been attending *Madaran* for almost a year.

Much of Akram's and Maryam's biographical information was common knowledge among the attendees. When a new woman would join, and after a few sessions, others would update her with member profiles, relaying details like marital status, number of children, hometown, and, crucially, the circumstances under which HIV was contracted. For *Madaran* participants, the subject of mode of contraction was both a mutual point of reference and common denominator. In some cases, a husband's extramarital relations and temporary marriage partnerships (of which his permanent wife had not been informed) were largely responsible for contraction. In other cases, women were infected via sexual activity with their spouses, not knowing about their husbands' IDU or HIV status. For some of the participants, the circumstances behind their HIV contraction— via the typically named reasons of spousal deceit, blood transfusion, drug use, and, in some cases, the cryptic "accidentally"—were mentioned far more during the workshops, informal conversations, and interviews than their HIV-positive status. Notably, members often distinguished the creative seamstress Farah, who discovered she was HIV-positive midway through her first pregnancy, after her husband, a hemophiliac, became HIV-positive as a result of an HIV-contaminated blood transfusion. Although she did not disclose her diagnosis to family members, she was an active participant in SPASDI's public awareness teach-ins. In the year I attended SPASDI meetings, it was uncommon to hear a mother admit to the group that she contracted the virus via drug usage; more often were stories of philandering husbands.

It was a SPASDI belief that by training *Madaran* members to be social workers for the general public, known as "peer trainers,"[122] they would facilitate informed discussions about HIV/AIDS facts and prevention. This would eventually lead to the destigmatization of their health status, for it would be regarded as an ordinary illness—similar to how cancer is understood today. SPASDI staff encouraged mothers to act as health and cultural ambassadors for HIV by speaking publicly about their condition and talking about HIV/ AIDS care and prevention to university students at Al-Zahra University or in front of seminary students at the *Howze-ye Elmi* in Qom, for instance. Hence HIV would not be considered a disease targeting marginalized communities but affecting the general public and not necessarily one targeting a particular social group, economic class, sexual practice, and lifestyle. (Notably, during my fieldwork, I only witnessed three of the same participants present their stories at SPASDI events.)

In what follows, I discuss two different leitmotifs on breastfeeding and *tamkin*, elaborating not only the coping strategies of women living with HIV but also the tensions that emerge when they attempt to fulfil SPASDI's larger advocacy goals.

Breastfeeding HIV-Negative Babies? The Desires and Pressures of Motherhood

Though I had promised not to mention HIV in the interviews, I was still keen to understand if and how it had altered any of the participants' perceptions of womanhood and their bodies. Given the authorities' restrictions on women's behavior and dress, and the level of discomfort that many had felt as a result, I speculated if HIV had added another layer. Did it factor into their constructions of motherhood, marriage, femininity, or dress, for instance? Moreover, given the "tainted character" associated with PLWH, did this health status change how they observed and judged the morality and modesty of others—or controversially, of their (deceased) husbands? In other words, did they maintain favorable memories of their husbands since their HIV-positive diagnosis?

Particularly important for my research was understanding the unique challenges of motherhood the participants faced, especially when bombarded by social expectations to breastfeed and national program encouraging breastfeeding for the sake of their children's health and survival. Though HIV-positive women can generally bear children, they must follow certain steps to reduce the possibility of the child contracting HIV to less than 2 percent,[123] for nearly one-third of infants born to HIV-infected mothers will contract the virus.[124] Until recently, HIV-positive women were recommended to follow additional preventive interventions—such as undergoing treatment with antiretroviral medications during pregnancy, labor, and delivery; delivering the child via Cesarean section; and *not* breastfeeding.[125] If breastfeeding is conducted, health experts estimate that between 10 to 20 percent of children will likely contract the disease.[126] Yet alongside this medical advice on preventing perinatal transmission of HIV infection, there is a swirl of mixed messages concerning women's maternal and familial obligations from an array of sources that collectively impact a woman's decision to breastfeed. There are also financial constraints under consideration: baby formula might be reasoned as an unnecessary, extra cost compared to milk provided the "natural" way, which is presumably free. Thus, in this regard, breastfeeding presents a moral dilemma: Is it ethically and morally responsible to do so when HIV-positive?

According to my interviews, this question was secondary to a woman's obligatory, maternal duties outlined by social norms and cultural codes. For, in some traditional families, if a woman refuses to nurse, it could potentially blemish her family's reputation or be regarded as a dishonorable act against family practice and advice. As is the case in many countries, cultural mandates dictate "if, when, where, and how long a child will receive human milk," surmises Stolzer.[127] In Iran, the discourse of breastfeeding is couched in the rhetoric of "mother's responsibility" and factors in the construction of a healthy, morally guided Islamic state. Maternal-child nursing is also legally protected and religiously sanctioned. Even Iran's personal status laws reflect the importance of breastfeeding in the preservation of Muslim families. Women are granted the legal right of financial maintenance for the length of time they breastfeed their children during marriage and can demand this compensation in case of divorce.[128] Likewise, religious treatises of *marja'e taqlid* are rife with extensive commentaries on breastfeeding practices.[129] These are based on Qur'anic and *hadith* literature, which, in the former, advises in most cases almost two years of exclusive breastfeeding,[130] and in the latter, recalls that the Prophet Muhammad was breastfed by his wet nurse for this period.[131]

On the domestic level, health ministry officials began campaigning against formula-use during the Iran–Iraq War, integrating references of Islamic religious tradition to promote the state's family planning policies. Wartime rationing raised the price of formula once the government limited its imports, and for many years it was not sold to the general public.[132] By 1991, domestic breastfeeding policy became fused with the MOHME-operated National Committee of Breastfeeding Promotion. After producing booklets and workshops on infant mortality and improving infant health, MOHME began designating hospitals as "baby friendly."[133] Via the *Tarh-e Bimarestan-e Doostdar-e Koudak* (Baby-friendly hospital initiative), the ministry set up a health network with a breastfeeding committee in each province. These initiatives were bolstered in 1995, when the legislature ratified the law, Promoting Breastfeeding and Supporting Mothers During the Nursing Period, whereby the import of any form of dried milk or supplementary nutrition for infants was allowed only with the government's permission, and in limited cases.[134] Almost ten years later, in 2004, MOHME increased efforts to promote breastfeeding in order to reduce growth abnormalities, to decrease the mortality rate, and to increase the number of "baby-friendly hospitals."

Interestingly, the state's aggressive promotion of breastfeeding on a national level presents unique dilemmas for HIV-positive women. Given the state and religious discourses on motherhood encouraging women to breastfeed, does this policy irresponsibly pressure women living with HIV to fulfil ideal motherhood roles at the (public health) risk of others and, more so, of their children? Indeed, breastfeeding is understood to be more than an endearing engagement between mother and child. This research demonstrates that breastfeeding was a key demarcation point between how certain HIV-positive women conceptualized their bodies in conflict with their personal desires, family traditions, and what they perceived as distinct religious and/or cultural traditions and values. Nursing a child was an essential rite of passage marking a woman's transition into a particular maternal, familial, and, in some cases, religious community. The coercion to mother and thus to breastfeed was articulated and reinforced by the state as cultural and religious norms.

Farah was the first person I asked about motherhood in general and breastfeeding in particular. I spoke with her one year before she became pregnant with her second child. During an informal conversation, she emphasized her desires to become pregnant again, to possibly breastfeed, and to have two healthy children. For Farah, the subject of breastfeeding was a deeply personal issue, and she recalled the struggle over whether to nurse her baby:

> I found out mid-pregnancy that I was HIV-positive. . . . My doctor advised me to not breastfeed. And when I gave birth after a C-section, my breasts were filled with milk. After two or three days, I became so upset. My doctor again said not to breastfeed, and to place ice on my breasts so that the milk would stop. This

feeling was so upsetting. I went into the shower and cried, holding the ice to my chest, and thinking, "Oh God, I don't know what the solution is, my breasts are so heavy with milk, and I'm not allowed to breastfeed." And now when I see someone giving milk to her child, my heart just aches . . . I also think being a woman—maybe this is a really traditional way of thinking, or old-fashioned— but this thought comes to me that woman and womanhood, a woman's entire value is giving birth, breastfeeding, raising children . . . these are all valuable for women. When I couldn't do this, I thought any mother would do anything for her child, and I haven't done this. . . . But then, when I feel this way, I think it's more valuable that my child is healthy and HIV-negative.

The following summer I saw Farah again; she was glowing, fully six-months pregnant. When I asked her if she was excited about giving birth, she beamed, and said that she hoped the baby would be born healthy.

Farah's situation was exceptional. For the majority of *Madaran*'s participants who became HIV-positive after bearing children, they no longer considered breastfeeding an option given the potential health risks to their children. Of the nine interviewees, only Farah had expressed a wish to expand her family. Yet they still emphasized the importance of breastfeeding to perceptions of self-worth, body image, and societal expectations of maternity. Both Masoumeh and Farah, for instance, mentioned that when a woman denied her breastfeeding responsibility for the sake of less consequential concerns—such as time management and maintaining perfect breast form—the baby's health would be jeopardized.

A recurring notion in these discussions was that the general recommendation stating that women should breastfeed to protect their children's health was in fact more like a tremendous expectation and moral imperative for women— irrespective of their health status. This pressure can have a disciplinary effect on women, influencing their decisions to breastfeed out of responsibility to their family and faith. As many of these interviews demonstrated, breastfeeding was mired in many presumptions about what a good mother and woman should do for her baby. For many of these women, they understood breastfeeding to be an expression of a cultural, economic, familial, and political norm accepted by the majority of Muslim-Iranian women. However, the consequences of these normative assumptions place a burden on Iranian women who, by virtue of their HIV-positive status, could place their children in danger if they do decide to breastfeed.

Masoumeh's Advice on Respecting Women and Observing Tamkin

On the very first day I joined the *Madaran* workshops, I was greeted by the tall, willowy Masoumeh. She was ostensibly the most enthusiastic and loquacious, doling out advice and telling anecdotes about raising her sons, her *sigheh* (temporary marriage) partnerships, HIV-treatment bureaucracy, and cooking, among many other topics. Originally from Kashan, she was raising her two teenage sons with the help of relatives after her husband, at age forty-one, died from an HIV-related illness. A former wearer of the *chador*, she stopped wearing it once her eyesight worsened, believing it compromised her mobility.[135]

Masoumeh was a woman with many plans—to remarry, to get a driver's license, and to find a job—which necessitated group discussion. On one occasion, she animatedly chatted about a young man who pursued her after spotting her in a driver's education class. Fearing that his intentions were dishonest and/or prurient, she located his number and used the opportunity to start a phone acquaintanceship. She insisted that her intentions were only to teach him how to seek relationships with women in a more "respectful manner."[136] As the group listened and sat in amazed silence, she described a particular conversation with him wherein she urged him to respect and regard her as a sister and nothing more. She also advised him on the benefits of contraception in preventing STDs. At that moment, it appeared that SPASDI's aim to transform these women into agents of social change had worked—for, without their intervention, would she have attempted to offer such words in the past?

Such optimism and self-satisfaction over this particular episode on respecting women were put under question when Masoumeh explained her opinions on modesty and morality. When I broached the subject of caring for one's body in relation to religious tenets, she responded,

> I'm religious, but a believer? To the first degree, the highest level? Yes, to the level that my hair should not be shown, or a man shouldn't see my waist [but] I'm not that strict. I'm also not so comfortable to uncover my neck in front of a *mard-e namahram*. I'm sensitive to my ankles . . . that men not see my legs. [I laugh, asking her why.] We think it's extremely inappropriate. We say if a man sees a woman's legs, it's like he's seeing your vagina. It makes no difference if a man sees either. [She laughs.] It's what we say. We say that from the ankles, he would understand what's going on up there and how it is. [She points to her groin.]

In addition to gender relations being clearly defined in her explanation, she discusses the role of women in preserving their modesty through their dress and movements, which should be observed and conducted in a multitasking manner. When walking down the street or praying, for instance, women should be clearly aware of their surroundings and especially of those who are looking at them. In fact, it is their responsibility to prevent being the center of attention.

Even though Masoumeh did not explicitly reference any religious sources for the connections she made between the ankle and the vagina, she implied that exposure of these body parts would result in the same offense: temptation and sin. This relationship is perhaps attributed to her acknowledgment of the Islamic concept on intimate bodily parts, known as *awrat*.[137] According to Shi'a understanding, the exposure of private parts, including women's bodies, save their faces and hands, is forbidden.[138] While Masoumeh engages *awrat* in her conceptualization of modesty and marital relations, she is also privileging her deference to her husband's expectations and observing *tamkin*. Hence, when she walked outside, she knew exactly what was at stake: In order to preserve her reputation and satisfy her husband, she should alter her dress, divert her eyes, and not seek out any illicit attention from the opposite sex. And to prevent other women from encountering a similar feeling of naked discomfort, she was instructing them to wear looser and longer clothing.

Evidently, Masoumeh internalized social norms and codes of morality that reveal a double standard between acceptable public behavior for men and women. It is worth noting that she did not advise that men, too, should look away—even though it is also religiously required for both sexes. Moreover, though she proudly spoke of sexual morality and modesty, and even of her efforts to discuss condom usage to a stranger, she did not mention any misgivings about her husband's failure to abide by the same advice. I quietly speculated if her contraction of HIV was the result of her husband's lack of respect for her as a woman, wife, and mother. For it was through his extramarital affairs and unprotected sexual relations that led to her becoming HIV-positive.

Closing Reflections

For this small albeit determined coterie of women, *Madaran* created a unique space for community-building and group support at the same time that it provided a respite from social isolation and ostracism. Just like many women around the globe, its members sought wider social acceptance and freedom from judgment. And like most people, they strove to remain healthy by having access to quality social and health services so that ultimately they could provide for their children and carry on with their lives. As demonstrated by the interviews of both Farah and Masoumeh, SPASDI's critical support had even encouraged some members to speak out, breaking taboos the moment they discussed sensitive issues like marital relations, sexuality, temporary marriage, poverty, and drug addiction, among others, in a titular Islamic Republic.

Though this interesting and rich material illuminates the highly complex and politically charged landscape in which a select group of HIV-positive women live and navigate, it offers only a preliminary glimpse and analysis of SPASDI's advocacy program turned social experiment whereby women living with HIV become agents of social change in the fight against AIDS. Yet the skepticism looms: suppose the government should adopt a similar program, would this unlikely group of social workers and HIV-educators radically impact sexual behavior? Would it force Iran's clerical authority to speak about the dangerous implications of *tamkin* in relation to HIV/AIDS, or even broach social realities underscoring the sexual promiscuity of married men?

Clearly SPASDI helps women cope and deal with their illness. However, the main intention of the center—to involve *Madaran* members in campaigns to educate the public about HIV/AIDS prevention and awareness and consequently initiate social change—has not yet materialized in transforming the discourse of the HIV/AIDS epidemic in Iran. As the interviews attest, many of the women, albeit loquacious when discussing marriage and modesty, had largely internalized government and religious ideology on gender roles, modesty, and morality, and had subsequently found temporary strategies to solve their own problems. Ensuring the health and well-being of their children, protecting their reputation, and staving off poverty were prioritized over SPASDI's aim to raise HIV-awareness, or even pressure the government to alter its public health policies. Hence for any radical change in HIV-awareness and prevention—one that is effective in the long term—the intervention from progressive legislation and support from authoritative Shi'a clerics are requisite. The latter, in particular, would have to address not only the importance of condom usage for HIV-positive spouses and also expanding the reasons supporting a woman's right to divorce (as they have in cases of a husband's drug use and impotence, for example) but also the notion of *tamkin*—by reconsidering if a woman's health should be endangered while sexually appeasing her husband.

CONCLUSION

This project commenced by boldly sidestepping certain markers of difference—principally, the oft-repeated assertion about grand ideological ruptures severing two consecutive government regimes in Iran. My aim was to inquire how scholarship of postrevolutionary Iran would transform if analyses centered instead on the continuity of gendered, social control and not its eruption or cessation in 1979. *Revolutionary Bodies* is intended to realize this objective, underscoring mutually compatible methods, concepts, and tools of discipline and enforcement related to sexuality that were similarly implemented throughout the revolutionary agendas of the Pahlavi and IRI regimes. What began as a curiosity about mutilated mannequins on an innocuous street in Tehran quickly developed into a larger exploration of the historical and conceptual regulation of Iranian women in general and female sexuality in particular in the last decades of the twentieth century until the first decade of the twenty-first. The flexibility in (patriarchal and Islamic discursive) interpretations of their simultaneous threat and allure has enabled the continuous structuring and restructuring of Iran's social policy and cultural reform agenda under two government regimes. Through it all, there was heavy investment in transforming gender, sex, and self; further, the technologies of discipline and reform were at times indistinguishable from one another during these consecutive periods.

So as to think expansively about the massive social engineering projects orchestrated and implemented by state apparatuses, much of the book's analysis is anchored to Valentine's articulation of bodily technologies, be they *Zan-e Rouz* magazine of the imperial Pahlavi, or chastity and modesty campaigns of the Islamic Republic. I entered a conceptual and historically situated tapestry of sorts, woven over five unique sites that bridged together Pahlavi-era state regulations to those of the cleric-led Islamic Republic. Individual chapters on a popular women's weekly, former red-light district *Shahr-e No*, temporary marriage or *sigheh*, public artworks depicting women, and a nongovernmental HIV-AIDS organization in Tehran demonstrate how bodily technologies act as pivots and points of departure for how clerics, the media, governmental bodies such as the Supreme Council for the Cultural Revolution, as well as other political and social actors, facilitate the sexual and social control of Iranian men and women. In most of these sites, disciplining "deviant" or "immoral" women by demanding their reform was one of the ways through which states sought to regain their authority and propose ideal societies for their publics. In others, regulation had taken the form of spatial cleansing and compulsory forgetting.

Evidently, the very methods employed to promote reform among women were used to restrict certain expressions and ways of living. Specific social and political identities were subdued through the outlining of normative and religiously and/or socially acceptable behaviors and appearances, separating from this ilk those considered deviant, backward, and/or morally reprehensible. In seeking the emancipation of its female citizens, Pahlavi reformers translated political and social liberation as the improving and refashioning of Iranian women's behavior, dress, social interactions, physical appearance, and pastimes. With Queen Farah Pahlavi at the helm of this effort, the project of cultivating a "modern" woman's desires had found its human embodiment to promote them—in the figure of a sophisticated and fashionable Iranian queen who traveled the globe and, in more quiet moments, read books to her children. Although educational reforms were part of the modernization program, they were sidelined in the face of the growing influence of popular women's magazines and television—emerging giants within Iran's mediascape that helped advertise desires, both consumer and sexual, to a broader audience. After 1979, supporters of Ayatollah Khomeini working within both industries slightly changed course; co-opting the rhetoric of reform from the previous regime, they began to encourage piety, motherhood, and revolutionary Islamic values for the modern Iranian woman. Promoting family values ground in Islamic discourse, they reinforced a model Islamic character of womanhood and motherhood, encouraging women to embrace a somewhat unrealistic and inaccessible gendered, religious, and political identity. Almost four decades later, the government ideology on gender roles, modesty, and morality has had lasting, at times detrimental, results, especially for Iranian women living on the margins whose exclusion is generally accepted as a default.

In this study, there are also clear mutations of these disciplinary technologies, recoded and revamped into ideological character prototypes and promoted as positive values. Though when praxis and statistical data have illuminated their contradictions in the postrevolutionary period, assertions about the necessity and relevance of these values ring hollow. While focusing on the intricate manner of their implementation, in particular, sociocultural spaces, other mini-narratives and discourses emerged, interlinking matters of public space, gender, sexuality, marriage, and public health. Through this resurfacing, there were discernible grey areas, speaking to formerly untold and peculiar collaborations between state bodies and the advertising industry and the global sex trade, among others. In the latter instance, when investigating Iran's prostitution policy during consecutive administrations, the tacit acceptance of the sexual exploitation of women—and its necessity for societal cohesion and male heterosexual release in both popular and state discourses—was undeniable. Official and clerical remonstrations to the contrary were never sufficient erasers of the sociohistorical narratives and sociological data illustrating that it was often impoverished and marginalized women who were left with very few options but to become *sigheh* for their economic survival. Think back to the development of Tehran's Razi Park leisure and educational compound: by constructing and advertising ahistorical narratives about this idyllic family gathering space, the postrevolutionary state concealed and denied certain age-old practices and asymmetrical power structures that once clamored so distinctly in the former red-light district. And so, unironically, decades after the latter's destruction, the reverberations of reviving "deviant" norms were being felt and observed on that site, reconstituted every time money was exchanged for (sexual) pleasure.

Iranian women continue to be uniquely positioned as both human bookends and conceptual targets of two revolutions—one, in the 1960s, pushing forward Iran's modern and Western reform; the other, since the 1980s, demanding a return to morality and religion. Iran's state reform agendas are united by hegemonic conceptualizations that posit women as boundary-making objects of the nation-state and naturally receptive to reform, guidance, and discipline from above. That they are expected to fall in line with such measures has endured to the present; since 2009 bursts of public demonstrations, campaigns, and violence on the ground and online suggest that reception will always be like tumbling back and forth down a two-way street. Perhaps the motivations behind many of these measures stemmed from earnest desires to pry open an ostensible "better life," to ameliorate that which was considered "backward" and unrefined, or to reset what had morally gone astray. Debates on the intentions and outcomes will persist in perpetuity, though lingering throughout is the question, was it worth it?

NOTES

Introduction

1 Documentary filmmaker Firouzeh Khosrovani had coined the disfigurement of mannequins in Tehran's storefronts as a "rough cut." *Rough Cut*, directed by Firouzeh Khosrovani (Tehran: n.p. 2007). See Nina Power, "Mannequins, Manners, and Mutilation," *Cabinet Magazine* 301 (Summer 2008): pp. 21–5; Fatemeh Sadeghi, "Foot Soldiers of the Islamic Republic's 'Culture of Modesty,'" *Middle East Report*, no. 250, The Islamic Revolution at 30 (Spring 2009), pp. 50–5.

2 No longer were guidance authorities *Gasht-e Ershad* surveilling public spaces for signs of public impropriety. During springtime, when rising temperatures translated into people wearing thinner layers of clothing and exposing more skin, the presence of plainclothes forces hanging around city intersections and stationed at the entrance of malls and major parks was expected. (For many Iranians, this meant bypassing such areas and pursuing alternate pathways and entrances.) Clearly, their hanging around such spaces was meant to remind denizens that flouting compulsory *hejab* and modesty ordinances would not be tolerated.

3 See Firoozeh Kashani-Sabet, *Frontier Fictions: Shaping the Iranian Nation, 1804–1946* (Princeton: Princeton University Press, 1999); Camron Michael Amin, "Selling and Saving 'Mother Iran': Gender and the Iranian Press in the 1940s," *International Journal of Middle East Studies* 33 (2001): pp. 335–61.

4 Ashraf Zahedi, "Contested Meaning of the Veil and Political Ideologies of Iranian Regimes," *Journal of Middle East Women's Studies* 3, no. 3 (Fall 2007): p. 90.

5 Payam-e Nur Majaleh, "*Farhang-e Efaf va Hejab; Rah-e Kar Nahadinehsazi, Gostaresh va Hefz-e Bavarha-ye Diny*," Hawzeh online, July–August 207, no. 184 and 185, accessed September 2, 2019, http://www.hawzah.net/fa/Magazine/View/3992/5197/47614.

6 See Ervand Abrahamian, *Iran between Two Revolutions* (Princeton: Princeton University Press, 1982); Asef Bayat, *Street Politics: Poor People's Movements in Iran* (New York: Columbia University Press, 1997); Kashani-Sabet (2011); Ali Ansari, *Iran under Ahmadinejad: The Politics of Confrontation* (Abingdon: Routledge, 2007) and *Iran, Islam and Democracy: The Politics of Managing Change* (London: Chatham House, 2006); Saïd Amir Arjomand, *After Khomeini: Iran under His Successors* (Oxford: Oxford University Press, 2009) and *The Turban for the Crown: The Islamic Revolution in Iran* (New York: Oxford University Press, 1988); Paidar, *Women and the Political Process in Twentieth-Century Iran* (Cambridge: Cambridge University Press, 1997); Nikki Keddie and Yann Richard, *Modern Iran: Roots and Results of Revolution* (New Haven: Yale University Press, 2003); Ziba Mir-Hosseini, *Islam and Gender: The Religious Debate in Contemporary Iran* (Princeton: Princeton University Press, 1999); and Hamid Dabashi, *Theology of Discontent: The Ideological Foundation of the Islamic Revolution in Iran* (New Brunswick: Transaction Publishers, 2006) and *Iran: A People Interrupted* (New York: New Press, 2008).

7   See Arjomand, *The Turban for the Crown*; Arjomand , *After Khomeini*; Dabashi, *Theology of Discontent*; Mir-Hosseini, *Islam and Gender*.

8   See also Misagh Parsa, *Social Origins of the Iranian Revolution* (New Brunswick: Rutgers University Press, 1989).

9   See Minoo Moallem, *Between Warrior Brother and Veiled Sister: Islamic Fundamentalism and the Politics of Patriarchy in Iran* (Berkeley: University of California, 2005); Valentine Moghadam, *Modernizing Women: Gender and Social Change in the Middle East* (Boulder: Lynne Rienner Publishers, Inc., 2003); Haleh Esfandiari, *Reconstructed Lives: Women & Iran's Islamic Revolution* (Baltimore: Johns Hopkins University Press, 1997).

10 See Janet Afary, *Sexual Politics in Modern Iran* (Cambridge: Cambridge University Press, 2009); Moallem, *Between Warrior Brother and Veiled Sister*; Moghadam, *Between Warrior Brother and Veiled Sister*; Hamideh Sedghi, *Women and Politics in Iran: Veiling, Unveiling, and Reveiling* (Cambridge: Cambridge University Press, 2007).

11 See Moghadam, *Modernizing Women*; Farzaneh Milani, *Veiling and Words: The Emerging Voices of Iranian Women Writers* (Syracuse: Syracuse University Press, 1992); Zahedi, "Contested Meaning of the Veil and Political Ideologies of Iranian Regimes," pp. 75–98.

12 See Afsaneh Najmabadi, *Women with Mustaches and Men without Beards: Gender and Sexual Anxieties of Iranian Modernity* (Berkeley: University of California, 2005). See also Mir-Hosseini, *Islam and Gender*; Ziba Mir-Hosseini, *Marriage on Trial: A Study of Islamic Family Law* (London: I.B. Tauris, 2000), pp. 72–83; Moallem, *Between Warrior Brother and Veiled Sister*; and Shireen Mahdavi, "Women and the Shii *Ulama* in Iran Author," *Middle Eastern Studies* 19, no. 1 (January 1983): p. 18.

13 See Najmabadi, *Women with Mustaches and Men without Beards*.

14 In the last section of this piece, on the study of gender politics of the Islamic Republic, Afary discusses the formation of Islamist women's movements and the emergence of "Islamic feminism" in reaction to stringent restrictions imposed by hard-line clerics. She surmises that through women's activism, press, and writings, new debates about their legal rights and status emerge, culminating in shifting gender roles and the pushing of traditional social limits. See Afary, *Sexual Politics in Modern Iran*.

15 See Kathryn Babayan and Afsaneh Najmabadi, eds., *Islamicate Sexualities: Translations across Temporal Geographies of Desire* (Boston: President and Fellows of Harvard College, 2008), Preface. See also Joseph Massad, *Desiring Arabs* (Chicago: University of Press, 2007).

   Hamid Dabashi has done seminal research on Iranian modern artist Shirin Neshat. See Hamid Dabashi, "Shirin Neshat: Transcending the Boundaries of an Imaginative Geography" in *The Last Word*, ed. Octavio Zaya (San Sebastian, Spain: Museum of Modern Art, 2005). He has also written about the figure of woman in postrevolutionary cinema as a site of contestation between "a metaphysics of concealment and an aesthetics of revelation." See Hamid Dabashi, "Body-less Faces: Mutilating Modernity and Abstracting Women in an 'Islamic Cinema,'" *Visual Anthropology* 10, no. 2 (1998): pp. 361–80. Per the subjects of female sexuality, marriage, and divorce in Iran, the works of both Mir-Hosseini and Shahla Haeri are some of the best analyses on these topics from the perspective of Islamic jurisprudence and civil and penal laws. See Shahla Haeri, *Law of Desire: Temporary Marriage in Iran* (London: I.B. Tauris & Co Ltd, 1989); Mir-Hosseini, *Islam and*

Gender; and Ziba Mir-Hosseini, *Marriage on Trial: A Study of Islamic Family Law* (London: I.B. Tauris, 2000).

16 See Babayan and Najmabadi, *Islamicate Sexualities*; and Massad, *Desiring Arabs*.

17 Babayan and Najmabadi, *Islamicate Sexualities*, p. 3.

18 Ibid., Preface.

19 See Massad, *Desiring Arabs*.

20 See Hammed Shahidian, "Contesting Discourses of Sexuality in Post-Revolutionary Iran," in *Deconstructing Sexuality in the Middle East: Challenges and Discourses*, ed. Pinar Ilkkaracan (Aldershot: Routledge, 2008), pp. 80–106.

21 See Kamran Talattof, *Modernity, Sexuality and Ideology in Iran: The Life and Legacy of Popular Iranian Female Artists* (Syracuse: Syracuse University Press, 2011).

22 See *Sexuality in Muslim Contexts: Restrictions and Resistance*, ed. Anissa Helie and Homa Hoodfar (London: Zed Books, 2012).

23 After the establishment of the Islamic Republic, *mut'a* was advocated as "evidence of Islamic understanding and foresight on matters of human sexuality." Haeri, *Law of Desire*, p. 6.

24 Ibid., p. 26.

25 So foundational is this work, that Fatemeh Sadeghi, a political scientist and denizen of Tehran, incorporates Haeri's discussion of the different kinds of *sigheh* arrangements to bolster her arguments on shifting sexuality discourse of young urban Iranian women in 2006.

26 See Roxanne Varzi, *Warring Souls: Youth, Media, and Martyrdom in Post-Revolution Iran* (Durham: Duke University Press, 2006); Pardis Mahdavi, *Passionate Uprisings* (Stanford: Stanford University Press, 2009); Shirin Saeidi, "Hero of Her Own Story: Gender and State Formation in Contemporary Iran" (PhD diss., Cambridge University, 2011).

27 Afsaneh Najmabadi, *Professing Selves: Transsexuality and Same-Sex Desire in Contemporary Iran* (Durham, NC: Duke University Press, 2014), p. 4.

28 Mahdavi, *Passionate Uprisings*, p. 3.

29 Professor of anthropology Soheila Shashahani is also credited for her work on representations of the body in addition to her ethnographic contributions of nomadic tribes in Iran, examining issues such as sexual division of labor. Shirin Ahmadnia is a professor of sociology who writes extensively on social problems in Iran, yet does not situate these issues within the paradigm of modernization theories of tradition versus modernity. See Soheila Shahshahani, "History of Anthropology in Iran," *Iranian Studies* 19, no. 1 (Winter 1986): pp. 65–86. See also Shahshahani, "Body as a Means of Non-Verbal Communication in Iran," *International Journal of Modern Anthropology*, Thought Short Report, 1 (2008): pp. 65–81.

30 I discuss this topic in Chapter 5.

31 See Fatemeh Sadeghi, "Negotiating with Modernity," *Comparative Studies of South Asia, Africa and the Middle East* 28, no. 2 (2008): pp. 250–9.

32 Ibid., p. 254.

33 Ibid.

34 Ibid., pp. 253–4.

35 Haeri, *Law of Desire*, p. 70.

36 Bernstein, Elizabeth and Laurie Schaffner, *Regulating Sex: The Politics of Intimacy and Identity* (New York: Routledge, 2005), p. xiii.

37 Ibid.

38 These values are outlined in the Preamble and "General Principles" sections of Iran's Constitution, specifically the first four articles. See Islamic Republic of Iran Constitution, amended July 28, 1989.

39 See *Islamic Republic of Iran Constitution*, Article 3.

40 Saeed Rahnema and Haideh Moghissi, "Clerical Oligarchy and the Question of 'Democracy' in Iran," Iran Chamber, 2001, accessed December 4, 2019, http://www .iranchamber.com/government/articles/clerical_oligarchy_democracy_iran.php.

41 Zohreh T. Sullivan explains,

> Gradually, as evidenced by the writings of Khomeini and Motahari, all differences withered into a single truth: the only acceptable woman in the Islamic state was the Muslim woman who was the "pillar of family," and who abided by all the laws laid down in the *shari'a*, who would accept the misogynist gender coding prescribed for her by the new government's version of Islam. See Zohreh T. Sullivan, "Eluding the Feminist, Overthrowing the Modern? Transformations in Twentieth-Century Iran," in *Remaking Women: Feminism and Modernity in the Middle East*, p. 233.

42 See Marnia Lazreg, "Feminism and Difference: The Perils of Writing as a Woman on Women in Algeria," *Feminist Studies* 14, no. 1 (Spring 1988): pp. 81–107.

43 Gill Valentine, *Social Geographies: Space and Society* (Essex: Pearson Education Ltd., 2001), p. 45.

44 Ibid.

45 Shannon Bell, *Reading, Writing, and Rewriting the Prostitute Body* (Bloomington: Indiana University Press, 1994), p. 2.

Chapter 1

1 Ronald Inglehart and Wayne E. Baker, "Modernization, Cultural Change, and the Persistence of Traditional Values," *American Sociological Review* 65, no. 1, Looking Forward, Looking Back: Continuity and Change at the Turn of the Millennium (February 2000): p. 19.

2 Annabelle Sreberny-Mohammadi and Ali Mohammadi, "Small Media for a Big Revolution: Iran," *International Journal of Politics, Culture, and Society* 3, no. 3, The Sociology of Culture (Spring 1990): p. 344.

3 *Zan-e Rouz* was not Iran's first women's magazine. By the time it launched, the women and girl's magazine *Ettela'at-e Banuvan* was already in circulation, published by the *Ettela'at* publishing house from March 1965 to April 1979. There is a century-old history of the publication of Iranian women's journals and newspapers that began in the early twentieth century. While the Iranian state had yet to channel its resources toward girls' education and raising female literacy rates—girls' education did not begin until 1918—wives of the Iranian elite began taking matters into their own hands. In 1910, the wife of a doctor published Iran's first women's newspaper, *Danesh* (Knowledge). They established girl-only schools, and began advertising the schools' openings in magazines specializing in women's issues. These publications catering to women audiences came on the heel of the Constitutional Revolution, marking the entrance of women's voices into political discourse. This period saw the publications of newspapers that soon became subscription-based journals. *Zaban-e zanan* (Mouthpiece of Women), founded by Sediqyeh Dowlatabadi, jumped

right into debates on trade agreements between Great Britain and Iran, *hejab*, and women's suffrage. Soon, *Jahan-e Zanan, Alam-e Nesvan, Jamiyat-e Nesvan*, and *Nameh-ye Banovan-e Iran* entered the world of print journalism, especially after Iran fell under the political control of Reza Shah. In these papers, constitutionalism was less discussed and instead, issues that appealed to women among the provinces increased. Journals began publishing short stories, discussing educational systems and midwifery programs found abroad, and highlighted topics considered gender-specific to women—such as child marriage and legal status. See Amin, "Selling and Saving 'Mother Iran,'" pp. 335–61.

4   Amir Taheri, "The Grand Old Man of Iranian Press Passes Away in America," Asharq alawsat, December 14, 2006, accessed October 4, 2011, http://www.asharq-e.com/news.asp?section=7&id=7333. *Kayhan* was launched between 1942 and 1943. Its former chief-editor Amir Taheri remarked, "Mesbahzadeh was a passionate technophile, always looking for new ways of doing things. Thanks to that passion, in 1974 *Kayhan* became one of the first three newspapers in the world to introduce electronic composition, four colour printing, and satellite transmission of news photos. In many areas of press technology, *Kayhan* was a decade ahead of leading American and European newspapers. Having installed the most advanced printing presses in the country, *Kayhan* managed to win large contracts for producing school textbooks along with dozens of magazines issued by various government departments." Ibid.

5   "*Bonyangozar-e Kayhan Dargozasht/Kayhan* Titan Passes Away," BBC Persian, November 11, 2006, accessed December 4, 2019, http://www.bbc.co.uk/persian/arts/story/2006/11/061125_mf_mesbahzadeh.shtml.

Mostafa Mesbahzadeh was the publisher and editor in chief, and Amir Taheri replaced him up until 1979, when *Kayhan* formed a new editorial board under the Islamic Republic. The establishment of *Zan-e Rouz* is closely tied to the success Mesbahzadeh was able to achieve in publishing *Kayhan*. Mesbahzadeh is quoted as having said, "We had created a space of freedom when the nation needed it." At his side was the political mentor Abdul-Rahman Faramarzi, an established lawyer and journalist, who took on various advisory and editorial roles while also financing the *Kayhan* project. Mesbahzadeh also turned to friends within the Pahlavi regime—a young Muhammad Reza Pahlavi is reported to have donated approximately $50,000.00 he borrowed from Queen mother to finance this venture. See Taheri, "The Grand Old Man of Iranian Press Passes Away in America."

6   See Haleh Esfandiari, *My Prison, My Home: One Woman's Story of Captivity in Iran* (New York: HarperCollins, 2009), pp. 39–40. During the 1970s, many of *Kayhan*'s employees were *Tudeh* members, including the deputy editor-in-chief. According to Haleh Esfandiari's memoirs, during the 1970s when state censorship had increased, Mesbahzadeh became protective of his staff of editors and journalists. They were under surveillance by the Shah's secret police SAVAK (*Sazeman-e Ettela'at va Amniyat-e Keshvar*), which had its own censorship office. Mesbahzadeh assisted jailed reporters by paying the salaries of fired journalists. In certain cases, he reemployed them under assumed names.

7   *Kayhan* was one of two leading newspapers reporting on world news, along with *Ettela'at*, which is Iran's oldest newspaper since 1926 and still in circulation. See Shahpour Ghasemi, "*Kayhan* Newspaper," Iran Chamber Society, 2006, accessed December 4, 2019, http://www.iranchamber.com/media/articles/*Kayhan*_newspaper.php.

8   See Sreberny-Mohammadi and Mohammadi, "Small Media for a Big Revolution: Iran," pp. 341–71.

9   Ghasemi, "*Kayhan* Newspaper."

10   Ibid.

11   Taheri, "The Grand Old Man of Iranian Press Passes Away in America."

12   *Kayhan*, October 4, 1958. Quote in Sreberny-Mohammadi and Mohammadi, *Small Media Big Revolution*, p. 87. "If the origins of Iranian radio lie initially in military control and later as an instrument of political hegemony, television began as private entrepreneurship, a classic multiplier of consumerist modernity, and was only later taken over by the state as an instrument of its modernization project. To discuss the development of television in Iran adequately, it is necessary to describe in more detail the advent of Muhammad Reza Shah to power and the developmentalist orientation that his state would pursue. But first came a hiatus in the strong state, which allowed an opposition to develop." Ibid., p 79.

13   Sreberny-Mohammadi and Mohammadi, *Small Media, Big Revolution*, p. 63.

14   Ibid. The shah's emphasis on improving "social knowledge" was first published in *Kayhan*, October 4, 1958. The comment was made during a public speech when he praised television broadcasting as a way to train the youth and improve social knowledge; the training details and definition of "social knowledge" were not made explicit.

15   For example, a parliamentary bill permitted a former RCA television representative to establish a television broadcast center based in Tehran, staffed by American directors and an Iranian staff. 1958 marked the inaugural year of this private television system, in which American-formatted programming was initially broadcast. Years later, regional television centers opened up in specialized locations throughout Iran, such as Abadan and Esfahan, cities known for their economic potential and foreign communities and where advertising could be rather lucrative. The government soon got involved, taking over Sabet Pasal's television monopoly and in 1966, Radio Television Melli Iran commenced broadcasting, the first time a national television network was established. See Ibid., pp. 61–7.

16   Esfandiari, *My Prison, My Home*, p. 39.

17   Ibid.

18   Marita Sturken and Lisa Cartwright, *Practices of Looking: An Introduction to Visual Culture* (Oxford: Oxford University Press, 2001), p. 189.

19   See *Zan-e Rouz*, Issue 1 (1344/1965).

20   Articles on beauty regimen included maintaining the right hairstyles specific to the shape of one's face and changing one's hair color according to European trends and *Vogue* magazine fashion advice. See *Zan-e Rouz*, Issue 597 (2535/1977), pp. 12–13.

21   *Zan-e Rouz*, Issue 657 (2536/1978), p. 91.

22   Ibid., pp. 20–1. In one section in particular, an Austrian hairdresser informs readers how to apply makeup on faces that possess short noses, broad chins, chubby faces, to name a few.

23   See Camron Michael Amin, *The Making of the Modern Iranian Women: Gender, State Policy and Popular Culture, 1865–1946* (Gainesville: University Press of Florida, 2002).

24   The 1968 coronation ceremony of Muhammad Reza Shah was near Shiraz, Iran— at Persepolis, the ancient capital of the Achaemenid Empire (550–330 BCE). World leaders convened in Persepolis for an ornate celebration of the 2500-year

anniversary of Persian monarchy. See Dabashi, *Iran: A People Interrupted*, p. 147. For Ayatollah Khomeini's criticism of the event, see Dabashi, *Theology of Discontent*, pp. 451–2.

25 See Houshang Chehabi, *Iranian Politics and Religious Modernism: The Liberation Movement of Iran under the Shah and Khomeini* (Ithaca: Cornell University Press, 1990); Mohammad Gholi Majd, *Resistance to the Shah: Landowners and Ulama in Iran* (Gainesville: University Press of Florida, 2000).

26 Ervand Abrahamian, *A History of Modern Iran* (Cambridge: Cambridge University Press, 2008), p. 131.

27 Paidar, *Women and the Political Process in Twentieth-Century Iran*, p. 149.

28 *Zan-e Rouz*, Issue 1 (1344/1965) "Introduction."

29 For example, by the second issue, a green-eyed model features on the cover page and is dressed in Western-looking clothing. The edition also has a section on the English rock band, the Beatles. See *Zan-e Rouz*, Issue 2.

30 Figure 1.2 is taken from a post on a Facebook fan page dedicated to Farah Pahlavi, entitled "Her Majesty Farah Pahlavi." The original source and photographer are unknown. See "Her Majesty Farah Pahlavi," Facebook, October 1, 2012, accessed April 15, 2019. https://www.facebook.com/pg/Her-Majesty-Farah-Pahlavi-128183 343902418/posts/.

31 In Figure 1.2, although there is a television in partial-view in the setting's background, the most pronounced details remain in the foreground, of the queen and her children.

32 Ibid., p. 26.

33 See Pierre Bourdieu, *Photography: A Middle-Brow Art*, trans. Shaun Whiteside (Stanford: Stanford University Press, 1990).

34 Sreberny-Mohammadi and Mohammadi, "Small Media for a Big Revolution," pp. 344–5.

35 See Ibid., p. 62. At the time, owning a television was an extraordinary event that typically Iran's establishment experienced. Television imports to Iran did not begin until 1958. Consumer demand for television sets jump-started in the 1950s, with the efforts of entrepreneurial businessman Habibollah Sabet Pasal, who, along with his Harvard-educated son, represented RCA in Iran. Selling receivers to Tehran's elite, he also sold television advertisements to local businessmen, establishing a privatized television system and, what some have argued, had its own "built-in modernizing potential."

36 The term "souvenir" is being used in the same manner as Bourdieu, when he describes the "festive moments" as reminders of cultural, religious, or holiday events; they authenticate past experiences and reinforce nostalgia. Bourdieu, *Photography: A Middle-brow Art*, p. 21.

37 For explication of the Iranian upper class and the overall politics of uneven socioeconomic development in Pahlavi Iran, see Abrahamian, *Iran Between Two Revolutions*, especially chapter 9, "The Politics of Uneven Development," pp. 432–5.

38 *Zan-e Rouz*, Issue 597 (2535/1977), pp. 8–9.

39 This column would only run for eight issues, set in a question and answer style format in which the interviewees' photographs were displayed on the very top of the magazine page and answers to questions such as "What is important to you? School? Money? or Love?" were presented underneath each woman's photograph. It is noteworthy that none of the women were pictured wearing veils. This is presumably

because they were not interviewed and/or were not sought out; one can only speculate. See *Zan-e Rouz*, Issue 1 (1344/1965), pp. 32–3.

40 Ibid.

41 *Zan-e Rouz*, Issue 595 (2535/1976): p. 22.

42 The article highlights the fasting rituals in "Rome, India, China, and even among Native Americans in the United States." It also informs the reader that just as Jesus Christ had fasted for forty days and nights prior to his death, Christians followed his guide; so, too, did Muslims "throughout the world, during the month of Ramadan" in recognition of the Prophet's fasting. The author also praises the copious benefits to withholding food.

43 The author insists that fasting may achieve a youthful glow, without the usage of expensive hormone treatments and plastic surgery.

44 A *chador* is a traditional Iranian garment; it is a long cloak covering a woman's body from head to ankle. The color black is often associated with the *chador*, although it comes in a variety of colors. It is considered a conservative method of veiling. See Paidar, *Women and the Political Process in Twentieth-Century Iran*, p. 215.

45 *Zan-e Rouz*, Issue 638 (2536/1978), p. 24.

46 *Zan-e Rouz*, Issue 597 (2535/1977), pp. 12–13.

47 In my interviews with Iranian women above the age of fifty (which I discuss in Chapter 5), the majority remembered that during their adolescence and young adulthood, they would not purchase ready-made bras and undergarments. They instead preferred to seek the services of a local seamstress to sew them customized brassieres. Purchasing imported undergarments was not common, they claimed.

48 *Zan-e Rouz*, Issue 1 (1344/1965). A section on improving homemaking skills featured in *Zan-e Rouz*'s very first issue.

49 "*Chehreh-ye Penhani va Seri-ye Shoma: Az Posht-e Cigar*," *Zan-e Rouz*, Issue 599 (Aban 2535/November 1976), pp. 18–19. This title roughly translates to "[Getting to Know] Your Hidden and Secret Face: From the Back of a Cigarette."

50 For example, if held in an upright position, this means that the person should be viewed as weak and having a nervous character. In another example, when the cigarette is held in between the pointer finger and thumb, this means that the person is considered unreliable. *Zan-e Rouz*, Issue 559 (Aban 2535/November 1976), p. 18.

51 Iran banned smoking scenes in film and television productions in 2011. Deputy director of the Islamic Republic of Iran Broadcasting (IRIB) urged managing directors of TV stations and film directors to emphasize the health setbacks of smoking. "IRIB Bans Smoking Scenes in Iranian Productions," *Mehr News*, May 1, 2011, accessed September 18, 2011, http://www.mehrnews.com/en/newsdetail.as px?NewsID=1226049.

52 Allan M. Brandt wrote a fascinating article on the recruitment of women to cigarette smoking in the first half of the twentieth century, when the cigarette was marketed as appealing to women and served "as a symbol for both feminists and flappers." See Allan M. Brandt, "Recruiting Women Smokers: The Engineering of Consent," *Journal of the American Medical Women's Association* 51, no. 1–2 (1996): pp. 63–6.

53 *Zan-e Rouz*, Issue 681 (Khordad 2537/June 1978), p. 22.

54 Abrahamian, *Iran between Two Revolutions*, p. 436. The Pahlavis had vast wealth, partly owning two machine tool factories, two car plants, two brick-manufacturing companies, three mining firms, three textile mills, and four construction companies. A nephew, Prince Shahram, was a "majority shareholder in eight large companies

that specialized in construction, insurance, cement, textiles, and transport." See Abrahamian, *Iran between Two Revolutions*, p. 437.

55 Ibid., p. 447.
56 Ibid., p. 446.
57 Paidar, p. 147.
58 See Shirin Deylami, "In the Face of the Machine: *Westoxification*, Cultural Globalization, and the Making of an Alternative Global Modernity," *Polity* 43 (2011): pp. 242–63.
59 See Roy Mottahedeh, *The Mantle of the Prophet: Religion and Politics in Iran* (Oxford: One World, 2000), p. 296. Other translations of *gharbzadegi* are "west-struckeness," "westitis," "Occidentosis," and "Euromania." The term "westoxified" is translated from the Persian adjective *gharbzadeh*, a descriptive term for a person, culture, and identity that has become stricken by Western exploitation, consumerism, and cultural hegemony. Although he did not coin the term, the concept was made popular by modernist writer and intellectual Jalal Al-e Ahmad. According to Said Arjomand, Al-e Ahmad borrowed the terminology from his mentor, a philosophy professor at the University of Tehran, Sayyid Ahmad Fardid. See Arjomand, *After Khomeini*, p. 73.
60 Valentine Moghadam, "Revolution, the State, Islam, and Women: Gender Politics in Iran and Afghanistan," *Social Text* 22 (Spring 1989): p. 45.
61 Afsaneh Najmabadi, "Hazards of Modernity and Morality: Women, State and Ideology in Contemporary Iran," in *Women, Islam, and the State*, ed. Deniz Kandiyoti (Philadelphia: Temple University Press, 1991), pp. 65.
62 Ervand Abrahamian, *A Modern History of Iran* (Cambridge: Cambridge University Press, 2008), p. xvii.
63 Paidar, *Women and the Political Process in Twentieth-Century Iran*, p. 168. Quoted in Najmabadi, "Hazards of Modernity and Morality: Women, State and Ideology in Contemporary Iran," pp. 65–6.
64 Shirin Sedigh Deylami, "Strangers Among Us: The Critique of Westoxification in Perso-Islamic Political Thought" (PhD diss., University of Minnesota, 2008), p. 50.
65 Although Ayatollah Motahhari (1920–79) was assassinated in 1979, he is considered the chief ideologue of Islamist groups in the revolution. He forged a friendship with Ayatollah Khomeini in the mid-1940s until his death. Khomeini referred to him as "The fruit of my life" at his funeral. See Dabashi, *Theology of Discontent*, p. 150. In the early 1960s and 1970s he became a prolific writer, penning *The Structure of Women's Rights in Islam* (1978) and a work for which he is most well-known, *Causes of Attraction to Materialism* in 1969, wherein he attacks Iranian secular intellectuals and begins to lodge a defense against Marxism. His writings were widely read during the revolutionary period. See Dabashi, *Theology of Discontent*, chapter 3.
66 Paidar, *Women and the Political Process in Twentieth-Century Iran*, p. 209.
67 Paidar observes that the leadership of the anti-Shah movement was fluid and unpredictable, whereby what was initially a revolutionary movement initiated by a small group of secular intellectuals developed into a diverse network of secular and religious members and ultimately by the summer of 1978 narrowed down to the leadership of Ayatollah Khomeini as the highest authority of this movement. See Ibid., pp. 198–200. For more on the diverse anti-Shah opposition and leadership, see Abrahamian, *A History of Modern Iran*; Arjomand, *The Turban for the Crown*; and Dabashi, *Theology of Discontent*.

68   See Paidar, pp. 224–33. As an example of scholars who concentrate on economic
      and cultural disruptions initiated by the revolution, see Farhad Nu'mani and Sohrab
      Behdad, *Class and Labor in Iran: Did the Revolution Matter?* (Syracuse: Syracuse
      University Press, 2006), p. 191. Ali Mirsepassi notes that a "generation of Western
      scholars" has interpreted the Iranian Revolution as "backward looking," in the
      framework of the French and British revolutions that are interpreted instead as
      breaking points between modernity and tradition. See Ali Mirsepassi, *Political Islam,
      Iran, and the Enlightenment: Philosophies of Hope and Despair* (London: Cambridge
      University Press, 2011), p. 164.

69   Ziba Mir-Hosseini, "The Conservative: Reformist Conflict over Women's Rights in
      Iran," *International Journal of Politics, Culture, and Society* 16, no. 1 (Fall 2002): p. 41.

70   Paidar, *Women and the Political Process in Twentieth-Century Iran,* p. 214.

71   Ibid., p. 231.

72   Kashani-Sabet, *Frontier Fictions*; Amin, "Selling and Saving 'Mother Iran.'"

73   See Mehrangiz Kar, "The Invasion of the Private Sphere in Iran," *Social Research* 70,
      no. 3 (Fall 2003): pp. 829–36.

74   Ibid. Quoted in Ali Reza Nobari, *Iran Experts* (Stanford: Stanford University Press,
      Iran America Documentation Group, 1978), p. 13.

75   Valentine M. Moghadam, "Gender and Revolutionary Transformation: Iran
      1979 and East Central Europe 1989," *Gender and Society* 9, no. 3 (June 1995):
      p. 342.

76   "Preamble," *Constitution of Islamic Republic of Iran.* For information on Khomeini's
      unique appropriation of Shi'i concepts and borrowed ideas from Third World
      populism, see Ervand Abrahamian, *Khomeinism: Essays on the Islamic Republic*
      (Berkeley: University of California Press, 1993), p. 17. After the overthrow of the
      monarchy, a national referendum on the question "Islamic Republic: Yes or No?"
      was held in March 1979. Almost 98 percent responded "yes," even though the ballot
      did not explain the definition of the terminology "Islamic Republic."

77   See Lois Beck and Guity Nashat, eds. *Women in Iran from 1800 to the Islamic
      Republic* (Champaign: University of Illinois Press, 2004); Parvin Paidar, *Women and
      the Political Process in Twentieth Century Iran*; Haleh Esfandiari, *Reconstructed Lives:
      Women and Iran's Islamic Revolution* (Baltimore: Johns Hopkins University Press,
      1997); Mahnaz Afkhami and Erika Friedl, eds., *In the Eye of the Storm: Women in
      Post-revolutionary Iran* (Syracuse: Syracuse University Press, 1994).

78   Arjomand, *After Khomeini*, pp. 22–3.

79   I explore the topic of public morality in greater detail in Chapter 4. At this point, I
      concentrate on contextualizing and analyzing the visual representation of a modest
      Muslim female character in postrevolutionary *Zan-e Rouz* editions.

80   For discussion on Khomeini's suspicions of the international press, see Sreberny-
      Mohammadi and Mohammadi, *Small Media, Big Revolution*, p. 134. Of Iran's
      domestic media, Khomeini wrote, "I have seen a number of them engaged in
      implementing the evil designs of the right or the left, most unjustly, in Iran . . . I
      hope that they will engage in service to God and the people." Ruhollah Khomeini,
      "We Shall Confront the World with Our Ideology," *MERIP Reports*, no. 88, Iran's
      Revolution: The First Year (June 1980): p. 25.

81   "Women in the Constitution," Preamble, *Islamic Republic of Iran Constitution*,
      adopted October 24, 1979, amended July 28, 1989.

82   Shahla Sherkat wrote about her experiences as a journalist and chief editor for
      Zan-e Rouz. She says the semipublic organization behind *Zan-e Rouz* terminated

her contract for "promoting modernist, Westernized and feminist tendencies." She later became founder and chief editor of influential feminist journal *Zanan*. See Shahla Sherkat, "Telling the Stories of Iranian Women's Lives," Nieman Reports, Summer 2009, accessed May 4, 2012, http://www.nieman.harvard.edu/reports/article/101473/Telling-the-Stories-of-Iranian-Womens-Lives.aspx.

83   Mehrangiz Kar, *Crossing the Red Line: The Struggle for Human Rights in Iran* (Costa Mesa: Blind Owl Press, 2007), p. 99. Kar writes that many women's publications after the revolution were published under the supervision of Qom and Mashhad-based seminaries, encouraging the "myth of Fatemeh, which had been transformed in the patriarchal minds of men who directed these publications into an order of obedience, contentment and silence for women." Ibid.

84   Ibid.

85   *Zan-e Rouz* published a commentary series on women's rights in Islam, penned by Grand Ayatollah Motahhari (a Khomeini colleague who authored many treatises, on subjects of *hejab* and women's rights in Islam). In one of the articles, he discusses the concepts of *hejab* and modesty. The article offers advice to women about preserving their modesty in order to best realize a good character. See *Zan-e Rouz*, Issue 1165 (Ordibehesht 1367/May 1988), pp. 11–12.

86   Zahedi, "Contested Meaning of the Veil and Political Ideologies of Iranian Regimes," p. 86.

87   *Zan-e Rouz*, Issue 750 (1358/1980), pp. 10–11, 56.

88   The Persian pronunciation of the Arabic term *ummah* is *ommat*, also transliterated as *ummat*.

89   See Dabashi and Chelkowski, *Staging a Revolution: The Art of Persuasion in the Islamic Republic of Iran*, pp. 101–2. Dabashi discusses the usage of Arabic *naskh* calligraphy in revolutionary posters and banners. He notes that the phrases are typically excerpted from the Qur'an and are thus regarded as the true utterances of God. Most Iranians would not have been literate enough in Arabic to understand its meaning, though, according to Dabashi, their presence would be immediately noticed, provoking awe in any Muslim. The inclusion of Arabic would have been regarded with semiotic wonder, as "Whatever is actually written in that Arabic cannot be but the Truth manifest." He explains, "Such Arabic phrases demand obedience by merely being there."

90   Shahidian, "Contesting Discourses of Sexuality in Post-Revolutionary Iran," p. 80.

91   I discuss the Islamic and state discourses of modesty in Chapter 4.

92   Shahidian, "Contesting Discourses of Sexuality in Post-Revolutionary Iran," p. 80.

93   See Lila Abu-Lughod, "Modesty Discourses," in *Encyclopedia of Women & Islamic Cultures: Family, Law and Politics*, ed. Suad Joseph and Afsaneh Najmabadi (Leiden: Koninklijke Brill NV, 2005), p. 496.

94   For an analysis of Motahhari's main ideas concerning women's roles in family and society, see Paidar, *Women and the Political Process in Twentieth-Century Iran*, pp. 175–8.

95   Ibid., p. 177.

96   In the article's photograph, a quarter of her face is shielded by a *chador*.

97   *Zan-e Rouz*, Issue 851 (1361/1982) pp. 46–8.

98   Ibid.

99   The concept of *awrat* (in the singular '*awra*) appears in the Qur'an to describe the private parts of men and women not to be exposed and the moment during the day

when male servants or children could not enter homes without permission. See Chapters 4 and 5, for a more detailed description of *awrat*.

100 There was no pamphlet or guidebook to demarcate the "look" of a modest iconography of women's bodies on the pages of magazines. The techniques for projecting modesty happened as a process of trial and error, which meant that initially, there were no standard representations of the figure of women in the first years after the revolution. For instance, in 1980 issues of *Zan-e Rouz*, women are pictured without a *hejab* and are photographed with men, to whom they are unrelated. In issues from 1985 to 1986, women are photographed almost always wearing an Islamic *hejab*.

101 Other techniques detected in postrevolutionary issues of *Zan-e Rouz* involved anatomizing women's bodies; instead of illustrating the body as it appeared from the outside, the body was broken down into anatomical parts, using detailed representations of women's internal organs. The effect of this representation is that the body is treated as an object of science, and it is prevented and disassociated from being an object of desire. In a section dedicated to "Medical Advice," found adjacent to the section "Family Health," anatomical drawings of a woman's orbital area and of a male figure's thyroid gland are illustrated. See *Zan-e Rouz*, Issue 1041 (16 Farvardin 1365/April 1985), pp. 26–7.

102 *Zan-e Rouz*, Issue 757, *Norooz* edition (5 Esfand 1358/February 24, 1980), pp. 28–9. Figure 1.10 is an atypical illustration. Subsequent illustrations found in this section depicted an individual man or woman exercising separately and not in pairs. This separation of the sexes speaks to the magazine's distinguishing between *mahram* and *namahram* relations by promoting physical activity that is homosocial. Even cartoon renditions of men and women should reflect this standard.

103 This heart formation pose reminds us of the heart in Figure 1.9, drawn inside the figure of the Muslim female prototype to symbolize her spiritual and emotional core.

104 Figure 1.11 and 1.12, see *Zan-e Rouz*, Issue 1093 (24 Aban 1365/November 15, 1986), p. 23. Figure 1.13, *Zan-e Rouz*, Issue 1112 (22 Farvardin 1366/April 11, 1987), p. 18.

105 Moallem, *Between Warrior Brother and Veiled Sister,* p. 28.

106 Mir-Hosseini, "The Conservative: Reformist Conflict over Women's Rights in Iran," p. 42. In 1983, appearing in public without a *hejab* was considered an offence against public morality, as stipulated in Article 102 of Islamic Punishments. The penalty advised for this activity was seventy-four lashes and fines.

107 *Zan-e Rouz*, Issue 735 (1358/1980), pp. 52–3.

108 Notice, too, that their legs are exposed, although this is understandable given that, in the first year after the revolution, wearing trousers and overcoats was not yet standard practice among Iranian women.

109 *Zan-e Rouz*, Issue 1098 (29 Azar 1365/December 20, 1986), p. 4.

110 See Afsaneh Najmabadi, "Power, Morality and the New Muslim Womanhood," in *The Politics of Social Transformation in Afghanistan, Iran, and Pakistan*, ed. Myron Weiner and Ali Banuazizi, pp. 366–89 (Syracuse: Syracuse University Press, 1994); Moallem, *Between Warrior Brother and Veiled Sister;* Varzi, *Warring Souls*; and Moghadam, *Modernizing Women;* Valentine Moghadam, *Modernizing Women: Gender and Social Change in the Middle East* (Boulder: Lynne Rienner Publishers, Inc., 2003); Valentine Moghadam, "Gender and Revolutionary Transformation: Iran 1979 and East Central Europe 1989," *Gender and Society* 9, no. 3 (June 1995): pp. 328–58; Sadeghi, "Negotiating with Modernity."

111 Dabashi and Chelkowski, *Staging a Revolution*, p. 88.
112 Dabashi, "Body-less Faces: Mutilating Modernity and Abstracting Women," p. 361.
113 Ibid., pp. 362–3.
114 Ibid., p. 362.

Chapter 2

1 A version of this chapter was published as "Red Lights in Parks: A Social History of *Park-e Razi*," in *Divercities: Competing Narratives and Urban Practices in Beirut, Cairo and Tehran*, eds. Nadia von Maltzahn and Monique Bellan. Institut Orient Beirut, OIS 3 (2015).
2 Akbar Varvayyi, "*Barrasi-ye Avamel-e Rouspigari-ye Kheyabani dar Tehran-e Bozorg/ The Investigation of the Causes of Street Prostitution in Greater Tehran,*" PhD diss., School of Law and Political Science, University of Tehran, 2008, p. 51.
3 District Four is the northeastern suburb of Tehranpars in Tehran, Iran.
4 Varvayyi, "*Barrasi-ye Avamel-e Rouspigari-ye Kheyabani dar Tehran-e Bozorg*/The Investigation of the Causes of Street Prostitution in Greater Tehran."
5 Ibid., p. 45.
6 Ibid.
7 The "concept of 'corruption,' has shifted since the 1979 revolution to include adultery, prostitution, homosexuality, drug trafficking, alcohol consumption, and common crimes such as murder and theft," explains Parvin Paidar. This concept of moral corruption will be discussed further in this chapter. See Paidar, *Women and the Political Process in Twentieth-Century Iran*, p. 345.
8 In Persian, *najeeb-khaneh* is an ironic term, often expressed sarcastically, to mean a prostitute's home. Its literal meaning refers to a place in which women are chaste and morally sound, as the term *najeeb* literally means chaste. The literal meaning appeals to the image of a woman who seeks her sexual desire within a family setting and framework; she is committed to her husband and typically her actions do not arouse gossip or suspicion. When a woman is referred to as *najeeb* in the context of *najeeb-khaneh*, then she is being humiliated for her supposedly unchaste behavior. It is a pejorative comment meant to discredit and/or question the woman's commitment to her family and husband, meaning that she cannot maintain a chaste role if she sells her body. By referring to her home as *najeeb-khaneh*, the utterance debases not only the woman's character but also the home environment in which she lives— ultimately humiliating the female and the family.
9 Gavin R. B. Hambly, "The Traditional Iranian City in the Qajar Period," in *Cambridge History of Iran*, eds. P. Avery, G. R.G. Hambly and C. Melville (Cambridge: Cambridge University Press, 2008), p. 543. For more information on the historical development of Tehran, see Ferydoon Firoozi, "Tehran: A Demographic and Economic Analysis," *Middle Eastern Studies* 10, no. 1 (January 1974): pp. 60–76.
10 Ali Madanipour, *Tehran: The Making of a Metropolis* (New York: John Wiley & Sons, Ltd., 1998), p. 5.
   See also Bayat, *Street Politics*, p. 25. Bayat describes Tehran in 1905 as a walled city of 19 square kilometers with 160,000 inhabitants; it grew to over 300,000 in the early 1930s. The wall was destroyed in 1930, and soon modern streets were constructed.

11 Willem Floor, *A Social History of Sexual Relations in Iran* (Washington DC: Mage Publishers, 2008), p. 257.

12 Ibid., p. 249.

13 The establishment of *Shahr-e No* was not unprecedented. According to Floor, Tehran had a special city quarter for prostitutes during Fath 'Ali Shah's reign (1798–1834), which was closed by Muhammad Shah (1834–48). See Willem Floor, "Venereal Disease in Iran (1855–2005): A Public Affair," *Comparative Studies of South Asia, Africa and the Middle East* 26, no. 2 (2006): p. 263.

14 The destruction of cinemas is also part of the discourse on the destruction of sex districts in Iran. Mob attacks on cinema houses had previously been reported after they were accused of showing foreign "sex" films. In August 1978, controversy swirled around the deathly blaze of Cinema Rex—a cinema house in a poor district of Abadan, Iran. While watching the film The Deer, starring Behrouz Vossoughi, cinemagoers found themselves trapped inside the movie house. There were more than 430 reported casualties. Soon accusations flew over the perpetrators' identities and political motivations. The Pahlavi regime pointed to anti-regime Islamists and the anti-Shah opposition blamed SAVAK for "arranging a 'Reichstag fire,'" by "locking the cinema doors, and sabotaging the local fire department," done to discredit Islamic militants. See Abrahamian, *Iran between Two Revolutions*, p. 513. In August 1980, twenty-six people were tried, leading to six executions. The revolutionary courts condemned Captain Monir Taheri as being the main arsonist; however, Amnesty International deemed the trial unfair and without due process. See "One Person's Story: Mr. Monir Taheri," Abdorrahman Boroumand Foundation, 2012, accessed August 15, 2011, http://www.iranrights.org/english/memorial-ca se--3246.php. For an investigative report on the fire, see Amnesty International, "Law and Human Rights in the Islamic Republic of Iran," February 1980, accessed January 3, 2012, http://www.iranomid.com/en/ARCHVS/TheIRIReport.pdf.

15 Saieed Bashirtash and Ebrahim Nabavi, "*Shahr-e No Atash Gereft va Rouspiyan Koshteh Shodand/Shahr-e No* on Fire and Prostitutes Killed," Radio Zamaneh, 9 Bahman 1387/January 29, 2009, accessed October 5, 2011, http://www.zamaaneh. com/revolution/2009/01.post_218.html.

16 Maryam Poya, *Women, Work and Islamism: Ideology and Resistance in Iran* (London: Zed Books, 1999), p. 68.

17 Article 138 of the Iranian IRI constitution administers the punishment for a convicted man is seventy-five lashes and exile where the offense took place for three months to a year. A convicted woman is typically sentenced with seventy lashes. See Iranian Penal Code, Book 2, *Hadd* Punishment, Part 4, Article 135.

18 Haeri, *Law of Desire*, p. 203.

19 Ibid.

20 Ibid.

21 The phrase is often found on Persian-language blogs and heard in street conversations. Taleghani's comment was made in early 1979 when he was asked about the fires destroying red-light districts in southern Tehran.

22 Vali Mahlouji, "Re-creating *Shahr-e No*: Kaveh Golestan and the Intimate Politics of the Marginal," n.d., accessed December 6, 2019, http://valimahlouji.com/recreating-shahr-e-no/.

23 Paul Stock, "History and the Uses of Space," in Paul Stock (ed.), *The Uses of Space in Early Modern History* (New York: Palgrave Macmillan, 2015), p. 8.

24 Michel Foucault, "Of Other Spaces," in *Diacritics* 16, no. 1 (Spring 1986), pp. 22–7.

25 The term *khalafkari* denotes delinquency and wrongdoing in one.

26 Sattareh Farman Farmaian, *Daughter of Persia* (London: Bantam Press, 1992), p. 301. Arak is a highly alcoholic spirit, often homemade.

27 There are a variety of Persian terms for STDs. Floor's translation of VD is *bimariha-yi jeldi*. A more common term is *amraz-e mogharebati*. Typically, *bimariha-yi jeldi* refers to diseases that affect the skin. For specific kinds of VD, syphilis is translated as *seflis* and gonorrhea is known as *suzak*.

28 "*Shahr-e No: Mazhar-e Fesad dar Qabl az Enqelab/Shahr-e No*: The Symbol of Moral Corruption before the Revolution," *Tahrikh-e Moaaser-e Iran*, 22 Ordibehesht 1387/ May 11, 2008, accessed November 21, 2011, http://bahman18.blogfa.com/post-11. aspx.

29 Firoozeh Kashani-Sabet, "The Politics of Reproduction: Maternalism and Women's Hygiene in Iran, 1896–1941," in *International Journal of Middle East Studies* 38 (2006), pp. 1–29.

30 Willem Floor, "Venereal Disease in Iran (1855–2005): A Public Affair," *Comparative Studies of South Asia, Africa and the Middle East* 26, no. 2 (2006): p. 269.

31 Willem Floor, *A Social History of Sexual Relations in Iran* (Washington DC: Mage Publishers, 2008), p. 389.

32 Firoozeh Kashani-Sabet, *Conceiving Citizens: Women and the Politics of Motherhood in Iran* (Oxford: Oxford University Press, 2011), p. 17.

33 According to Floor, Hedayatollah Hakim-Olahi was an investigative reporter who based his findings on hospital data in the report, *Ba Man beh Shahr-e No Biyaid/Come with Me to Shahr-e No*. Quoted in Floor, *A Social History of Sexual Relations in Iran,* pp. 269, 388.

34 See Floor, "Venereal Disease in Iran (1855–2005): A Public Affair," pp. 268–70. See also Cyrus Schayegh, *Who Is Knowledgeable Is Strong* (Berkeley: University of California Press, 2009), p. 140.

35 Floor, *A Social History of Sexual Relations in Iran,* p. 386.

36 Ibid., p. 253.

37 Ibid., p. 388.

38 Ibid., p. 391.

39 Muge Ozbek, "The Regulation of Prostitution in Beyoglu (1875–1915)," *Middle Eastern Studies* 46, no. 4 (July 2010): p. 555.

40 Ibid.

41 Ibid.

42 See Jo Doezema, "Loose Women or Lost Women? The Re-emergence of the Myth of White Slavery in Contemporary Discourses of Trafficking in Women," *Gender Issues* 18, no. 1 (January 1, 2000): pp. 23–50.

43 Ozbek, "The Regulation of Prostitution in Beyoglu (1875–1915)," p. 555.

44 Ibid., p. 557.

45 Mary Gibson, *Prostitution and the State in Italy, 1860–1915* (Rutgers, NJ: Rutgers, the State University, 1986), p. 24. See also Alain Corbin, *Women for Hire*, trans. Alan Sheridan (Cambridge: Harvard University Press, 1990).

46 "France, Second Empire," *Encyclopedia of Prostitution and Sex Work*, vol. 1, ed. Melissa Hope Ditmore (Westport: Greenwood Press, 2006), p. 171.

47 Britain's Vagrancy Act of 1824 found that "every common prostitute wandering in the public streets . . . and behaving in a riotous or indecent manner . . . shall be deemed an idle and disorderly person." See Lynda Nead, *Myths of Sexuality:*

Representations of Women in Victorian Britain (Oxford: Basil Blackwell Publishing, 1990), p. 115.

48   Mary Lyndon Shanley, *Feminism, Marriage, and the Law in Victorian England* (Princeton: Princeton University Press, 1993), p. 92.

49   Opposing public campaigns were launched to extend and repeal the Contagious Diseases Acts. Proponents of the acts sought to extend its provisions to the civilian population while repeal organizations argued that the acts were gender-biased, effectively demonstrating the double standards between men and women. Suspected of spreading venereal disease, women underwent mandatory health checks only to be quarantined for several months if they were found carrying a venereal disease. By 1886, the acts were repealed, as a result of efforts by moralist and feminist organizations concerned about human rights violations. See Judith Walkowitz, *Prostitution and Victorian Society: Women, Class, and the State* (Cambridge: Cambridge University Press, 1980); Mary Poovey, *Uneven Developments: The Ideological Work of Gender in Mid-Victorian England* (Chicago: University of Chicago Press, 1988), p. 199; Margaret Hamilton, "Opposition to the Contagious Diseases Acts, 1864–1886," *Albion: A Quarterly Journal Concerned with British Studies* 10, no. 1 (Spring 1978): pp. 14–27.

50   Phillipa Levine, *Prostitution, Race and Politics: Policing Venereal Disease in the British Empire* (London: Routledge, 2003), p. 162.

51   James Francis Warren, *Ah Ku and Karayuki-san: Prostitution in Singapore, 1870–1940* (Singapore: Singapore University Press, 2003), p. 104.

52   Hakim-Olahi, *Ba Man beh Shahr-e No Biyaid*, vol. 2, pp. ii–iv. Quoted in Floor, *A Social History of Sexual Relations in Iran*, pp. 390–1. Floor mentions this 1946 book by Hakim-Olahi, who implored the Shah's government to contain the syphilis outbreak in Tehran. Hakim-Olahi recommended that the red-light district be relocated to a new site under direct police and public health provision. Prostitutes and their homes would be examined daily and would require health cards.

53   There were plans to conduct a national survey of the spread of syphilis. According to the 1949 *Report on Seven-Year Development Plan for the Plan Organization of the Imperial Government of Iran*, the government intended to conduct a survey to determine the incidence of syphilis in a "more vigorous attack upon venereal disease." Public health officers estimated that for different cities and villages, the percentage of infection ranged from 20 to 90 percent. Overseas Consultants, *Report on Seven-Year Development Plan for the Plan Organization of the Imperial Government of Iran* (Tehran: n.p., 1949), p. 61.

54   Floor, *A Social History of Sexual Relations in Iran*, p. 277. As researched by Floor, a 1945 article in *Mard-e Emruz* newspaper argued that Iran should follow the Turkish example of "placing prostitutes under police control for public health reasons." The article based its arguments on permitting prostitution and temporary marriage as "sexual outlets for males." Ibid., pp. 389–90.

55   Ibid., p. 392.

56   For information about the concerted efforts to blame prostitutes in Iran for venereal disease, see Cyrus Schayegh, "Criminal-Women and Mother-women: Sociocultural Transformations and the Critique of Criminality in Early Post-World War II in Iran," *Journal of Middle East Women's Studies* 2, no. 3 (Fall, 2006): pp. 5–6. Kashani-Sabet includes one exceptional, "forward-thinking" instance when an Iranian doctor contributed to a hygiene journal, suggesting that infected persons use condoms. However, he dismissed the method in part, stating that it was not a completely

trustworthy method. He also did not specify if both men and women should use condoms. See Kahsani-Sabet, "The Politics of Reproduction: Maternalism and Women's Hygiene in Iran, 1896–1941," pp. 17–18.

57 Kurush Shahbaz, "Iran's White Revolution," *World Affairs* 126, no. 1 (Spring 1963): p. 18.

58 Ibid., p. 19. In this executive order, the Shah asserts the government's improvements in state infrastructure through programs focusing on economic development, progress, anti-corruption, and public cooperation.

59 Shireen Mahdavi, "Women and the Shii *Ulama* in Iran," *Middle Eastern Studies* 19, no. 1 (January 1983): p. 17.

60 Princess Ashraf Pahlavi was a highly contested political figure from the Pahlavi regime, especially for her involvement in Iran's 1953 coup d'etat. A self-described women's rights and human rights activist, she wrote two memoirs in English, *Faces in a Mirror: Memoirs in Exile* (1980) and *Time for Truth* (1995). During the state-administered reforms of women's status of the Pahlavi dynasty, she became president of the High Council of Women's Organizations of Iran (*Shura-ye Aliye Jamiyat-e Zanan Iran*). After the High Council dissolved in 1966, Ashraf became founder and president of the Women's Organization of Iran (WOI). See Paidar, *Women and the Political Process in Twentieth-Century Iran.*

61 Floor, *A Social History of Sexual Relations in Iran*, p. 265. The Fourth Development Plan was implemented from 1968–73. For more information on the White Revolution's development programs, see Afsaneh Najmabadi, *Land Reform and Social Change in Iran* (Salt Lake City: University of Utah Press, 1987); Keith Watson, "The Shah's White Revolution-Education and Reform in Iran," *Comparative Education* 12, no. 1 (Mar. 1976): pp. 23–36.

62 Ibid., p. 264.

63 Indeed, there were efforts by the opposition Tudeh party to confront prostitution. The Tudeh-led Democratic Association of Women (DAW) adopted a 1946 declaration of aims and objectives in which "the struggle against prostitution and moral decadence" was addressed. It is not clear, however, what practical measures were taken to confront prostitution. See Paidar, *Women and the Political Process in Twentieth-Century Iran*, p. 125.

64 Khosrou Mansourian, interview by K.S. Batmanghelichi, New York, November 15, 2011.

65 Floor, *A Social History of Sexual Relations in Iran*, p. 265.

66 Afsaneh Najmabadi, "Iran's Turn to Islam: From Modernism to a Moral Order," *Middle East Journal* 41, no. 2 (Spring, 1987): p. 213.

67 Floor, *A Social History of Sexual Relations in Iran*, p. 263. A crucial point to note: scholars such as Valentine Moghadam have written about the capitalist mode of production's influence on women's work in Iranian society. For information related to the historical industrialization of Iran from the late Qajar period to the Pahlavi regime, see Moghadam's article "Hidden from History? Women Workers in Modern Iran," *Iranian Studies* 33, no. 3/4 (Summer–Autumn, 2000): p. 380. Moghadam states, "In the late Qajar period, Iran experienced a slow transition from a pre-industrial, traditional, and predominantly feudal society and economy to one where capitalist relations were emerging along with the appearance of modern factories. Issawi's economic history of Iran (Issawi, 1971) documents the kinds of factories that were built during this period, including many that failed (e.g., Issawi, 1971: 47 and chapter 6)."

68 Floor, "Venereal Disease in Iran (1855–2005): A Public Affair," p. 263. This is also verified in Paidar, *Women and the Political Process in Twentieth-Century Iran*, p. 41.

69 Ibid., p. 263.

70 Talattof, *Modernity, Sexuality and Ideology in Iran*, p. 57.

71 General Zahedi (1897–1963) was Mohammad Mossadeq's former Minister of the Interior and an instrumental coup leader, who participated as early as October 1951 and up until August 1953 in the American and British-led overthrow of Mossadeq. See Ervand Abrahamian, "The 1953 Coup in Iran," *Science & Society* 65, no. 2 (Summer, 2001): pp. 182–215, 199–201.

72 Hereafter I will use the terms *Qal'eh*, *Qal'eh Shahr-e No*, and *Qal'eh Zahedi*, interchangeably.

73 Foucault, "Of Other Spaces," pp. 22–7.

74 Ibid., p. 24.

75 Ibid., p. 27.

76 Floor, *A Social History of Sexual Relations in Iran*, p. 258.

77 Information about Tehran's *qal'eh* or red-light district, in the area known as *Shahr-e No*, is available through various reports, documentaries, newspaper clippings, and photojournalist documentation of both underground and state-administered sex trafficking during the Pahlavi era. A two-part, black-and-white documentary film, entitled, *Qal'eh*, directed by Kamran Shirdel and produced by the Iran's Ministry of Culture and Art from 1966 until 1980 and the "*Shahr-e No 1975–1977*" exhibition of photographer Kaveh Golestan were referenced for this section. See *Qaleh 1965– 1980/Shahr-e No Quarter 1965–1980*, directed by Kamran Shirdel (Tehran: Ministry of Culture and Art, 1980).

78 The north side of the area was located near Farabi Hospital, which is still located south of Ghazvene Square. Surface area estimate provided by Floor, *A Social History of Sexual Relations in Iran*, p. 259.

79 Floor states that *Shahr-e No* was founded in 1881. This cannot be independently verified by Persian sources from the era. Ibid., p. 259.

80 Dr. Mehdi Montazarqha'em, *Rouspigari dar Iran/Prostitution in Iran* (Tehran: Daneshgah-Ulume Behzisti va Tavanbakhshi, 1384/2005), p. 15.

81 Ja'far Shahri, *Tarikh-e Ijtimai-e Tehran dar Qarn-e 13/The Social History of Tehran in the 13th Century* (Tehran: Rasa Publishing, 1368/1989), p. 469.

82 Ibid, p. 470.

83 Floor, *A Social History of Sexual Relations in Iran*, p. 263. It is doubtful that these young girls and women were brought into the district of their own volition. Najmabadi wrote a seminal book on the 1905 raiding of villages, in the Quchan province, where young girls were sold into sex slavery by villagers who had trouble paying their taxes. Other girls were reportedly stolen by Turkmen tribes. The event caused a public outcry after the villagers attempted to seek help from the parliamentary government to no avail. See Afsaneh Najmabadi, *The Story of the Daughters of Quchan* (Syracuse: Syracuse University Press, 1998).

84 Ja'far Shahri, *Tehran-e Qadim* (Tehran: Moein Publishing, 24 Azar 1376/December 24, 1997). This five-volume work by Shahri (1914–94) offers a social history of Tehran during the late nineteenth to mid-twentieth centuries. More on Shahri's life can be found in the chapter "Ja'far Shahri" in Abbas Milani's *Eminent Persians: The Men and Women Who Made Modern Iran 1941–1979*, pp. 893–8.

85 Since 1979 when prostitution was banned, there are very few sources in Persian about the extent to which prostitution has spread in Iran. Independent scholars, both lay and professional, have commented about the taboo nature of this topic and

thus it is unlikely that their writings would have passed government censors in the publication sector of the Ministry of Islamic Culture and Guidance. According to Tehran-based NGO SPASDI director Mansourian, Sattereh Farman Farmaian wrote the only comprehensive study of Tehran's *Shahr-e No* to date. Additionally, there are available blog posts about the history of the red-light district. See "*Shahr-e No: Mazhar-e Fesad dar Qabl az Engelab/Shahr-e No*: The Symbol of Moral Corruption before the Revolution," Tahrikh-e Moaaser-e Iran, 22 Ordibehesht 1387/May 11, 2008, accessed November 21, 2011, http://bahman18.blogfa.com/post-11.aspx. It is worth noting that the opening lines of this article commence with a discussion about American and English colonialism and the decadent culture that it encourages in their colonies. The author argues that English and Americans in Iran also promoted this kind of corruption and decadence through the establishment of this brothel district, which, according to the article, took place during Muhammad Ali Shah Qajar's reign. See "*Shahr-e No*," Ahari Qorbat-Neshin (blog), August 9, 2011, accessed July 1, 2012, http://aharii.wordpress.com/2011/08/09/%D8%B4%D9%8 7%D8%B1%D9%86%D9%88/. See also Payvand, "Photos: Tehran's Brothel District Shahr-e-Noh 1975–77 by Kaveh Golestan," http://payvand.com/blog/blog/2010/1 2/10/photos-tehrans-brothel-district-shahr-e-no-1975-77-by-kaveh-golestan/.

86 Sattareh Farman Farmaian is often praised as the "Mother of Social Work" in Iran. A memoir of her life, coauthored by Dona Munker, is found in *Daughter of Persia: A Woman's Journey from Her Father's Harem Through the Islamic Republic* (New York: Doubleday, 1992). Born and raised into a large, aristocratic family in Tehran, she finished her university education in social work at University of Southern California. (She was the first Iranian graduate of USC.) Thereafter, she returned to Iran to establish in 1958, with the Shah's approval, Iran's very first School of Social Work. At the time, there was no word for the term "social work," so Farman Farmaian invented the term *madadkar*, meaning "one who helps." *Daughter of Persia: A Woman's Journey from Her Father's Harem Through the Islamic Republic*, p. 211. As a critic of both the Pahlavi regime and Khomeini, she was arrested by revolutionary forces in 1979 and soon immigrated to the United States. She died in May 2012.

87 Farman Farmaian, *Rouspigari dar Shahr-e No-e Tehran/Prostitution in Tehran's Shahr-e No, 49/6/25*, especially pp. 17–24. Her work is also referenced in interviews I conducted in the summer of 2011 in Tehran. In an interview with sociology professor Shirin Ahmadnia, she verified the prominence of her work. Shirin Ahmadnia, interview by K. S. Batmanghelichi, personal interview, Tehran, Iran, July 3, 2010.

88 Ibid., p. 60.

89 The ASHA, now called the American Sexual Health Association, is a nonprofit organization dedicated to heightening public awareness about sexual health, including providing information about sexual rights, STDs, and health-care providers. Although established in 1914 to control and prevent VD, drug addiction, and prostitution, by the 1960s, ASHA expanded its programs to include treating and rehabilitating drug addicts. See "American Social Health Association Records, 1905–2005," Social Welfare History Archives, University of Minnesota Libraries, 2002, accessed December 10, 2011, http://special.lib.umn.edu/findaid/xml/sw0045 .xml.

90 Other sites Farman Farmaian researched included public streets, houses outside of *Qal'eh Shahr-e No*, night entertainment spots, discotheques in southern Tehran, and *qowdha* (holes), or garbage dumps in south Tehran, which appeared more like

slums. Prostitutes lived and worked in some of the deep crevices of the *qowdha*. Ibid., pp. 22–3.

91 Although there was no law criminalizing prostitution, there was a Pahlavi-era law criminalizing acts committed against social morality. According to Section 3, Article 211 of the *Qanoun-e Mojazat-e Ommumi* (Pahlavi Criminal Code), ratified in 1924, the law stipulates, "Any person who participates in an act, which is against social morality, will be imprisoned from one month to one year, or will be fined from 25 to 500 tomans." Adultery, homosexuality (man having sex with men), rape, and incest were treated as crimes, punishable by death in Section 3, Article 207. See *Qanoun-e Mojazat-e Ommumi*, 1304/1924, Section 3, Article 207, 211.

92 Quoted in Payvand, "Photos: Tehran's Brothel District *Shahr-e No* 1975–77 by Kaveh Golestan," Payvand.com, December 10, 2010, accessed December 12, 2012, http://payvand.com/blog/blog/2010/12/10/photos-tehrans-brothel-district-shahr-e-no-1975-77-by-kaveh-golestan/.

93 See Farman Farmaian, *Rouspigari dar Shahr-e No-e Tehran/Prostitution in Tehran's Shahr-e No, 49/6/25*, p. 14.

94 One researcher in particular, Khosrou Mansourian, whom I discuss later in this chapter, insisted that most prostitutes only worked in the quarters and left the citadel for homes located in surrounding areas. Mansourian, interview by K.S. Batmanghelichi, Tehran, July 17, 2011.

95 Vivid images of this district are found in the photo compilation of Masoud Benhoud and Hojat Sepahvand. See *Kaveh Golestan 1950–2003: Recording the Truth in Iran* (Ostfildern, Germany: Hatje Canz Publishers, 2007).

96 Ibid., p. 14.

97 Mansourian, interview by K.S. Batmanghelichi, Tehran, July 17, 2011. Khosrou Mansourian was a researcher for Farman Farmaian's report on *Shahr-e No*.

98 Ibid.

99 According to an online report of currency exchange rates from 1979, one US dollar was equivalent to 70 rials or 7 tomans. See "Iran Currency Exchange Rate History: 1975–2012," Farsinet.com, accessed July 3, 2012, http://www.farsinet.com/toman/exchange.html.

100 There are contesting reports about the daily salary of prostitutes from this period. Khosrou Mansourian stated in our interview that prostitutes made between 400 and 500 tomans for each session. However, his answer differs from the statement of a *Qal'eh Shahr-e No* prostitute who was interviewed for the documentary film; she stated that children were prostituted for 40 to 50 tomans per hour. In addition, Willem Floor uses Farman Farmaian's report to note that the average daily income of a *Shahr-e No* prostitute was 743 riyals, a price that is significantly lower than Mansourian's estimate. It is likely that Mansourian was using 2011 currency exchange rates to estimate their salaries. In October 2011, one US dollar was equivalent to 10,700 rials or 1,070 tomans. See Floor, *A Social History of Sexual Relations in Iran*, p. 264. It is also worth noting that whatever money a *Shahr-e No* prostitute earned would be divided according to rent and food expenses, as well as divided among the madams and other prostitutes residing in each house.

101 Floor, *A Social History of Sexual Relations in Iran*, p. 263.

102 The price estimate of children, according to a *Shahr-e No* prostitute, is found in the aforementioned film, "A Documentary about Prostitution in *Qal'eh Shahr-e No*, Tehran," directed by Kamran Shirdel and produced by the Iran's Ministry of Culture and Art from 1966 until 1980. Farman Farmaian also interviewed prostitutes

who were younger than age fifteen. See Farman Farmaian, *Ruspargari dar Shahr-e Tehran/Prostitution in Tehran, 49/6/25*, Table 58, p. 93.

103 In an August 10, 2011 interview I conducted with 26-year-old Forough A.—whose name has been altered to protect her identity—she recounted a story of a grandfather who, as a teenager, had fallen in love with a young girl living inside *Shahr-e No*. Because this girl could not leave the premises on her own, the young man and a group of his friends entered the district, carrying extra men's clothing. After getting dressed as a young boy, the girl left the "citadel" with them and soon after, the young girl and boy married. Forough A., interview by K.S. Batmanghelichi, personal interview, Tehran, Iran, August 10, 2011.

104 For information about police tactics see film *Qal'eh Shahr-e No, Tehran*.

105 See *Kaveh Golestan 1950–2003: Recording the Truth in Iran*. For literacy rates of *Shahr-e No* prostitutes, see Farman Farmaian, *Rouspigari dar Shahr-e No-e Tehran/Prostitution in Tehran's Shahr-e No, 49/6/25*, Table 37.

106 Farman Farmaian, *Daughter of Persia*, p. 301. Farman Farmaian explains, "Many were wives or village girls who had been lured or abducted from their homes and sold into the brothels, so that they were beyond the pale of respectable society and could never return to their families." Ibid., p. 301.

107 Farman Farmaian interviewed 1,180 prostitutes and tallied how many were married. In *Shahr-e No*, 893 were married compared to 287 who were single. Farman Farmaian, *Rouspigari dar Shahr-e No-e Tehran/Prostitution in Tehran's Shahr-e No, 49/6/25*, Table 20, p. 63.

108 Khosrou Mansourian, interview by K.S. Batmanghelichi, personal interview, Tehran, Iran, July 17, 2011.

109 Ibid. I conducted two interviews with Mansourian in July and November 2011 in Tehran and New York, respectively.

110 "*Shahr-e No: Mazhar-e Fesaad dar Qabl az Enqelab/Shahr-e No*: The Manifestation of Moral Corruption before the Revolution," Tahrikh-e Moaaser-e Iran, 22 Ordibehesht 1387/May 11, 2008, accessed November 21, 2011, http://bahman18.blogfa.com/post-11.aspx. See also Floor, *A Social History of Sexual Relations in Iran*, pp. 262–3.

111 "*Shahr-e No: Mazhar-e Fesaad dar Qabl az Enqelab/Shahr-e No*: The Manifestation of Moral Corruption before the Revolution," Tahrikh-e Moaaser-e Iran. This sentiment was also verified by Khosrou Mansourian in a November 2011 interview.

112 Farman Farmaian, *Rouspigari dar Shahr-e No-e Tehran/Prostitution in Tehran's Shahr-e No, 49/6/25*, Table 34, p. 75.

113 Jo Doezema, "Forced to Choose: Beyond the Voluntary v. Forced Prostitution Dichotomy," in *Global Sex Workers*, eds. Kamala Kempadoo and Jo Doezema (New York: Routledge, 1998), p. 35.

114 Farman Farmaian, *Rouspigari dar Shahr-e No-e Tehran/Prostitution in Tehran's Shahr-e No, 49/6/25*, Table 16, p. 60.

115 This comment about political corruption in *Shahr-e No* was stated by both Fatemeh Sadeghi (the daughter of former Islamic revolutionary judge Khalkhali) and Khosrou Mansourian during our personal interviews. Fatemeh Sadeghi, interview by K.S. Batmanghelichi, personal interview, Tehran, Iran, October 1, 2011.

116 "*Pari Bolandeh Kist?/*Who Is Pari Bolandeh?" Mahitaabe, 2010, accessed July 15, 2011, http://mahitaabe.blogspot.com/2010/04/blog-post_25.html.

117 *Mahram* is an Islamic *shari'a* legal terminology that describes kin who cannot have sexual relations or get married as it would be considered both illegal and incestuous. A *mahram* relationship can also be one established by blood, milk, marriage, or

sexual union. See Jane Khatib-Chahidi, "Sexual Prohibitions, Shared Space and 'Fictive' Marriages in Shi'ite Iran," in *Women and Space: Ground Rules and Social Maps*, ed. Shirley Ardener (Oxford, Bloomsbury, 1997), p. 114.

118 Nashat adds, "After the abdication of Reza Shah in 1941, when the rule prohibiting the veil was abandoned, many women returned to it. But the trend was not completely reversed since the present-day *chador* bears only a remote resemblance to the elaborate veil of yesteryear." See Guity Nashat, "Women in the Islamic Republic in Iran," *Iranian Studies* 13, no. 1/4, Iranian Revolution in Perspective (1980): p. 167.

119 In 1953, one of the most prominent traditional athletes, Shaban Ja'fari, was a ringleader of the CIA-financed riots that accompanied the military coup d'état of 1953 against Prime Minister Mohammad Mosaddeq. See Houchang Chehabi, "zur-kana," *Encyclopedia Iranica*, August 15, 2006, accessed December 6, 2019, http://www.iranicaonline.org/articles/zur-kana.

120 Though this photograph cannot be truly verified, a number of online Persian sources have posted a snapshot of what appears to be Pari Bolandeh. In a black-and-white photograph apparently taken the day of the coup d'etat, she is photographed along with a group of men, waving a rod in the air while holding onto the car door. See *Kayhan*, Issue 10700 (20 Dey 1390/January 10, 2012), front cover.

121 The details about her execution are not clear. It was reported by *Kayhan* newspaper that she was killed by firing squad. According to the Omid Foundation of Human Rights, "The Revolutionary Tribunal of Tehran charged Ms. Sakineh Qasemi with 'corruption on earth.' Based on the *Kayhan* report, Ms. Qasemi was executed by a firing squad on July 12, 1980. However, according to the received electronic form, she was hanged in front of the *Shekufeh-ye No* cabaret in Tehran." See Boroumand Foundation, "One Person's Story: Ms. Sakineh Qasemi," Abdorrahman Boroumand Foundation, 2012, accessed August 15, 2011, http://www.iranrights.org/english/memorial-case--3246.php.

122 *Kayhan*, Issue 10755, "*Be Hokm-e Dadgahha-ye Enqelab-e Eslami: Seh Zan va Chahar Mard Tirbaran Shodand*/The Islamic Revolutionary Courts Executed 3 Women and 4 Men by Firing Squad," (21 Tir 1358/July 12, 1979), front cover. See also Maryam Hosseinkhah, *The Execution of Women in Iranian Criminal Law: An Examination of the Impact of Gender on Laws Concerning Capital Punishment in the New Islamic Penal Code* (New Haven, CT: Iran Human Rights Documentation Center, 2012), p. 28.

123 Boroumand Foundation, "One Person's Story: Mr. Monir Taheri," Abdorrahman Boroumand Foundation.

124 The photograph of "Pari Bolandeh" can be found in the same *Kayhan* article, announcing her execution. See "*Be Hokm-e Dadgahha-ye Enqelab-e Eslami: Seh Zan va Chehar Mard Tirbaran Shodand*/The Islamic Revolutionary Courts Executed Three Women and Four Men by Firing Squad," *Kayhan*, Issue 10755.

125 Payvand, "Photos: Tehran's Brothel District *Shahr-e-No* 1975–77 by Kaveh Golestan," Payvand.com, December 12, 2010, accessed August 20, 2011, http://payvand.com/blog/blog/2010/12/10/photos-tehrans-brothel-district-shahr-e-no-1975-77-by-kaveh-golestan/.

126 All interviews for this project followed International Review Board regulations, approved by Columbia University and the US Department of Health and Human Services.

127   Eager to hear personal accounts of the site, I conducted interviews specifically about *Shahr-e No* with ten Iranians (three women and seven men) in June and October 2011. The interviewees were all Tehran residents above the age of forty (except for 35-year-old Farhad). I had met each respondent through word of mouth, and most of the interviews took place in the privacy of their homes. Notably, among the respondents, there was only one person who felt sympathy for the prostitutes and/or acknowledged the role that they had played. Farhad, a web designer whose older cousins would tell him about their *Shahr-e No* dalliances, lamented the site's demolition and the consequences this had had for Iranian society. Farhad explained that once the quarter had been destroyed, the public soon forgot about its prostitutes and in some respects, they were made redundant. When I asked him to elaborate, he said that before the revolution, prostitutes were generally believed to work primarily at one site; now sex work had dispersed throughout Tehran, with others willing to participate and with little institutional regulation and intervention.

128   Because of this sensitive subject, I employ vague terminology to protect the names and identities of the interviewees and their family members.

129   Mansourian, interview by author, New York, November 15, 2011. Mansourian disputed the claim that male laborers were the most frequent patrons, stating that men from various social strata and political persuasions used *Shahr-e No*'s services.

130   In her memoirs, Farman Farmaian details her role in the November 1978 torching of *Qal'eh*—which, to her surprise, was lauded by Ayatollah Mahmoud Taleghani. Fearing for the lives of the women and children at the welfare center of *Qal'eh*, she and her social work colleagues ran to the district, carrying buckets of water to put out the fire while also insisting that the police and fire stations help. She then realized they had not entered the quarters because "it was better to let the *Qal'eh* burn than to antagonize the 'beards.'" "Beards" was the nickname for the most fanatical of the clerical supporters who Farman Farmaian witnessed carrying torches and cans of kerosene, intent on "punishing a few miserable women for the sins of the 'imperialists.'" See Farman Farmaian, *Daughter of Persia*, pp. 301–2.

131   Kar, *Crossing the Red Line*, p. 181.

132   "30 Years Ago on This Day," Radio Zamaneh, 8 Bahman 1387/January 27, 2009, accessed September 11, 2011, http://zamaaneh.com/revolution/2009/01/post_218.ht ml. Quoted in *Ettela'at*, "*Beh Atash Keshidan-e 'Qal'eh-ye Shahr-e No' va Koshtan-e Rouspeyan/Shahr-e No* Quarter Set on Fire and Prostitutes Killed," 9 Bahman 1357/ January 29, 1979.

133   Khalkhali was sworn into office as Head of the Revolutionary Courts on the 24th of Bahman 1357 (February 13, 1979).

134   Pahlavi-era movies and novels are two domains in which *Shahr-e No* characters have been sustained in the public memory—yet interviews of former patrons and inhabitants who lived in *Qal'eh*'s surrounding areas offer personal, nonfictional accounts of the social life, networks, and inter-dynamics of the quarter and its inhabitants.

135   See "Introduction to Farabi Eye Hospital," Tehran University of Medical Sciences, n.d., accessed November 1, 2019, http://medicine.tums.ac.ir/college/en/page/farabi-hospital.

136   For information on the impact of quick urbanization of Tehran city from a study of satellite images of the capital's urban development, see S. Z. Shahraki, Z. Arzjani, and N. Ahmadifard, "A Systematic Study of the Impact of Urbanization of Tehran

City on Agricultural and Garden Land Use," *Crop Research (Hisar)* 37, no. 1/3 (2009): pp. 307–11.

137 Located nearby are *Park-e Khanevadeh* (Family Park) and the miniature Ghazvene Square.

138 "*Ahamiyat-e Faza-ye Sabz va Ta'sir-e Un bar Ravan-e Ensan*/The Importance of Green Space and Its Effect on Human Mentality," Parks and Green Space Organization Tehran Municipality, n.d., accessed June 26, 2012, http://parks.tehran. ir/LinkClick.aspx?fileticket=wBH9D6Qm7Uw%3d&tabid=101&mid=481.

139 Fariba Abdelkhah has studied how municipal parks and gardens, especially in Tehran, offer a public, communal space in which different social groups and classes of society coexist and share in their "favourite consumption and leisure practices," such as picnicking, socializing with friends, family gatherings, sports, and selling crafts. However public parks are also sites on which varied social practices and groups interact and rival one another. Parks are often where local authorities, neighbors, and Revolutionary Guard members observe and, at times, enforce the moral code demanded by the regime. See Abdelkhah, *Being Modern in Iran*, pp. 19–20.

140 The structures of the culture center began in 2002 but were completed in 2005, and thereafter the center was given various names, from Sports Cultural Center, and then Art and Youth Cultural Center, to now Razi Cultural Center.

141 "Fifty Ambassadors, First Secretaries Guests of Iran Arts Garden-Museum," Tehran Municipality online, June 26, 2012, accessed July 1, 2012, http://en.tehran.ir/defau lt.aspx?tabid=77&ArticleId=747. In 2019, the organization cited its presence in over 400 centers.

142 "Comprehensive Chronology of Islamic Revolution Published," Tehran Municipality online, February 8, 2012, accessed June 14, 2012, http://en.tehran.ir/ViewArticle/tab id/77/ArticleId/523/Comprehensive-Chronology-of-Islamic-Revolution-Publishe d.aspx.

143 "*Yek Mohit-e Kamelan Farhangi Baraye Noh Hafte*/A Cultural Environment for 9 Weeks," *Hamshahri News*, 1388 Tir 22/July 13, 2009, accessed June 4, 2012, http:// www.hamshahrionline.ir/news-85383.aspx.

144 Hamid Naficy, *A Social History of Cinema, Volume 1: The Artisan Era, 1897–1941* (Durham: Duke University Press, 2011), p. 260.

145 Robert Sack, *Homo Geographicus: A Framework for Action, Awareness, and Moral Concern* (Baltimore: Johns Hopkins University Press, 1997), p. 32.

146 Here, the 1979 Revolution is identified as an Islamic revolution, eliminating the existence of any oppositional, secular forces that participated in the fall of the Pahlavi regime.

147 "*Mo'arefi-ye Manteqe-ye 11*/Introducing District 11," Cultural Arts Organization for Tehran Municipality, date unknown, accessed July 1, 2012, http://razi.farhangs ara.ir/%D9%85%D8%B9%D8%B1%D9%81%D9%8A%D9%85%D9%86%D8%B7 %D9%82%D9%87.aspx.

148 "Razi Cultural Center in Tehran," Press TV, October 29, 2015, accessed November 1, 2019, https://www.youtube.com/watch?v=SL2a6XaYuNA.

149 I visited the park with a female friend, as my family and I had safety concerns because I was unfamiliar with the area. Moreover, it is not typical for a female— regardless of her age, origin, or religious disposition—to visit parks unaccompanied in Iran. It would invite unwanted attention from strangers, including the park police, who would be curious about my reasons for doing so.

150 The interviews took place in the afternoons of Wednesday and Thursday on August 24 and 25, 2011. I spent eight hours each day at Park-e Razi.

151 I think that my female gender might have impacted what information male interviewees felt comfortable in sharing with me. Moreover, I realize that the topics of *Shahr-e No* and prostitution are considered taboo and thus not easily broached in public, and among strangers.

152 I was not successful in interviewing the women they described as former *Shahr-e No* prostitutes. There is thus no way to verify that indeed the women were (1) prostitutes or (2) had worked in *Shahr-e No*. I must therefore rely on their words. However, I did seek out additional sources for verification. The park's guards were reticent in verifying the interviewees' claims. After leaving the park, I telephoned the local police, asking for any information about the frequency of prostitution in the area. They did not respond to my requests. Thereafter, I contacted *Khaneh-ye Khorshid* (Sun House), a women's advocacy center and safe haven for female runaways and addicts located on Shush Avenue in south-central Tehran. The center provides methadone treatment, gynecological and psychological services for women, and provides basic necessities, such as food and clothing. I wanted more information elaborating how prostitution operates in Razi Park. I spoke with one of the volunteer staff members (who is a university student in social work). She confirmed that in parks located in poorer areas of Tehran, such as Razi Park, prostitution is common. More so, many female addicts temporarily reside in them with their children because of the available facilities, such as the public toilets, and because they have no stable housing. The staff member did not know if any of the prostitutes were formerly *Shahr-e No* residents. She also was not aware that Razi Park was the former site of *Shahr-e No*.

Chapter 3

1 On the subject of the Islamization of Tehran's public sphere as an Islamic space filled with Islamic objects, in the postrevolutionary period, see Varzi, *Warring Souls*, p. 108.

2 *Ettela'at, Enqelab* Edition, 10 Bahman 1357/January 30, 1979, accessed November 9, 2011, http://i47.tinypic.com/14jxncl.jpg.

3 The distinction between *mahram* and *namahram* has been explained as distinctions in kin relationships that determine one's relationship (and thus marriageability) to the opposite sex. In *shar'ia* (Islamic legal) terminology, *mahram* are kin who are unmarriageable, such as females with permanent blood relations to their fathers, grandfathers, brothers, sons, grandsons, uncles and nephews. One can become *mahram* to the opposite sex through marriage; thus in-laws, such as the father, son, stepfather and stepson, will be considered *mahram. Namahram* then refers to all others who can potentially marry one another; "therefore, veiling regulations should be sustained." Quoted from footnote in Fataneh Farahani, *Diasporic Narratives of Sexuality: Identity Formation among Iranian-Swedish Women* (Stockholm: Stockholm Universitet, 2007), p. 166. I again address the mahram/*namahram* paradigm in relation to space in Chapter 4.

4 Paidar, *Women and Political Process in Twentieth-Century Iran*, p. 345.

5   *Ettella'at*, December 22, 1998. Quoted in Hammed Shahidian, *Women in Iran: Gender Politics in the Islamic Republic*, vol. 2 (Westport: Greenwood Press, 2002), p. 166.

6   Najmabadi, "Iran's Turn to Islam: From Modernism to a Moral Order," p. 215.

7   Paidar explains, "The Council of the Islamic Revolution which had been set up in the final month of the Revolution by Ayatollah Khomeini presided over the immediate transitional tasks. The revolutionary leadership kept some parts of the pre-Revolutionary state machinery intact and replaced others with the institutions which were conceived during the Revolution." See Paidar, *Women and the Political Process in Twentieth-Century Iran*, p. 221.

8   See Abrahamian, *Iran between Two Revolutions*; Paidar, *Women and the Political Process in Twentieth-Century Iran*; Dabashi, *Theology of Discontent*; and Najmabadi, "Hazards of Modernity and Morality: Women, State and Ideology in Contemporary Iran"; Najmabadi, *The Story of the Daughters of Quchan*.

9   See *Islamic Republic of Iran Constitution*, Article 3, note 12 and16; Article 4.

10 State universities and government ministries were closed. The Pahlavi-era parliament and the senate were also dissolved during the early years of the postrevolutionary period.

11 Shaul Bakhash, "The Islamic Republic of Iran, 1979–1989," *The Wilson Quarterly (1976–)* 13, no. 4 (Autumn1989): p. 54.

12 Abrahamian, *Iran between Two Revolutions*, p. 536.

13 "*Mujtahid*," *Encyclopedia of Islam*, Second Edition, Brill Volume VII, p. 295, column 2. A *mujtahid* is "one who possesses the aptitude to form his own judgment on questions concerning the *shari'a*, using personal effort (*idjtihād* [*q.v.*]) in the interpretation of the fundamental principles (*uṣūl* [*q.v.*]) of the *shari'a*."

14 Mehran Tamadonfar, "Islam, Law, and Political Control in Contemporary Iran," *Journal for the Scientific Study of Religion* 40, no. 2 (June 2001): p. 217.

15 The 1982 Islamic Penal Code was originally ratified by the *Majles*'s (Parliament) Legal and Judicial Council and then passed by the Guardian Council for a period of five years. It was revised and reapproved by the Islamic Consultancy Parliament on July 30, 1991 and ratified by the High Expediency Council on November 28, 1991. For the English translation of the text, see MEHR website, accessed January 11, 2012, http://mehr.org/Islamic_Penal_Code_of_Iran.pdf.

16 Paidar, *Women and the Political Process in Twentieth-Century Iran*, p. 187.

17 Erving Goffman, *Stigma* (New York: Simon & Shuster, 1991), p. 2.

18 Ibid., p. 143.

19 Ibid., p. 3.

20 Ibid., p. 23.

21 Sarah Kingston, *Prostitution in the Community* (London: Routledge, 2013), p. 14.

22 Quoted in Ibid., p. 14. Original excerpt from Gail Pheterson, "The Whore Stigma: Female Dishonor and Male Unworthiness," *Social Text*, no. 37 (1993): pp. 39–64. doi:10.2307/466259.

23 Bell, *Reading, Writing, and Rewriting the Prostitute Body*, p. 2.

24 Ibid., pp. 1–2.

25 Ibid., p. 2.

26 Ibid., p. 40.

27 Ibid.

28 Paidar writes, "The Pahlavi Dynasty Was Labeled as the 'Spreader of Prostitution' and the 'Corrupter of Women and Family.'" Paidar, *Women and the Political Process in Twentieth-Century Iran*, p. 217.

29 See Floor, *A Social History of Sexual Relations in Iran*, 2008; Paidar, *Women and the Political Process in Twentieth-Century Iran*; Najmabadi, *Women with Mustaches and Men without Beards*; Firoozeh Kashani-Sabet, *Conceiving Citizens Women and the Politics of Motherhood in Iran* (Oxford: Oxford University Press, 2011).
30 Mahdavi, "Women and the Shii *Ulama* in Iran Author," p. 18.
31 See Kashani-Sabet, *Conceiving Citizens Women and the Politics of Motherhood in Iran*.
32 Kashani-Sabet, "The Politics of Reproduction: Maternalism and Women's Hygiene in Iran, 1896–1941," p. 14. See also Kashani-Sabet, *Conceiving Citizens Women and the Politics of Motherhood in Iran*.
33 Schayegh, "Criminal-Women and Mother-Women," p. 1.
34 Ibid. p. 2.
35 Ibid., p. 12.
36 Colloquial terminology exhibits a wider range for the term prostitute, including the terms *jendeh*, *fahesheh*, and *zanikeh*.
   Prostitution is not limited to female prostitutes. According to the news website Baztab-e Emruz, male prostitutes can be found in sport facilities and recreational centers in wealthy districts of Tehran. See "*Khahesh-e Sen-e Ruspigari*/A Decrease in Prostitution Age," Baztab-e Emruz, 24 Tir 1391/ July 14, 2012, accessed July 25, 2012, http://baztab.net/fa/news/10972/.
37 Socially harmed women are also referred to as "special women." See Radio Zamaneh, "*Sarpoush bar Vaqiyati Oryan*/Covering Up the Naked Truth," RadioZamaneh.com, 30 Tir 1391/ July 20, 2012, accessed July 27, 2012, http://www.radiozamaneh.com/society/khiyaban/2012/07/20/17202. See also Shahidian, "Contesting Discourses of Sexuality in Post-Revolutionary Iran," p. 186.
38 Shahidian, "Contesting Discourses of Sexuality in Post-Revolutionary Iran," p. 186.
39 Payvand, "Iran Juggles with Taboos, Holds First of Prostitutes and Police," Payvand.com, December 7, 2002, accessed January 12, 2012, http://www.netnative.com/news/02/dec/1032.html.
40 Hamideh Sadeghi offers a higher unofficial estimate of 84,000 prostitutes living in Tehran. See Sedghi, *Women and Politics in Iran*, p. 239.
41 Parto Parvin and Arash Ahmadi, "Iran Sets Sights on Tackling Prostitution," BBC News, July 26, 2012, accessed July 27, 2012, http://www.bbc.co.uk/news/world-middle-east-18966982.
42 In many cases, reticence to speak about prostitution is the norm; however, there are instances when Iranian authorities flatly deny the existence of prostitutes in Iran. In a well-known case, BBC reporter Sue Lloyd-Roberts (who was granted permission by the Ministry of Islamic Guidance to report on social change in Iran) was deported in December 2002 from Iran after interviewing and photographing female prostitutes. Officials told her, "We are deporting you tomorrow morning because you have taken pictures of prostitutes. . . . This is not a true reflection of life in our Islamic Republic. We don't have prostitutes." Nasrin Alavi detailed the incident in the book *We Are Iran*. See Nasrin Alavi, *We Are Iran* (London: Portobello Books Ltd, 2005), p. 156 and "Iran's Youth Reveal Anger and Sadness," BBC News, December 10, 2002, accessed January 12, 2012, http://news.bbc.co.uk/1/hi/world/middle_east/2563413.stm.
43 Kayvan Bozorgmehr, "Head of Sociology Association of Iran Announces: Drop in Prostitution Age in Iran," Roozonline, June 15, 2011, accessed January 12, 2012, http:

//www.roozonline.com/english/news3/newsitem/article/drop-in-prostitution-ag
e-in-iran.html.

44   Original source from the now-banned *Nowrooz*, September 17, 2001, Issue14. Per
      Zargooshi's results, "The majority of the prostitutes and *sigheh* wives in Iran exchange
      sex for survival. Being uneducated survival sex workers, they accept risky sex
      behaviours easily. *Sigheh* wives are an important source of infection. The very high
      rate of persistent infection despite standard treatments is disturbing. Our ideal is a
      world in which nobody is obliged to enter commercial sex work. In the meantime,
      however, there is an urgent need to offer medical care and education to sex workers
      as needy patients in a safe and unprejudiced environment. Denying the presence of
      such realities as prostitution and sexually transmitted diseases (STDs) because of their
      disagreement with scant claims and official propaganda, does not eradicate the facts
      but results in catastrophic public health problems." See J. Zargooshi, "Characteristics of
      Gonorrhea in Kermanshah, Iran," *Sex Transmission Infection Journal* 78, no. 6 (2002):
      pp. 460–1, accessed August 21, 2011, http://www.ncbi.nlm.nih.gov/pubmed?term=
      characteristics%20of%20gonorrhea%20in%20kermanshah#.

45   Parvin and Ahmadi, "Iran Sets Sights on Tackling Prostitution."

46   See Sholeh Shahrokhi, *Dokhtarane Farari: An Anthropological Investigation on Youth
      Runaways, Teen Prostitution, Cross-Dressing and Other Sexual Practices of Adolescent
      Girls in Tehran, Iran* (Berkeley, CA: University of Berkeley, 2008). See also Ahmad
      Kalateh Sadati, et al. "Experience of Violence among Street Prostitutes: A Qualitative
      Study in Shiraz, Iran," *Journal of Iinjury & Violence Research* 11, no. 1 (2019): pp.
      21–8. doi:10.5249/jivr.v11i1.865.

47   See "*Tanforoushi baraye Afzayesh-e Keyfiyat-e Zendegi*/Prostitution for the Purpose
      of Improving Quality of Life," *Salamat News*, 22 Azar 1390/December 2, 2011,
      accessed January 20, 2012, http://salamatnews.com/viewNews.aspx?ID=38047&cat=
      12. See also "*Sazman-e Behzisti: Bish az Panjah Darsad-e Kargaran-e Jensi, Zanan-e
      Mote'ahel Hastand*/State Welfare Organization: More than 50 Percent of Sex Workers
      Are Married Women," BBC Persian, December 12, 2011, accessed December 6,
      2019, http://www.bbc.co.uk/persian/iran/2011/12/111212_l21_sex_worker_iran.s
      html.

48   "*Tanforoushi baraye Afzayesh-e Keyfiyat-e Zendegi*/Prostitution for the Purpose of
      Improving Quality of Life," *Salamat News*.

49   "*Sazman-e Behzisti: Bish az Panjah Darsad-e Kargaran-e Jensi, Zanan-e Mote'ahel
      Hastand*/State Welfare Organization: More than 50 Percent of Sex Workers Are
      Married Women," BBC Persian.

50   Amnesty International, *Iran: End Executions by Stoning Report* (London: Amnesty
      International Publications, 2008), p. 7.

51   "*Sazman-e Behzisti: Bish az Panjah Darsad-e Kargaran-e Jensi, Zanan-e Mote'ahel
      Hastand*/State Welfare Organization: More than 50 Percent of Sex Workers Are
      Married Women," BBC Persian.

52   The article compares the medium age to figures from 1969, but it does not state
      explicitly what the medium age is in year 2012. See "*Tanforoushi baraye Afzayesh-e
      Keyfiyat-e Zendegi*/Prostitution for the Purpose of Improving Quality of Life,"
      Salamat News.

53   Muhammad Ali Zam, *Bahar* newspaper, July 2, 2000. Quoted in Alavi, *We Are Iran*
      (London: Portobello Books Ltd, 2005), p. 158.

54   "*Tanforoushi baraye Afzayesh-e Keyfiyat-e Zendegi*/Prostitution for the Purpose of
      Improving Quality of Life," *Salamat News*.

55　"*Sazeman-e Behzisti: Bish az Panjah Darsad-e Kargaran-e Jensi, Zanan-e Mote'ahel Hastand*/State Welfare Organization: More than 50 Percent of Sex Workers Are Married Women," BBC Persian.

56　Ibid.

57　"Postscript: Female Sex Workers and Fear of Stigmatisation," *Sex Transmission Infection Journal* 81 (2005): p. 180.

58　The news and analysis website Ghanoon stated that "cyber" prostitution was increasingly popular among Iran's youth, who turn to the internet to arrange services. "It said 55% of 'cyber prostitutes' are aged 16 to 25," the report said. See Parvin and Ahmadi, "Iran Sets Sights on Tackling Prostitution." For a study on e-prostitution in Iran, see conference paper by Mohamed Tavakol and Abbas Faghih, "Sociological Study of E-Dating and E-Prostitution in Iran," XVIII ISA World Congress of Sociology, 2014.

59　Tehran Bureau correspondent, "Experts Say Generation Gap Leading Cause of Runaways, Prostitution in Iran," *The Guardian.com*, October 10, 2014, accessed November 20, 2019, https://www.theguardian.com/world/iran-blog/2014/oct/10/iran-prostitution-sex-work-runaways.

60　Ibid. Agence France Press reported in May 2001 that Tehran police had closed down a brothel, arresting twenty-five people. The same year, India's *The Hindu* reported from Iranian newspaper *Omid-e Jahan* that Iran would no longer hand out passports to Iranian women expelled from Gulf countries—they were accused of involvement in prostitution rings. In the same article, twenty-nine brothels were reported closed, all located in northern Tehran. See Sohrab Morovati, "Iranian Police Declare War on Prostitution," Agence France Presse, May 22, 2002, accessed January 12, 2012, http://www.uri.edu/artsci/wms/hughes/war_on_prostitution.

61　Morovati, "Iranian Police Declare War on Prostitution."

62　Alavi, *We are Iran,* p. 153. In raids of brothels of Mashad, journalist Sohrab Morovati reported that about 150 people, including 44 women, were arrested; eight brothels were shut down and items believed to aid in procuring prostitutes, such as mobile phones, cars, motorcycles, alcohol, and pornographic films were also confiscated. See Morovati, "Iranian Police Declare War on Prostitution," Agence France Presse.

63　Ibid.

64　Kesava Menon, "Flesh Is Weaker in Moralistic Iran," *The Hindu*, January 27, 2001, accessed December 4, 2019, http://www.hindu.com/2001/01/28/stories/03280009.htm.

65　Paidar explains, "While lower-class women were portrayed as passive victims of the regime's oppression, affluent women were condemned as sex-objects, accomplices of the Shah and oppressors of lower-class women." See Paidar, *Women and the Political Process in Twentieth-Century Iran,* p. 171.

66　Paidar, *Women and the Political Process in Twentieth-Century Iran,* p. 217.

67　Ibid.

68　Shahidian, *Women in Iran*, p. 186.

69　For instance, in the section "Women in the Constitution" of the Islamic Republic's national constitution, it affirms, "The family is the fundamental unit of society and the main center for the growth and edification of human being. . . . It is the duty of the Islamic government to provide the necessary facilities for the attainment of this goal. This view of the family unit delivers woman from being regarded as an object or instrument in the service of promoting consumerism and exploitation. Not only does woman recover thereby her momentous and precious function of motherhood, rearing of ideologically committed human beings, she also assumes a pioneering social role and becomes the fellow struggler of man in all vital areas of life. Given the weighty responsibilities that woman thus assumes, she is accorded in Islam great value and nobility." See *Islamic Republic of Iran Constitution*, Preamble.

70 The integration of the "prostitute" and the "whore" are still part of the political discourse in Iran; in particular, the term "whore" has become a facile insult directed at women who are accused of participation in projects or displaying attitudes considered unacceptable and immoral by the regime. As recent as January 2012, Iran's Council of Public Culture announced its decision to disband the established Cinema House—a nongovernmental filmmaker's guild in Iran. Conservative director Farajollah Salahshour (director of film *The Prophet Joseph*) denounced the association as a whorehouse. Soon after, news reports and the blogosphere were speculating over the exposure of nubile actress Golfshifteh Farahani, who posed semi-topless (her hands strategically covering her nipples) in the French film magazine *Madame Le Figaro*. The reaction from Iranian authorities was neither pleasant nor tongue-in-cheek. Iranian authorities informed her, had she decided to return to Iran from her current residence in Paris, she would not be welcomed to her home country. For Salahshour quote, see "*Salahshour: Cinema-ye Iran Fahesheh-khaneh Ast*/Salahshour: Iran's House of Cinema Is a Whorehouse," *Aftab News*, 23 Mehr 23 1390/October 15, 2011, accessed February 14, 2014, http://aftabnew s.ir/vdcepp8zwjh8xoi.b9bj.html. See also "*Vezarat-e Ershad Khaneh-ye Cinema ra Monhal Kard*/Ministry of Culture Dissolves House of Cinema," BBC Persian, January 3, 2012, accessed December 4, 2019, http://www.bbc.co.uk/persian/iran/2 012/01/120103_l06_khaneyecinema_shut_down.shtml.

   See also "Chare-ee joz Enhelal-e Khane-ye Cinema Nadashtim/We Had No Choice But to Disband the House of Cinema," Fars News Agency, 21 Azar 1390 / December 12, 2011, accessed February 13, 2012, http://farsnews.com/newstext.p hp?nn=13901121000539.

71 See Nashat, "Women in the Islamic Republic of Iran," pp. 165–94. Original quote from Khomeini, *Jomhouri Eslami*, 16 Ordibehesht 1359/May 6, 1980.

72 Shahidian, "Contesting Discourses of Sexuality in Post-Revolutionary Iran," p. 186.

73 The penal code is based on a system of four different types of crimes, which are subject to four different types of punishments. They are *hodoud, qesas, ta'zir*, and *diyat*. Hodoud (singular, *hadd*) are acts prohibited by God, with mandatory penalties defined by the Qur'an. *Qesas* are crimes against a victim and his or her family; the decision of retribution lies with the victim's family in cases of murder. *Ta'zir* crimes are acts for which no specific penalties are mentioned in the Qur'an, leaving it up to the judge's discretion. *Diyat* punishment refers to a form of payment or compensation, payable to the victim or his or family. Tamadonfar, "Islam, Law, and Political Control in Contemporary Iran," p. 213.

74 Islamic Republic of Iran Penal Code, Book 2, *Hadd* punishment, Part 4, Articles 135–8. The colloquial term for pimping is *jakeshi kardan*; a pimp is a *jakesh*. Both terms are considered derogatory and thus not used in polite speech.

75 Clause 637 and 638 of the penal code concerns those caught having sex for money. According to Amnesty International, "Under Iranian law, capital offenses include adultery by married people, incest, rape, four convictions of an unmarried person for fornication, three convictions for drinking alcohol, or four convictions for homosexual acts among men." Prostitution is included in facilitating the fornication between unmarried persons. See "Iran: The Last Executioner of Children," Amnesty

International, June 27, 2007, accessed February 13, 2012, http://www.amnesty.org.uk
/news_details.asp?NewsID=17401.

76 Stoning punishments are administered for primarily adultery cases, and Articles
172 and 198 of the constitution authorize judges to issue stoning as a possible
sentence. See Shadi Sadr, "The 'End of Stoning': Islamic Republic Style," *Huffington
Post: The Blog*, March 13, 2012, accessed December 4, 2019, http://www.huffingto
npost.com/shadi-sadr/iran-stoning_b_1335809.html.

77 Tamadonfar, "Islam, Law, and Political Control in Contemporary Iran," p. 213.

78 Ibid., p. 212. For instance, in the case of adultery (which is a capital offense and
penalized as a *hodoud* crime), four credible witnesses must testify that they observed
a man and woman naked under the sheets or saw them engaging in the act of
intercourse. See *Islamic Republic of Iran Criminal Code*, Articles 76, 77, 78, and 79.

79 Floor, *A Social History of Sexual Relations in Iran*, p. 277.

80 Haeri, *Law of Desire*, p. 100.

81 *Kayhan*, Issue 82. Quoted in Paidar, p. 346.

82 Yeganeh, "Women, Nationalism, and Islam in Contemporary Political Discourse in
Iran," p. 16.

83 Haeri, *Law of Desire*, p. 100.

84 See Nashat, "Women in the Islamic Republic of Iran," pp. 165–94.

85 Shahidian, *Women in Iran: Gender Politics in the Islamic Republic*, vol. 2, p. 186.

86 Haeri, *Law of Desire*, p. 100.

87 His research also discusses the hygiene practices of prostitutes and their average
weekly salaries. It contributes pivotal historical details about *Shahr-e No*'s former
inhabitants, especially during a time when the research topic would have been
deemed taboo. However, being that the thesis project was approved and conducted
during the reformist administration of President Mohammed Khatami, it is probable
that university professors were more at liberty to approve controversial doctoral
dissertations in the social sciences. See Akbar Varvayyi, "*Barrasi-ye Avamel-e
Rouspigari-ye Kheyebani dar Tehran-e Bozorg*/The Investigation of the Causes of
Street Prostitution in Greater Tehran".

88 The most destitute of the prostitutes were the *qod-neshin*, a terminology for a
prostitute residing in the poorest and dirtiest areas of Tehran, such as Shush Square
in south Tehran. In this area, prostitutes were known to wear *chadors* and were
managed by a *riess* (boss), whom they called *Maman*. See Varvayyi, "Barrasi-ye
Avamel-e Rouspigari-ye Kheyebani dar Tehran-e Bozorg/The Investigation of the
Causes of Street Prostitution in Greater Tehran," pp. 44–8.

89 Ibid.

90 Ibid.

91 Floor's statement is based on the section "Penance *Sigheh*" from Haeri's *Law of
Desire*, p. 99. Floor, *A Social History of Sexual Relations in Iran*, p. 265.

92 Ibid. Similar rehabilitation programs were reported for "harmed women" in recent
years. According to Shahidian, in 2000, newspaper *Iran* reported that 350 prostitutes
were taken to similar centers, and the number of prostitutes was higher than
the previous year. See Shahidian, "Contesting Discourses of Sexuality in Post-
Revolutionary Iran," p. 186.

93 Paidar, *Women and the Political Process in Twentieth-Century Iran*, p. 278.

94 Ibid., p. 279. For a detailed explanation, see Haeri, *Law of Desire*, pp. 99–100.

95 Ibid., p. 278. Quoted in Amnesty International Report, 1987. The details of this
situation are not explicated in this report. Haeri also does not provide further details.

96   That women should assume operational roles during Iran's war effort is a theme
      Ayatollah Khomeini identifies as an example of female sacrifice in the name of a
      revolutionary cause. Women volunteers were crucial to Khomeini's directive for
      a national mobilization army of 20 million; women thus received participated in
      a range of activities servicing the war effort, some of whom received noncombat
      military and first-aid training. See Afsaneh Najmabadi, "Power, Morality, and the
      New Muslim Womanhood," in *The Politics of Social Transformation in Afghanistan,*
      Iran, and Pakistan, ed. Myron Weiner and Ali Banuazizi (Syracuse: Syracuse
      University Press, 1994), pp. 382–3.

97   Excerpt is from Khomeini's speech, delivered to a group of women in honor of
      Women's Day. See "Ruhollah al-Musawi al-Khomeini Women's Day Speech," Iran
      Chamber Society, 25 Farvardin 1361/April 14, 1982, accessed December 4, 2019,
      http://www.iranchamber.com/history/rkhomeini/books/women_position_khom
      eini.pdf.

98   See Roxanne Varzi, "Iran's Pieta: Motherhood, Sacrifice and Film in the Aftermath of
      the Iran-Iraq War," *Feminist Review* 88 (2008): pp. 86–98.

99   Haeri, *Law of Desire*, p. 210.

100   Shahla Haeri, "Power of Ambiguity: Cultural Improvisations on the Theme of
      Temporary Marriage," *Iranian Studies* 19, no. 2 (Spring 1986), p. 144.

101   The official legal terminology for *sigheh* in Arabic is *nikah al-mut'a*, which has
      been literally translated as a pleasure or enjoyment marriage. See Shahla Haeri,
      "Temporary Marriage and the State in Iran: An Islamic Discourse on Female
      Sexuality," *Social Research* 59, no. 1, Religion and Politics (Spring, 1992): pp. 201–23.

102   See Ziba Mir-Hosseini, "Sexuality, Rights, and Islam: Competing Gender Discourses
      in Postrevolutionary Iran," in *Women in Iran from 1800 to the Islamic Republic*, eds.
      Lois Beck and Guity Nashat (Champaign: University of Illinois Press, 2004), p. 207.

103   Jurist al-Hilli was a thirteenth-century *mujtahid* (*Shi'a* legal scholar and jurist)
      whose works were fundamental in shaping Twelver Shi'a legal doctrines. Mir-
      Hosseini, "Sexuality, Rights, and Islam: Competing Gender Discourses in
      Postrevolutionary Iran," p. 207.

104   Haeri, *Law of Desire*, p. 17.

105   Ibid., p. 1.

106   Ibid., pp. 2, 54–5.

107   Ibid., p. 54. According to Shi'a Grand Ayatollah Sistani, "It is permissible for a
      man and a woman to recite the formula of the temporary marriage (*mut'a*), after
      having agreed on the period of marriage and the amount of *Mehr* (another form
      of dowry or *mehrieh* in Persian). Hence, if the woman says: *Zawwajtuka nafsi fil*
      muddatil ma'lumati 'alal mahril ma'lum (i.e. I have made myself your wife for an
      agreed period and agreed mahr), and then the man immediately responds thus:
      Qabiltu azzewaja lenafsi hakaza (i.e. I have accepted the marriage as was agreed.),
      the marriage will be in order. And the marriage will also be in order if they appoint
      other persons to act as their representatives." See "Fixed-Time Marriage," Grand
      Ayatollah al-Uzma Seyyed al-Sistani website, date not published, accessed July 2,
      2012, http://www.sistani.org/index.php?p=616687&id=1190.

108   Haeri, "Power of Ambiguity: Cultural Improvisations on the Theme of Temporary
      Marriage," p. 124.

109   This period of abstinence is known as *'idda*. See Ibid., pp. 57–8.

110   In a temporary union, a woman can only have one temporary marriage at any
      one time, whereas a Muslim man is allowed as many *sigheh* wives as he desires,

in addition to the four permanent wives he is legally permitted to marry. The possibility of a limitless number of female *sigheh* is just one area of ambiguity in which women's rights activists demand justice and review. Other questions concern the disenfranchisement of women and the status of wife, especially when a legal system allows a prostitute to bear the same title and status as that of a temporary wife who bears legitimate children with her *sigheh* partner.

111　Ayatollah Murtiza Motahhari, "The Rights of Women in Islam: Fixed-Term Marriage," part 3, *Mahjubi* (October/November 1981): pp. 52–6. Quoted in Haeri, *Law of Desire*, p. 96.

112　Mahdavi, "Women and the *Shi'i Ulama* in Iran," p. 22. See also Haeri, "Power of Ambiguity: Cultural Improvisations on the Theme of Temporary Marriage," p. 124. According to Qur'an 4:24, the verse reads, "Women already married, other than your slaves, God has ordained all this for you. Other women are lawful to you, so long as you seek them in marriage, with gifts from your property, looking for wedlock rather than fornication. If you wish to enjoy women through marriage, give them their bride-gift—this is obligatory—though if you should choose mutually, after fulfilling this obligation, to do otherwise [with the bride-gift], you will not be blame: God is all knowing and all wise. See *The Qur'an*, trans. by M. A. S. Abdel Haleem (Oxford: Oxford University Press, 2005), p. 53.

113　Haeri, "Power of Ambiguity: Cultural Improvisations on the Theme of Temporary Marriage," p. 124. For an explanation of pre-Islamic Arabia practices of temporary marriage, see I. K. A. Howard, "Mut'a Marriage Reconsidered in the Context of the Formal Procedures for Islamic Marriage," *Journal of Semitic Studies 20 (1975)*: pp. 82–92.

114　Haeri, "Power of Ambiguity: Cultural Improvisations on the Theme of Temporary Marriage," pp. 81–3. Another circumstance worth mentioning is the usage of *sigheh* for the purposes of procreation. For instance, in the event that a wife has abnormal menstrual cycles or cannot naturally conceive, a Muslim man may seek out the sexual services of a number of unmarried women. See Haeri, "Cultural Improvisations on the Theme of Temporary Marriage," pp. 136–7.

115　For instance, when a male and female want to remain in nonsexual contact and the woman remains unveiled in his presence, their agreement should stipulate the nonsexual nature of their interaction.

116　A temporary marriage requires no witnesses or registration, although in Iran, some clerics encourage the registration of *sigheh* unions.

117　In *sigheh* marriage, children conceived during these unions are considered legitimate.

118　Haeri, *Law of Desire*, p. 4.

119　Ibid., p. 64.

120　Ibid., especially pp. 23, 167, 203.

121　Ibid., p. 203.

122　Ibid., p. 64.

123　Ibid., p. 203.

124　Ibid.

125　Mir-Hosseini, "Sexuality, Rights, and Islam: Competing Gender Discourses in Postrevolutionary Iran," p. 207.

126　Haeri, "Temporary Marriage and the State in Iran: An Islamic Discourse on Female Sexuality," p. 202.

127 What constitutes husband and wife in Islamic legal terminology faces an entirely different reality in practice, wherein these terms carry many discrepancies in the domain of temporary marriage. In both permanent and temporary unions, the husband (*hamsar* or *shohar* in Persian) occupies an identifiable, stable status. The role of husband is identifiable as a singular individual in that heterosexual relationship. Yet the term "wife" appears more ambiguous by virtue of its non-singularity; the term "wife" can apply to more than one woman as her role as spouse can be replicated by the presence of another female spouse. Hence, a Muslim wife can be, officially and in accordance to *shari'a*, one of four permanent wives, provided that just treatment by the husband is extended equally among the other wives. Indeed, multiple wives married to one man in a permanent union only constitute a very small segment of Iranian society.

128 This crisis was also blamed on the alleged increase in the age of marriage, which had gone from 18.4 in 1966 to 19.7 in 1986, according to a 1988 report by the SCI. See Paidar, *Women and the Political Process in Twentieth-Century Iran,* pp. 284–5.

129 See *Ebtekar News*, "*Mokhalefan-e Ezdevaj-e Movaqat Cheh Migouyand?*/What Do the Opponents of Temporary Marriage Say?," Issue 949 (12 Tir 1386/July 3, 2007); "'*Tarvij-e Ezdevaj-e Movaqat' va Ma-vane'e-e Shar'ei va Orfi*/Promoting Temporary Marriage and Religious and Common Obstacles," BBC Persian, 15 Khordad 1396/ June 5, 2007, accessed December 4, 2019, http://www.bbc.co.uk/persian/iran/story/ 2007/06/070605_ka-short-marriage.shtml.

130 *Ettela'at*, Issue 18, 14 Aban 1364/November 5, 1985. Quoted in Paidar, *Women and the Political Process in Twentieth-Century Iran*, p. 285.

131 Paidar, *Women and the Political Process in Twentieth-Century Iran*, p. 285.

132 *Kayhan*, Issue 25. Quoted in Paidar, *Women and the Political Process in Twentieth-Century Iran*, p. 285.

133 *Zan-e Rouz*, Issue 1045 (Azar 1364/November 1985), pp. 4–5, 52–3, 58. Haeri mentions this interview in Footnote 60 of her article, "Power of Ambiguity: Cultural Improvisations on the Theme of Temporary Marriage," pp. 123–54.

134 "60 Minutes," CBS, interview with Hojatoleslam Ali Akbar Hashemi Rafsanjani, March 8, 1997, accessed June 5, 2011, http://www.youtube.com/watch?v=P-ojq-O_Ecc.

135 Haeri, "Marriage and the State in Iran: An Islamic Discourse on Female Sexuality," p. 205.

136 Haeri, "Temporary Marriage and the State in Iran: An Islamic Discourse on Female Sexuality," pp. 203–6.

137 Paidar, *Women and the Political Process in Twentieth-Century Iran*, p. 286.

138 For studies on Iran's macroeconomic trends in the 1990s, including unemployment rates of men and women, see Parvin Alizadeh, *The Economy of Iran: The Dilemmas of an Islamic State* (London: I.B. Tauris, 2000) and for the 2000s, see Ali Ghessari, ed., *Contemporary Iran: Economy, Society, Politics* (Oxford: Oxford University Press, Inc., 2009).

139 "'*Tarvij-e Ezdevaj-e Movaqat va Ma-vane'-e Shar'ei Orfi*/Promoting Temporary Marriage and Religious and Customary Obstacles." Pourmohammadi was Interior minister from August 2005 until August 2008. According to a report from Human Rights Watch, he was implicated in the 1988 execution of Iranian prisoners in Evin prison when he was a representative of the Ministry of Information, in charge of determining executions. See Human Rights Watch report of the accusations levied against him: Human Rights Watch, "Pour-mohammadi and the 1988 Prison

Massacres," HRW.org, December 2005, accessed December 4, 2019, http://www.hrw.org/legacy/backgrounder/mena/iran1205/2.htm.

140   Ibid.

141   Robert Tait, "Iranian Minister Backs Temporary Marriage to Relieve Lust of Youth," *The Guardian*, June 3, 2007, accessed December 4, 2019, http://www.guardian.co.uk/world/2007/jun/04/iran.roberttait.

142   Haeri, *Law of Desire*, p. 96.

143   Shahidian, "Contesting Discourses of Sexuality in Post-Revolutionary Iran," p. 186.

144   Quote originally from *Etemad* newspaper, though excerpted in Nazila Fathi, "To Regulate Prostitution, Iran Ponders Brothels," *New York Times*, August 28, 2002, accessed November 20, 2011, http://www.nytimes.com/2002/08/28/world/to-regulate-prostitution-iran-ponders-brothels.html.

145   "*Rahandazi-ye Khaneh-ye Efaf baraye-e Tarvij-e 'Sigheh' dar Shahroud ba Estefadeh az Yek Veblog*/A Chastity House Established in Shahroud Advocating *Sigheh* via Blog," Al-Arabiya, January 8, 2011, accessed December 4, 2019, http://www.alarabiya.net/articles/2011/01/08/132677.html.

146   Floor, "Venereal Disease in Iran (1855-2005): A Public Affair," p. 273.

147   Floor writes that conservative newspaper *Afarinesh* published a few details about the program. Ibid.

148   Established in 2001 in Tehran, WomeninIran opened after reformist newspapers were targeted and shut down by the government. An online venture, WomeninIran consisted of women journalists and academics writing on topics that championed women's rights causes on the internet. Their stories were often written anonymously and integrated UN international conventions, such as the Universal Declaration of Human Rights and the Convention for the Elimination of Discrimination Against Women (CEDAW). Writing in both Persian and English, they covered domestic news, provided investigative reports, and highlighted stories of human rights abuses such as domestic violence, the situation of female prisoners, and women's right to enter soccer stadiums—topics that were normally considered taboo and thus not covered in the main press. Information from WomeninIran website and their former researcher Leila Mouri.

149   WomeninIran, "*Tarh-ha-ye Jaygozin-e Khaneh-ha-ye Efaf*?/Alternative Plans for Chastity Houses?" WomeninIran.com, 2 Mehr 1381/September 24, 2002, accessed November 22, 2011, http://www.womeniniran.com/news/02-07-81/1-02-07-81.htm.

150   "*Tarh-ha-ye Jaygozin-e Khaneh-ha-ye Efaf*?/Alternative Plans for Chastity Houses?" WomeninIran.com.

151   Ibid.

152   Alavi, *We Are Iran,* p. 157.

153   Charles Recknagel and Azam Gorgin, "Iran: Proposal Debated for Solving Prostitution with 'Chastity Houses,'" *Pars Times*, August 7, 2002.

154   WomeninIran, "*Tarh-ha-ye Jaygozin-e Khaneh-ha-ye Efaf*?/Alternative Plans for Chastity Houses?"

155   Ibid. Their protests were launched following reports that housewives were becoming infected with HIV after having only sexual contact with their husbands—meaning that they were participating in sexual relations outside of their permanent marriage in the form of *sigheh* and/or extramarital affairs.

156   Ibid.

157   Ibid.

158   Ibid., p. 157.

159   Nadya Labi, "Married for a Minute," *Mother Jones*, March/April 20120, accessed
       November 10, 2011, http://www.motherjones.com/politics/2010/03/temporary-m
       arriage-iran-islam.

160   Ibid.

161   Haeri, *Law of Desire*, p. 2.

162   Haeri, "Power of Ambiguity: Cultural Improvisations on the Theme of Temporary
       Marriage," p. 125.

163   Haeri, *Law of Desire*, p. 5.

164   Ziba Mir-Hosseini, "A Response to Shahla Haeri's *Review of Marriage on Trial, A
       Study of Islamic Family Law in Iran and Morocco*," *International Journal of Middle
       East Studies* 30, no. 3 (August 1998): pp. 470–1.

165   Labi, "Married for a Minute."

166   Haeri's article on the *sigheh mu'ta* provides a more thorough account of this
       practice. Interestingly enough, there is a debate between Mir-Hosseini and Haeri
       over the general practice of temporary marriage, which is worth reading. See Mir-
       Hosseini, "A Response to Shahla Haeri's Review of *Marriage on Trial, A Study of
       Islamic Family Law in Iran and Morocco*" and Shahla Haeri, "A Reply to Ziba Mir-
       Hosseini," *International Journal of Middle East Studies* 30, no. 3 (August 1998): pp.
       471–2.

167   Paidar, *Women and the Political Process in Twentieth-Century Iran,* p. 286. Quoted in
       Haeri, *Law of Desire*, p. 165.

168   Haeri, *Law of Desire*, p. 50.

169   Mir-Hosseini explains, "*mut'a* marriage is stigmatized and socially unacceptable,
       involves no celebration, establishes no common residence, and is often done in
       secrecy." See Mir-Hosseini, "A Response to Shahla Haeri's Review of *Marriage on
       Trial*" and Haeri, *Law of Desire*.

170   The feminist journal was closed by the authorities in February 2007.

171   Elaine Sciolino, "Love Finds a Way in Iran: 'Temporary Marriage,'" October 4, 2000,
       accessed September 12, 2011, http://www.library.cornell.edu/colldev/mideast/tmp
       mrig.htm.

172   See "*Sigheh: Niyaz-e Mali, Mabna- ye Tahghir-e Zan-e Irani/Sigheh*: Financial Need,
       the Reason for the Denigration of Iranian Women," *Gozaresh* 215, no. 19 (Bahman
       1388/February 2009): p. 10.

173   Ibid.

174   Ibid. The authors also note that this financial stress is gender-related; women, they state,
       have much more difficulty entering the workforce than men. In my own interviews
       conducted in 2011 in Tehran, I spoke with two women who mentioned that they had
       entered *sigheh* as a way to sustain a romantic relationship with married men, who had no
       intentions of divorcing their permanent wives. Both women were professional women in
       their mid-thirties who were in *sigheh* relationships with older men.

175   Ibid., p. 11.

176   Ibid. As for the male demographic that participates in a *sigheh* relationship, *Gozaresh*
       reported that only 3 percent of men are believed to be against *sigheh*. As for the
       men who are generally associated with entering into *sigheh* partnerships, *Gozaresh*
       does not positively characterize them. Male participants to *sigheh* are described
       as *vashy*—a term in Persian that connotes both wild and violent characteristics.
       With their *sigheh* spouses, they engage in *gheir materof-e jensi* (nonstandard sex,
       presumably meaning risky sexual positions) and often believe that by making threats

and using money as their advantage, they can behave in any manner with these women. Married men, in particular, are portrayed negatively, as their reasons for *sigheh* partnerships are based on their wives' alleged failures: for instance, husbands describe their wives as being sexually cold or emotionless, or they do not become sexually aroused by their husbands. In no manner did the husbands admit to their own personal failures or misgivings.

177 Ibid. Only in 2011 did the Ministry of Culture and Islamic Guidance and the Ministry of Health and Human Services permit the release of a sexual education DVD detailing how to have pleasurable sex between spouses, entitled *Ashnayeh Mahboub* (The Beloved Companion). Upon its release and within the time span of one month, the DVD was no longer available across Tehran pharmacies; the video is now available online.

178 *Mehriyeh* is a payment owed to the wife upon marriage that is typically requested in the event of a divorce. It is an essential condition for the legality of marriage and also a wife's right to request. For an in-depth explanation of *mehriyeh*, see Mir-Hosseini, *Marriage on Trial*, pp. 72–83. See also Zahra Tizro, *Domestic Violence in Iran: Women, Marriage and Islam*, pp. 39–44.

179 "*Sigheh: Niyaz-e Mali, Mabna- ye Tahghir-e Zan-e Irani/Sigheh*: Financial Need, the Reason for the Denigration of Iranian Women," *Gozaresh*.

180 In January 2012, rising inflation caused the value of gold coins to skyrocket. The number of *sekeh* (gold coins) is often the bargaining factor in the formulation of *mehrieh* in a permanent marriage contract. Legally speaking, *mehrieh* is one of the most important structural components of the traditional Islamic marriage and must be indicated in the marriage contract itself. The groom's acceptance of *Mehrieh* is often determined by the number of *sekeh* he agrees to pay the bride in case of emergency or the dissolution of marriage. This agreement is sound provided that the union is consummated "*Afzayesh-e Ezdevaj-e Movaqat pa-be-pa-ye Qeimat-e Sekeh*/The Rise in Temporary Marriage on Pace with the Rise in Gold Coins," Asr-e Iran, 5 Bahman 1390/January 25, 2012, accessed December 4, 2019, http://www.asriran.com/fa/news/198672/افزایش-ازدواج-موقت-پا-به-پای-قیمت-سکه.

181 See Parvaneh Hooshmand, "Sexualities. Practices. Iran," in *Encyclopedia of Women in Islamic Cultures: Family, Law and Politics* 3, ed. Suad Joseph and Afsaneh Najmabadi (Leiden: Brill Publishing, 2005), pp. 384–6.

182 Ibid., p. 385.

183 Ibid.

184 Permanently married women are not permitted to enter *sigheh* relationships, be they sexual or nonsexual. Haeri explains, "A fictive nonsexual *sigheh* with a married woman is . . . perceived to be threatening because it symbolically infringers on the husbands' exclusive right of ownership to his wife's wifely duties and, for that matter, poses a threat to the purity of his seed." See Haeri, *Law of Desire*, p. 93.

185 "*Mokhalefan-e Ezdevaj-e Movaqat Cheh Migouyand?*/What Do the Opponents of Temporary Marriage Say?".

 The government does not publish recent statistics about the status of *sigheh* usage among Iranians.

186 Fatemeh Sadeghi, "'Temporary Marriage' and the Economy of Pleasure," trans. Frieda Afary, Tehran Bureau online, March 15, 2010, accessed December 4, 2019, http://www.pbs.org/wgbh/pages/frontline/tehranbureau/2010/03/temporary-marr iage-and-the-economy-of-pleasure.html.

Chapter 4

1 One of the IRI's founding fathers, Hojjat al-Eslam Ali Akbar Hashemi Rafsanjani (1934–2017) was the fourth president of Iran from 1989 to 1997.

2 *Kayhan*, airmail edition, 23 Bahman 1364/ February 12, 1986. Quoted in Najmabadi, "Iran's Turn to Islam: From Modernism to a Moral Order," p. 215.

3 Najmabadi, "Iran's Turn to Islam: From Modernism to Moral Order," p. 204.

4 Nashat, "Women in the Islamic Republic of Iran," p. 185.

5 *Kayhan*, March 14, 1983. Quoted in Haleh Afshar, "Women, State and Ideology in Iran," *Third World Quarterly* 7, no. 2 (April 1985): pp. 265–6.

6 Shahidian, "Contesting Discourses of Sexuality in Post-Revolutionary Iran," pp. 97, 99. See also Najmabadi, "Power, Morality and the New Muslim Womanhood."

7 "lokht," *Sulayman Hayyim New Persian-English Dictionary* (Tehran: Librairie-imprimerie Beroukhim, 1934–6).

8 Zahedi, "Contested Meaning of the Veil and Political Ideologies of Iranian Regimes," p. 89.

9 Mir-Hosseini, *Islam and Gender*, p. 7.

10 Moghadam, "Revolution, the State, Islam, and Women," p. 45.

11 See Benjamin Forest and Juliet Johnson, "Unraveling the Threads of History: Soviet-Era Monuments and Post-Soviet National Identity in Moscow," *Annals of the Association of American Geographers* 92, no. 3 (September 2002): p. 524.

12 After public protest, the statue was repaired and still remains in the same square in central Tehran.

13 Abrahamian, *A History of Modern Iran*, p. 177.

14 The term "body" refers to individual and whole representations or features of the physical structure of a person, such as hair or limbs.

15 For more on the division between private and public space within an Islamic context, see Fatima Mernissi, *The Veil and the Male Elite: A Feminist's Interpretation of Women's Rights in Islam* (New York: Basic Books, 1991).

16 Although this chapter focuses on the conceptualization of public space in the Shi'a Iranian context, there are other formations of public space, as they are practiced and constructed in other contexts of the region, which are also worth future consideration. See Shirley Ardener, ed., *Women and Space: Ground Rules and Social Maps* (New York: St. Martin's Press, 1981). For an analysis of spatial divisions in the Algerian context, see Doria Cherifati-Merabtine, "Algeria at a Crossroads: National Liberation, Islamization, and Women," in *Gender and National Identity: Women and Politics in Muslim Societies*, ed. Valentine Moghadam (London: Zed Books, 1994), pp. 40–62.

17 Jane Khatib-Chahidi, "Sexual Prohibitions, Shared Space, and Fictive Marriages in Shi'ite Iran," in *Women and Space: Ground Rules and Social Maps*, ed. Shirley Ardener (New York: St. Martin's Press, 1981), p. 112. See also Haeri, *Law of Desire*, p. 76.

18 Khatib-Chahidi, "Sexual Prohibitions, Shared Space, and Fictive Marriages in Shi'ite Iran," p. 114.

19 Ibid.

20 Khatib-Chahidi describes four categories of *mahram* persons: blood relatives (including half brothers and sisters, maternal and paternal aunts and uncles), milk relatives (meaning children breastfed by a nonbiological woman and including

her own biological children), relatives by marriage, and relationships arising from illegitimate sexual unions. Ibid., pp. 116–17.

21 Ibid., p. 114.

22 Haeri, *Law of Desire*, p. 76.

23 Reza Arjmand, *Public Urban Space, Gender and Segregation: Women-only Urban Parks in Iran* (New York: Routledge, 2017), pp. 7–8.

24 Ziba Mir-Hosseini has published several interviews with prominent and high-ranking Shi'a *mujtahids* who offer differing opinions on "guarding one's gaze" with respect to observing *hejab*. See Mir-Hosseini, *Islam and Gender*, pp. 44–5, 76.

   In Persian, the word *tahrik* refers to bodily provocation in which a man or woman's desires are aroused and thus this arousal triggers an inclination toward that object or person of desire; this instigates or provokes such feelings and, in many cases, bodily reaction (or arousal of the sexual organs), in him or her.

25 Dabashi, "Body-Less Faces: Mutilating Modernity and Abstracting Women in an 'Islamic Cinema,'" p. 377.

26 According to Shi'a discourse on sexuality, the natural disposition of a heterosexual gaze is wanton and lustful when not confined to an Islamic marital framework. Controlling this gaze thus involves reigning in unrestrained male and female sexualities. The Qur'an (24:30 and 24:31) instructs believing men and women to lower their gaze and guard their modesty. For more on the discourse of the gaze in Islamic texts, see Mir-Hosseini, *Islam and Gender*, pp. 64, 68, 94.

27 Ibid.

28 Haggai Ram, "Multiple Iconographies: Political Posters in the Iranian Revolution," in *Picturing Iran: Art, Society and Revolution*, ed. Shiva Balaghi and Lynn Gumpert (London: I.B. Tauris, 2002), p. 90.

29 See Arjomand, *After Khomeini*; Abrahamian, *Iran between Two Revolutions*; Abrahamian, *A History of Modern Iran*; Rostam-Povey, *Women, Power and Politics in 21st Century Iran*.

30 For instance, in Tehran, a bronze statue of a veiled mother (sculpted by Zahra Rahnavard) is erected in Mothers' Square (also called Mohseni Square) at Mirdamad Boulevard. At Imam Khomeini Square (formerly Toupkhaneh Square during the Pahlavi period), there is a monument honoring Iran's pre-Islamic and imperial dynasty, and on top of that structure is a metal sculpture of the word God in Arabic. Hassan Abad Square in the traditional business (Moniriyeh) district of Tehran was renamed to the 31st of Shahrivar Square, however this name did not stick, and the square is still referred to by its original name. The 31st of Shahrivar (September 30) marks the day Iraqi forces launched an air and ground invasion of Iran.

31 "*Gozaresh-ha az Voghou-e 'Dargeeri' dar Meydan-e Baharestan-e Tehran Hekayat Darad*/Reports of Outbreaks in Tehran's Baharestan Square," BBC Persian, 3 Tir 1388/ June 24, 2009, accessed August 11, 2011, http://www.bbc.co.uk/persian/iran/2 009/06/090624_nm_demonstraion.shtml.

32 Hamid Dabashi has written extensively about the tumultuous period after the reelection of President Mahmoud Ahmadinejad in June 2009. See Hamid Dabashi, *The Green Movement in Iran* (New Brunswick: Transaction Publishers, 2011).

33 The media reported two people were killed by Iranian Revolutionary Guards Corps' forces during anti-regime protests following gas price hikes in November 2019. See Saeed Dadeghi, "Map of the Protests," Radio Zameneh.com, 29 Aban 1398/ November 20, 2019, accessed November 24, 2019, https://www.radiozamaneh. com/475235.

34 Baharestan Square was already well-known for holding opposition rallies during the prescient days of democratically elected Prime Minister Mohammed Mossadegh (1882–1967), who was overthrown in a British and American-orchestrated coup d'état.

35 Fars News Agency, http://www.aerocenter.ir/forum/showthread.php?t=3772. See also "*Namayesh-e Moushak-e Shahab-e Seh dar Meydan-e Baharestan-e Tehran*/The Exhibition of Shahab-Three Missile in Tehran's Baharestan Square," BBC Persian, 3 Mehr 1387/September 24, 2008, accessed December 6, 2019, http://www.bbc.co.uk /persian/iran/story/2008/09/080924_mg-shahab3.shtml.

36 For more information on Ayatollah Modarres (1870–1937), see Abrahamian, *Iran between Two Revolutions*.

37 See Afsaneh Monfared, "Baharestan," Encyclopedia Islamica.com, date not published, accessed July 5, 2012, http://www.encyclopaediaislamica.com/madkhal2 .php?sid=2184.

38 Ibid.

39 *Zan-e Rouz*, Issue 853 (Bahman 1360/February 1982), "*Begoo! Begoo!*," p. 62.

40 I was not successful in locating other photographs of this statue; moreover, public recollection of it had also waned.

41 See photograph of "*Mojassameh-ye Azadi-ye Shahenshahi dar Meydan-e Baharestan*," in section "*Begoo! Begoo!*" of *Zan-e Rouz*, Issue 853 (Bahman 1360/February 1982), p. 62.

42 The term used in this text is *desaar*, an Arabic term for clothing and dress. The author of the complaint did not use the more common Persian word *poushesh*.

43 The IRP, an important parliamentary party, was first led by cleric Mohammed Husayn Beheshti, and it was disbanded by the regime in 1987.

44 Parsa, *Social Origins of the Iranian Revolution*, pp. 297–8.

45 For more on the IRI's state goals, see *Islamic Republic of Iran Constitution*, amended July 28, 1989, Article 3.

46 *Awrat* is mentioned several times in the Qur'an, as well as in hadith literature. In Persian, the term is known as *awrat*, while in Arabic, the term is pronounced as *awra*. See Qur'an 24: 58 *Sura al-Nur* and Qur'an 33:13, *Sura al-Ahzab*.

47 For more on the concept of *awrat*, see Haideh Moghissi, *Women and Islam: Social Conditions, Obstacles, and Prospects* (New York: Routledge, 2005), pp. 81–3. Moghissi provides a contextual analysis of the many uses of *awrat* in the Qur'an and *hadith* literature, which has often been associated with women's bodily weakness. She argues that a more suitable definition should be "inviolate vulnerability," as reference to the broader notions of Arabo-Islamic sanctity and privacy of the home and family.

48 According to Ja'far al-Saddiq, men's *awrat* is considered to be their genitals and buttocks.

49 Grand Ayatollahs, known by their honorary titles of *Ayatollah al-Uzma*, are the highest sources of emulation in Shi'a Islam. They offer specialist interpretations of Islamic texts and law and publish their interpretations in *resaleh*, which ideally should demonstrate their expert knowledge as Shi'a *mujtahid*.

50 Ayatollah Ruhollah Khomeini, *Tahrir al-Vasileh*, vol. 1, Chapter 129, lines 3–11.

51 Sadr, "*Ahkam-e Lebas*/Clothing Regulations," p. 229.

52 Sadr., p. 230. Grand Ayatollahs have even deliberated over exercise clothing, for its tightness on the body presents potential challenges in preserving modesty and Islamic chastity and might elicit sexual arousal in male and female observers.

53 For more information about Ayatollah Muhammad Bahjat, who died in 2009, see Yasin Jibouri, "*Uswat al-Aarifeen*. A Look at the Life of Ayatollah Bahjat," Ahlul Bayt Digital Islamic Library Project, 2005, accessed March 15, 2012, http://www.al-islam.org/uswat_alarifin/. For Behjat's *resaleh*, which is published online, see http://www.aviny.com/Ahkam/ResalehBahjat/index.aspx.

54 Ibid.

55 Recall the burning down of Cinema Rex in Abadan, Iran, which I discuss in Chapter 2 of this book, in a section describing the attempts to set *Shahr-e No* district ablaze in the first days of the revolution.

56 In the early history of Islam, according to Islamic and Christian sources, there is an oft-quoted story of an attack on images and statues, marking an "outbreak of iconoclasm," during Yazid II. b. 'Abd al-Malik Caliphate (720–4). See G. R. D. King, "Islam, Iconoclasm, and the Declaration of Doctrine," *Bulletin of the School of Oriental and African Studies, University of London* 48, no. 2 (1985): p. 267.

57 Yusuf al-Qardawi, *The Lawful and the Prohibited in Islam* (Oak Brook, IL: American Trust Publications, 1999), pp. 98–9.

58 See *"Hormat-e Mojassamehsazi va Naqqashi*/The Sanctity of Sculpting and Painting," *Kavoshi Now dar Fiqh-e Eslami* 4 (Summer and Fall 1374/1995): pp. 62–4.

59 See Grand Ayatollah Naser Makarem Shirazi, "Comments on Exceptions on Sculptures and Statues," date not published, accessed July 12, 2012, http://makarem.ir/websites/farsi/estefta/?mit=1121.

60 See *"Setiz ba Mojassameh*/The Struggle with Statues," BBC Persian, August 26, 2002, accessed September 20, 2011, http://www.bbc.co.uk/persian/arts/020826_mj-mojassame.shtml.

61 See Ehsan Yarshater, *"Namayeshgah-e Bienal-e Naqqashi va Peykarsazi dar Kakh-e Abyaz," Sokhan* 9, no. 1 (1958): pp. 82–4.

62 Habibollah Ayatollahi, *The Book of Iran: The History of Iranian Art* (Tehran: Organization for Islamic Culture and Communications & Center for International-Cultural Studies, 2003), p. 307.

63 The 1950s was also the decade in which the faculty of Fine Arts in Tehran University, which had opened an arts academy in 1940 modeled after France's Beaux Arts, developed a full university degree curriculum. See Maryam Ekhtiar and Marika Sardar, "Modern and Contemporary Art in Iran," in *Heilbrunn Timeline of Art History* (New York: The Metropolitan Museum of Art, 2000).

64 *"Setiz ba Mojassameh*/The Struggle with Statues," BBC Persian.

65 Tabatabai (*d.* 2008) was a poet, avant-garde painter, and sculptor. Ziapour (*d.* 1999) was a modern-art pioneer in painting. Tanavoli (*b.* 1937) is considered one of Iran's greatest modern-art painters and sculptors.

66 Ibid. In the same article, BBC Persian reported that in 1980, many statues considered anti-revolutionary were destroyed. As recently as 2002, Ayatollah Jannati urged attendants of Tehran's Friday prayer to destroy the statue of "Kaveh Ahangar" in Esfahan because it was anti-revolutionary.

67 According to the sculpture's title, it is presumed that the artwork depicts a male creature playing a flute.

68 The City Theatre is a theater complex situated at the northwest corner of Daneshjou Park in central Tehran.

69 *"Mard-e Neylabakzan-e Ta'atre-e Shahr dar Kojast?*/Where Is *The Flute Player* at City Theater?" *Rooznameh Aftab-e Yazd*, 28 Aban 1386/November 19, 2007, accessed February 14, 2012, http://www.magiran.com/npview.asp?ID=1523682.

70 "*Mojassameh-ye Mard-e Neylabakzan Bazsazi Mishavad/The Flute Player* under Repair," *Rooznameh Iran*, 13 Aban 1386/December 4, 2007, accessed February 14, 2012, p. 24, http://www.magiran.com/npview.asp?ID=1531840. Mohassess did not comply. Most of his public works of art were destroyed after the revolution. According to his website, he subsequently destroyed all remaining artworks in Iran. See "Biography: Part One of Bahman Mohassess," Bahman Mohassess Foundation, 2012, accessed February 13, 2012, http://bahmanmohassess.com/life/biography-part-one/.

71 *Mard-e Neylabakzan, Hamchenan Montazer-e Mohasses Ast/*The Flute-Playing Male Statue Is Still Waiting for Mohasses," *Aftab News*, 21 Esfand 1386/ March 11, 2008, accessed February 14, 2012, http://www.aftabir.com/news/view/2008/mar/11/ مرد-نی-لبك-زن-همچنان-منتظر-محصص-است/c5c1205239299_art_culture_art_statue.php.

72 Ibid.

73 "*Setiz ba Mojassameh/* The Struggle with Statues," BBC Persian.

74 The history of the communist movement in Iran begins in the late nineteenth century and early twentieth century with the rapid growth of industry and rising discontent against despotism. Iran's Tudeh Party, the oldest political party in Iran, is believed to be the first organized Communist Party in the Middle East; it became factionalized during the Pahlavi years. Immediately after the revolution, communist supporters became opposed to Khomeini's consolidation of power, for the new leadership did not include representatives of the left parties. For more on the factionalism of opposition parties in the early years of the postrevolutionary period, see Farhang Jahanpour, "The Rise and Fall of the Tudeh Party," *The World Today* 40, no. 4 (April 1984): p. 153.

75 "*Setiz ba Mojassameh/*The Struggle with Statues," BBC Persian.

76 Ibid.

77 Ibid.

78 Ibid.

79 According to Iranian reformer and philosopher Abdelkarim Soroush, "The Iranian state may be the first ever case of a state that intends to make society religious." See Masoud Behnoud, "The Ideal Islamic State: An Unattainable Quest," Abdolkarim Soroush website, January 8, 2006, accessed July 10, 2011, http://www.drsoroush .com/English/News_Archive/E-NWS-20060108-TheIdealIslamicState-AnUnatta inableQuest.html.

80 Nader Entessar, "Criminal Law and the Legal System in Revolutionary Iran," *Boston College Third World Law Journal* 8, no. 1 (January 1988): p. 100.

81 See Ameneh Youssefzadeh, "The Situation of Music in Iran since the Revolution: The Role of Official Organizations," *British Journal of Ethnomusicology* 9, no. 2 (2000): pp. 35–61. *Gasht-e Ershad* is part of the police force, under the supervision of the security forces, the Ministry of the Interior, and Ayatollah Ali Khamenei. In the large and bustling squares heading to northern Tehran, *Gasht-e Ershad* is the expected presence monitoring public spaces, especially during the summer months. Wherever crowds of different socioeconomic backgrounds and religious persuasions gather and intermix, *Gasht-e Ershad* is likely found to remind them of both sexual difference and observance of the separation of the sexes. At the entrance of parks, such as midtown Laleh Park and uptown Mellat Park, a *Gasht-e Ershad* representative, with walkie-talkie in hand, reminds passersby to observe Islamic custom.

82 Entessar, "Criminal Law and the Legal System in Revolutionary Iran," p. 100. See also "Iran: New 'Morality Police' Units Generate Controversy," RFERF, July 25, 2002, accessed June 14, 2012, http://www.rferl.org/content/article/1100367.html.

83 See *Mosavabat-e Comisiyon-e Siasatgozari dar Omour-e Ejraee-ye Mobarezeh-ye Farhangi ba Mazaher-e Fesad 6877/The Ratification of Policy-Making Commission Regarding Executive Affairs of Cultural Struggle with the Symbols of Corruption 6877*, Islamic Republic of Iran Ministry of the Interior, 19 Ordibehesht 1371/ May 9, 1992.

84 Ibid., Objective 4.

85 "*Tarvij-e Farhang-e Efaf va Hejab dar Asar-e Honari Mored-e Nazar Gharar Girad/* Encouraging a Culture of Chastity and *Hejab* in Works of Art Being Considered," *Mehr News*, 17 Dey 1390/ January 7, 2012, accessed March 13, 2012, http://www .mehrnews.com/fa/NewsDetail.aspx?NewsID=1503379. Since 2009, the Minister of Culture and Islamic Guidance is Seyyed Mohammad Hosseini.

86 Ibid.

87 Abrahamian, *A Modern History of Iran*, pp. 186–8.

88 See Ali Gheissari and Kaveh-Cyrus Sanandaji, "New Conservative Politics and Electoral Behavior in Iran," in *Contemporary Iran: Economy, Society, Politics* (Oxford: Oxford University Press, 2009), p. 2. For a midterm assessment of Khatami's first presidential term and a description of the sociopolitical environment in Iran during the period, see Jahangir Amuzegar, "Khatami and the Iranian Economy at Mid-Term," *Middle East Journal* 53, no. 4 (Autumn 1999): pp. 534–52.

89 See Afary, *Sexual Politics in Modern Iran* and Farideh Farhi, "Religious Intellectuals, the 'Woman Question,' and the Struggle for the Creation of a Democratic Public Sphere in Iran," *International Journal of Politics, Culture, and Society* 15, no. 2 (Winter 2001): pp. 315–39.

90 In 1982 the Supreme Council was known as the *Setad-e Enqelab-e Farhangi* (Headquarter of the Culture Revolution) and from 1982 to 1987, the membership of the Khomeini-appointed Council did not change. Circa 1375, the Council became known by its present name. Its membership is generally divided into three groups all of whom Khamenei appoints: honorary, legal authorities and ministries, and individual members. On 21 Esfand 1381/March 12, 2003, new membership was inducted for three-year terms. The last induction of members took place on 17 Khordad 1390/June 7, 2011. The President, Head of Judiciary, Speaker of Parliament, MCIG, and the Ministry of Health and Medical Education are members of the Supreme Council. For a government narrative in Persian of the Supreme Council of the Cultural Revolution, see Secretariat of the Office of the Supreme Council of the Cultural Revolution, "Introducing the Supreme Council," date unknown, accessed March 13, 2012, http://www.iranculture.org/fa/Default.aspx?cu rrent=viewDoc&currentID=1338.

91 See Paidar, *Women and the Political Process in Twentieth-Century Iran*, p. 314.

92 Supreme Council of the Cultural Revolution, *The Principles, Foundations, and Executing Methods in Developing a Culture of Chastity*, 14 Bahman 1376/February 3, 1998, Article 10.

93 An Arabic term that entered Persian via Islamic sources, the word *efaf* in Persian has been translated as "chastity," "modesty," and "virtue." I have chosen the translation of "modesty" (from the phrase "culture of modesty"), as it best illustrates propriety in dress, speech, and/or conduct. Although imperfect in encapsulating all aspects of these aforementioned terms, it still conveys forms of self-restraint, avoidance, and/or rejection of temptation, behavior, and acts that are viewed as unlawful, unvirtuous, and lust-driven—all of which are invoked in the term.

94 Ibid.

95 For a brief discussion of the committee's inaugural years, see Keddie and Richard, *Modern Iran: Roots and Results of Revolution*, p. 250. See also Paidar, *Women and the Political Process in Twentieth-Century Iran*, pp. 320–1 and Arjomand, *After Khomeini*, p. 69.

96 See *Ousul va Mabani va Ravesh-ha-ye Ejraee-ye Gostaresh-e Farhang-e Efaf/The Principles, Foundations, and Executing Methods in Spreading a Culture of Chastity*, Supreme Council of the Cultural Revolution, 14 Bahman 1376/February 3, 1998.

97 Negar Mottahedeh, *Displaced Allegories: Post-Revolutionary Iranian Cinema* (Durham: Duke University Press, 2008), p. 2.

98 *Ousul va Mabani va Ravesh-ha-ye Ejraee-ye Gostaresh-e Farhang-e Efaf*, Objective 5.

99 See *Rahbord-ha-ye Gostaresh-e Farhang-e Efaf/Guidelines of Developing or Spreading a Culture of Chastity*, Supreme Council of the Cultural Revolution, 13 Dey 1384/ July 26, 2005. I point to other objectives outlined in the text: Objective 38 comments on producing a culture of chastity through fashion. Objective 45 designates that fabrics and clothing that promote anti-Islamic values will not be imported to Iran. Objective 30 clarifies that there is no conflict with women wearing the *hejab* and being active in society.

100 Ibid., Objective 8.

101 See *Qanoun-e Rahkar-ha-ye Ejraee-ye Gostaresh-e Farhang-e Efaf va Hejab/The Law of Executing Solution for Developing a Culture of Hejab and Chastity*, Supreme Council of the Cultural Revolution, 4 Mordad 1384/January 2006.

102 Ibid., Introduction, 2006.

103 Ibid.

104 Mal-veiling means wearing the veil in a manner in which Islamic *hejab* is not fully observed; one typical example is when the head is not covered, revealing a person's hair. According to Fatemeh Sadeghi, bad-*hejab* is translated as "misveiled," describing girls who wear *hejab* in order to "accommodate themselves to Iranian legal requirements yet intentionally disregard the spirit if not precisely the letter of the law." See Sadeghi, "Negotiating with Modernity: Young Women and Sexuality in Iran," p. 250.

105 Ibid., "General Policies and Methods," Objective 3.

106 Ibid., Objective 8.

107 Sadr, p. 66.

108 See Supreme Council of the Cultural Revolution, *Qanoun-e Rahkar-ha-ye Ejraee-ye Gostaresh-e Farhang-e Efaf va Hejab*, "Policies and Solutions," Objective 4, accessed March 13, 2012, http://www.effat.ir/fa/index.php?option=com_content&view=art icle&id=1222306:-1&catid=85:1390-02-26-19-41-09&Itemid=108.

109 Ibid., "General Policies and Methods."

110 *Qanoun-e Gostaresh-e Rahkarha-ye Ejraee-ye Efaf va Hejab/Law for the Spreading of the Method of Executing Hejab and Chastity*, "Security Forces," Duty 1.

111 Ibid., Duty 9.

112 Ibid., Duty 2.

113 University settings are not exempt from these regulations on the body. Explicit guidelines are frequently published by semiofficial online Fars News Agency, which publishes new dress codes prohibiting particular forms of dress, including body jewelry and headgear that are not paired with some form of a *hejab*. Directed at both men and women, the dress code would ensure all transgressors would not be allowed entrance into university grounds. These dress regulations banned the wearing of bright-colored clothing, tight or shortened slacks, and tattoos that were

visible to the human eye. As women would be prohibited from dressing in tight clothing, men would also be ordered to follow similar modes of propriety. They were also forbidden from wearing shorts, body jewelry, and sleeves that were considered too short.

114   "*Mankan-ha-ye Sineh Borideh dar Vitrine-ha-ye Iran*/Cut-off Breasts of Mannequins in Iran's Windowships," Radio Farda, 12 Azar 1385/December 3, 2006, accessed June 5, 2012, www.radiofarda.com/content/f2_mancan/269913.html.

115   "Iran's Catwalk Ban Is Only the Beginning," RFERL, September 20, 2008, accessed July 4, 2012, http://www.rferl.org/content/Iran_Catwalk_Ban_Only_The_Begin ning/1201610.html.

116   These guidelines were an extension of clothing regulations, *Qanoun-e Samandehi-ye Mode va Lebas*, devised in 2007 (1385). For more information about the "Guidelines For Fashion and Dress Shows" from the MCIG, see "*Sharayet va Zavabet-e Bargozari-ye Namayeshga-he Mode va Lebas dar Keshvar Eblagh Shod*/Conditions and Regulations on the Exhibition of Fashion and Clothing in the Country Announced," Fars News Agency, 14 Shahrivar 1387/ September 4, 2008, accessed July 1, 2012, http://www.farsnews.com/newstext.php?nn=8706140288.

117   Ibid.

118   Additionally, during any designer exhibition, it is required that appropriate music should be played, which should be "well-matched to Islamic and Iranian culture," and according to one news report, "should not prompt models to move or walk in an inappropriate manner." See "Iran's Catwalk Ban is Only the Beginning," RFERL.

119   According to a December 2006 Radio Farda news report, sales dropped by 20 percent in comparison to the previous year. See "*Mankan-ha-ye Sineh Borideh dar Vitrine-ha-ye Iran*/Cut-off Breasts of Mannequins in Iran's Windowships," Radio Farda.

120   I interviewed four clothing managers in Haft-e Tir in July 2010 and June 2011. They detailed how they would maneuver through Gasht-e *Ershad*'s policies. The managers did not want to provide their names and preferred that I report only on the general procedural interactions between them and the Ministry of Cultural and Islamic Guidance.

121   See Fataneh Farahani, *Diasporic Narratives of Sexuality: Identity Formation Among Iranian-Swedish Women* (Stockholm: Stockholm Universitet, 2007), pp. 138–40.

122   Mehrangiz Kar, "Death of a Mannequin," in *My Sister, Guard Your Veil; My Brother, Guard Your Eyes: Uncensored Iranian Voices*, ed. Lila Azam Zanganeh (Boston: Beacon Press, 2006), p. 32.

123   Quoted in Kar, *Crossing the Red Line*, p. 35. See also Farahani, *Diasporic Narratives of Sexuality*, p. 140.

124   As reported on its website, since 1989, the company Manken-e Yaran (also known as Yaran Company) has been the first and largest producer, distributor, and exporter of male and female mannequins in Iran. With over ten offices across the country, Manken-e Yaran advertises and sells mannequins online through an Iran-based web address to domestic and regional customers. Noticeably, some of the male mannequins are advertised without clothing. Female mannequins, by contrast, are all pictured with clothing; however, not all of them have veils. See Manken-e Yaran, accessed July 4, 2012, http://www.yarancompany.com/index.html.

125   Kar, "Death of a Mannequin," p. 35.

126   Ibid.

127 "*Mankan-ha-ye Sineh Borideh dar Vitrine-ha-ye Iran*/Cut-off Breasts of Mannequins in Iran's Windowships," Radio Farda.
128 Power, "Mannequins, Manners, and Mutilation."
129 Registering modesty involved a deliberate process of Islamic reform, the subjects of Chapters 1, 2, and 3 of this work.
130 Mehri Honarbin-Holliday, "Autonomous Minds and Bodies in Theory and Practice: Women Constructing Cultural Identities and Becoming Visible through Art," in *Women, Power and Politics in 21st Century Iran*, eds. Tara Povey and Elaheh Rostami-Povey (London: Ashgate Publishing, Ltd., 2012), pp. 53–72, p. 56.
131 Honarbin-HollidayIbid., p. 56.
132 Asef Bayat, "Tehran: Paradox City," *New Left Review* 66 (November/December 2010): p. 114.
133 Ibid.
134 Bayat comments, "More dramatically, it still retains the structural and architectural palimpsest of the Shah's time, but this is overlaid with a veneer of post-revolutionary ideology, some significant redevelopment and the footprints of globalization. More dramatically, it has been transformed from below by population growth, immigration and informal development." Ibid., p. 120.

Chapter 5

1 A version of this chapter was published in the article, "Women and Sexuality in Contemporary Iran: When HIV Meets Government Morality," *Anthropology of the Middle East* 9, no. 2, Special Issue: Sexuality, Culture and Public Politics in the Middle East (December 2014): pp. 108–24.
2 Robert Crawford, "The Boundaries of the Self and the Unhealthy Other: Reflections on Health, Culture and AIDS," *Social Science & Medicine* 38, no. 10. (1994): p. 1347.
3 Ibid., p. 1355.
4 See National AIDS Committee Secretariat and Iran Ministry of Health and Medical Education (MOHME), "Islamic Republic of Iran AIDS Progress Report: Monitoring of the United Nations General Assembly Special Session on HIV and AIDS," March 2012, accessed August 1, 2014, http://www.unaids.org/en/dataanalysis/knowyou rresponse/countryprogressreports/2012countries/IRIran%20AIDS%20Progres s%20Report%202012%20English%20final1_1.pdf.
5 Ibid.
6 UNAIDS, "Women, Girls, Gender Equality and HIV Fact Sheet," February 2012, accessed March 1, 2012, http://www.unaids.org/en/media/unaids/contentassets/doc uments/factsheet/2012/20120217_FS_WomenGirls_en.pdf
7 UNAIDS, "AIDSinfo: Epidemiological Status Islamic Republic of Iran," accessed November 5, 2013, http://www.unaids.org/en/dataanalysis/datatools/aidsinfo/. For more on this topic, see UNAIDS, *Standing Up, Speaking Out: Women and HIV in the Middle East and North Africa* (New York: Joint United Nations Programme on HIV/ AIDS UNAIDS, 2012), pp. 8–12, 29.
8 Minoo Mohraz, "All That Families Must Know About the Red Ribbon/*Hameh Unche Khanevadeha Bayad darbar-ye Ruban-e Ghermez Bedanand*," *Aftab online*, 23 Azar/ December 2014, accessed March 8, 2015, http://www.aftabir.com/articles/view/hea lth_therapy/ illness/c13_1418505983p1.php/.

9   Iran Daily, "Official: Training Needed to Reduce AIDS," December 1, 2014, accessed December 4, 2019, http://www.iran-daily.com/News/56546.html.

10 Notably, the cited figure is much lower than the number given in a UNAIDS (2012a) report, which finds that Iran has approximately 71,000 PLWH—the highest number in the Middle East. The latest Iranian official statistics reported a total of 30,183 people with HIV at the end of 2015. See Mostafa Shokoohi, Mohammad Karamouzian, Mehdi Osooli, Hamid Sharifi, Noushin Fahimfar, Ali Akbar Haghdoost, Omid Zamani, and Ali Mirzazadeh, "Low HIV Testing Rate and Its Correlates among Men Who Inject Drugs in Iran," *International Journal of Drug Policy* 32 (2016): pp. 64–9.

11 Mohammad Hossein Nikman, "United Nations High-Level Meeting on HIV/AIDS Statement," statement by United Nations from Acting Health Minister of the Islamic Republic of Iran, United Nations High-level Meeting on HIV/AIDS New York, June 9, 2011, http://www.un.org/en/ga/aidsmeeting2011/pdf/iran.p df, accessed December 4, 2019. MOHME reported that up to twenty-five centers countrywide would be created to provide "a safe haven for them where information, education, HIV counselling and testing, harm reduction, care and support can be provided without the fear of stigma and discrimination." Already localized support centers, known as *Bashgah-e Yaraneh-e Mosbat* (Positive Clubs) and affiliated with *Tanzim-e Khanevadeh-ye Jomhouri-ye Islami* (Family Planning Association of the Islamic Republic of Iran), were set up for HIV-positive patients, focusing on HIV harm reduction and creating local strategies for the problems of stigma and discrimination.

12 Khosrou Mansourian, interview by author, Tehran, July 2011.

13 For more on *tamkin* and *nafaqa*, see Ziba Mir-Hosseini, "*Tamkin*: Stories from a Family Court in Iran," in *Everyday Life in the Muslim Middle East*, eds. D. L. Bowen and E. Early (Indianapolis: Indiana, 2002), pp. 136–50.

14 Shahidian, *Women in Iran*, p. 56.

15 Vida Nassehi-Behnam, "Iran and Afghanistan: Islamic Law," in *Encyclopedia of Women and Islamic Cultures: Family, Law and Politics*, eds. Suad Joseph and Afsaneh Najmabadi, vol. 2 (Leiden: Brill, 2005), p. 118.

16 UNAIDS, "Women, Girls, Gender Equality and HIV Fact Sheet," February 2012, p. 8, accessed December 4, 2019, http://www.unaids.org/en/media/unaids/contentasset s/documents/factsheet/2012/20120217_FS_WomenGirls_en.pdf

17 Nikman, "United Nations High-level Meeting on HIV/AIDS Statement," *Supra note* 25.

18 See Pardis Mahdavi, "Who Will Catch Me if I Fall? Health and the Infrastructure of Risk in Urban Tehran," in *Contemporary Iran*, ed. Ali Gheissari (New York: Oxford University Press, 2009); UNDP Iran "The Prevention and Control of HIV/AIDS in Iran," February 2010, accessed April 12, 2012, http://www.undp.org.ir/index.php/pr oject-highlights/481-27-february-2011-the-prevention-and-control-ofhivaids-In-ir an; and *Zanan*, "*Zanan va AIDS dar Iran: Az Enkar ta Paziresh*/Women and AIDS in Iran: From Denial to Acceptance," pp. 50–5.

19 Janne Bjerre Christensen, *Drugs, Deviancy, and Democracy in Iran: The Interaction of State and Civil Society* (New York: Palgrave Macmillan, 2011), p. 135. Kamiar Alaie also confirmed this statement in a telephone interview with the author.

20 Ibid. See also Islamic Republic of Iran Penal Code, Book 2, "*Hadd* Punishment for Adultery."

21 Abdollah Javadi-Amoli, Your Daily Muslim, 2012, accessed March 8, 2015, http://
    yourdailymuslim.com/2013/03/18/yourdaily-muslim-abdollah-javadi-amoli/.

22 Ayatollah Yousef Saanei, "*Fatwas: Amouzesh-e Ommumi dar Pishgiri az AIDS*/Public
    Education about AIDS Prevention," n.d., accessed June 1, 2012, http://www.feqh
    .org/fa/estefta/estefta46.htm.

23 Mahdavi, "Who Will Catch Me If I Fall? Health and the Infrastructure of Risk in
    Urban Tehran," p. 157.

24 As of April 2014, parliamentary legislation was under way to slash contraceptive
    services and dissuade contraceptive use in an attempt to boost Iran's birth rate (see
    Saeed Kamali-Dehghan), "Iran Considers Ban on Vasectomies in Drive to Boost
    Birthrate," *The Guardian.co.uk*, April 15, 2014, accessed December 1, 2019, http://
    www.theguardian.com/world/2014/apr/15/iran-ban-vasectomies-birthrate.

25 See Mir-Hosseini, *Islam and Gender*.

26 Personal communication with Homa Hoodfar, September 4, 2014.

27 See Kamyar Ghabili, Mohammadali Shoja, and Pooya Kamran, "The Iranian Female
    High School Students' Attitude Towards People with HIV/AIDS: A Cross-Sectional
    Study," *AIDS Research and Therapy* 5, no. 15 (July 2008), doi: 10.1186/1742-6405-
    5-15; A. Mohammadpour, Yekta, Z. P., Nasrabadi, N. and M. M., "Coming to
    Terms with a Diagnosis of HIV in Iran: A Phenomenological Study," *Journal of
    the Association of Nurses in AIDS Care* 20, no. 4 (July/August 2009): 249–59, doi:
    10.1016/j.jana.2009.03.003; and A. Tavoosi, A. Zaferani, A. Enzevaei, P. Tajik, and
    Z. Ahmadinezhad, "Knowledge and Attitude Towards HIV/AIDS Among Iranian
    Students," *BMC Public Health* 4, no. 17 (May 2004), doi:10.1186/1471-2458-4-17.

28 See Afary, *Sexual Politics in Modern Iran*; Haeri, *Law of Desire: Temporary Marriage
    in Shi'i Iran*.

29 *Anjoman-e Hemayat va Yari-ye Aseeb Didegan-e Ejtemai-i*/Society for the Protection
    and Assistance of Socially Disadvantaged Individuals/SPASDI "About Us: History,"
    2010, accessed July 20, 2014, http://spasdi.ir/#!/page_CONTENT1

30 Robert Prus, *Symbolic Interaction and Ethnographic Research: Intersubjectivity and
    the Study of Human Lived Experience* (Albany: SUNY Press, 1995), p. 2.

31 In 2012 when this research was conducted, Mansourian was the main director until
    2015, when he was arrested. As of 2017, Mansourian is credited online as being
    part of the SPASDI management team. The NGO's general director and chairman as
    of 2019 is Dr. Mohammad Javad Haghshenas. See SPASDI, "Management," January
    17, 2017, accessed December 4, 2019, http://spasdi.ir/index.php/en/about-us-en/
    management-en.

32 In Iran's HIV/AIDS reports to UNDP, the first cases of HIV were documented in
    1985. See UNDP Iran, "The Prevention and Control of HIV/AIDS in Iran," February
    27, 2011, accessed April 12, 2012, http://www.undp.org.ir/index.php/project-high
    lights/481-27-february-2011-the-prevention-and-control-of-hivaids-in-iran.
    Researcher Pardis Mahdavi states that HIV was first detected in 1986. See Mahdavi,
    "Who Will Catch Me If I Fall? Health and the Infrastructure of Risk for Urban
    Young Iranians," p. 157. Journal *Zanan* claims the first detected case was reported in
    1987 caused by contaminated blood during a transfusion. See "*Zanan va AIDS dar
    Iran: Az Enkar ta Paziresh*/Women and AIDS in Iran: From Denial to Acceptance,"
    Zanan 135 (Shahrivar 1385/September 2006): pp. 50–5.

33 UNDP Iran, "The Prevention and Control of HIV/AIDS in Iran," February 2010,
    accessed April 12, 2012, http://www.undp.org.ir/index.php/project-highlights/481
    -27-february-2011-the-prevention-and-control-ofhivaids-In-iran.

34 For more information about the organization and its operations in the provinces see Ramin Mehrdad, "Health System in Iran," *Japan Medical Association Journal* 52, no. 1 (2009): pp. 69–73.

35 *Monitoring of the United Nations General Assembly Special Session on HIV and AIDS*, National AIDS Committee Secretariat, Iran MOHME, February 2010, p. 14.

36 In the many medical publications I reviewed for this chapter, I noticed that in Iran's official reports of its domestic HIV/AIDS epidemic, the same list of characters (also known as subpopulations participating in high-risk behaviors) are mentioned as participating in unhealthy, high-risk activities, and thus by this kind of categorization, government resources are allocated to specific groups for treatment, prevention, and study. This group historically included female sex workers, inmates, intravenous drug addicts, and men who have sex with men; in the past decade (between 2001 and 2008), studies surveyed truck drivers, sailors, and pregnant women.

37 The term "IDU" stands for "intravenous drug user" or "injected drug user." According to a UNAIDS 2002 report, most HIV transmission in the country occurred among its estimated 200,000–300,000 IDUs, of which 65 percent of the known and reported HIV cases in Iran were IDU-attributed. Figures were first reported in 2002 by Iran's Ministry of Health and published in Ali Rowhani Rahbar, Kaveh Khoshnood, and Sahar Rooholamini, "Prevalence of HIV Infection and Other Blood-Borne Infections in Incarcerated and Non-incarcerated Injection Drug Users (IDUs) in Mashhad, Iran," *International Journal of Drug Policy* 15 (2004): p. 151.

Studies find that Iranian drug users seeking treatment use opium and heroin. (Opium usage has significantly decreased but injection of a form of methamphetamine is on the rise.) However very little is known about the characteristics and risk profiles of Iran's IDUs. A 2006 study attempted to describe the correlation between harm reduction needs of IDUs and others at a high risk of HIV infection. See Emran Razzaghi, Afarin Rahimia Movaghar, Traci Craig Green, and Kaveh Khoshnood, "Profiles of Risk: A Qualitative Study of Injecting Drug Users in Tehran, Iran," *Harm Reduction Journal* 3, no. 12 (March 18, 2006): p. 2. Another 2006 study conducted on patterns of drug use among IDUs found that specific information on IDUs in Iran—such as their high-risk behavior—is insufficient and as such, has yet to lead to the creation of specific health promotion and intervention strategies specific to these populations. Additionally, researchers find that the specific data on IDU, such as help seeking and blood-borne virus risk behavior is insufficient to allow such tailoring of health promotion and intervention strategies. They also question if government agencies can adequately facilitate the monitoring of risk-factor trends over time. See Carolyn Day, Bijan Nassirimanesh, Anthony Shakeshaft, and Kate Dolan, "Patterns of Drug Use among a Sample of Drug Users and Injecting Drug Users Attending a General Practice in Iran," *Harm Reduction Journal* 3, no. 1 (2006): p. 2.

38 Christensen, *Drugs, Deviancy, and Democracy in Iran*, p. 134.

39 Homeira Fallahi, Sedigheh Sadat Tavafian, Farideh Yaghmaie, and Ebrahim Hajizadeh, "Stigma, Discrimination, and the Consequences of HIV-AIDS for People Living with It in Iran," *Life Science Journal* 8, no. 4 (2011): p. 503. Because of the high infection rates reported among the incarcerated, the MOHME and nongovernmental health agencies concentrated on controlling sexually transmitted infections (STI) in prisons. A 2002 voluntary study conducted in a local prison

in Iran's Fars province reported that "30% and 78% prevalence rates of HIV and hepatitis C virus (HCV) infection among incarcerated drug users, respectively." See Bijan Nassirimanesh, "Proceedings of the Abstract for the Fourth National Harm Reduction Conference," Harm Reduction Coalition, Seattle (2002). Of the population sampled, shared needles and razors, along with used needles and unhygienic conditions for tattooing, were reported to be common conduits of disease transmission.

40   Emran Razzaghi, Afarin Rahimi Movaghar, Traci Craig Green, and Kaveh Khoshnood, "Profiles of Risk: A Qualitative Study of Injecting Drug Users in Tehran, Iran," *Harm Reduction Journal* 3, no. 12 (March 18, 2006), doi: 10.1186/1477-7517-3-12. The needle exchange program was established in the late 1990s, at the time distinguishing Iran as the only country in the Middle East and North Africa to offer needle exchange services in some of its prisons. As of September 2011, the needle exchange program was ongoing and UNAIDS reported 679 sites for needle exchange compared to 21 sites in Afghanistan. See *Middle East and North Africa Regional Report on AIDS 2011*, UNAIDS, accessed March 5, 2012, p. 21, http://www.unaids.or g/en/media/unaids/contentassets/documents/unaidspublication/2011/JC2257_UNA IDS-MENA-report-2011_en.pdf.

In a one-year period, 6,022,834 free needles and syringes were distributed. On average, between twenty-six and thirty-five needles and syringes are distributed per IDU per year. See *Islamic Republic of Iran: Monitoring of the United Nations General Assembly Special Session on HIV and AIDS Report*, National AIDS Committee Secretariat, Iran MOHME, March 2012, p. 25.

41   See Razzaghi et al., "Profiles of Risk: A Qualitative Study of Injecting Drug Users in Tehran, Iran," pp. 1–13.

42   Ibid., p. 11. Prisoners and their families were informed about HIV risks and given condoms; in certain prisons, pilot programs administering clean syringes were offered to IDUs. Prisoners' wives, who became directly infected through conjugal visits with incarcerated IDUs and/or contaminated blood contact, also received some information and training about the disease.

43   Christensen, *Drugs, Deviancy, and Democracy in Iran*, pp. 135–6. Article 1 of Iran's Anti-Narcotics Law, as amended in 1997, punishes anyone "using drugs in any form or manner except for cases provided for by law." Article 2 specifies the punishments for each offense, taking into account the defendant's criminal record. Depending on the number of kilograms found in his/her possession, for the first offense, fines and lashes are administered; by the fourth offense, the death penalty is administered. Article 42 notes that judiciary power is permitted to request that drug-related convicts attend special detoxification camps to aid in rehabilitation rather than prisons. See "The Anti-Narcotics Law of the Islamic Republic of Iran," November 8, 1997, accessed April 25, 2012, http://www.unhcr.org/refworld/docid/4c35b0a52 .html.

It was reported that in January 2005, justice minister Ayatollah Mohammad Esma'il Shoushtari instructed prosecutors to ignore punitive judicial laws germane to drug offences and defer to health ministry officials on treating drug-addicted convicts. See Amir Arsalan Afkhami, "From Punishment to Harm Reduction: Resecularization of Addiction in Contemporary Iran," in *Contemporary Iran: Economy, Society, Politics*, ed. Ali Gheissari (Oxford: Oxford University Press, 2009), p. 207; Karl Vick, "AIDS Crisis Brings Radical Change in Iran's Response to Heroin Use," *Washington Post*, July 5, 2005.

44   Christensen, *Drugs, Deviancy, and Democracy in Iran,* p. 135.

45   For an extensive discussion of modern-day techniques employed by Western penal systems, which elaborate disciplinary power structures, see Foucault, *Discipline and Punish.*

46   Afkhami, "From Punishment to Harm Reduction: Resecularization of Addiction in Contemporary Iran," p. 200. In capital criminal cases, drug addicts were also charged with *mohareb ba khoda* (at war with God).

47   Christensen, *Drugs, Deviancy, and Democracy in Iran,* p. 135. See also Afkhami, "From Punishment to Harm Reduction: Resecularization of Addiction in Contemporary Iran," p. 200.

48   Dr. Mohammad Hossein Nikman, "United Nations High-Level Meeting on HIV/ AIDS Statement," (statement to United Nations from Acting Health Minister of the Islamic Republic of Iran, June 8–10, 2011, New York), accessed April 12, 2012, http://www.un.org/en/ga/aidsmeeting2011/pdf/iran.pdf. There is also a thirty-member National AIDS Committee which assists in coordination and management of the AIDS Plan that the Ministry of Health attests has an "active participation and administration of the government." See *Islamic Republic of Iran Progress Report: Monitoring of the United Nations General Assembly Special Session on HIV and AIDS,* National AIDS Committee Secretariat, MOHME, March 2012, accessed April 12, 2012, p. 54, http://www.unaids.org/en/dataanalysis/monitoringcountryprogress/p rogressreports/2012countries/ce_IR_Narrative_Report.pdf.

49   See Mahdavi, "Who Will Catch Me If I Fall? Health and the Infrastructure of Risk for Urban Young Iranians," p. 158.

50   Positive Clubs are affiliated with *Tanzim-e Khanevadeh-ye Jomhouri-ye Islami* (Family Planning Association of the Islamic Republic of Iran).

51   See "The Prevention and Control of HIV/AIDS in Iran," UNDP Iran, February 27, 2011, accessed April 12, 2012, http://www.undp.org.ir/index.php/hivaids-tb-malari a/481-27-february-2011-the-prevention-and-control-of-hivaids-in-iran/.

52   Standard HIV/AIDS treatment is Antiretroviral Therapy (ART), which was introduced internationally in 1996. See World Health Organization, *Antiretroviral Therapy for HIV Infection in Adults and Adolescents: Recommendations for Public Health Approach 2010 Revision* (Geneva: WHO, 2010). In Iran, the estimated number of people eligible for ART is 26,000—compared to 22,000 in Pakistan, 25,000 in Somalia, and 93,000 in Sudan. See *UNAIDS Middle East and North Africa Regional Report on AIDS 2011,* pp. 52–3.

53   Other services included the following: information, education, assessment, family and group counseling, methadone maintenance, and the provision of sterile needles and syringes and condoms. See Rahbar, "Prevalence of HIV Infection and Other Blood-borne Infections in Incarcerated and Non-incarcerated Injection Drug Users (IDUs) in Mashhad, Iran," p. 152. "Triangular clinics" were established as part of a comprehensive nationwide policy to provide prevention and treatment. The first triangular clinic was established in Kermanshah's central prison in October 2000. It demonstrated that by "grouping the three service areas together, it was possible to deliver a responsive, comprehensive and integrated service to drug users, their local community and people living with HIV, including drug users and their families." See *UNAIDS Middle East and North Africa Regional Report on AIDS 2011,* p. 31.

54   Clinics such as ones established in Mashhad by the Central Prison of Mashhad offered programs for HIV/AIDS, drug dependence, and STD. See Rowhani

Rahbar et al., "Prevalence of HIV Infection and Other Blood-Borne Infections in Incarcerated and Non-incarcerated Injection Drug Users (IDUs) in Mashhad, Iran," p. 152. The government even augmented its spending in the fight against rising HIV/AIDS infections. For 2004–5, they pledged about $14 million. By March 2009, it spent 309,174,961,000 rials ($38 million) for HIV/AIDS control programs, accounting to a 16.2 percent increase in spending, according to the MOHME. Financial commitments were pledged for "all members of the general population, especially high-risk groups and prisoners." According to the MOHME's 2012 monitoring reports prepared for UNAIDS, the "allocation of funds, sex, age, ethnic and religious background and profession have not been a factor." See *Monitoring of the United Nations General Assembly Special Session on HIV and AIDS, National AIDS Committee Secretariat*, Iran MOHME, p. 22; "The Prevention and Control of HIV/AIDS in I.R. Iran, Phases 1& 2," UNDP Iran, 2011, accessed April 30, 2012, http://www.undp.org.ir/index.php/component/content/article/4 03. Ongoing, joint Iran and UNDP efforts pledged almost $15.9 million dollars in a two-phase education project designed to control HIV prevalence and incidence.

55 Afkhami, "From Punishment to Harm Reduction," pp. 203–4.

56 Kamiar Alaie (HIV/AIDS expert and medical doctor), interview by author, telephone interview, New York, NY., June 26, 2012.

57 Afkhami, "From Punishment to Harm Reduction," pp. 204–6.

58 The Iranian media has also broadcast some programs for "the elimination of discrimination and stigma against people living with HIV/AIDS." See *Islamic Republic of Iran Country Report: Monitoring of the United Nations General Assembly Special Session on HIV and AIDS*, National AIDS Committee Secretariat, Ministry of Health and Education, February 2010, p. 33, accessed April 18, 2012, http:// www.unaids.org/fr/dataanalysis/monitoringcountryprogress/2010progressrepo rtssubmittedbycountries/file,33662,fr.pdf. ISNA usually publishes HIV/AIDS statistics that are accompanied interviews with Ministry of Health officials who confirm these numbers. The articles do not report any information about how the data is calculated or provide data about sexual behaviors in the general public that might contribute to rising HIV rates of infection. It is also worth mentioning that MNA is run by Islamic Ideology Dissemination Organization, headed by Seyyed Mehdi Khamoushi, which recently launched "Wikifeqh," an online information site for Islamic Religious Law. See "Wikifeqh," Islamic Ideology Dissemination Organization, accessed April 18, 2012, http://wikifeqh.ir/wiki/index.php. In 2006, funding allocated to media programs through IRIB was set at $254,00.00. See "Declaration of Commitment," *Islamic Republic of Iran Country Report: Monitoring of the United Nations General Assembly Special Session on HIV and AIDS*, Office of the Under-Secretary for Health, MOHME, Centre for Disease Management, January 2006, accessed June 1, 2012, http://data.unaids.org/pub/report/2006/2006_countr y_progress_report_iran_en.pdf.

59 See "The Prevention and Control of HIV/AIDS in Iran," UNDP Iran, February 27, 2011.

60 Conflicting media sources reported that Iran had removed World AIDS Day from their state calendar. State-affiliated newspaper *Etemad* reported on March 12, 2012 that the new regulations, approved by the Supreme Council of Revolution, permitted the official state calendar to hold occasions "of importance to different layers of the nation" and that "strengthen 'Iranian national identity.'" It was reported that the ruling was approved and signed by council chair and Iranian president

Mahmoud Ahmadinejad, in August 2009. This report disputes the actual events. According to Iran's UNDP, the official holiday was celebrated at the Iranian Health Ministry in 2010, 2011, and 2012. Iran's English-language satellite channel Press TV broadcast the short-program, "Getting to Zero," about a Tehran-based World AIDS Day conference. See Golnaz Esfandiari, "Iran Reportedly Removes World AIDS Day from State Calendar," *RFERL*, March 17, 2012, accessed June 4, 2012, http://www .rferl.org/content/iran_takes_world_aids_day_off_calendar/24518879.html. "Iran Marks World AIDS Day," Press TV, November 30, 2011, accessed June 4, 2012, http: //www.presstv.ir/detail/213079.html.

61 Interviews in Tehran with Fatemeh S. (SPASDI social worker) and K. Mansourian (SPASDI director), interview by author, September 21, 2011, Tehran, Iran.

62 In official reports of its domestic HIV/AIDS epidemic, the same list of characters (also known as subpopulations participating in high-risk behaviors) are mentioned as participatory in unhealthy, high-risk or at-risk activities, and thus, by this kind of categorization, government resources are allocated to specific groups for treatment, prevention, and study. This group typically included female sex workers, inmates, intravenous drug addicts, and men who have sex with men. Between 2001 and 2008, studies surveyed truck drivers, sailors, and pregnant women.

63 By 2011, nearly 38 percent of registered teachers in Iran had been trained in HIV/ AIDS awareness and prevention. "The Prevention and Control of HIV/AIDS," UNDP Iran, February 27, 2011.

64 Qom is the largest center for Shi'a scholarship in the world.

65 Hannah Allam, "Iran's AIDS-Prevention Program among World's Most Progressive," *Knight Rider*, April 14, 2006, accessed December 4, 2019, https://www.mcclatchydc. com/latest-news/article24454495.html. The pamphlet was mainly designed by Dr. Arash Alaei, who helped improve HIV/AIDS awareness in Kermanshah province after a government-testing program confirmed the rising rates of infections among drug addicts from its ex-convict and prisoner populations, which was subsequently found present among the wives and children of Kermanshah's addicts. Allam reported that the handbook was no longer in distribution, after the election of President Ahmadinejad.

66 *Islamic Republic of Iran Progress Report: Monitoring of the United Nations General Assembly Special Session on HIV and AIDS*, March 2012, p. 34. Research studies conducted in different geographic areas across Iran and published between the years 2001 and 2011, document the current attitudes, behaviors, and knowledge about HIV/AIDS. In general, many of the studies identify discriminatory attitudes toward HIV/AIDS patients. They report to the misconceptions about contraction, curability, and prevention that have contributed to the spread of misinformation about the illness, along with fomenting anxieties about the virus's alleged threat to society. The reasons for this misinformation have been attributed to poor media attention to the issue; the application of certain spurious religious beliefs; the limited and inconsistent HIV/AIDS education for student populations; and the reticence of parents, teachers, physicians, and nurses to discuss the issue to their respective communities. Negative attitudes of the illness are also attributed to religious beliefs. In a 2010 study on the attitudes of a selection of Shiraz high school students, researchers concluded that "loyalty to Islamic religious beliefs have an important role on attitudes towards the disease." See Tavoosi et al., "Knowledge and Attitude towards HIV/AIDS among Iranian Students"; See Mohammad Reza Mohammadi et al., "Reproductive Knowledge, Attitudes and Behavior among Adolescent Males in Tehran, Iran,"

International Family Planning Perspectives 32, no. 1 (2006) and C. A. Yazdi, K. Aschbacher, A. Arvanta, H. M. Naser, A. Abdollahi, M. Mousavi, M. R. Narmani, M. Kianpishe, F. Nicfallah, and A. K. Moghadam, "Knowledge, Attitudes and Sources of Information Regarding HIV/AIDS in Iranian Adolescents," *AIDS Care* 18, no. 8 (November 2006): pp.1004–10; M. Movahed and S. Shoaa, "On Attitude Towards HIV/AIDS Among Iranian Students: Case Study: High School Students in Shiraz City," *Pakistan Journal of Biological Sciences* 13, no. 6 (March 2010): p. 275.

67 See Anahita Tavoosi et al., "Knowledge and Attitude towards HIV/AIDS among Iranian Students."

68 *Guidelines for Measuring National HIV Prevalence*, UNAIDS/WHO Working Group on Global HIV/AIDS and STI Surveillance, 2005, p. 5, accessed April 10, 2012, http://www.unaids.org/en/media/unaids/contentassets/dataimport/pub/manual/2005/20050101_gs_guidemeasuringpopulation_en.pdf

69 *Guidelines for Measuring National HIV Prevalence*, UNAIDS/WHO, p. 5.

70 Ibid.

71 "Monitoring of the United Nations General Assembly Special Session on HIV and AIDS," National AIDS Committee Secretariat, MOHME, February 2010, p. 19, accessed April 10, 2012, http://www.unaids.org/fr/dataanalysis/monitoringcountryprogress/2010progressreportssubmittedbycountries/file,33662,fr.pdf.

72 See "Epidemiological Fact Sheet on HIV/AIDS and Sexually Transmitted Infections: 2004 Update for Iran," UNAIDS/WHO, pp. 1–14, accessed April 10, 2012, http://data.unaids.org/publications/Fact-Sheets01/iran_en.pdf.

73 See "Declaration of Commitment," *Islamic Republic of Iran Country Report: Monitoring of the United Nations General Assembly Special Session on HIV and AIDS*, Office of the Under-Secretary for Health, MOHME, Centre for Disease Management, January 2006.

74 "Epidemiological Fact Sheet on HIV and AIDS 2008 Update," IRI, October 2008, p. 4, accessed April 13, 2012, http://apps.who.int/globalatlas/predefinedReports/EFS2008/full/EFS2008_IR.pdf.

75 "Monitoring of the United Nations General Assembly Special Session on HIV and AIDS," National AIDS Committee Secretariat, MOHME, February 2010, p. 19, accessed April 3, 2012, http://www.unaids.org/fr/dataanalysis/monitoringcountryprogress/2010progressreportssubmittedbycountries/file,33662,fr.pdf.

76 *Islamic Republic of Iran Progress Report: Monitoring of the United Nations General Assembly Special Session on HIV and AIDS*, p. 15.

77 The researchers explain, "In 2003, officially there were 5086 Iranians living with HIV/AIDS, of which, 4838 were male and 248 were female." See Tavoosi et al., "Knowledge and Attitude towards HIV/AIDS among Iranian Students."

78 See Golnaz Esfandiari, "Iran: Tehran Begins to Confront the 'Time Bomb' of HIV/AIDS," *RFERL*, November 10, 2003, accessed April 2, 2012, http://www.rferl.org/content/article/1104954.html.

79 *HIV/AIDS in Iran (Cumulative Statistics) Tehran 2004 Report*, Iran Center for Disease Management, Office of the Deputy for Public Health, MOHME of the I.R. Iran, 2004. In Persian.

80 "*Zanan va AIDS dar Iran: Az Enkar ta Paziresh*/Women and AIDS in Iran: From Denial to Acceptance," *Zanan*.

81 "*Amar-e Vagh'ei-ye Mobtalayan be AIDS dar Iran*/Real Statistics of AIDS Cases in Iran," *Farda News*, 7 *Azar* 1388/November 28, 2009, accessed April 30, 2012, http://www.fardanews.com/fa/news/96834/.

82 Ibid.

83 Ibid.

84 *Islamic Republic of Iran Progress Report: Monitoring of the United Nations General Assembly Special Session on HIV and AIDS*, National AIDS Committee Secretariat, MOHME, March 2012, p. 48, accessed April 13, 2012, http://www.unaids.org/en/dataanalysis/monitoringcountryprogress/progressreports/2012countries/ce_IR_Narrative_Report.pdf.

85 Ibid., pp. 15, 72.

86 Mina Rasheed, "Iran: HIV/AIDS—More than a Social Taboo," *Payvand News online*, February 2, 2009, accessed March 21, 2012, http://www.payvand.com/news/09/feb/1346.html.

87 UNAIDS, "Islamic Republic of Iran."

88 See Hamid Dabashi, *Shi'ism: A Religion of Protest* (Boston: Belknap Press of Harvard University Press, 2011); Moojan Momen, *An Introduction to Shi'i Islam: The History and Doctrines of Twelver Shi'ism* (New Haven: Yale University Press, 1985).

89 "The Prevention and Control of HIV/AIDS in I.R. Iran, Phases 1& 2," UNDP Iran, 2011.

90 *UNAIDS Middle East and North Africa Regional Report on AIDS 2011*, p.73.

91 According to The Global Fund website, "The Global Fund is an international financing institution dedicated to attracting and disbursing resources to prevent and treat HIV and AIDS, TB and malaria." See The Global Fund, "Who We Are." The Global Fund to Fight AIDS, Tuberculosis and Malaria, 2012, accessed April 30, 2012, http://www.theglobalfund.org/en/about/whoweare/.

92 Ibid, p. 73.

93 See S. Kalkhoran and L. Hale, "AIDS Education in an Islamic Nation: Content Analysis of Farsi-language AIDS-Education Materials in Iran," *Promotion & Education* 15, no. 3 (September 2008).

94 Lorestan Province is located in Western Iran. "*Behtarin Noskhe-ye Mobarezeh ba AIDS Din-e Eslam Ast*/The Best Prescription in the Fight Against AIDS Is Islam." Fars News Agency, 15 *Azar* 1389/December 6, 2010, accessed April 30, 2012, http://www.farsnews.com/newstext.php?nn=8909151208.

95 Ibid.

96 See Kalkhoran and Hale, "AIDS Education in an Islamic Nation: Content Analysis of Farsi-language AIDS-Education Materials in Iran," pp. 21–5.

97 National AIDS Committee Secretariat (MOHME), *Islamic Republic of Iran AIDS Progress Report*, March 2015, p. 8, accessed December 1, 2019, https://www.unaids.org/sites/default/files/country/documents/IRN_narrative_report_2015.pdf.

98 See Ali Montazeri, "AIDS Knowledge and Attitudes in Iran: Results from a Population-Based Survey in Tehran," *Patient Education and Counseling* 57 (2005): pp. 199–203.

99 See Mohammadi et al., "Reproductive Knowledge, Attitudes and Behavior among Adolescent Males in Tehran, Iran," pp. 35–44.

100 See Tavoosi et al., "Knowledge and Attitude Towards HIV/AIDS among Iranian Students." A. Feizzadeh, "Evidence-Based Approach to HIV/AIDS Policy and Research Prioritization in Islamic Republic of Iran," *Eastern Mediterranean Health Journal* 16, no. 3 (March 2010): pp. 259–65. C. A. Yazdi et al., "Knowledge, Attitudes and Sources of Information Regarding HIV/AIDS in Iranian Adolescents," *AIDS Care* 18, no. 8 (Nov. 2006): pp. 1004–10.

101 Mahdavi, "Who Will Catch Me If I Fall? Health and the Infrastructure of Risk for Urban Young Iranians," pp. 157–8.

102   Rasheed, "Iran: HIV/AIDS—More than a Social Taboo".

103   For more on temporary and permanent marriage, see Chapter 3.

104   Nikman, "United Nations High-Level Meeting on HIV/AIDS Statement," *Supra note* 25.

105   *UNAIDS Middle East and North Africa Regional Report on AIDS 2011*, p. 11.

106   SPASDI began raising awareness and offering public outreach, speaking on university campuses and in government ministries and agencies, to better assist children with disabilities. Their social programs have expanded to meet the demand of natural disasters (they helped facilitate emergency aid to earthquake victims in Bam, an ancient city where roughly 70 percent was destroyed). *Anjoman-e Hemayat va Yari-ye Aseeb Didegan-e Ejtemai-i*/Society for the Protection and Assistance of Socially Disadvantaged Individuals, "AIDS Special Services: Activities for AIDS Victims: Single Mother Families and Children," n.d., accessed December 4, 2019, http://spasdi.ir/en/?p=52.

107   Mansourian is also credited for his contribution to the seminal research report, authored by Sattareh Farman Farmaian, on the living conditions of prostitutes in the former Pahlavi-era red-light district *Shahr-e No*. See Chapter 2 of this book.

108   Ibid.

109   MOHME reports concur with Mansourian's assessment. According to Iran's March 2012 monitoring report, "HIV-positive persons who are known to engage in high-risk behaviors tend to refrain from accessing counseling centers, laboratories, mental health specialists, and other services; consulting these services could potentially result in their public identification." See *Islamic Republic of Iran Progress Report: Monitoring of the United Nations General Assembly Special Session on HIV and AIDS*, p. 61.

110   In one meeting, a SPASDI social worker predicted that the societal treatment of those who have HIV/AIDS would improve just as it had for those afflicted by syphilis, which, almost fifty years earlier, was a common STD in rural and urban communities. For more on the syphilis epidemic in early twentieth-century Iran, see Chapter 2 of this book.

111   "AIDS Special Services: Activities for AIDS Victims: Single Mother Families & Children," SPASDI, August 1, 2010, accessed April 14, 2012, http://spasdi.ir/en/?p=52.

112   Mansourian's son is my good friend.

113   Of the twenty-two questions from the questionnaire, only eight questions were allowed. I also distributed a confidentiality form in Persian that explained their rights and a description of my project and credentials.

114   This questionnaire had approximately thirty questions and provided me with an open framework to consult as I followed topical trajectories in our conversations. These questions covered topics of motherhood, health awareness, and breastfeeding practices. For each female participant, I asked, for example, "What is your opinion of your body?" or "In your opinion, what do you imagine or feel about the male or female body?" As a way to both clarify and focus my subject, I asked women about their relationships with their breasts, for example, through their individual reflections on ideal breast size, body maintenance, intimate encounters, nursing, and as a gendered marker of a female physical form. Because the topic of "breasts" served as the common denominator for all of the women, many of the participants spoke candidly about body satisfaction, breastfeeding, and ideal breast size, to name a few.

115 All interviews were recorded and took place at the SPASDI office in Tehran, in a private room adjacent to the meeting room on the third floor. I took all measures to safeguard and disguise their identities.

116 S. Nayeri, SPASDI board member, email with author, August 2, 2014.

117 A *chador* is a long garment, also described as an open cloak, worn by Iranian women in observance of Islamic *hejab*.

118 I recall a particular lecture on the narrative of *Musa* (Moses) and Bani Israel. Mansourian had encouraged the participants to believe in their collective efforts—to increase HIV/AIDS awareness and destigmatize the disease—even though the end goal, which Mansourian had compared to Qur'anic and Biblical accounts about the parting of the Red Sea, seemed an impossible feat. He said, "You must have faith even in a path where there is no faith. We must make ourselves stronger in the face of societal problems." Excerpt taken from workshop on July 26, 2011 at SPASDI headquarters in Tehran.

119 CD4 cells are clusters of white blood cells or lymphocytes and are an important part in fortifying the immune system. A low CD4 count means the immune system is weakened and thus the ability to fight off infections is compromised. HIV most often infects and becomes part of these cells; when infections form, these cells multiply and make more copies of HIV. See *The Body: The Complete HIV/AIDS Resource Fact Sheet, CD4 (T-Cell Tests)*, The Body.com, March 29, 2012, accessed April 14, 2012, http://www.thebody.com/content/6110/cd4-t-cell-tests.html#anchor251.

120 "AIDS Special Services: Activities for AIDS Victims: Single Mother Families & Children," SPASDI.

121 CD4 cells are white blood cells that are essential to fortifying the human immune system.

122 See United Nations Social Development Work, "Society for the Protection and Assistance of Socially Disadvantaged Individuals," November 30, 2016, accessed December 4, 2019, https://unsdn.org/2016/11/30/society-for-the-protection-and-assistance-of-socially-disadvantaged-individuals/.

123 Association of Nurses in AIDS Care, "Clinical Management of the HIV-Infected Infant and Child," in *ANAC's Core Curriculum for HIV/AIDS Nursing*, ed. B. Swanson (Sudbury, MA: Jones and Bartlett Publishers, LLC, 2010), pp. 307–28.

124 UNICEF advised, "The longer a child is breastfed by an HIV mother, the higher the risk of HIV infection. Breastfeeding for six months has about one third of the risk of breastfeeding for two years." See HIV/AIDS Unit UNICEF, *HIV and Infant Feeding: The Facts* (New York: UNICEF, 2002).
   In November 2009, WHO released new recommendations on infant feeding by HIV-positive mothers, based on new evidence that showed a combination of exclusive breastfeeding and the use of antiretroviral treatment. WHO stated it could "significantly reduce the risk of transmitting HIV to babies through breastfeeding." See WHO, "Breast Is Always Best, Even for HIV-Positive Mothers," *Bulletin of the WHO* 88, no. 1 (January 2010): pp. 1–80, accessed December 4, 2019, https://www.who.int/bulletin/volumes/88/1/10-030110/en/

125 See Majid Tarahomi, et al., "Preventing Mother-to-Child Transmission of HIV/AIDS: Do Iranian Pregnant Mothers Know about It?" *Journal of Reproduction and Infertility* 11, no. 1 (April–June 2010): pp. 53–57. For more on HIV and reproductive decisions, see also D. B. Barnes, "Reproductive Decisions for Women with HIV:

Motherhood's Role in Envisioning a Future," *Qualitative Health Research Journal* 19, no. 4 (April 2009): pp. 481–91.

126 National AIDS Trust, "HIV Facts: The Basics," 2012, accessed April 20, 2012, http://www.nat.org.uk/HIV-Facts/The-basics.aspx.

127 J. Stolzer, "Breastfeeding: An Interdisciplinary Review," *International Review of Modern Sociology* 32, no. 1 (Spring 2006): p. 109.

128 Islamic Republic of Iran Judiciary Family Law, *Qanoun-e Tarvij-e Taghziye ba Shir-e Madar va Hemayat az Madaran dar Doran-e Shirdehi*/Law Encouraging Breastfeeding and the Protection of Mothers during Breastfeeding, Azar 22 1374/2006 (Tehran: Ganjdanesh Publishing): pp. 295–8.

129 Rules on breastfeeding are routinely discussed by religious scholars as part of their various formal treatise as well as their sermons.

130 B. Olang, Khalil Farivar, Abtin Heidarzadeh, Birgitta Strandvik, and Agneta Yngve, "Breastfeeding in Iran: Prevalence, Duration and Current Recommendations," *International Breastfeeding Journal* 4, no. 8. (2009). doi: 10.1186/1746-4358-4-8.

131 Suckling is mentioned in *Sura* IV: 23 and *Sura* II: 233 of the Qur'an and *sunna*. Mothers are advised to breastfeed their babies for a complete course of two years, with a minimum of six months to ensure child's survival (for more, see Avner Giladi), *Infants, Parents and Wet Nurses: Medieval Islamic Views on Breastfeeding and their Social Implications* (Leiden: Brill, 1999).

132 Mohsen Maddah, "Breastfeeding Rates in Iran: Why Is There Such a Large Gap between Iran and Other Countries?," *Journal of Human Lactation* 24, no. 149 (April 2009), doi: 10.1177/0890334408316087.

133 "Baby friendly" is the rough translation of *doostdar-e koudak*. See Ibid.

134 Only pharmacies were allowed to distribute formula or dried milk. This policy, however, is not strictly enforced as formula can be easily found at corner stores (quoted in "Shirin Ebadi Book Excerpts," *BadJens Iranian Feminist Newsletter*, September 2004, accessed June 1, 2012, http://www.badjens.com/ebadi.html.

135 When a woman wears a *chador*, she places both hands inside this garment in an effort to cover her body. As a result, her hands may not move freely, making multitasking difficult. When carrying items, she uses her teeth to hold onto the cloth.

136 The participants to this discussion understood that the young man desired to have casual sex with her.

137 Haideh Moghissi provides a contextual analysis of the many uses of *awrat* in the Qur'an and *hadith* literature. She argues that a more suitable definition should be "inviolate vulnerability," as reference to the broader notions of Arabo-Islamic sanctity and privacy of the home and family. See Moghissi, *Women and Islam*.

138 According to Jafar al-Saddiq, men's *awrat* is their buttocks. For information on Ayatollah Khomeini's discussion of *awrat* in the treatise *Tahrir al-Vasileh*, see Ruhollah Khomeini, *Tahrir al-Vasileh*, vol. 1, Chapter 129, lines 3–11.

BIBLIOGRAPHY

Persian Sources

"*Afzayesh-e Ezdevaj-e Movaqat pa-be-pa-ye Qeimat-e Sekeh*/The Rise in Temporary Marriage on Pace with the Rise in Gold Coins." Asrir-e Iran, 5 Bahman 1390/ December 4, 2019. Accessed January 27, 2012. http://www.asriran.com/fa/ news/198672/افزایش-ازدواج-موقت-پا-به-پای-قیمت-سکه.

"*Ahamiyat-e Faza-ye Sabz va Ta'sir-e Un bar Ravan-e Ensan*/The Importance of Green Space and Its Effect on Human Mentality." Parks and Green Space Organization Tehran Municipality, n.d. Accessed June 26, 2012. http://parks.tehran.ir/LinkClick.aspx?filetic ket=wBH9D6Qm7Uw%3d&tabid=101&mid=481.

Ali Mohammadi, Fariborz. *Danestaniha-ye Jensi va Rahnemudha-ye A'emeh-ye Athar/ Sexual Knowledge and the Guidance from the Pure Imams*. Tehran: Rastin, 1387/2009.

"*Amar-e Vagh'ei-ye Mobtalayan be AIDS dar Iran*/Real Statistics of AIDS Cases in Iran." *Farda News*, 7 Azar 1388/November 28, 2009. Accessed April 30, 2012. http://www. fardanews.com/fa/news/96834/.

Azar, Shabnam. "*Sikut-e felezi neylabakzan*/Metallic Silence of The Flute Player." Radio Zamaneh, 9 Mordad 1389/ July 31, 2010. Accessed February 14, 2012. http://zamaaneh .com/morenews/2010/07/post_1349.html.

"*Bahman Mohasses: Pishro va Mardomgoriz*/Bahman Mohasses: Pioneer and Misanthrope." BBC Persian, January 29, 2010. Accessed February 12, 2012. http://www .bbc.co.uk/persian/arts/2010/07/100729_l11_bahman_mohasses.shtml.

"*Barrasi-ye Naqsh-e Eslam dar Mobareze alay-he AIDS*/Investigating the Role of Islam in the Struggle against AIDS." BBC Persian, December 4, 2006. Accessed April 30, 2012. http://www.bbc.co.uk/persian/tajikistan/story/2006/12/061204_rm_islam_aids.shtml.

Bashirtash, Saied and Ebrahim Nabavi. "*Shahr-e No Atash Gereft va Rouspiyan Koshteh Shodand*/Shahr-e No on Fire and Prostitutes Killed." Radio Zamaneh, 9 Bahman 1387/ January 29, 2009. Accessed October 5, 2011. http://www.zamaaneh.com/revolution/ 2009/01.post_218.html.

"*Behtarin Noskhe-ye Mobarezeh ba AIDS Din-e Eslam Ast*/The Best Prescription in the Fight against AIDS Is Islam." Fars News Agency, 15 Azar 1389/ December 6, 2010. Accessed April 30, 2012. http://www.farsnews.com/newstext.php?nn=8909151208.

"*Bonyangozar-e Kayhan Dargozasht*/Kayhan Titan Passes Away." BBC Persian, November 11, 2006. Accessed December 4, 2019. http://www.bbc.co.uk/persian/arts/story/2006/ 11/061125_mf_mesbahzadeh.shtml.

"*Chalesh-e Vazir-e Behdasht ba Sazman-e Nezam Pezeshki*/Minister of Health's Challenges with the Medical Council of the Islamic Republic of Iran." *Afkar News*, 21 Ordibehesht 1391/ May 10, 2012. Accessed May 20, 2012. http://www.ghatreh.com/news/ nn9805044/چالش-وزیر-بهداشت-سازمان-نظام-پزشکی.

"*Chare-ee joz Enhelal-e Khane-ye Cinema Nadashtim*/We Had No Choice But to Disband the House of Cinema." Fars News Agency, 21 Azar 1390/December 12, 2011. Accessed February 13, 2012. http://farsnews.com/newstext.php?nn=13901121000539.

"*Ezharat-e Ayatollah Javadi Amoli darbaraye Hamjesbazi-ye Qanouni dar Gharb*/Statements of Ayatollah Javadi-Amoli about the West's Legalizing Homosexuality." *Khabar News*, 28 Farvardin 1391/ April 16, 2012. Accessed April 20, 2012. http://www.khabaronline.ir/detail/208221/culture/religion.

Farman Farmaian, Sattareh. *Rouspigari dar Shahr-e No-e Tehran, 49/6/25/Prostitution in Tehran's Shahr-e No, 49/6/25*. Tehran: Amouzeshgah-e 'Ahli-ye Khadamat-e Ejtimaei, 1349/1970.

Freud, Sigmund. *Ravankavi va Tahrim-e Zaneshouee ba Maharem/Pyschoanalysis and the Incest Taboo*, 3rd ed. Translated by Nasser al-din Saheb al-Zamani. Tehran: Mo'asseseh-ye 'Ataee, 1966.

"*Gharb va Jonoub-e Tehran dar Sho'le-ye Atash*/Western and Southern Tehran on Fire." *Ettela'at*, 10 Bahman 1357/ February 10, 1979. Accessed November 9, 2011. http://i47.tinypic.com/14jxncl.jpg.

"*Gozaresh-ha az Voqou-e 'Dargiri' dar Meydan-e Baharestan-e Tehran Hekayat Darad*/Reports of Outbreaks in Tehran's Baharestan Square." BBC Persian, 3 Tir 1388/ June 24, 2009. Accessed August 11, 2011. http://www.bbc.co.uk/persian/iran/2009/0 6/090624_nm_demonstraion.shtml.

Grand Ayatollah Yousef Saanei. "*Amouzesh-e Ommumi dar Pishgiri az AIDS*/Public Education about AIDS Prevention." *Fatwas*. Accessed June 1, 2012. http://www.feqh.org/fa/estefta/estefta46.htm.

Hakim-Olahi, Hedayatollah. *Ba Man Beh Shahr-e No Biyaeed*. Vol. 2. Tehran: N.p., 1326/1947.

"*Hormat-e Mojassamehsazi va Naqqashi*/The Sanctity of Sculpting and Painting." *Kavoshi Now dar Fiqh-e Eslami* 4 (Summer and Fall 1374/1995): pp. 62–4.

"*Kahesh-e Senn-e Ruspigari*/A Decrease in Prostitution Age." Baztab-e Emruz, 24 Tir 1391/ July 14, 2012. Accessed July 25, 2012. http://baztab.net/fa/news/10972/.

Khomeini, Ayatollah Ruhollah. *Sima-ye Zan dar Kalam-e Emam Khomeini/Women as Depicted in Imam Khomeini's Words*. Tehran: Ministry of Islamic Guidance, 1369/1990.

Khomeini, Ayatollah Ruhollah. *Tahrir al-Vasileh*, vol. 1, Chapter 129.

Khomeini, Ayatollah Ruhollah. "Women's Day Speech." 25 Farvardin 1361/April 14, 1982.

Khomeini, Ayatollah Ruhollah. *Velayat-e Faqih: Hokomat-e Eslami/Velayat-e Faqih and Islamic Government*. Tehran: Entesharat-e Amir Kabir, 1360/1981.

M., Mina and Hassan Kh. *Razha-ye Movafaghiyat dar Rabete-ye Jensi/Secrets of Success in Sexual Relations*. 3rd ed. Tehran: 1388/2009.

Makarem Shirazi, Naser. "Comments on Exceptions of Sculptures and Statues." n.d. Accessed July 12, 2012. http://makarem.ir/websites/farsi/estefta/?mit=1121.

"*Mankan-ha-ye Sineh Borideh dar Vitrine-ha-ye Iran*/Cut-off Breasts of Mannequins in Iran's Windowshops." Radio Farda, 12 Azar 1385/December 3, 2006. Accessed June 5, 2012. http://www.radiofarda.com/content/f2_mancan/269913.html.

"*Mard-e Neylabakzan-e Ta'atr-e Shahr dar Kojast?*/Where Is the Flute Player of City Theater?" *Rooznameh Aftab-e Yazd*, 28 Aban 1386/ November 19, 2007. Accessed February 14, 2012. http://www.magiran.com/npview.asp?ID=1523682.

"*Mard-e Neylabakzan, Hamchenan Montazer-e Mohasses Ast*/The Flute Player is Still Waiting for Mohasses." *Aftab News*, 21 Esfand 1386/ March 11, 2008. Accessed February 14, 2012. http://www.aftabir.com/news/view/2008/mar/11/c5c1205239299_ art_culture_art_statue.php/مرد-نی-لبك-زن-همچنان-منتظر-محصص-است.

Monfared, Afsaneh. "Baharestan." Encyclopedia Islamica.com, n.d. Accessed July 5, 2012. http://www.encyclopaediaislamica.com/madkhal2.php?sid=2184.

Montazarqha'em, Mehdi. *Rouspigari dar Iran*/Prostitution in Iran. Tehran: Daneshgah-e Oloum-e Behzisti va Tavanbakhshi, 1384/2005.

"*Mo'arefi-ye Manteqeh-ye 11*/Introducing District 11." Cultural Arts Organization for Tehran Municipality, n.d. Accessed July 1, 2012. http://razi.farhangsara.ir/%D9%85%D 8%B9%D8%B1%D9%81%D9%8A%D9%85%D9%86%D8%B7%D9%82%D9%87.aspx.

"*Mo'arefi-ye Shoura-ye 'Ali-ye Enqelab-e Farhangi*/Introducing the Supreme Council of the Revolutionary Council." Office of the Supreme Council of the Cultural Revolution. Accessed March 13, 2012. http://www.iranculture.org/fa/Default.aspx?current=view Doc&currentID=1331.

"*Mojassameh-ye Mard-e Neylabakzan Bazsazi Mishavad*/The Statue of Flute-playing Man Being Repaired." *Rooznameh-ye Iran*, 13 Azar 1386/December 4, 2007. Accessed February 14, 2012. http://www.magiran.com/npview.asp?ID=1531840.

"*Mokhalefan-e Ezdevaj-e Movaqat Cheh Migouyand*?/What Do the Opponents of Temporary Marriage Say?" *Ebtekar News*, Issue 949 (12 Tir 1386/ July 3, 2007).

"*Namayesh-e Moushak-e Shahab-e Seh dar Meydan-e Baharestan-e Tehran*/The Exhibition of Shahab-Three Missile in Tehran's Baharestan Square." BBC Persian, 3 Mehr 1387/September 24, 2008. Accessed December 6, 2019. http://www.bbc.co.uk/persian/i ran/story/2008/09/080924_mg-shahab3.shtml.

Najmabadi, Mahmud. *Bala-ye Azim-e Nasl-e Bashar: Seflis va Souzak/The Great Disaster of the Human Race: Syphilis and Gonorrhea*. Tehran: Firdūsi, 1927.

Naser, Bahonar and Homayoun Mohammadi. *Gozargah-ha-ye Tablighat-e Bazargani az Aghaz ta Eslam/The Passage of Commercial Advertising from the Beginning to Islam*. Tehran: Pajouheshgah-e Farhang, Honar va Ertebatat: 1388/2009.

"*Navad va No Darsad-e Bimaran-e Jadid-e AIDS az Tariq-e Ravebet-e Jensi Mobtala Shodand*/99 Percent of New AIDS Infections through Sexual Relations." Fars News Agency, 9 Khordad 1391/ May 29, 2012. Accessed June 3, 2012. http://www.farsnews. com/newstext.php?nn=13910309000837.

"*Negah-e beh Rouspigari dar Iran*/A Glance at Prostitution in Iran/A Glance at Prostitution in Iran." Pyknet.net. Accessed August 10, 2011. www.pyknet.net/1384/jaftej/01esfan/ 62/pag/37ruspi.htm.

"*Negarani az Bazgasht-e Mojaddad Moj-e AIDS dar Zendanha-ye Iran*/Worries for the Return of the AIDS Epidemic Wave among Prisoners in Iran." *Emruz News*, 13 Esfand 1390/ March 3, 2012. Accessed April 19, 2012. http://www.emruznews.com/2012/03/ post-9499.php.

"*Nokat-e Mohem darbare-ye Shir Dadan*/Important Points about Breastfeeding." MOHME, date unknown. Accessed May 13, 2012. http://bzhc.qums.behdasht.gov.ir/index.aspx?s iteid=183&pageid=31393&pro=nobak.

Osul va Mabani va Ravesh-ha-ye Ejraee-ye Gostaresh-e Farhang-e Efaf/The Principles, Foundations, and Methods in Spreading a Chaste Culture. Shura-ye Aali-ye Enqelab-e Farhangi, 1376 Farvardin 14/ February 3, 1998.

"*Pari Bolandeh Kist*?/Who Is Pari Bolandeh?" Mahitaabe (blog), 2010. Accessed July 15, 2011. http://mahitaabe.blogspot.com/2010/04/blog-post_25.html.

Payam-e Nur Majaleh, "Farhang-e Efaf va Hejab; Rah-e Kar Nahadinehsazi, Gostaresh va Hefz-e Bavarha-ye Diny," Hawzeh online, July–August 2007, no. 184 and 185. Accessed September 2, 2019. http://www.hawzah.net/fa/Magazine/View/3992/5197/47614.

"*Qal'eh Shahr-e No 1965–1980/Shahr-e No* Quarter 1965–1980." Iran Ministry of Culture and Art. Directed by Kamran Shirdel. Tehran: N.p., 1980.

"*Rahandazi-ye Khane-ye Efaf baraye-e Tarvij-e 'Sigheh' dar Shahroud ba Estefadeh az Yek Veblog*/A Chastity House Established in Shahroud Advocating *Sigheh* via Blog."

Al-Arabiya, January 8, 2011. Accessed December 4, 2019. http://www.alarabiya.net/articles/2011/01/08/132677.html.

Sadeghi, Fatemeh. *"Chera Hejab*/Why the Hejab?" Meydaan.org, 25 Ordibehesht 1387/May 14, 2008. Accessed March 14, 2012. http://www.meydaan.com/Showarticle.aspx?arid=548.

Sadr, Shadi. *Majmoueh-ye Qavanin va Moqararat-e Pousesh dar Jomhouri-ye Eslami-ye Iran/The Collection of Rules and Regulations of Dress in the Islamic Republic of Iran.* Tehran: Ketab-e Nili, 1388/2009.

"Salahshour: Cinema-ye Iran Fahesheh-khaneh Ast/Salahshour: Iran's House of Cinema is a Whorehouse." *Aftab News*, 23 Mehr 1390/ October 15, 2011. Accessed February 14, 2014. http://aftabnews.ir/vdcepp8zwjh8xoi.b9bj.html.

"Sarpoush bar Vaqiyati Oryan/Covering Up the Naked Truth." RadioZamaneh, 30 Tir 1391/ July 20, 2012. Accessed July 27, 2012. http://www.radiozamaneh.com/society/khiyaban/2012/07/20/17202.

"Sazman-e Behzisti: Bish az Panjah Darsad-e Kargaran-e Jensi, Zanan-e Mote'ahel Hastand/State Welfare Organization: More than 50 Percent of Sex Workers Are Married Women." BBC Persian, December 12, 2011. Accessed December 6, 2019. http://www.bbc.co.uk/persian/iran/2011/12/111212_l21_sex_worker_iran.shtml.

"Setiz ba Mojassameh/The Struggle with Statues." BBC Persian, August 26, 2002. Accessed September 20, 2011. http://www.bbc.co.uk/persian/arts/020826_mj-mojassame.shtml.

"Shahr-e No: Mazhar-e Fesad dar Qabl az Enqelab/Shahr-e No: The Symbol of Moral Corruption before the Revolution." Tahrikh-e Moaaser-e Iran, 22 Ordibehesht 1387/May 11, 2008. Accessed November 21, 2011. http://bahman18.blogfa.com/post-11.aspx.

"Shahr-e No." Ahari Qorbat-Neshin (blog), August 9, 2011. Accessed July 1, 2012. http://aharii.wordpress.com/2011/08/09/%D8%B4%D9%87%D8%B1%D9%86%D9%88/.

Shahri, Ja'far. *Tarikh-e Ejtemaei-ye Tehran dar Qarn-e 13/The Social History of Tehran in the 13th (20th) Century.* Tehran: Rasa Publishing, 1368/1989.

Shahri, Ja'far. *Tehran-e Qadim/Old Tehran.* Tehran: Moein Publishing, 1376/ 1997.

"Sharayet va Zavabet-e Bargozari-ye Namayeshga-he Mode va Lebas dar Keshvar Eblagh Shod/Conditions and Regulations on the Exhibition of Fashion and Clothing in the Country Announced." Fars News Agency, 14 Shahrivar 1387/September 4, 2008. Accessed July1, 2012. http://www.farsnews.com/newstext.php?nn=8706140288.

"Sigheh: *Niyaz-e Mali*, *Mabna- ye Tahghir-e Zan-e Irani*/Sigheh: Financial Need, the Reason for the Denigration of Iranian Women." *Gozaresh* 215, no. 19 (Bahman 1388/February 2009): pp. 10–11.

"Tanforoushi baraye Afzayesh-e Keyfiyat-e Zendegi/Prostitution for the Purpose of Improving Quality of Life." *Salamat News*, 22 Azar 1390/ December 2, 2011. Accessed January 20, 2012. http://salamatnews.com/viewNews.aspx?ID=38047&cat=12.

"'Tarvij-e Ezdevaj-e Movaqat' va Mavan'e-e Shar-ei va Orfi/'Promoting Temporary Marriage' and Religious and Common Obstacles." BBC Persian, 15 Khordad 1396/June 5, 2007. Accessed December 4, 2019. http://www.bbc.co.uk/persian/iran/story/2007/06/070605_ka-short-marriage.shtml.

"Tarvij-e Farhang-e Efaf va Hejab dar 'Asar-e Honari Mored-e Nazar Gharar Girad/Encouraging a Culture of Chastity and *Hejab* in Works of Art Being Considered." *Mehr News*, 17 Dey 1390/ December 24, 2011. Accessed March 13, 2012. http://www.mehrnews.com/fa/NewsDetail.aspx?NewsID=1503379.

"*Tarh-ha-ye Jayegozin-e Khaneha-ye Efaf?*/Alternative Plans for Chastity Houses?" Women in Iran online, 2 Mehr 1381/ September 24, 2002. Accessed November 22, 2011. http://www.womeniniran.com/news/02-07-81/1-02-07-81.htm.

Varvayyi, Akbar. "*Barrasi-ye Avamel-e Rouspigari-ye Kheyabani dar Tehran-e Bozorg*/The Investigation of the Causes of Street Prostitution in Greater Tehran." Ph.D diss., University of Tehran, School of Law and Political Science, 2008.

"*Vezarat-e Ershad Khaneh-ye Cinema ra Monhal Kard*/Ministry of Culture Dissolves House of Cinema." BBC Persian, January 3, 2012. Accessed December 4, 2019. http://www.bbc.co.uk/persian/iran/2012/01/120103_l06_khaneyecinema_shut_down.shtml.

"*Yek Mohit-e Kamelan Farhangi Baraye Noh Hafte*/A Cultural Environment for 9 Weeks." *Hamshahri News*, 1388 Tir 22/ July 13, 2009. Accessed June 4, 2012. http://www.hamshahrionline.ir/news-85383.aspx.

Zam, Muhammad Ali. *Bahar* newspaper, July 2, 2000.

"*Zanan va AIDS dar Iran: Az Enkar ta Paziresh*/Women and AIDS in Iran: From Denial to Acceptance." *Zanan* 135 (Sharivar 1385/September 2006): pp. 50–5.

Periodicals

Ettela'at,

Issue "*Beh Atash Keshidan-e 'Qal'eh-ye Shahr-e No' va Koshtan-e Rouspeyan/Shahr-e No* Quarter Set on Fire and Prostitutes Killed." (9 Bahman 1357/ January 29, 1979).
Enqelab Edition (10 Bahman 1357/ January 30, 1979).
Issue 18 (14 Aban 1364/November 5, 1985).
Issue (1 Dey 1377/ December 22, 1998).

Kayhan

Issue (12 Mehr 1337/ October 4, 1958).
Issue 10755. "*Beh Hokm-e Dadgah-ha-ye Enqelab-e Eslami: Seh Zan va Chahar Mard Tirbaran Shodand*/The Islamic Revolutionary Courts Executed Three Women and Four Men by Firing Squad." (21 Tir 1358/ July 12, 1979).
Issue 11053 (2 Mordad 1359/ July 24, 1980), p. 2.
Issue (23 Esfand 1361/ March 14, 1983).
Issue, airmail edition (23 Bahman 1364/ February 12, 1986).
Issue 10700 (20 Dey 1390/ January 10, 2012), front cover.
Issue 19858 (29 Bahman 1388/ February 18, 2010).

Zan-e Rouz/Today's Women

Issue 1 (1344/1965), cover page, "Introduction," pp. 32–3.
Issue 9 (1344/1965) p. 32.
Issue 559 (Aban 2535/ November 1976), p. 18.
Issue 595 (2535/1976), p. 22.
Issue 597 (2535/ 1977), pp. 8–9, 12–13.
Issue 599 (Aban 2535/November 1976), pp. 18–19.
Issue 638 (2536/1978), p. 24.

Issue 650 (2536/1978).

Issue 657 (2536/1978), p. 91.

Issue 681 (Khordad 2537/June 1978), p. 22.

Issue 735 (1358/1980), pp. 52–3.

Issue 748 (21 Dey 1358/January 11, 1980), pp. 38–9, 42.

Issue 750 (1358/1980), pp. 10–11, 56.

Issue 757 Norooz edition (5 Esfand 1358/ February 24, 1980), pp. 28–9.

Issue 851 (1361/1982) pp. 46–8.

Issue 853 (Bahman 1360/February 1982), "*Begoo! Begoo!*," p. 62.

Issue 1041 (16 Farvardin 1365/April 5, 1985), pp. 26–7.

Issue 1045 (Azar 1364/November 1985), pp. 4–5, 52–3, 58.

Issue 1093 (24 Aban 1365/November 15, 1986), p. 23.

Issue 1098 (29 Azar 1365/December 20, 1986), p. 4.

Issue 1112 (22 Farvardin 1366/April 11, 1987), p. 18.

Issue 1117 (Ordibehesht 1366/May 16, 1987), pp. 12–13, 26.

Issue 1165 (Ordibehesht 1367/May 1988), pp. 11–12.

English Sources

Abrahamian, Ervand. *A History of Modern Iran*. Cambridge: Cambridge University Press, 2008.

Abrahamian, Ervand. *Iran between Two Revolutions*. Princeton: Princeton University Press, 1982.

Abrahamian, Ervand. *Khomeinism: Essays on the Islamic Republic*. Berkeley: University of California Press, 1993.

Abrahamian, Ervand. "The 1953 Coup in Iran." *Science & Society* 65, no. 2 (Summer 2001): pp. 182–215.

Abrahamian, Ervand. *The Iranian Mojahedin*. New Haven: Yale University Press, 1989.

Abu-Lughod, Lila. "Fieldwork of a Dutiful Daughter." *Arab Women in the Field: Studying Your Own Society*, edited by Soraya Altorki & Camillia Fawzi El-Solh, pp. 139–61. Syracuse: Syracuse University Press, 1988.

Abu-Raddad, Laith. "Characterizing the HIV/AIDS Epidemic in the Middle East and North Africa: Time for Strategic Action." World Bank, June 2010. Accessed April 14, 2012. http://web.worldbank.org/WBSITE/EXTERNAL/COUNTRIES/MENAEXT/0 ,,contentMDK:22632787~pagePK:146736~piPK:146830~theSitePK:256299,00.html.

Afary, Janet. *Sexual Politics in Modern Iran*. Cambridge: Cambridge University Press, 2009.

Afkhami, Amir Arsalan. "From Punishment to Harm Reduction: Resecularization of Addiction in Contemporary Iran." In *Contemporary Iran: Economy, Society, Politics*, edited by Ali Gheissari, pp. 194–210. Oxford: Oxford University Press, 2009. Afshar, Haleh. "Women, State and Ideology in Iran." *Third World Quarterly* 7, no. 2(April 1985): pp. 256–78.

Afkhami, Mahnaz. "Women in Post-Revolutionary Iran: A Feminist Perspective." In *In the Eye of the Storm: Women in Post-Revolutionary Iran*," edited by Mahnaz Afkhami and Erika Friedl, pp. 5–18. London: I.B. Tauris Publishers, 1994.

Aghajanian, Akbar. "Family Planning and Contraceptive Use in Iran, 1967–1992." *International Family Planning Perspectives* 20, no. 2 (June 1994): pp. 66–9.

Ahmed, Leila. *Women and Gender in Islam: Historical Roots of a Modern Debate*. New Haven: Yale University Press, 1993.

"AIDS Special Services: Activities for AIDS Victims: Single Mother Families & Children." SPASDI, August 1, 2010. Accessed April 14, 2012. http://spasdi.ir/en/?p=52.

Alavi, Nasrin. *We are Iran*. London: Portobello Books Ltd, 2005.

Alcoff, Linda Martin. *Visible Identities, Race, Gender, and the Self*. New York: Oxford University Press, 2006.

Alizadeh, Parvin. *The Economy of Iran: The Dilemmas of an Islamic State*. London: I.B. Tauris, 2000.

Allam, Hannah. "Iran's AIDS-Prevention Program among World's Most Progressive." Knight Rider, April 14, 2006. Accessed December 4, 2019. https://www.mcclatchydc.com/latest-news/article24454495.html.

Altorki, Soraya and Camillia Fawzi El-Solh. *Arab Women in the Field: Studying Your Own Society*. Syracuse: Syracuse University Press, 1988.

"American Social Health Association Records, 1905–2005." Social Welfare History Archives, University of Minnesota Libraries, 2002. Accessed December 10, 2011. http://special.lib.umn.edu/findaid/xml/sw0045.xml.

Amin, Camron Michael. "Selling and Saving 'Mother Iran': Gender and the Iranian Press in the 1940s." *International Journal of Middle East Studies* 33 (2001): pp. 335–61.

Amin, Camron Michael. *The Making of the Modern Iranian Women: Gender, State Policy and Popular Culture, 1865–1946*. Gainesville: University Press of Florida, 2002.

Amnesty International. *Iran: End Executions by Stoning Report*. London: Amnesty International Publications, 2008.

Amnesty International. "Law and Human Rights in the Islamic Republic of Iran Report." Amnesty International, February 1980. Accessed January 3, 2012. http://www.iranomid.com/en/ARCHVS/TheIRIReport.pdf.

Amnesty International. "Iran: The Last Executioner of Children." Amnesty International, June 27, 2007. Accessed February 13, 2012. http://www.amnesty.org.uk/news_details.asp?NewsID=17401.

Amuzegar, Jahangir. "Khatami and the Iranian Economy at Mid-Term." *Middle East Journal* 53, no. 4 (Autumn 1999): pp. 534–52.

Anderson, Stephanie. "Cliches of Australian Aborigines: Photography and Raciology, Paris, 1885." In *Reading Images, Viewing Texts: Cross-disciplinary Perspectives*, edited by Louise Maurer and Roger Hillman, pp. 13–30. Berne: Peter Lang S.A., 2006.

Anjoman-e Hemayat va Yari-ye Aseeb Didegan-e Ejtemai-i/Society for the Protection and Assistance of Socially Disadvantaged Individuals (SPASDI). "AIDS Special Services: Activities for AIDS Victims: Single Mother Families and Children." n.d. Accessed December 4, 2019. http://spasdi.ir/en/?p=52.

Anjoman-e Hemayat va Yari-ye Aseeb Didegan-e Ejtemai-i/Society for the Protection and Assistance of Socially Disadvantaged Individuals (SPASDI). "Management." SPASDI.org, January 17, 2017. Accessed December 4, 2019. http://spasdi.ir/index.php/en/about-us-en/management-en.

Ansari, Ali. *Iran, Islam and Democracy: The Politics of Managing Change*. London: Chatham House, 2006.

Ansari, Ali. *Iran under Ahmadinejad: The Politics of Confrontation*. Abingdon: Routledge, 2007.

Ansari, Ali. "The Myth of the White Revolution: Mohammad Reza Shah, 'Modernization' and the Consolidation of Power." *Middle Eastern Studies* 37, no. 3 (July 2001): pp. 1–24.

Apple, Rima. *Mothers & Medicine: A Social History of Infant Feeding 1890–1950*. Madison: The University of Wisconsin Press, 1987.

Arjmand, Reza. *Public Urban Space, Gender and Segregation: Women-Only Urban Parks in Iran*. New York: Routledge, 2017.

Arjomand, Said Amir. *After Khomeini: Iran under His Successors*. Oxford: Oxford University Press Inc., 2009.

Arjomand, Said Amir. *The Turban for the Crown: The Islamic Revolution in Iran*. Oxford: Oxford University Press, 1988.

Arnold, Thomas. "Symbolism and Islam." *The Burlington Magazine for Connoisseurs* 54, no. 307 (October 1928): pp. 154–6.

Arondekar, Anjali R. *For the Record: On Sexuality and the Colonial Archive in India*. Durham: Duke University Press, 2009.

Assistance of Socially Disadvantaged Individuals (SPASDI). "AIDS Special Services: Activities for AIDS Victims: Single Mother Families and Children." n.d. Accessed December 4, 2019. http://spasdi.ir/en/?p=52.

Avery, Peter, Gavin Hambly, and Charles Melville, eds. *The Cambridge History of* Iran, *Volume 7: From Nadir Shah to the Islamic Republic, Volume 7*. Cambridge: Cambridge University Press, 1991.

Ayatollahi, Habibollah. *The Book of Iran: The History of Iranian Art*. Tehran: Organization for Islamic Culture and Communications & Center for International-Cultural Studies, 2003.

Babayan, Kathryn and Afsaneh Najmabadi, eds. *Islamicate Sexualities: Translations across Temporal Geographies of Desire*. Boston: President and Fellows of Harvard College, 2008.

"Biography: Part One." Bahman Mohassess Foundation, 2012. Accessed February 13, 2012. http://bahmanmohassess.com/life/biography-part-one.

Bakhash, Shaul. "The Islamic Republic of Iran, 1979–1989." *The Wilson Quarterly (1976-)* 13, no. 4 (Autumn 1989): pp. 54–62.

Barnes, DB. "Reproductive Decisions for Women with HIV: Motherhood's Role inEnvisioning a Future." *Qualitative Health Research Journal* 19, no. 4 (April 2009): pp. 481–91.

Barnett, Tony and Alan Whiteside. *AIDS in the Twenty-First Century: Disease and Globalization*. New York: Palgrave Macmillan, 2002.

Barry, Kathleen. *The Prostitution of Sexuality*. New York and London: New York University Press, 1995.

Bartlett, Allison. *Breastwork: Rethinking Breastfeeding*. Sydney: University of New South Wales Press, Ltd., 2005.

Bayat, Asef. *Street Politics: Poor People's Movements in Iran*. New York: Columbia University Press, 1997.

Bayat, Asef. "Tehran: Paradox City." *New Left Review* 66 (November/ December 2010): pp. 99–122.

Behnoud, Masoud. "The Ideal Islamic State: An Unattainable Quest." Abdolkarim Soroush online, January 8, 2006. Accessed July 10, 2011. http://www.drsoroush.com/English/News_Archive/E-NWS-20060108-TheIdealIslamicState-AnUnattainableQuest.html.

Bell, Emma, Promise Mthembu, Sue O'Sullivan, and Kevin Moody. "Sexual and Reproductive Health Services and HIV Testing: Perspectives and Experiences of Women and Men Living with HIV and AIDS." *Reproductive Health Matters* 15: 29, Supplement: Ensuring Sexual and Reproductive Health for People Living with HIV: Policies, Programmes and Health Services (May 2007): pp. 113–36.

Bell, Shannon. *Reading, Writing, and Rewriting the Prostitute Body*. Bloomington: Indiana University Press, 1994.

Blum, Linda. "Mothers, Babies, and Breastfeeding in Late Capitalist America: The Shifting Contexts of Feminist Theory." *Feminist Studies* 19, no. 2 (Summer 1993): pp. 291–311.

Bochner, Arthur. "Embracing Contingencies of Lived Experience in the Study of Close Relationships." Keynote lecture to the International Conference on Personal Relationships, Oxford University, 1990.

Boroujerdi, Mehrzad. *Iranian Intellectuals and the West: The Tormented Triumph of Nativism*. Syracuse: Syracuse University Press, 1996.

Bosworth, Clifford, E. Van Donzel, W. P. Heinrichs, and Ch Pellat. *Encyclopedia of Islam*, Second Edition, Volume VII. London: Brill Academic Publishing, 1993.

Bourdieu, Pierre. *Photography: A Middle-Brow Art*. Translated by Shaun Whiteside. Stanford, CA: Stanford University Press, 1990.

Bozorgmehr, Kayvan. "Head of Sociology Association of Iran Announces: Drop in Prostitution Age in Iran." Roozonline, June 15, 2011. Accessed January 12, 2012. http://www.roozonline.com/english/news3/newsitem/article/drop-in-prostitution-age-in-iran.html.

Brandt, Allan. "Recruiting Women Smokers: The Engineering of Consent." *Journal of the American Medical Women's Association* 51, no. 1–2 (1996): pp. 63–6.

Bucar, Elizabeth. *Creative Conformity: The Feminist Politics of U.S. Catholic and Iranian Shi'i Women*. Washington, DC: Georgetown University Press, 2011.

Butler, Judith. *Gender Trouble: Feminism and Subversion of Identity*. New York: Routledge, 1999.

Butler, Judith. "Performative and Gender Constitution: An Essay in Phenomenology and Feminist Theory." *Theatre Journal* 40, no. 4 (December 1988): pp. 519–31.

Butler, Judith. *Subjects of Desire*. New York: Columbia University Press, 1999.

Butler, Judith. "Subjects of Sex/Gender/Desire." In *The Cultural Studies Reader*, edited by Simon During, pp. 340–54. New York: Routledge, 1993.

Carter, Pam. *Feminism, Breasts and Breast-Feeding*. New York: St. Martin's Press, 1995.

Chehabi, Houshang. "zur-kana." *Encyclopedia Iranica*, August 15, 2006. Accessed December 6, 2019. http://www.iranicaonline.org/articles/zur-kana.

Chehabi, Houshang. *Iranian Politics and Religious Modernism: The Liberation Movement of Iran under the Shah and Khomeini*. Ithaca: Cornell University Press, 1990.

Chehabi, Houshang. "Stating the Emperor's New Clothes: Dress Codes and Nation-Building under Reza Shah." *Iranian Studies* 26, no. ¾ (Summer–Autumn 1993): pp. 209–29.

Chelkowski, Peter J. and Hamid Dabashi. *Staging a Revolution: The Art of Persuasion in the Islamic Republic of Iran*. New York: New York University Press, 1999.

Cherifati-Merabtine, Doria. "Algeria at a Crossroads: National Liberation, Islamization, and Women." In *Gender and National Identity: Women and Politics in Muslim Societies*, edited by Valentine Moghadam, pp. 40–62. London: Zed Books, 1994.

Choay, Françoise. *The Invention of the Historic Monument*. Cambridge: Cambridge University Press, 2001.

Christensen, Janne Bjerre. *Drugs, Deviancy and Democracy in Iran: The Interaction of State and Civil Society*. London: I.B. Tauris, 2011.

Cichocki, Mark. *Living with HIV: A Patient's Guide*. North Carolina: McFarland & Company, Inc., 2009.

Corbin, Alain. *Women for Hire*, translated by Alan Sheridan. Cambridge: Harvard University Press, 1990.

Crawford, Robert. "The Boundaries of the Self and the Unhealthy Other: Reflections on Health, Culture and AIDS." *Social Science & Medicine* 38, no. 10 (1994): pp. 1347–65.

Dabashi, Hamid. "Body-Less Faces: Mutilating Modernity and Abstracting Women in an 'Islamic Cinema.'" *Visual Anthropology* 10, no. 2 (1998): pp. 361–80.

Dabashi, Hamid. "In the Absence of the Face." *Social Research* 67, no. 1 (Spring 2000): pp. 127–85.

Dabashi, Hamid. *Iran: A People Interrupted*. New York: New Press, 2008.

Dabashi, Hamid. *Shi'ism: A Religion of Protest*. Boston: Belknap Press of Harvard University Press, 2011.

Dabashi, Hamid. "Shirin Neshat: Transcending the Boundaries of an Imaginative Geography." In *The Last Word*, edited by Octavio Zaya. San Sebastian, Spain: Museum of Modern Art, 2005.

Dabashi, Hamid. *The Green Movement in Iran*. New Brunswick: Transaction Publishers, 2011.

Dabashi, Hamid. *Theology of Discontent: The Ideological Foundation of the Islamic Revolution in Iran*. New Brunswick: Transaction Publishers, 2006.

Dadeghi, Saeed. "Map of the Protests." Radio Zameneh.com, 29 Aban 1398/ November 20, 2019. Accessed November 24, 2019. https://www.radiozamaneh.com/475235.

Dalla, Rochelle L. et al. *Global Perspectives on Prostitution and Sex Trafficking*. Lanham: Lexington, 2011.

Day, Carolyn, Bijan Nassirimanesh, Anthony Shakeshaft, and Kate Dolan. "Patterns of Drug Use among a Sample of Drug Users and Injecting Drug Users Attending a General Practice in Iran." *Harm Reduction Journal* 3, no. 1 (2006): pp. 1–5.

Deleuze, Gilles. *Cinema 2: The Time-Image*. Translated by Hugh Tomlinson and Robert Galeta. Minneapolis: University of Minnesota Press, 1989.

Derrida, Jacques. *Archive Fever: A Freudian Impression*. Translated by Eric Prenowitz. Chicago: University of Chicago Press, 1995.

Doezema, Jo. "Forced to Choose: Beyond the Voluntary v. Forced Prostitution Dichotomy." In *Global Sex Workers*, edited by Kamala Kempadoo and Jo Doezema, pp. 34–50. New York: Routledge, 1998.

Doezema, Jo. "Loose Women or Lost Women? The Re-emergence of the Myth of White Slavery in Contemporary Discourses of Trafficking in Women." *Gender Issues* 18, no. 1 (January 2000): pp. 23–50.

Douglas, Mary. "The Two Bodies." In *Natural Symbols: Explorations in Cosmology*, pp. 69–87. London and New York: Routledge, 1996.

"Dr. Minoo Mohraz Stresses on the Prevention of Diseases such as HIV/AIDS for Maintaining a Healthy Society." *Tehran University of Medical Sciences Public Relations News*, December 7, 2011. Accessed June 1, 2012. http://publicrelations.tums.ac.ir/english/news/detail.asp?newsID=29111.

Ekhtiar, Maryam and Marika Sardar. "Modern and Contemporary Art in Iran." *Heilbrunn Timeline of Art History*. New York: The Metropolitan Museum of Art, 2000.

Ellis, Carolyn, Michael C. Flaherty, and Michael G. Flaherty, eds. *Investigating Subjectivity: Research on Lived Experience*. London: Sage Publications Ltd., 1992.

"Epidemiological Fact Sheet on HIV and AIDS 2008 Update." Islamic Republic of Iran, October 2008. Accessed April 13, 2012. http://apps.who.int/globalatlas/predefinedReports/EFS2008/full/EFS2008_IR.pdf.

"Epidemiological Fact Sheet on HIV/AIDS and Sexually Transmitted Infections: 2004 Update for Iran." UNAIDS/WHO, pp. 1–14. Accessed April 10, 2012. http://data.unaids.org/publications/Fact-Sheets01/iran_en.pdf.

Encyclopedia of Islam, Second Edition, s.v. "*rada*" or "rida."

Entessar, Nader. "Criminal Law and the Legal System in Revolutionary Iran." *Boston College Third World Law Journal* 8, no. 1 (January 1988): pp. 91–102.

Esfandiari, Golnaz. "Iran Reportedly Removes World AIDS Day from State Calendar." *RFERL*, March 17, 2012. Accessed June 4, 2012. http://www.rferl.org/content/iran_t akes_world_aids_day_off_calendar/24518879.html.

Esfandiari, Golnaz. "Iran: Tehran Begins to Confront the 'Time Bomb' of HIV/AIDS." RFERL, November 10, 2003. Accessed April 2, 2012. http://www.rferl.org/content/a rticle/1104954.html.

Esfandiari, Haleh. *My Prison, My Home: One Woman's Story of Captivity in Iran*. New York: HarperCollins, 2009.

Esfandiari, Haleh. *Reconstructed Lives: Women & Iran's Islamic Revolution*. Baltimore: Johns Hopkins University Press, 1997.

Ewen, Stuart. *Captains of Consciousness Advertising and the Social Roots of the Consumer Culture*. New York: Basic Books, 2001.

Falah, Homeira, Ghazi-Walid, and Caroline Rose Nagel. *Geographies of Muslim Women: Gender, Religion, and Space*. New York: Guilford, 2005.

Fallahi, Sedigheh Sadat Tavafian, Farideh Yaghmaie, and Ebrahim Hajizadeh. "Stigma, Discrimination, and the Consequences of HIV-AIDS for People Living with It in Iran." *Life Science Journal* 8, no. 4 (2011): pp. 503–10.

Farahani, Fataneh. *Diasporic Narratives of Sexuality: Identity Formation among Iranian-Swedish Women*. Stockholm: Stockholm University, 2007.

Farhi, Farideh. "Religious Intellectuals, the 'Woman Question,' and the Struggle for the Creation of a Democratic Public Sphere in Iran." *International Journal of Politics, Culture, and Society* 15, no. 2 (Winter 2001): pp. 315–39.

Farman Farmaian, Sattareh. *Daughter of Persia: A Woman's Journey from Her Father's Harem through the Islamic Revolution*. New York: Anchor Book, 1993.

Fathi, Nazila. "To Regulate Prostitution, Iran Ponders Brothels." *New York Times*, August 28, 2002. Accessed November 20, 2011. http://www.nytimes.com/2002/08/28/world/ to-regulate-prostitution-iran-ponders-brothels.html.

Feizzadeh, A. "Evidence-Based Approach to HIV/AIDS Policy and Research Prioritization in Islamic Republic of Iran." *Eastern Mediterranean Health Journal* 16, no. 3 (March 2010): pp. 259–65.

Fendall, N. R. E. "A Comparison of Family Planning Programs in Iran and Turkey." *HSMHA Health Reports* 86, no. 11 (November 1971): pp. 1011–24.

Fetterman, D. M. *Ethnography: Step-by –Step*. 3rd ed. Thousand Oaks: Sage, 2002.

Floor, Willem. *A Social History of Sexual Relations in Iran*. Washington DC: Mage Publishers, 2008.

Floor, Willem. "The Art of Smoking in Iran and Other Uses of Tobacco." *Iranian Studies* 35, no. 1–3 (Winter, Spring, Summer 2002): pp. 47–85.

Floor, Willem. "Venereal Disease in Iran (1855–2005): A Public Affair." *Comparative Studies of South Asia, Africa and the Middle East* 26, no. 2 (2006): pp. 260–78.

Forest, Benjamin and Juliet Johnson. "Unraveling the Threads of History: Soviet-Era Monuments and Post-Soviet National Identity in Moscow." *Annals of the Association of American Geographers* 92, no. 3 (September 2002): pp. 524–47.

Foucault, Michel. *Discipline and Punish: The Birth of the Prison*. London: Penguin Group, 1991.

Foucault, Michel. *The Archaeology of Knowledge*. Translated by A. M. Sheridan Smith. New York: Pantheon, 1972.

Foucault, Michel. *The History of Sexuality, Vol. 2: The Use of Pleasure*. Translated by R. Hurley. London: Penguin, 1985.

Foucault, Michel. *The Order of Things: An Archaeology of the Human Sciences*. Routledge: New York, 1970.

Foucault, Michel. "The Subject and Power." *Critical Inquiry* 8, no. 4 (Summer 1982): pp. 777–95.

Foucault, Michel and Jay Miskowiec. "Of Other Spaces." *Diacritics* 16, no. 1 (Spring 1986): pp. 22–7.

Fuch Ebaugh, Helen Rose. *Becoming an Ex: The Process of Role Exit*. Chicago: University of Chicago Press, 1988.

Garber, Marjorie. *Vested Interests: Cross-Dressing and Cultural Anxiety*. New York: Routledge, 1997.

Ghasemi, Shahpour. "*Kayhan* Newspaper." Iran Chamber Society, 2006. Accessed December 4, 2019. http://www.iranchamber.com/media/articles/kayhan_newspaper.php.

Goffman, Erving. "Embodied Information in Face-to-Face Interaction." In *The Body: A Reader*, edited by Mariam Fraser and Monica Greco, pp. 82–8. Routledge: New York, 2005.

Goffman, Erving. *Stigma*. New York: Simon & Shuster, 1991.

Gholi Majd, Mohammad. *Resistance to the Shah: Landowners and Ulama in Iran*. Gainesville: University Press of Florida, 2000.

The Global Fund. "Who We Are." The Global Fund to Fight AIDS, Tuberculosis and Malaria, 2012. Accessed April 30, 2012. http://www.theglobalfund.org/en/about/whoweare/.

Grondahl, Paul. "Doctor Released from Iranian Prison." *Times Union*, June 13, 2011. Accessed March 20, 2012. http://www.timesunion.com/local/article/Doctor-released-from-Iranian-prison-I-struggle-1420477.php#ixzz1PXaIeC00.

Haeri, Shahla. "A Reply to Ziba Mir-Hosseini." *International Journal of Middle East Studies* 30, no. 3 (August 1998): pp. 471–2.

Haeri, Shahla. *Law of Desire: Temporary Marriage in Iran*. London: I.B. Tauris & Co Ltd, 1989.

Haeri, Shahla. "Marriage and the State in Iran: An Islamic Discourse on Female Sexuality." *Social Research* 49, no. 1, *Religion and Politics* (Spring 1992): pp. 201–23.

Haeri, Shahla. "Power of Ambiguity: Cultural Improvisations on the Theme of Temporary Marriage." *Iranian Studies* 19, no. 2 (Spring 1986): pp. 123–54.

Haghayeghi, Mehrdad. "Politics and Ideology in the Islamic Republic of Iran." *Middle Eastern Studies* 29, no. 1 (January 1993): pp. 36–52.

Hakakian, Roya. *Journey from the Land of No*. New York: Crown Publishers, 2004.

Hamilton, Margaret. "Opposition to the Contagious Diseases Acts, 1864–1886." *Albion: A Quarterly Journal Concerned with British Studies* 10, no. 1 (Spring 1978): pp. 14–27.

Hays, Sharon. *The Cultural Contradictions of Motherhood*. New Haven: Yale University Press, 1996.

Helie, Anissa and Homa Hoodfar, eds. *Sexuality in Muslim Contexts: Restrictions and Resistance*. London: Zed Books, 2012.

Hirschman, Elizabeth C. and Craig J. Thompson. "Why Media Matter: Toward a Richer Understanding of Consumers' Relationships with Advertising and Mass Media." *Journal of Advertising* 26, no. 1 (Spring 1997): pp. 43–60.

"HIV Facts: The Basics." National AIDS Trust, 2012. Accessed April 20, 2012. http://www.nat.org.uk/HIV-Facts/The-basics.aspx.

HIV/AIDS in Iran (Cumulative Statistics) Tehran 2004 Report. Iran Center for Disease Management, Office of the Deputy for Public Health, Ministry of Health and Medical Education of the I.R. Iran, 2004.

Honarbin-Holliday, Mehri. "Autonomous Minds and Bodies in Theory and Practice: Women Constructing Cultural Identities and Becoming Visible through Art." In *Women, Power and Politics in 21st Century Iran,* edited by Tara Povey and Elaheh Rostami-Povey, pp. 53–72. London: Ashgate Publishing, Ltd., 2012.

Honarbin-Holliday, Mehri. *Becoming Visible in Iran.* London: Tauris Academic Studies, 2008.

Hooshmand, Parvaneh. "Sexualities. Practices. Iran." *Encyclopedia of Women in Islamic Cultures: Family, Law and Politics* 3, edited by Suad Joseph and Afsaneh Najmabadi, pp. 384–6. Leiden: Brill Publishing, 2005.

Hosseinkhah, Maryam. *The Execution of Women in Iranian Criminal Law: An Examination of the Impact of Gender on Laws Concerning Capital Punishment in the New Islamic Penal Code.* New Haven: Iran Human Rights Documentation Center, 2012.

Howard, I. K. A. "Mut'a Marriage Reconsidered in the Context of the Formal Procedures for Islamic Marriage." *Journal of Semitic Studies* 20 (1975): pp 82–92.

Inglehart, Ronald and Wayne E. Baker. "Modernization, Cultural Change, and the Persistence of Traditional Values." *American Sociological Review* 65, no. 1, Looking Forward, Looking Back: Continuity and Change at the Turn of the Millenium (February 2000): pp. 19–51.

"Introduction to Farabi Eye Hospital." Tehran University of Medical Sciences, n.d. Accessed November 1, 2019. http://medicine.tums.ac.ir/college/en/page/farabi-hospital.

"Iran Anti-vice Chief in 'Brothel.'" BBC News, April 16, 2008. Accessed August 21, 2011. http://news.bbc.co.uk/2/hi/middle_east/7350165.stm.

"Iran Crisis: Live." The Guardian.co.uk, June 19, 2009. Accessed July 31, 2011. http://www.guardian.co.uk/news/blog/2009/jun/19/iran-unrest.

"Iran Crisis: Live." The Guardian.co.uk, June 24, 2009. Accessed January 1, 2012. http://www.guardian.co.uk/news/blog/2009/jun/24/iran-crisis.

"Iran Currency Exchange Rate History: 1975–2012." Farsinet.com. Accessed July 3, 2012. http://www.farsinet.com/toman/exchange.html.

"Iran-Iran: AIDS Awareness to Include Schools." IRIN News, June 25, 2002. Accessed April 30, 2012. http://www.irinnews.org/Report/40944/IRAN-IRAN-AIDS-awareness-to-include-schools.

"Iran Intensifies Campaign against HIV." Fars News Agency, November 11, 2008. Accessed June 1, 2012. http://english.farsnews.com/newstext.php?nn=8709061775.

"Iran Juggles with Taboos, Holds First of Prostitutes and Police." Payvand.com, December 7, 2002. Accessed January 12, 2012.http://www.netnative.com/news/02/dec/1032.html.

"Iran Marks World AIDS Day." Press TV, November 30, 2011. Accessed June 4, 2012. http://www.presstv.ir/detail/213079.html.

"Iran: New 'Morality Police' Units Generate Controversy." RFERF, July 25, 2002. Accessed June 14, 2012. http://www.rferl.org/content/article/1100367.html.

"Iran's Youth Reveal Anger and Sadness." BBC News, December 10, 2002. Accessed January 12, 2012. http://news.bbc.co.uk/1/hi/world/middle_east/2563413.stm.

"Iranian Artist Bahman Mohasses Dies at 79." *Tehran Times*, July 3, 2010. Accessed February 12, 2012. http://old.tehrantimes.com/index_View.asp?code=223931.

"IRIB Bans Smoking Scenes in Iranian Productions." *Mehr News*, May 1, 2011. Accessed September 18, 2011. http://www.mehrnews.com/en/newsdetail.aspx?NewsID=1226049.

Gatens, Moira. *Imaginary Bodies: Ethics, Power and Corporeality*. London and New York: Routledge, 1996.

Gheissari, Ali and Kaveh-Cyrus Sanandaji. "New Conservative Politics and Electoral Behavior in Iran." In *Contemporary Iran: Economy, Society, Politics*, edited by Ali Gheissari, pp. 275–98. Oxford: Oxford University Press, 2009.

Giladi, Avner. *Infants, Parents and Wet Nurses: Medieval Islamic Views on Breastfeeding and their Social Implications*. Leiden and Boston: Brill, 1999.

Gillespie, Alex and Flora Cornish. "Intersubjectivity: Towards a Dialogical Analysis." *Journal of the Theory of Social Behaviour* 40, no. 1 (2009): pp. 19–46.

Grondahl, Paul. "Doctor Released from Iranian Prison." *Times Union*, June 13, 2011. Accessed March 20, 2012. http://www.timesunion.com/local/article/Doctor- released-from-Iranian-prison-I-struggle-1420477.php#ixzz1PXaIeC00.

Grosz, Elizabeth. *Volatile Bodies: Toward a Corporeal Feminism*. Indianapolis: Indiana University Press, 1994.

Herek, Gregory, Keith Widaman, and John Capitanio. "When Sex Equals AIDS: Symbolic Stigma and Heterosexual Adults' Inaccurate Beliefs about Sexual Transmission of AIDS." *Social Problems* 52, no. 1 (2005): pp. 15–37.

Jahanpour, Farhang. "The Rise and Fall of the Tudeh Party." *The World Today* 40, no. 4 (April 1984): pp. 152–9.

Jenkins, Thomas. "Emotional Prostheses: Bodily Technologies for Emotional Expression." ThomasJenkins.net, 2008. Accessed September 9, 2011. http://www.thomasjenkins.net/prostheses/EmotionalProstheses.pdf.

Jibouri, Yasin. "*Uswat al-Aarifeen*. A Look at the Life of Ayatollah Bahjat." Ahlul Bayt Digital Islamic Library Project, 2005. Accessed 15 March 2012. http://www.al-islam.org/uswat_alarifin/.

Kabbash, I. A. et al. "Needs Assessment and Coping Strategies of Persons Infected with HIV in Egypt." *Eastern Mediterranean Health Journal* 14, no. 6 (2008): pp. 1–13.

Kalkhoran, Sara and Lauren Hale. "AIDS Education in an Islamic Nation: Content Analysis of Farsi-language AIDS-education Materials in Iran." *Promotion & Education Journal* 15, no. 3 (2008): pp. 21–5.

Kamali Dehghan, Saeed. "Homosexuals are Inferior to Dogs and Pigs, Says Iranian Cleric." The Guardian.co.uk, April 18, 2012. Accessed April 20, 2012. http://www.guardian.co.uk/world/iran-blog/2012/apr/18/iran-cleric-condemns- homosexuality.

Kamali Dehghan, Saeed. "Iran Considers Ban on Vasectomies in Drive to Boost Birthrate." The Guardian.co.uk, April 15, 2014. Accessed December 1, 2019. http://www.theguardian.com/world/2014/apr/15/iran-ban-vasectomies-birthrate.

Kar, Mehrangiz. *Frontier Fictions: Shaping the Iranian Nation, 1804–1946*. Princeton: Princeton University Press, 1999.

Kar, Mehrangiz. "The Invasion of the Private Sphere in Iran." *Social Research* 70, no. 3 (Fall 2003): pp. 829–36.

Kar, Mehrangiz. *Crossing the Red Line: The Struggle for Human Rights in Iran*. Costa Mesa: Mazda Publishing, 2006.

Kar, Mehrangiz. "Death of a Mannequin." In *My Sister, Guard Your Veil; My Brother, Guard Your Eyes: Uncensored Iranian Voices*, edited by Lila Azam Zanganeh, pp. 30–7. Boston: Beacon Press, 2006.

Kar, Mehrangiz. "The Politics of Reproduction: Maternalism and Women's Hygiene in Iran, 1896–1941." *International Journal of Middle Eastern Studies* 38 (2006): pp. 1–29.

Kashani-Sabet, Firoozeh. *Conceiving Citizens: Women and the Politics of Motherhood in Iran*. Oxford: Oxford University Press, 2011.

Kashani-Sabet, Firoozeh. "The Politics of Reproduction: Maternalism and Women's Hygiene in Iran, 1896–1941." In *International Journal of Middle East Studies* 38 (2006): pp. 1–29.

Kates, Steven and Glenda Shaw-Garlock. "The Ever Entangling Web: A Study of Ideologies and Discourses in Advertising to Women." *Journal of Advertising* 28, no. 2 (Summer 1999): pp. 33–49.

Kaveh Golestan 1950-2003: Recording the Truth in Iran. Ostfildern, Germany: Hatje Canz Publishers, 2007.

Keddie, Nikki and Yann Richard. *Modern Iran: Roots and Results of Revolution*. New Haven: Yale University Press, 2003.

Kempadoo, Kamala, and Jo Doezema. *Global Sex Workers: Rights, Resistance, and Redefinition*. New York: Routledge, 1998.

Khatib-Chahidi, Jane. "Sexual Prohibitions, Shared Space and 'Fictive' Marriages in Shi'ite Iran." *Women and Space: Ground Rules and Social Maps*, edited by Shirley Ardener, pp. 112–34. Oxford: Bloomsbury, 1997.

Khomeini, Ruhollah. *According to the Tahrir al-Vasilah of Ayatollah 'Uzma Imam Khomeini*. Translated by Laleh Bakhtiar. Tehran: Foreign Department of Bonyad Ba'that, 1986.

Khomeini, Ruhollah. "We Shall Confront the World with Our Ideology." *MERIP Reports*, no. 88. Iran's Revolution: The First Year (June 1980): pp. 22–5.

Khosrovani, Firouzeh. *Rough Cut*. Tehran: n.p. 2007.

Kian-Thiebaut, Azadeh. *Les Femmes Iraniennes entre Islam, Etat et Famille*. Paris: Maisonneuve et Larose, 2002.

Kilvington, Judith, Sophie Day, and Helen Ward. "Prostitution Policy in Europe: A Time of Change?" *Feminist Review* 67, Sex Work Reassessed (Spring 2001): pp. 78–93.

Kingston, Sarah. *Prostitution in the Community*. London: Routledge, 2013.

Labi, Nadya. "Married for a Minute." *Mother Jones*, March/April 20120. Accessed November 10, 2011. http://www.motherjones.com/politics/2010/03/temporary-marriage-iran-islam.

Lambek, Michael. "Taboo as Cultural Practice among Malagasy Speakers." *Man* 27, no. 2 (June 1992): pp. 245–66.

Lawrence, R. A. *Breastfeeding: A Guide for the Medical Profession*. Princeton: Mosby, 1994.

Lazreg, Marnia. "Feminism and Difference: The Perils of Writing as a Woman on Women in Algeria." *Feminist Studies* 14, no. 1 (Spring 1988): pp. 81–107.

Lazreg, Marnia. *Questioning the Veil: Open Letters to Muslim Women*. Princeton: Princeton University Press, 2009.

LeCompte, Margaret and Jean Schensul. *Designing and Conducting Ethnographic Research*. London: AltaMira Press, 2010.

Lefebvre, Henri. *The Production of Space*. Translated by Donald Nicholson-Smith. Oxford: Blackwell Publishing, 1991.

Leiss, William, Stephen Kline, Sut Jhally and Jacqueline Botterill. *Social Communication in Advertising: Persons, Products and Images of Well-Being*. London: Routledge, 1997.

Leslie, D. A. "Global Scan: The Globalization of Advertising Agencies, Concepts, and Campaigns." *Economic Geography* 71, no. 4 (October 1995): pp. 402–26.

Levin, David Michael. *The Body's Recollection of Being*. London: Routledge, 1985.

Levine, Phillipa. *Prostitution, Race and Politics: Policing Venereal Disease in the British Empire*. London: Routledge, 2003.

Liamputtong, P., N. Haritavorn, and N. Kiatgying-Angsulee. "HIV and AIDS, Stigma and AIDS Support Groups: Perspectives from Women Living with HIV and AIDS in Central Thailand." *Social Science & Medicine* 69 (2009): pp. 862–8.

Madanipour, Ali. *Tehran: The Making of a Metropolis*. New York: John Wiley & Sons, Ltd., 1998.

Maddah, Mohsen. "Breastfeeding Rates in Iran: Why Is There Such a Large Gap between Iran and Other Countries." *Journal of Human Lactation* 24, no. 149 (April 2008), doi: 10.1177/0890334408316087.

Mahdavi, Pardis. *Passionate Uprisings*. Stanford: Stanford University Press, 2009.

Mahdavi, Pardis. "Who Will Catch Me If I Fall? Health and the Infrastructure of Risk for Urban Young Iranians." In *Contemporary Iran: Economy, Society, Politics*, edited by Ali Gheissari, pp. 150–93. Oxford: Oxford University Press, 2009.

Mahdavi, Shireen. "Women and the *Shii Ulama* in Iran." *Middle Eastern Studies* 19, no. 1 (January 1983): pp. 17–27.

Mahlouji, Vali. "Re-creating *Shahr-e No*: Kaveh Golestan and the Intimate Politics of the Marginal," n.d. Accessed December 6, 2019. http://valimahlouji.com/recreating-shahr -e-no/.

Makhlouf Obermeyer, Carla. "Reproductive Choice in Islam: Gender and State in Iran and Tunisia." *Studies in Family Planning* 25, no. 1 (January-February 1994): pp. 41–51.

Marcus, Michelle I. "Dressed to Kill: Women and Pins in Early Iran." *Oxford Art Journal* 17, no. 2 (1994): pp. 3–15.

Massad, Joseph. *Desiring Arabs*. Chicago: University of Press, 2007.

May, Tim. *Qualitative Research in Action*. London: SAGE, 2002.

Maynard, Mary and June Purvis. *Researching Women's Lives from a Feminist Perspective*. London: Taylor & Francis, 1994.

Maynes, Mary Jo., Jennifer L. Pierce, and Barbara Laslett. *Telling Stories: The Use of Personal Narratives in the Social Sciences and History*. Ithaca: Cornell University Press, 2008.

Mazo Karras, Ruth. "The Regulation of Brothels in Later Medieval England." *Signs* 14, no. 2 (Winter 1989): pp. 399–433.

McLarney, Ellen. "The Burqa in Vogue: Fashioning Afghanistan." *Journal of Middle East Women's Studies* 5, no. 1 (Winter 2009): pp. 1–20.

Mehrdad, Ramin. "Health System in Iran." *Japan Medical Association Journal* 52, no. 1 (2009): pp. 69–73.

Mehryar, Amir, Shirin Ahmad-Nia, and Shahla Kazemipour. "Reproductive Health in Iran: Pragmatic Achievements, Unmet Needs, and Ethical Challenges in a Theocratic System." *Studies in Family Planning* 38, no. 4 (December 2007): pp. 352–61.

Menon, Kesava. "Flesh Is Weaker in Moralistic Iran." *The Hindu*, January 27, 2001. Accessed December 4, 2019. http://www.hindu.com/2001/01/28/stories/03280009.htm.

Mercer, Ramona. *Becoming a Mother: Research on Maternal Identity from Rubin to the Present*. New York: Springer, 1995.

Merleau-Ponty, Maurice. *Phenomenology of Perception*. Translated by Routledge and Kegan Paul. New York: Routledge, 2002.

Merleau-Ponty, Maurice. "The Invisible and the Invisible." In *Maurice Merleau-Ponty: Basic Writings*, edited by Thomas Baldwin. London: Routledge, 2004.

Merleau-Ponty, Maurice. "The Phenomenology of Perception.'" In *Maurice Merleau-Ponty: Basic Writings*, edited by Thomas Baldwin. London: Routledge, 2004.

Mernissi, Fatima. *The Veil and the Male Elite: A Feminist's Interpretation of Women's Rights in Islam*. New York: Basic Books, 1991.

Michels, Dia and Naomi Baumslag. *Milk, Money, and Madness: The Culture and Politics of Breastfeeding*. Bergen & Garvey Trade: Westport, CT, 1995.

Milani, Abbas. *Eminent Persians: The Men and Women Who Made Modern Iran 1941– 1979*. Volume 2. Syracuse: Syracuse University Press, 2008.

Milani, Farzaneh. *Veiling and Words: The Emerging Voices of Iranian Women Writers*. Syracuse: Syracuse University Press, 1992.

Mir-Hosseini, Ziba. "Divorce, Veiling and Feminism in Post-Khomeini Iran." In *Women and Politics in the Third World*, edited by Haleh Afshar, pp. 142–70. London: Routledge, 1996.

Mir-Hosseini, Ziba. "A Response to Shahla Haeri's Review of *Marriage on Trial, A Study of Islamic Family Law in Iran and Morocco*." *International Journal of Middle East Studies* 30, no. 3 (August 1998): pp. 469–75.

Mir-Hosseini, Ziba. *Islam and Gender: The Religious Debate in Contemporary Iran*. Princeton: Princeton University Press, 1999.

Mir-Hosseini, Ziba. "The Conservative: Reformist Conflict over Women's Rights in Iran." *International Journal of Politics, Culture, and Society* 16, no. 1 (Fall 2002): pp. 37–53.

Mir-Hosseini, Ziba. *Marriage on Trial: A Study of Islamic Family Law*. London: I.B. Tauris, 2000.

Mir-Hosseini, Ziba. "Muslim Women's Quest for Equality: Between Islamic Law and Feminism." *Critical Inquiry* 32, no. 4 (Summer 2006): pp. 629–45.

Moallem, Minoo. *Between Warrior Brother and Veiled Sister: Islamic Fundamentalism and the Politics of Patriarchy in Iran*. Berkeley: University of California, 2005.

"Modesty Discourses." In *Encyclopedia of Women & Islamic Cultures: Family, Law, and Politics*, edited by Suad Joseph and Afsaneh Najmabadi, pp. 494–8. Leiden: Koninklijke Brill NV, 2005.

Moghadam, Valentine. "Gender and Revolutionary Transformation: Iran 1979 and East Central Europe 1989." *Gender and Society* 9, no. 3 (June 1995): pp. 328–58.

Moghadam, Valentine. "Hidden from History? Women Workers in Modern Iran." *Iranian Studies* 33, no. 3/4 (Summer–Autumn 2000): pp. 377–401.

Moghadam, Valentine. *Modernizing Women: Gender and Social Change in the Middle East*. Boulder: Lynne Rienner Publishers, Inc., 2003.

Moghadam, Valentine. "Revolution, the State, Islam, and Women: Gender Politics in Iran and Afghanistan." *Social Text* 22 (Spring 1989): pp. 40–61.

Moghissi, Haideh. *Women and Islam: Social Conditions, Obstacles, and Prospects*. New York: Routledge, 2005.

Mohammadi, Mohammad Reza et al. "Reproductive Knowledge, Attitudes and Behavior among Adolescent Males in Tehran, Iran." *International Family Planning Perspectives* 32, no. 1 (March 2006): pp. 35–44.

Mohammadpour, Ali et al. "Coming to Terms with a Diagnosis of HIV in Iran: A Phenomenological Study." *Journal of the Association of Nurses in AIDS Care* 20, no. 4 (July/August 2009): pp. 249–59.

Moin, Baquer. *Khomeini: Life of the Ayatollah*. London: I.B. Tauris & Co Ltd, 1999.

Momen, Moojan. *An Introduction to Shi'i Islam: The History and Doctrines of Twelver Shi'ism*. New Haven: Yale University Press, 1985.

Montazeri, Ali. "AIDS Knowledge and Attitudes in Iran: Results from a Population-based Survey in Tehran." *Patient Education and Counseling* 57 (2005): pp. 199–203.

Moore, Tami. "The Bartering of Female Sexuality." In *Global Perspectives on Prostitution and Sex Trafficking*, edited by Rochelle Dalla, Lynda M. Baker, John DeFrain, and Celia Williamson, pp. 277–90. London: Lexington Books, 2011.

Morovati, Sohrab. "Iranian Police Declare War on Prostitution." Agence France Presse, May 22, 2002. Accessed January 12, 2012. http://www.uri.edu/artsci/wms/hughes/war_on_prostitution.

Mottahedeh, Negar. *Displaced Allegories: Post-Revolutionary Iranian Cinema*. Durham: Duke University Press, 2008.

Mottahedeh, Roy. *The Mantle of the Prophet: Religion and Politics in Iran*. Oxford: One World, 2000.

Movahed, M. and S. Shoaa. "On Attitude Towards HIV/AIDS Among Iranian Students (Case Study: High School Students in Shiraz City)." *Pakistan Journal of Biological Sciences* 13, no. 6 (March 2010): pp. 271–8.

Naficy, Hamid. *A Social History of Cinema, Volume 1: The Artisan Era, 1897–1941*. Durham: Duke University Press, 2011.

Najibullah, Farangis. "Iran's Catwalk Ban Is Only the Beginning." RFERL, September 20, 2008. Accessed July 4, 2012. http://www.rferl.org/content/Iran_Catwalk_Ban_Only_The_Beginning/1201610.html.

Najmabadi, Afsaneh. "Iran's Turn to Islam: From Modernism to a Moral Order." *Middle East Journal* 41, no. 2 (Spring 1987): pp. 202–17.

Najmabadi, Afsaneh. *Land Reform and Social Change in Iran*. Salt Lake City: University of Utah Press, 1987.

Najmabadi, Afsaneh. "Hazards of Modernity and Morality: Women, State and Ideology in Contemporary Iran." In *Women, Islam, and the State*, edited by Deniz Kandiyoti, pp. 48–76. Philadelphia: Temple University Press, 1991.

Najmabadi, Afsaneh. "Power, Morality and the New Muslim Womanhood." In *The Politics of Social Transformation in Afghanistan, Iran, and Pakistan*, edited by Myron Weiner and Ali Banuazizi, pp. 366–89. Syracuse: Syracuse University Press, 1994.

Najmabadi, Afsaneh. "The Erotic *Vatan* [Homeland] as Beloved and Mother: To Love, to Possess, and to Protect." *Comparative Studies in Society and History* 39, no. 3 (July 1997): pp. 442–67.

Najmabadi, Afsaneh. *The Story of the Daughters of Quchan*. Syracuse: Syracuse University Press, 1998.

Najmabadi, Afsaneh. *Women with Mustaches and Men without Beards: Gender and Sexual Anxieties of Iranian Modernity*. Berkeley: University of California, 2005.

Najmabadi, Afsaneh. *Professing Selves: Transsexuality and Same-Sex Desire in Contemporary Iran*. Durham, NC: Duke University Press, 2014.

Nashat, Guity. "Women in the Islamic Republic in Iran." *Iranian Studies* 13, no. 1/4, Iranian Revolution in Perspective (1980): pp. 165–94.

Nashat, Guity and Lois Beck, eds. *Women in Iran from 1800 to the Islamic Republic*. Champaign: University of Illinois Press, 2004.

Nassirimanesh, Bijan. "Proceedings of the Abstract for the Fourth National Harm Reduction Conference." Harm Reduction Coalition, Seattle, 2002.

Nast, Heidi J. and Steve Pile. *Places Through the Body*. London: Routledge, 1998.

"National AIDS Trust Press Release." National AIDS Trust, February 2011. Accessed April 20, 2012. http://www.nat.org.uk/News-and-Media/PressReleases/2011/February/MORI%20survey%20%20knowledge%20and%20attitud es%20to%20HIV.aspx.

Nead, Lynda. *Myths of Sexuality: Representations of Women in Victorian Britain*. Oxford: Basil Blackwell Publishing, 1990.

Nikman, Dr. Mohammad Hossein. "United Nations High-level Meeting on HIV/AIDS Statement." Statement to the United Nations from Acting Health Minister of the Islamic Republic of Iran, June 8–10, 2011. New York. Accessed December 4, 2019. http://www.un.org/en/ga/aidsmeeting2011/pdf/iran.pdf.

Nobari, Ali Reza. *Iran Experts*. Stanford: Stanford University Press, Iran America Documentation Group, 1978.

Nolen, Stephanie. *28 Stories of AIDS in Africa*. Toronto: Vintage Canada, 2008.

Nu'mani, Farhad and Sohrab Behdad. *Class and Labor in Iran: Did the Revolution Matter?* Syracuse: Syracuse University Press, 2006.

Olang, B., Khalil Farivar, Abtin Heidarzadeh, Birgitta Strandvik, and Agneta Yngve. "Breastfeeding in Iran: Prevalence, Duration and Current Recommendations." *International Breastfeeding Journal* 4, no. 8 (2009), doi:10.1186/1746-4358-4-8.

"One Person's Story: Mr. Monir Taheri." Abdorrahman Boroumand Foundation, 2012. Accessed August 15, 2011. http://www.iranrights.org/english/memorial-case-- 3246.php.

"One Person's Story: Ms. Sakineh Qasemi." Abdorrahman Boroumand Foundation, 2012. Accessed August 15, 2011. http://www.iranrights.org/english/memorial-case-- 3246.php.

Osanloo, Arzoo. *The Politics of Women's Rights in Iran*. Princeton: Princeton University Press, 2009.

Overseas Consultants, *Report on Seven-Year Development Plan for the Plan Organization of the Imperial Government of Iran*. Tehran: n.p., 1949.

Oxford English Dictionary, s.v. "archon." Accessed September 12, 2011. http://www.oed.com/view/Entry/10427?rskey=Wf7iu6&result=2&isAdvanced=false#eid.

Ozbek, Muge. "The Regulation of Prostitution in Beyoglu (1875–1915)." *Middle Eastern Studies* 46, no. 4 (July 2010): pp. 555–68.

Paidar, Parvin. *Women and the Political Process in Twentieth-Century Iran*. Cambridge: Cambridge University Press, 1997.

Palmer, Gabrielle. *The Politics of Breastfeeding*. London: Pandora Press, 1988.

Parkes, Peter. "Milk Kinship in Islam. Substance, Structure, History." *Social Anthropology* 13, no. 3 (2005): pp. 307–29.

Parsa, Misagh. *Social Origins of the Iranian Revolution*. New Brunswick: Rutgers University Press, 1989.

Parvin, Parto and Arash Ahmadi. "Iran Sets Sights on Tackling Prostitution." BBC News, July 26, 2012. Accessed July 27, 2012. http://www.bbc.co.uk/news/world-middle-east-1 8966982.

"Photos: Tehran's Brothel District *Shahr-e-No* 1975-77 by Kaveh Golestan." Payvand.com, December 12, 2010. Accessed August 20, 2011. http://payvand.com/blog/blog/2010/1 2/10/photos-tehrans-brothel-district-shahr-e- no-1975-77-by-kaveh-golestan/.

Polk, William R. "The Nature of Modernization: The Middle East and North Africa." *Foreign Affairs* 44, no. 1 (October 1965): pp. 100–110.

Poovey, Mary. *Uneven Developments: The Ideological Work of Gender in Mid-Victorian England*. Chicago: University of Chicago Press, 1988.

"Postscript: Female Sex workers and Fear of Stigmatisation." *Sex Transmission Infection Journal* 81 (2005): pp. 180–8.

Poya, Maryam. *Women, Work and Islamism: Ideology and Resistance in Iran*. London: Zed Books, 1999.

"Pour-mohammadi and the 1988 Prison Massacres." Human Rights Watch, December 2005. Accessed December 4, 2019. http://www.hrw.org/legacy/backgrounder/mena/i ran1205/2.htm.

Power, Nina. "Mannequins, Manners, and Mutilation." *Cabinet Magazine* 301 (Summer 2008): pp. 21–5.

Prus, Robert C. *Symbolic Interaction and Ethnographic Research: Intersubjectivity and the Study of Human Lived Experience*. Albany: State University of New York Press, 1996.

al-Qardawi, Yusuf. *The Lawful and the Prohibited in Islam*. Oak Brook: American Trust Publications, 1999.

The Qur'an. Translated by M. A. S. Abdel Haleem. Oxford: Oxford University Press, 2005.

Rahbar, Ali Rowhani, Kaveh Khoshnood, and Sahar Rooholamini. "Prevalence of HIV Infection and Other Blood-borne Infections in Incarcerated and Non-incarcerated Injection Drug Users (IDUs) in Mashhad, Iran." *International Journal of Drug Policy* 15 (2004): pp. 151–5.

Rahnema, Saeed and Haideh Moghissi. "Clerical Oligarchy and the Question of 'Democracy' in Iran." Iran Chamber Society, 2001. Accessed December 4, 2019. http://www.iranchamber.com/government/articles/clerical_oligarchy_democracy_ iran.php.

Rahimi-Movaghar, A., et al. "HIV Prevalence Amongst Injecting Drug Users in Iran: A Systematic Review of Studies Conducted During the Decade 1998–2007." *International Journal of Drug Policy* (2011).

Rahmati-Najarkolaei, F., Sh. Niknami, F. Aminshokravi, M. Bazargan, Ahmadi, A. Hadjizadeh, et al. "Experiences of Stigma in Healthcare Settings among Adults Living with HIV in the Islamic Republic of Iran." *Journal of the International AIDS Society* 13, no. 27 (2010): pp. 1–11.

Rajaee, Farhang. *The Iran-Iraq War: The Politics of Aggression*. Gainesville: University of Florida Press, 1993.

Ram, Haggai. "Multiple Iconographies: Political Posters in the Iranian Revolution." In *Picturing Iran: Art, Society and Revolution*, edited by Shiva Balaghi and Lynn Gumpert, pp. 90–101. London: I.B. Tauris, 2002.

Rasheed, Mina. "Iran: HIV/AIDS—More than a Social Taboo." *Payvand News*, February 2, 2009. Accessed March 21, 2012. http://www.payvand.com/news/09/feb/1346.html.

"Razi Cultural Center in Tehran." Press TV, October 29, 2015. Accessed November 1, 2019. https://www.youtube.com/watch?v=SL2a6XaYuNA.

Razzaghi, Emran, Afarin Rahimi Movaghar, Traci Craig Green, and Kaveh Khoshnood. "Profiles of Risk: A Qualitative Study of Injecting Drug Users in Tehran, Iran." *Harm Reduction Journal* 3, no. 12 (March 18, 2006): pp. 1–13.

Recknagel, Charles and Azam Gorgin. "Iran: Proposal Debated for Solving Prostitution with 'Chastity Houses.'" *Pars Times*, August 7, 2002.

Roberts, Nickie. *Whores in History: Prostitution in Western Society*. London: HarperCollins, 1992.

Rostami-Povey, Elaheh. "The Women's Movement in Its Historical Context." In *Women, Power and Politics in 21st Century Iran*, edited by Tara Povey and Elaheh Rostami-Povey, pp. 17–34. London: Ashgate Publishing, Ltd., 2012.

Rowhani Rahbar, Ali et al. "Prevalence of HIV Infection and Other Blood-borne Infections in Incarcerated and Non-incarcerated Injection Drug Users (IDUs) in Mashhad, Iran." *International Journal of Drug Policy* 15 (2004): pp. 151–5.

Rubin, Reva. "Attainment of the Maternal Role. Part 1: Processes." *Nursing Research* 16 (Summer/Fall 1967): pp. 237–65.

Sadati, Ahmad Kalateh et al. "Experience of Violence among Street Prostitutes: A Qualitative Study in Shiraz, Iran." *Journal of Injury & Violence Research* 11, no.1 (2019): pp. 21–8. doi:10.5249/jivr.v11i1.865.

Sadeghi, Fatemeh. "Negotiating with Modernity." *Comparative Studies of South Asia, Africa and the Middle East* 28, no. 2 (2008): pp. 250–9.

Sadeghi, Fatemeh. "'Temporary Marriage' and the Economy of Pleasure." Translated by Frieda Afary. *Tehran Bureau* online, March 15, 2010. Accessed December 4, 2019. http://www.pbs.org/wgbh/pages/frontline/tehranbureau/2010/03/temporary- marriage-and-the-economy-of-pleasure.html.

Sadr, Shadi. "The 'End of Stoning': Islamic Republic Style." *Huffington Post: The Blog*, March 13, 2012. Accessed December 4, 2019. http://www.huffingtonpost.com/shadi-sadr/iran-stoning_b_1335809.html.

Saiedi, Shirin. "Hero of Her Own Story: Gender and State Formation in Contemporary Iran." PhD diss., Cambridge University, 2011.

Schayegh, Cyrus. *Who Is Knowledgeable Is Strong*. Berkeley: University of California Press, 2009.

Schayegh, Cyrus. "'A Sound Mind Lives in a Healthy Body': Texts and Contexts in the Iranian Modernists' Scientific Discourse of Health, 1910s-40s." *International Journal of Middle East Studies* 37, no. 2 (May 2005): pp. 167–88.

Schayegh, Cyrus. "Criminal-Women and Mother-Women: Socio-Cultural Transformations and the Critique of Criminality in Early Post-World War II Iran." *Journal of Middle East Women's Studies* 2, no. 3 (Fall 2006): pp. 1–21.

Schayegh, Cyrus. "Modeling Marriage: Family Magazines in Iran." Bad Jens.com. September 2004.

Sciolino, Elaine. "Love Finds a Way in Iran: 'Temporary Marriage.'" *New York Times*, October 4, 2000. Accessed September 12, 2011. http://www.library.cornell.edu/colldev/mideast/tmpmrig.htm.

Sedghi, Hamideh. *Women and Politics in Iran: Veiling, Unveiling, and Reveiling*. Cambridge: Cambridge University Press, 2007.

Sedigh Deylami, Shirin. "In the Face of the Machine: *Westoxification*, Cultural Globalization, and the Making of an Alternative Global Modernity." *Polity* 43 (2011): pp. 242–63.

Sedigh Deylami, Shirin. "Strangers Among Us: The Critique of *Westoxification* in Perso-Islamic Political Thought." PhD diss., University of Minnesota, 2008.

"Select *Fatwas* of Ayatollah Makarem Shirazi on Marriage and Family." Islamopedia Online. Accessed June 1, 2012. http://www.islamopediaonline.org/*fatwa*/select-*fatwas*-ayatollah-makarem-shirazi-marriage-and-family.

al-Serouri, A. W. et al. "AIDS Awareness and Attitudes among Yemeni Young People Living in High-Risk Areas." *Eastern Mediterranean Health Journal* 16, no. 3 (2010): pp. 242–50.

Shahbaz, Kurush. "Iran's White Revolution." *World Affairs* 126, no. 1 (Spring 1963): pp. 17–21.

Shahidian, Hammed. "Contesting Discourses of Sexuality in Post-Revolutionary Iran." In *Deconstructing Sexuality in the Middle East: Challenges and Discourses*, edited by Pinar Ilkkaracan, pp. 80–106. Aldershot: Routledge, 2008.

Shahidian, Hammed. *Women in Iran: Gender Politics in the Islamic Republic*. Volume 2. Westport: Greenwood Press, 2002.

Shahraki, S. Z. Arzjani, and N. Ahmadifard. "A Systematic Study of the Impact of Urbanization of Tehran City on Agricultural and Garden Land Use." *Crop Research (Hisar)* 37, no. 1/3 (2009): pp. 307–11.

Shahrokhi, Sholeh. *Dokhtarane Farari: An Anthropological Investigation on Youth Runaways, Teen Prostitution, Cross-Dressing and Other Sexual Practices of Adolescent Girls in Tehran, Iran*. Berkeley, CA: University of Berkeley, 2008.

Shahrokhi, Sholeh. "Body as a Means of Non-Verbal Communication in Iran." *International Journal of Modern Anthropology*, Thought Short Report (2008): pp. 65–81.

Shahshahani, Soheila. "History of Anthropology in Iran." *Iranian Studies* 19, no. 1 (Winter 1986): pp. 65–86.

Shanley, Mary Lyndon. *Feminism, Marriage, and the Law in Victorian England*. Princeton: Princeton University Press, 1993.

Shaw, Rhonda. "Performing Breastfeeding: Embodiment, Ethics & the Maternal Subject." *Feminist Review* 78 (November 1, 2004): doi:10.1057/palgrave.fr.9400186.

Sherkat, Shahla. "Telling the Stories of Iranian Women's Lives." *Nieman Reports*, Summer 2009. Accessed May 4, 2012. http://www.nieman.harvard.edu/reports/article/101473/Telling-the-Stories-of-Iranian-Womens-Lives.aspx.

Shilts, Randy. *And the Band Played On: Politics, People, and the AIDS Epidemic*. New York: Macmillan, 2007.

"Shirin Ebadi Book Excerpts." *BadJens Iranian Feminist Newsletter*, September 2004. Accessed June 1, 2012. http://www.badjens.com/ebadi.html.

Shokoohi, Mostafa, Mohammad Karamouzian, Mehdi Osooli, Hamid Sharifi, Noushin Fahimfar, Ali Akbar Haghdoost, Omid Zamani, and Ali Mirzazadeh. "Low HIV Testing Rate and Its Correlates among Men Who Inject Drugs in Iran." *International Journal of Drug Policy* 32 (2016): pp. 64–9.

Sreberny-Mohammadi, Annabelle. "Small Media for a Big Revolution: Iran." *International Journal of Politics, Culture, and Society* 3, no. 3, The Sociology of Culture (Spring 1990): pp. 341–71.

Sreberny-Mohammadi, Annabelle and Ali Mohammadi. *Small Media Big Revolution: Communication, Culture and the Iranian Revolution*. Minneapolis: University of Minnesota Press, 1994.

Stearns, Cindy A. "Breastfeeding and the Good Maternal Body." *Gender and Society* 13, no. 3 (June 1999): pp. 308–25.

Stolberg, Sheryl Gay, and Robert Pear. "Wary Centrists Posing Challenge in Health Care Vote." *New York Times*, February 27, 2010. Accessed February 28, 2012. http://www.nytimes.com/2010/02/28/us/politics/28health.html.

Stolzer, J. "Breastfeeding: An Interdisciplinary Review." *International Review of Modern Sociology* 32, no. 1 (Spring 2006): pp. 103–28.

Sturken, Marita and Lisa Cartwright. *Practices of Looking: An Introduction to Visual Culture*. Oxford: Oxford University Press, 2009.

Sulayman Hayyim New Persian-English Dictionary. Tehran: Librairie-imprimerie Beroukhim, 1934–1936.

Sullivan, M. J. *Paraplegic Bodies: Self and Society*. New Zealand: University of Auckland, 1996.

Sullivan, M. J. "Paraplegic Bodies: Self and Society." PhD dissertation, University of Auckland, New Zealand, 1996.

Sullivan, Zohreh. "Eluding the Feminist, Overthrowing the Modern? Transformations in Twentieth-Century Iran." In *Remaking Women: Feminism and Modernity in the Middle East*, edited by Lila Abu Lughod, pp. 215–42. Princeton: Princeton University Press, 1998.

Tadiar, Neferti Xina. "Filipinas 'Living in a Time of War." In *Body Politics*, edited by Odine de Guzman, pp. 1–19. Manila: University Center for Women's Studies, University of the Philippines, 2002.

Taheri, Amir. "The Grand Old Man of Iranian Press Passes Away in America." *Asharq alawsat*, December 14, 2006. Accessed October 4, 2011. http://www.asharq-e.com/n ews.asp?section=7&id=7333.

Tait, Robert. "Iranian Minister Backs Temporary Marriage to Relieve Lust of Youth." *The Guardian*, June 3, 2007. Accessed December 4, 2019. http://www.guardian.co.uk/worl d/2007/jun/04/iran.roberttait.

Talattof, Kamran. *Modernity, Sexuality, and Ideology in Iran: The Life and Legacy of a Popular Female Artist*. Syracuse: Syracuse University Press, 2011.

"Taleban Dismisses Statue Outcry." BBC News, February 27, 2011. August, 30, 2011. http://news.bbc.co.uk/2/hi/south_asia/1192195.stm.

Tamadonfar, Mehran. "Islam, Law, and Political Control in Contemporary Iran." *Journal for the Scientific Study of Religion* 40, no. 2 (June 2001): pp. 205–19.

Tavakol, Mohamed and Abbas Faghih. "Sociological Study of E-Dating and E-Prostitution in Iran." Unpublished paper, XVIII ISA World Congress of Sociology, July 13–19, 2014.

Tavoosi, Anahita et al. "Knowledge and Attitude Towards HIV/AIDS Among Iranian Students." *BMC Public Health* 4, no. 17 (2004). doi:10.1186/1471-2458-4-17.

Tehran Bureau correspondent. "Experts Say Generation Gap Leading Cause of Runaways, Prostitution in Iran." *The Guardian.com*, October 10, 2014. Accessed November 20, 2019. https://www.theguardian.com/world/iran-blog/2014/oct/10/iran-prostitution-s ex-work-runaways.

Tehran Municipality. "Fifty Ambassadors, First Secretaries Guests of Iran Arts Garden-Museum." Tehran Municipality online, June 26, 2012. Accessed July 1, 2012. http://en.tehran.ir/default.aspx?tabid=77&ArticleId=747.

Tehran Municipality. "Comprehensive Chronology of Islamic Revolution Published." Tehran Municipality online, February 8, 2012. Accessed June 14, 2012. http://en.tehra n.ir/ViewArticle/tabid/77/ArticleId/523/Comprehensive- Chronology-of-Islamic-Rev olution-Published.aspx.

Tehran's Baharestan Square, December 22, 2010. Accessed December 12, 2011. http://www.panoramio.com/photo/45391444. Photographer unknown.

Tehran's Baharestan Square, June 27, 2011. Accessed December 12, 2011. http://www.panoramio.com/photo/54834343. Photo courtesy of Saied Mahmoud Javadi.

"The Body: The Complete HIV/AIDS Resource Fact Sheet, CD4 (T-Cell Tests)." The Body. com, March 29, 2012. Accessed April 14, 2012. http://www.thebody.com/content/6110/ cd4-t-cell-tests.html#anchor251.

"The Prevention and Control of HIV/AIDS in Iran." UNDP Iran, February 27, 2011. Accessed April 12, 2012. http://www.undp.org.ir/index.php/hivaids-tb- malaria/48 1-27-february-2011-the-prevention-and-control-of-hivaids-in-iran/.

"The Prevention and Control of HIV/AIDS in I.R. Iran, Phases 1& 2." UNDP Iran, 2011. Accessed April 30, 2012. http://www.undp.org.ir/index.php/component/content/arti cle/403.

"The Prevention and Control of HIV/AIDS." UNDP Iran, February 27, 2011. Accessed June 19, 2012. http://www.undp.org.ir/index.php/hivaids-tb-malaria/481-27- february-2011-the- prevention-and-control-of-hivaids-in-iran.

"Thirty Years Ago on This Day." Radio Zamaneh, 8 Bahman 1387/January 27, 2009. Accessed September 11, 2011. http://zamaaneh.com/revolution/2009/01/post_218.html.

Tizro, Zahra. *Domestic Violence in Iran: Women, Marriage and Islam*. New York: Routledge, 2011.

Tober, Diane M., Mohammad-Hossein Taghdisi, and Mohammad Jalali. "'Fewer Children, Better Life' or 'As Many as God Wants'?: Family Planning among Low-Income Iranian and Afghan Refugee Families in Isfahan, Iran." *Medical Anthropology Quarterly* 20, no. 1, Medical Anthropology in the Muslim World: Ethnographic Reflections on Reproductive and Child Health (March 2006): pp. 50–71.

Tohidi, Nayereh. "Modernity, Islamization, and Women in Iran." In *Gender and National Identity: Women and Politics in Muslim Societies*, edited by Valentine M. Moghadam, pp. 110–47. London: Zed Books, 1994.

Torab, Azam. *Performing Islam: Gender and Ritual in Iran*. London: Brill Academic Publishing, 2006.

UNAIDS, *Global Report Fact Sheet 2010 Middle East and North Africa*. UNAIDS. Accessed April 14, 2012. http://www.unaids.org/documents/20101123_FS_mena_em_en.pdf.

UNAIDS. *Islamic Republic of Iran Country Overview*, 2009. Accessed April 12, 2012. http://www.unaids.org/en/regionscountries/countries/islamicrepublicofiran/.

UNAIDS. *Middle East and North Africa Regional Report on AIDS 2011*. Accessed March 5, 2012. http://www.unaids.org/en/media/unaids/contentassets/documents/unaidspublication/2011/JC2257_UNAIDS-MENA-report-2011_en.pdf.

UNAIDS/WHO. *Epidemiological Fact Sheets on HIV/AIDS and Sexually Transmitted Infections for Iran*, 2004 Update, pp. 1–14.

UNICEF. "HIV and Infant Feeding: The Facts." New York: UNICEF, 2002.

UNICEF. "Infant Feeding and HIV: Risks and Benefits of Breastfeeding." New York: UNICEF, 2002. Accessed April 12, 2012. http://www.unicef.org/nutrition/23964_infantfeeding.html.

United Nations Social Development Work. "Society for the Protection and Assistance of Socially Disadvantaged Individuals." November 30, 2016. Accessed December 4, 2019. https://unsdn.org/2016/11/30/society-for-the-protection-and-assistance-of- socially-disadvantaged-individuals/.

United States Department of State. *2012 Trafficking in Persons Report-Iran*, Refworld-UNHCR website, June 19, 2012. Accessed July 12, 2012. http://www.unhcr.org/refworld/country,,USDOS,,IRN,,4fe30cc0c,0.html.

Valentine, Gill. *Social Geographies: Space and Society*. Essex: Pearson Education Ltd., 2001.

Varzi, Roxanne. "Iran's Pieta: Motherhood, Sacrifice and Film in the Aftermath of the Iran-Iraq War." *Feminist Review* 88, War (2008): pp. 86–98.

Varzi, Roxanne. *Warring Souls: Youth, Media, and Martyrdom in Post-Revolution Iran*. Durham: Duke University Press, 2006.

Vick, Karl. "AIDS Crisis Brings Radical Change in Iran's Response to Heroin Use." *Washington Post*, July 5, 2005.

Walkowitz, Judith. *Prostitution and Victorian Society: Women, Class, and the State*. Cambridge: Cambridge University Press, 1980.

Warren, James Francis. *Ah Ku and Karayuki-san: Prostitution in Singapore, 1870-*. Singapore: Singapore University Press, 2003.

Watson, Keith. "The Shah's White Revolution-Education and Reform in Iran." *Comparative Education* 12, no. 1 (March 1976): pp. 23–36.

Weiner, Myron and Ali Banuazizi. *The Politics of Social Transformation in Afghanistan, Iran, and Pakistan*. Syracuse: Syracuse University Press, 1994.

Weiss, Gail. *Body Images: Embodiment as Intercorporeality*. New York and London: Routledge, 1999.

"Women, Girls, Gender Equality and HIV Fact Sheet." UNAIDS, February 2012. Accessed December 4, 2019. http://www.unaids.org/en/media/unaids/contentassets/documents/factsheet/2012/20120217_FS_WomenGirls_en.pdf.

World Health Organization. *Antiretroviral Therapy for HIV Infection in Adults and Adolescents: Recommendations for Public Health Approach 2010 Revision*. Geneva: WHO, 2010.

World Health Organization. "Breast Is Always Best, Even for HIV-Positive Mothers." *Bulletin of the WHO* 88, no. 1 (January 2010): pp. 1–80. Accessed December 4, 2019. https://www.who.int/bulletin/volumes/88/1/10-030110/en/.

World Health Organization. *International Code of Marketing of Breast-milk Substitutes*. Geneva: World Health Organization, 1981.

Yazdi, C. A., K. Aschbacher, A. Arvanta, H. M. Naser, A. Abdollahi, M. Mousavi, M. R. Narmani, M. Kianpishe, F. Nicfallah, and A. K. Moghadam. "Knowledge, Attitudes and Sources of Information Regarding HIV/AIDS in Iranian Adolescents." *AIDS Care* 18, no. 8 (November 2006): pp. 1004–10.

Yeganeh, Nahid. "Women, Nationalism, and Islam in Contemporary Political Discourse in Iran." *Feminist Review* 44, Nationalism and National Identities (Summer 1993): pp. 3–18.

Young, Iris Marion. *On Female Body Experience: 'Throwing Like a Girl' and Other Essays*. Oxford: Oxford University Press, 2005.

Youssefzadeh, Ameneh. "The Situation of Music in Iran since the Revolution: The Role of Official Organizations." *British Journal of Ethnomusicology* 9, no. 2 (2000): pp. 35–61.

Zahedi, Ashraf. "Contested Meaning of the Veil and Political Ideologies of Iranian Regimes." *Journal of Middle East Women's Studies* 3, no. 3 (Fall 2007): pp. 75–98.

Zamani, Saman et. al. "Prevalence of HIV/HCV/HBV Infections and Drug-Related Risk Behaviours Amongst IDUs Recruited Through Peer-Driven Sampling in Iran." *International Journal of Drug Policy* 21 (2010): pp. 493–500.

Zargooshi, J. "Characteristics of Gonorrhea in Kermanshah, Iran." *Sex Transmission Infection Journal* 78, no. 6 (2002): pp. 460–1.

Legal Documents

"The Anti-Narcotics Law of the Islamic Republic of Iran." November 8, 1997. Accessed April 25, 2012. http://www.unhcr.org/refworld/docid/4c35b0a52.html.

Dabir-e Shora-ye 'Aali-ye Enqelab-e Farhangi/Head of the Supreme Council of the Cultural Revolution, 5 Esfand 1363/ February 24, 1988.

Islamic Republic of Iran, *Qanoun-e Mojazat-e Islamic/Islamic Penal Code*, 1991. http://mehr.org/Islamic_Penal_Code_of_Iran.pdf.

Iran Ministry of the Interior. *Mosavebat-e Comisiyon-e Siasatgozari dar Omour-e Ejraee-ye Mobarezeh-ye Farhangi ba Mazaher-e Fesad/The Ratification of Policymaking Commission regarding Executive Affairs of the Cultural Struggle with Symbols of Corruption* 6877, 19 Ordibehesht 1371/ May 9, 1992.

"Preamble." Islamic Republic of Iran Constitution, December 3, 1979, amended July 28, 1989.

Social Council of Tehran Province. "The Executive Bylaw Concerning the Struggle Against Mal-veiling." Article 3: A to D.

Supreme Council of the Cultural Revolution. *The Principles, Foundations, and Executing Methods in Developing a Culture of Chastity*, 14 Bahman 1376/ February 3, 1998.

Supreme Council of the Cultural Revolution. *Ousul va Mabani va Ravesh-ha-ye Ejraee-ye Gostaresh-e Farhang-e Efaf/The Principles, Foundations, and Executing Methods in Spreading a Culture of Chastity.* 14 Bahman 1376/February 3, 1998.

Supreme Council of the Cultural Revolution. *Qanoun-e Tarvij-e Taghziye ba Shir-e Madar va Hemayat az Madaran dar Doran-e Shirdehi/Law Encouraging Breastfeeding and the Protection of Mothers during Breastfeeding.* Islamic Republic of Iran Judiciary, Family Law, 1374 Azar 22. Tehran: Ganjdanesh Publishing, 1385/2006. pp. 295–8.

Supreme Council of the Cultural Revolution. *Qanoun-e Rahkar-ha-ye Ejraee-ye Gostaresh-e Farhang-e Efaf va Hejab.* "Policies and Solutions." Objective 4, Supreme Council of the Cultural Revolution. Accessed March 13, 2012. http://www.effat.ir/fa/index.php?option=com_content&view=article&id=1222306:-1&catid=85:1390-02-26-19-41-09&Itemid=108.

Supreme Council of the Cultural Revolution. *Rahbord-ha-ye Gostaresh-e Farhang-e Efaf/ Guidelines of Developing or Spreading a Culture of Chastity,* 13 Dey 1384/ July 26, 2005.

Ministry of Culture and Islamic Guidance. *Qanoun-e Samandehi-ye Mode va Lebas/ Regulations on Re-organizing Fashion and Clothing,* 12 Dey 1385/ January 2, 2007 and 20 Dey 1385/ January 10, 2007. Accessed July 4, 2012. http://honari.farhang.gov.ir/rules-rule7-fa.html.

Ministry of Culture and Islamic Guidance. *Qanoun-e Samandehi-ye Mode va Lebas/ Regulations on Re-organizing Fashion and Clothing,* 12 Dey 1385/ January 2, 2007 and 20 Dey 1385/ January 10, 2007. Accessed July 4, 2012. http://honari.farhang.gov.ir/rules-rule7-fa.html.

Islamic Republic of Iran Judiciary. *Qanoun-e Tarvij-e Taghziye ba Shir-e Madar va Hemayat az* Madaran dar Duran-e Shirdahi/Law Encouraging Breastfeeding and the Protection of Mothers during Breastfeeding. Family Law, 1374 Azar 22/ December 13, 1995. Tehran: Ganjdanesh Publishing, 1385/2006.

Islamic Republic of Iran Penal Code. Book 2. "*Hadd* Punishment for Adultery." *Qanoun-e Mojazat-e Ommumi/Pahlavi Criminal Code,* 1304/1924.

Resolution WHA27.43. *Handbook of Resolutions and Decisions of the World Health Assembly and the Executive Board,* Volume II, 4 ed. World Health Assembly: Geneva, 1981.

Interviews

Ahmadnia, Shirin. Interview by author. Personal interview. Tehran, Iran, July 3, 2010.

Alaie, Kamiar. Interview by author. Telephone. New York, NY., June 26, 2012.

A., Forough. Interview by author. Personal interview. Tehran, Iran, August 10, 2011.

Mansourian, Khosrou. Interview by author. Personal interview. Tehran, Iran, July 17, 2011 and November 15, 2011.

Sadeghi, Fatemeh. Interview by author. Personal interview. Tehran, Iran, October 1, 2011.

S. Fatemeh (SPASDI social worker). Interview by author. Personal interview. Tehran, Iran, September 21, 2011.

Reports

Guidelines for Measuring National HIV Prevalence, UNAIDS/WHO Working Group on Global HIV/AIDS and STI Surveillance, 2005. Accessed April 10, 2012. http://www.

unaids.org/en/media/unaids/contentassets/dataimport/pub/manual/2005/200501
01_gs_guidemeasuringpopulation_en.pdf

*Islamic Republic of Iran Country Report: Monitoring of the United Nations General
Assembly Special Session on HIV and AIDS, Declaration of Commitment*. Office of the
Under-Secretary for Health, Ministry of Health and Medical Education, and Centre for
Disease Management, January 2006. Accessed June 1, 2012. http://data.unaids.org/pu
b/report/2006/2006_country_progress_report_iran_en.pdf.

*Islamic Republic of Iran Country Report: Monitoring of the United Nations General
Assembly Special Session on HIV and AIDS*. National AIDS Committee Secretariat,
Ministry of Health and Education, February 2010. Accessed April 18, 2012. http://
www.unaids.org/fr/dataanalysis/monitoringcountryprogress/2010progressreportssu
bmittedbycountries/file,33662,fr..pdf.

*Islamic Republic of Iran Progress Report: Monitoring of the United Nations General
Assembly Special Session on HIV and AIDS*, National AIDS Committee Secretariat, Iran
Ministry of Health and Medical Education, February 2010. Accessed April 14, 2012.
http://www.unaids.org/en/dataanalysis/monitoringcountryprogress/progressreports/
2010countries/iran_2010_country_progress_report_en.pdf.

*Iran Progress Report: Monitoring of the United Nations General Assembly Special Session on
HIV and AIDS*. National AIDS Committee Secretariat and Ministry of Health and
Medical Education, March 2012. Accessed April 12, 2012. http://www.unaids.org/en/
dataanalysis/monitoringcountryprogress/progressreports/2012countries/ce_IR_Narra
tive_Report.pdf.

Islamic Republic of Iran AIDS Progress Report, National AIDS Committee Secretariat and
Ministry of Health and Medical Education, March 2015. Accessed December 1, 2019.
https://www.unaids.org/sites/default/files/country/documents/IRN_narrative_repor
t_2015.pdf.

"Monitoring of the United Nations General Assembly Special Session on HIV and AIDS."
National AIDS Committee Secretariat and Ministry of Health and Medical Education,
February 2010. Accessed April 10, 2012. http://www.unaids.org/fr/dataanalysis/mo
nitoringcountryprogress/2010progressreportssubmittedbycountries/file,33662,fr..pdf

"The Prevention and Control of HIV/AIDS in I.R. Iran, Phases 1& 2." UNDP Iran, 2011.
Accessed April 30, 2012. http://www.undp.org.ir/index.php/component/content/arti
cle/403.

INDEX

Note: Page numbers followed by 'n' refer to notes.

* 9 7 8 1 3 5 0 1 9 5 3 8 7 *